The Cambridge Handbook of
Information and Computer Ethics

Information and Communication Technologies (ICTs) have profoundly changed many aspects of life, including the nature of entertainment, work, communication, education, health care, industrial production and business, social relations and conflicts. They have had a radical and widespread impact on our moral lives and hence on contemporary ethical debates. *The Cambridge Handbook of Information and Computer Ethics* provides an ambitious and authoritative introduction to the field, with discussions of a range of topics including privacy, ownership, freedom of speech, responsibility, technological determinism, the digital divide, cyber warfare and online pornography. It offers an accessible and thoughtful survey of the transformations brought about by ICTs and their implications for the future of human life and society, for the evaluation of behaviour, and for the evolution of moral values and rights. It will be a valuable book for all who are interested in the ethical aspects of the information society in which we live.

Luciano Floridi is Professor and Research Chair in Philosophy of Information, University of Hertfordshire; Fellow of St Cross College, Oxford University; and UNESCO Chair in Information and Computer Ethics. His publications include *Philosophy and Computing: An Introduction* (1999) and *The Blackwell Guide to the Philosophy of Computing and Information* (2004).

The Cambridge Handbook of
Information and Computer Ethics

EDITED BY

Luciano Floridi

CAMBRIDGE
UNIVERSITY PRESS

CAMBRIDGE UNIVERSITY PRESS
Cambridge, New York, Melbourne, Madrid, Cape Town, Singapore,
São Paulo, Delhi, Dubai, Tokyo

Cambridge University Press
The Edinburgh Building, Cambridge CB2 8RU, UK

Published in the United States of America by Cambridge University Press, New York

www.cambridge.org
Information on this title: www.cambridge.org/9780521888981

First published 2010

Printed in the United Kingdom at the University Press, Cambridge

A catalogue record for this publication is available from the British Library

ISBN 978-0-521-88898-1 Hardback
ISBN 978-0-521-71772-4 Paperback

Contents

Contributors

Alison Adam is Professor of Science, Technology and Society in the School of English, Sociology, Politics and Contemporary History at University of Salford, UK.

Colin Allen is Professor of History and Philosophy of Science and Professor of Cognitive Science in the College of Arts and Sciences at Indiana University, Bloomington, USA.

John Arquilla is Professor of Defense Analysis at the United States Naval Postgraduate School.

Philip Brey is Professor of Philosophy of Technology and Chair of the Department of Philosophy of the University of Twente.

Terrell Ward Bynum is Professor of Philosophy and Director of the Research Center on Computing and Society at Southern Connecticut State University, USA.

Stephen Clarke is a James Martin Research Fellow in the Programme on the Ethics of the New Biosciences at the University of Oxford.

Charles Ess is Professor of Philosophy and Religion, Distinguished Professor of Interdisciplinary Studies, Drury University, Missouri, USA, and Professor MSO, Information and Media Studies Department, Aarhus University, Denmark.

Luciano Floridi is Professor of Philosophy at the University of Hertfordshire, where he holds the Research Chair in Philosophy of Information, and Fellow of St Cross College, University of Oxford.

Adam Henschke is currently working on his PhD at Charles Sturt University, at the Centre for Applied Philosophy and Public Ethics.

Bernd Carsten Stahl is a Reader in Critical Research in Technology in the Centre for Computing and Social Responsibility at De Montfort University, Leicester, UK.

John Sullins is an Associate Professor at Sonoma State University, part of the California State University system.

Herman T. Tavani is Professor of Philosophy at Rivier College (USA) and President of the International Society for Ethics and Information Technology.

May Thorseth is Associate Professor in the Department of Philosophy, NTNU Norwegian University of Science and Technology, and Director of Programme for Applied Ethics.

Jeroen van den Hoven is Professor of Moral Philosophy at Delft University of Technology and Vice Dean of the Faculty of Technology, Policy and Management. He is Scientific Director of the Centre for Ethics and Technology of the Three Technical Universities in the Netherlands.

John Weckert is Professor of Computer Ethics at Charles Sturt University, and Professorial Fellow at the Centre for Applied Philosophy and Public Ethics, Charles Sturt University, University of Melbourne and the Australian National University.

Vincent Wiegel is Senior Researcher in Philosophy at the Delft University of Technology, the Netherlands. He is Programme Manager of the DesignForValues research programme.

Preface

Luciano Floridi

Information and Communication Technologies (ICTs) have profoundly altered many aspects of life, including the nature of entertainment, work, communication, education, health care, industrial production and business, social relations and conflicts. As a consequence, they have had a radical and widespread impact on our moral lives and hence on contemporary ethical debates. Consider the following list: PAPA (privacy, accuracy, intellectual property and access); 'the triple A' (availability, accessibility and accuracy of information); ownership and piracy; the digital divide; infoglut and research ethics; safety, reliability and trustworthiness of complex systems; viruses, hacking and other forms of digital vandalism; freedom of expression and censorship; pornography; monitoring and surveillance; security and secrecy; propaganda; identity theft; the construction of the self; panmnemonic issues and personal identity; new forms of agency (artificial and hybrid), of responsibility and accountability; roboethics and the moral status of artificial agents; e-conflicts; the re-prioritization of values and virtues... these are only some of the pressing issues that characterize the ethical discourse in our information societies. They are the subject of information and computer ethics (ICE), a new branch of applied ethics that investigates the transformations brought about by ICTs and their implications for the future of human life and society, for the evolution of moral values and rights, and for the evaluation of agents' behaviours.

Since the seventies, ICE has been a standard topic in many curricula. In recent years, there has been a flourishing of new university courses, international conferences, workshops, professional organizations, specialized publications and research centres. However, research, and the corresponding teaching materials, have so far been largely influenced by professional and technical approaches, addressing mainly applied problems in legal, social and technological contexts. This trend is understandable. ICE emerged in recent decades not as a mere intellectual exercise, or something cooked up in the ivory tower of academia, but as an increasingly felt need for clarifications and guidelines in the ethically messy world generated by the fastest changes ever experienced by humanity. This bottom-up process has given to ICE an enviable platform of real and substantial evidence with which to work, from industry standards to social issues, from political decisions to legal requirements. However, this wealth of empirical data and grounding problems has come at a theoretical cost. Today, ICE is like a pyramid: it has a very large empirical base, but a rather slim top of theoretical insights. To use a different metaphor, imagine three runners on a typical oval track. In information societies around the world we find that one of the runners is well ahead, and that is technology and its applications. ICT has outpaced the second runner, represented by national and international legal systems and legislation, which are following, rather than leading, the race in almost any technological context. Last comes our conceptual understanding, the third runner. In ICT, we often innovate first, then try to regulate, and finally seek to understand what is actually happening. In theory, we all know perfectly well that the safest and most reasonable way of proceeding would be exactly the opposite. In practice, each runner requires different amounts of resources: *thinking* is always a slower process than *deciding*, which inevitably takes more time than *doing*. This book seeks to redress the situation. It is an attempt to give a substantial push to the third runner, to make sure that the distance between technology and the full, conceptual comprehension of it is as short as possible. For this reason, it is entirely and exclusively dedicated to conceptual approaches to ICE.

The book provides a philosophical introduction to the most important conceptual issues in ICE. It is to be hoped that it will serve as a groundbreaking resource as well as a timely, comprehensive review for both students and general readers alike. It is meant to engage a wide audience, from undergraduates, who need to study the new computational and informational turn in ethics, to teachers in need of a reliable textbook, to researchers interested in broadening their expertise, and to members of the general public, who might be curious about the ethical aspects of the information society in which they live.

The book comprises fifteen newly commissioned chapters. Each of them provides an authoritative, philosophical survey of the fundamental themes, problems, arguments and theories, which constitute the innovative field of ICE. Combining the virtues of careful scholarship and lucid exposition, each chapter is planned to be usable as a self-standing introduction to its topic. In line with a more theoretical approach, examples are used to illustrate and substantiate conceptual analyses, not to support a mere case-based approach, which often turns out to be insufficiently enlightening and generalizable. The first chapter is an introduction explaining the nature of the new paradigm in applied ethics. The chapters are followed by an epilogue in which I have outlined the possible development of the field, in a world increasingly globalized.

The book does not provide purely abstract discussions with no practical applications, but rather offers a broad and objective introduction to the conceptual understanding of the real-world problems that affect life in the information society, in a style that is both accessible and didactically useful. Here is a quick guide to its contents.

Part I   **Introduction and background**

The first two chapters guide the reader, from a top-down perspective, towards a critical and informed appreciation of the moral problems discussed in ICE.

Chapter 1 Ethics after the Information Revolution, Luciano Floridi

Keywords: computer revolution, infosphere, inforgs.

This chapter provides a general introduction to the field, its origins and scope.

Chapter 2 The historical roots of information and computer ethics, Terrell Ward Bynum

Keywords: history of computer ethics, professional ethics, Norbert Wiener.

This chapter outlines the development of the field, starting with the work of Norbert Wiener and the computer revolution in the fifties. The historical perspective is not only scholarly interesting but also important to introduce and contextualize the development of the philosophical problems discussed in the following chapters.

Part II   **Ethical approaches**

Still moving towards the specific issues investigated by computer ethics, the three chapters in this section introduce the ethical theories and methodologies commonly used in the area.

Chapter 3 Values in technology and disclosive computer ethics, Philip Brey

Keywords: disclosive computer ethics, ethics of design, interdisciplinary research, value-sensitive design.

The chapter introduces disclosive computer ethics, one of the new approaches that has been developed within the field. Disclosive computer ethics is independent of the usual approaches in normative ethics. It shows how one of the important tasks of computer ethics is to uncover values and moral decisions embedded in ICT artefacts and practices. The chapter also covers recent investigations into design procedures and their ethics.

Chapter 4 The use of normative theories in computer ethics, Jeroen van den Hoven

Keywords: applied ethics, Aristotle, Consequentialism, Deontologism, Kant, Rawls, Virtue Ethics.

The chapter analyses how standard ethical positions, especially Virtue Ethics, Deontologism and Consequentialism, and their methodologies have been used and adapted in order to deal with issues arising in computer ethics. Topics discussed here comprise whether any particular approach is more amenable to application to computer-related ethical issues; which values and normative guidelines have been more successful among professionals; what sort of ICT moral issues, if any, may not be subject to an ethical analysis in terms of the old paradigms and may require radical innovations; how ethics may help to approach, formulate and solve ICT moral problems.

Chapter 5 Information ethics, Luciano Floridi

Keywords: artificial agents, environmental ethics, foundation of computer ethics, information ethics.

Since the nineties, a new approach to computer ethics, known as information ethics, has been developed by several researchers and especially by the IEG (Information Ethics Group) in Oxford. Information ethics may be briefly described as an extension of environmental ethics to artificial contexts (cyberspace, or more generally the so-called infosphere) inhabited by artificial agents. This chapter outlines the nature and scope of information ethics, some of the difficulties it faces in its application to practical issues in computer ethics, and the criticisms that have been brought against it.

Part III   Ethical issues in the information society

This section is dedicated to specific topics and problems, in ICE, characterizing social and individual life in the information society. These are organized by dividing them into standard thematic areas and hence six chapters.

Chapter 6 Social issues in computer ethics, Bernd Carsten Stahl

Keywords: ownership, intellectual property, copyright and open source software.

The computer revolution, by de-materializing artefacts, products and services and transforming them in strings and streams of digits, has profoundly affected concepts such as *ownership, intellectual property, copyright,* fair sharing and use, as well as voluntary collaboration and *open source software.* This chapter discusses some of the classic problems arising in these contexts.

Chapter 7 Rights and computer ethics, John Sullins

Keywords: freedom of speech and pornography; privacy, surveillance and trust.

This chapter continues the previous analysis by investigating individuals' rights in the information society. The information society is built on information and communication technologies. Precisely because the exchange of data and information is so facilitated, some problems that have affected individuals in the past acquire macroscopic dimensions. The chapter discusses the classic issue of how freedom of speech and its potential abuse (especially pornography and politically, socially or religiously discriminating contents) may be ethically regulated. It then investigates several theories of informational privacy, which have been developed to tackle the problems arising in environments which are at risk of being dominated by 'Big Brother' or 'Panopticon' strategies (the surveillance society).

Chapter 8 Conflict, security and computer ethics, John Arquilla

Keywords: cryptography, cyber terrorism, hacktivism, information warfare.

Information has always played a crucial role in warfare and in national security issues. Naturally, information warfare – namely the use and management of information resources in pursuit of a competitive advantage over an opponent – has followed the development both of information technologies and of society. The more advanced the former are, and the closer the latter is to being an information society, the more important information warfare and security become. Society has been using ICT not only to develop but also to defend itself from internal and external threats (terrorism and war). How is this changing the nature of security and conflicts? What are the ethical issues involved? This chapter deals with these fundamental questions by discussing, among others, topics such as the collection of tactical information, the reliability of vital information and their sources, and the spreading of propaganda or disinformation among the enemy.

Chapter 9 Personal values and computer ethics, Alison Adam

Keywords: community, diversity, gender, personal identity.

ICT, digital environments and virtual communities allow the creation of entirely new scenarios for the construction and re-definition of one's self and for the analysis of gender issues. The cyborg, post-humanist debate has expanded our understanding of the moral questions posed in contexts where individuals have so much more freedom to characterize and shape themselves in a variety of ways. At the same time, social constructions have acquired an entirely new and challenging dimension, thanks to online services such as myspace.com and role games such as *World of Warcraft*. This chapter investigates the new challenges posed by ICT and the consequent ethical debate about personal identity and community, gender issues and diversity.

Chapter 10 Global information and computer ethics, Charles Ess and May Thorseth

Keywords: equal access, digital divide, deliberative democracy, East–West issues, globalization, pluralism.

ICT is often synonymous with globalization. It is not by chance that the information society is identified as a transcultural and transnational phenomenon. This chapter focuses on the global, ethical transformations brought about by ICT in three contexts. First, the development of a deliberative democracy based on the possibility of a technologically sustainable participation of all members of a community, in a distributed environment (this includes, for example, phenomena such as electronic voting systems and feedback mechanisms and web-based political campaigns). Second, the moral and political problems caused by a technological neo-colonialism coming from the information society and affecting non-ICT-based communities. This topic is related to the digital divide. A person's livelihood and welfare increasingly depend on familiarity with, and ability to use, ICT. How is the information society coping with the new issues posed by *equal access* to ICT systems for people with disabilities, and by the gap between those with regular, effective access to digital technologies and those without? And finally, the debate on pluralism and diversity, that is, whether different cultures (the simplified polarization here is often Eastern vs. Western cultures) might be able to tolerate, if not appreciate, each other in contexts where ICT forces them to interact. A classic example is represented by the different ways in which cultures may assess the importance and value of privacy.

Chapter 11 Computer ethics and applied contexts, John Weckert and Adam Henschke

Keywords: applied ethics, bioethics, business ethics, environmental ethics medical ethics.

ICE, seen as a branch of applied ethics, is really a transdisciplinary field, which touches on several issues also discussed in other areas of applied ethics. ICT plays a key role in bioethics, business ethics, environmental ethics and medical ethics. This chapter investigates these areas of overlapping ethical concerns, to identify the key problems that can be fruitfully approached from an ICE perspective, including biometrics and genetics, the use of computers and computerized control systems in workplaces, environmental issues caused by the IT revolution, and the relation between IT and ethical dilemmas in medical contexts.

Part IV   Ethical issues in artificial contexts

This section is dedicated to specific topics and problems, in ICE, characterizing artefacts and synthetic environments. These have been organized into three chapters.

Chapter 12 The ethics of IT artefacts, Vincent Wiegel

Keywords: intentionality, technological artefacts, values.

Researchers in STS (Science and Technology Studies) have long argued that human artefacts, their uses and the practices that they generate, or in which they are embedded, have significant ethical implications. In this chapter, the value-ladenness of technological artefacts is investigated by extending the STS approach to digital products and tools.

Chapter 13 Artificial life, artificial agents, virtual realities: technologies of autonomous agency, Colin Allen

Keywords: AI, ALife, artificial reality.

ICT has not only modified the reality which we inhabit, it has also created new realities, new agents and new ways of exploring the world of life. These, in turn, have caused old moral issues to be revisited (e.g. responsibility, moral artificial agency) and generated new issues (e.g. action at distance, known as telepresence, virtual crimes). The chapter covers the debates on the ethics of artificial intelligence applications, on the nature of moral life in artificial reality environments, and ethical implications of Alife (artificial life) studies.

Chapter 14 On new technologies, Steve Clarke

Keywords: distributed computing, nano-technology, new emerging technologies.

Nano-technologies and distributed computing (such as RFID tags) promise to blur the boundary between the real (offline) and the virtual (online) by blending the two types of environment into a single 'infosphere'. This radical transformation is already heralding the evolution of new ethical problems, concerning, for example, risk assessment, decisional delegation and heteronomous control. This chapter explores the ethical issues that are arising from these new emerging technologies.

Part V   Metaethics

Chapter 15 The foundationalist debate in computer ethics, Herman T. Tavani

Keywords: uniqueness debate, foundation of computer ethics.

As all new disciplines, computer ethics has generated a lively debate on its status as an independent field of philosophical research. Is computer ethics just ethics applied to ICT-related problems? Or does it give rise to a new, independent field of investigation? Is it just another branch of applied ethics, or should it be seen as a version of professional ethics? In this chapter, the debate and the various positions are analysed, in order to provide the reader with clear grasp of the various perspectives from which the main conceptual issues in the field have been approached. It is a difficult and theoretical topic, which advanced students may wish to study only at the end of their course.

Acknowledgements

Many people contributed to the realization of this book. I am very much indebted to Hilary Gaskin and her team at Cambridge University Press for their outstanding editorial help. This book would have been impossible without their friendly and professional support and feedback. The authors are to be congratulated for their excellent chapters, and thanked for the constructive patience they exercised against what must have seemed sometimes like editorial harassment. I am most grateful to all of them for their intellectual contributions. Penny Driscoll, my personal assistant, provided vital help in editing the final bibliography and other parts of the book. The anonymous referees offered some excellent input, which proved very valuable. Finally, I owe to Kia, my wife, the environmental happiness within which this book developed. Without her, some editorial problems would have turned into nasty troubles instead of exciting challenges.

Part I

Introduction and background

1 Ethics after the Information Revolution

Luciano Floridi

1.1 Introduction: history as the information age

Humanity has organized its history according to many metrics. Some are natural and circular, relying on seasons and planetary motions. Some are social or political and linear, being determined, for example, by the succession of Olympic Games, the number of years since the founding of the city of Rome (*ab urbe condita*), or the ascension of a king. Still others are religious and have a V-shape, counting years before and after a particular event (e.g. the birth of Christ). There are larger periods that encompass smaller ones, named after influential styles (Baroque), people (Victorian era), particular circumstances (Cold War) or some new technology (Nuclear age). What all these and many other metrics have in common is that they are all *historical*, in the strict sense that they all depend on the development of systems to record events and hence accumulate and transmit information about the past. It follows that history is actually synonymous with the information age, since *prehistory* is the age in human development that precedes the availability of recording systems. Hence, one may further argue that humanity has been living in various kinds of information societies at least since the Bronze Age, the era that marks the invention of writing in different regions of the world, and especially in Mesopotamia. Comparing the computer revolution to the printing revolution would be misleading not because they are unrelated, but because they are actually phases of a much wider, macroscopic process that has spanned millennia: the slow emergence of the information society since the fourth millennium BC. And yet, this is not what we normally mean when talking about the information age. Typically, we have in mind something much more limited in scope and closer in time. There may be many explanations, but one seems more convincing than any other: only very recently has human progress and welfare begun to depend mostly on the successful and efficient management of the information life cycle.[1] So the long period of time that

---

[1] A typical life cycle includes the following phases: occurring (discovering, designing, authoring, etc.), processing and managing (collecting, validating, modifying, organizing, indexing, classifying, filtering, updating, sorting, storing, networking, distributing, accessing, retrieving, transmitting, etc.) and using (monitoring, modelling, analysing, explaining, planning, forecasting, decision-making, instructing, educating, learning, etc.).

the information society has taken to surface should not be surprising. Imagine a historian writing in a million years from now. She may consider it normal, and perhaps even elegantly symmetrical, that it took roughly six millennia (from its beginning in the Neolithic, tenth millennium BC, until the Bronze Age) for the agricultural revolution to produce its full effect, and then another six millennia (from the Bronze Age until the end of the second millennium AD) for the information revolution to bear its main fruit. During this span of time, information technologies evolved from being mainly recording systems, to being also communication systems (especially after Gutenberg), to being also processing systems (especially after Turing). As I will explain below, they have begun to play the role of re-ontologizing systems. Thanks to this evolution, nowadays the most advanced economies are highly dependent, for their functioning and growth, upon the pivotal role played by information-based, intangible assets, information-intensive services (especially business and property services, communications, finance and insurance, and entertainment) as well as information-oriented public sectors (especially education, public administration and health care). For example, all G7 members qualify as information societies because, in Canada, France, Germany, Italy, Japan, United Kingdom, and the United States of America, at least 70% of the Gross Domestic Product (GDP) depends on intangible goods, which are information-based, rather than material goods, which are the physical output of agricultural or manufacturing processes.

The almost sudden burst of a global information society, after a few millennia of relatively quieter gestation, has generated new and disruptive challenges, which were largely unforeseeable only a few decades ago. Needless to say, Information and Communication Technologies (ICTs) have been changing the world profoundly, irreversibly and problematically since the fifties, at a breathtaking pace, and with unprecedented scope, making the creation, management and utilization of information, communication and computational resources vital issues. As a quick reminder, and in order to have some simple, quantitative measure of the transformations experienced by our generation, consider the following findings.

In a recent study, researchers at Berkeley's School of Information Management and Systems estimated that humanity had accumulated approximately 12 exabytes[2] of data in the course of its entire history until the commodification of computers, but that it had produced more than 5 exabytes of data just in 2002, 'equivalent in size to the information contained in 37,000 new libraries the size of the Library of Congress book collections' (Lyman and Varian 2003). In 2002, this was almost 800 MB of recorded data produced per person. It is like saying that every newborn baby came into the world with a

---

[2] One exabyte corresponds to 1,000,000,000,000,000,000 bytes or 10^{18}.

burden of 30 feet of books, the equivalent of 800 MB of data on paper. This exponential escalation has been relentless: 'between 2006 and 2010...the digital universe will increase more than six fold from 161 exabytes to 988 exabytes'.[3]

Not feeling under pressure would be abnormal. The development of ICT has not only brought enormous benefits and opportunities but also greatly outpaced our understanding of its conceptual nature and implications, while raising problems whose complexity and global dimensions are rapidly expanding, evolving and becoming increasingly serious. A simple analogy may help to make sense of the current situation. Our technological tree has been growing its far-reaching branches much more widely, rapidly and chaotically than its conceptual, ethical and cultural roots. The lack of balance is obvious and a matter of daily experience in the life of millions of citizens dealing with information-related ethical issues. The risk is that, like a tree with weak roots, further and healthier growth at the top might be impaired by a fragile foundation at the bottom. As a consequence, today, any advanced information society faces the pressing task of equipping itself with a viable philosophy and ethics of information. Applying the previous analogy, while technology keeps growing bottom-up, it is high time we start digging deeper, top-down, in order to expand and reinforce our conceptual understanding of our information age, of its nature, its less visible implications and its impact on human and environmental welfare, and thus give ourselves a chance to anticipate difficulties, identify opportunities and resolve problems, conflicts and dilemmas.

It is from such a broad perspective that I would like to invite the reader to approach this volume. The chapters constituting it perfectly complement each other. Written by leading experts in the area, they tackle some of the key issues in information and computer ethics (ICE). Since the authors need no introduction, and the contents of the chapters are outlined in the preface, in the rest of this introductory chapter my contribution will be to discuss some conceptual undercurrents, which flow beneath the surface of the literature on ICE, and may be seen surfacing in different places throughout this book. In discussing them, I shall focus, more generally, on the potential impact of ICT on our lives. And since there would be no merit in predicting the obvious, I will avoid issues such as rising concerns about privacy and identity theft, spamming, viruses, or the importance of semantic tagging, online shopping and virtual communities. Nor will I try to steal ideas from those who know better than I do the future development of the actual technologies (see for example O'Reilly 2005, Microsoft-Research 2005, *Nature* 2006). I will, instead,

---

[3] Source: 'The Expanding Digital Universe: A Forecast of Worldwide Information Growth Through 2010', white paper – sponsored by EMC – IDC, www.emc.com/about/destination/digital_universe/

stick to what philosophers do better, conceptual engineering, and seek to capture the silent *Weltanschauung* that might be dawning on us.

1.2   ICT as re-ontologizing technologies

In order to grasp the ICT scenarios that we might witness and experience in the near future, and hence the sort of ethical problems we might be expected to deal with, it is useful to introduce two key concepts at the outset, those of 'infosphere' and of 're-ontologization'.

Infosphere is a neologism I coined some years ago (Floridi 1999a) on the basis of 'biosphere', a term referring to that limited region on our planet that supports life. It denotes the whole informational environment constituted by all informational entities (thus including informational agents as well), their properties, interactions, processes and mutual relations. It is an environment comparable to, but different from, cyberspace (which is only one of its sub-regions, as it were), since it also includes offline and analogue spaces of information. We shall see that it is also an environment (and hence a concept) that is rapidly evolving.

Re-ontologizing is another neologism that I have recently introduced in order to refer to a very radical form of re-engineering, one that not only designs, constructs or structures a system (e.g. a company, a machine or some artefact) anew, but one that also fundamentally transforms its intrinsic nature, that is, its ontology or essence. In this sense, for example, nano-technologies and biotechnologies are not merely re-engineering but actually re-ontologizing our world.

Using the two previous concepts, it becomes possible to formulate succinctly the following thesis: ICTs are re-ontologizing the very nature of (and hence what we mean by) the infosphere, and here lies the source of some of the most profound transformations and challenging problems that our information societies will experience in the close future, as far as technology is concerned.

The most obvious way in which ICTs are re-ontologizing the infosphere concerns the transition from analogue to digital data and then the ever-increasing growth of our informational space. Both phenomena are very familiar and require no explanation, but a brief comment may not go amiss.

Although the production of analogue data is still increasing, the infosphere is becoming more digital by the day. A simple example may help to drive the point home: the new Large Hadron Collider built at the CERN (http://lhc.web.cern.ch/lhc/) to explore the physics of particles produces about 1.5 GB data per second, or about 10 petabytes of data annually, a quantity of data a thousand times larger than the Library of Congress's print collection and at least twice as large as Google's whole data storage, reported to be approximately 5 petabytes in 2004 (Mellor 2004).

This radical re-ontologization of the infosphere is largely due to the fundamental convergence between digital resources and digital tools. The ontology of the information technologies available (e.g. software, databases, communication channels and protocols, etc.) is now the same as (and hence fully compatible with) the ontology of their objects. This was one of Turing's most consequential intuitions: in the re-ontologized infosphere, there is no longer any substantial difference between the *processor* and the *processed*, so the digital deals effortlessly and seamlessly with the digital. This potentially eliminates one of the most long-standing bottlenecks in the infosphere and, as a result, there is a gradual erasure of *ontological friction*.

Ontological friction refers to the forces that oppose the flow of information within (a region of) the infosphere, and hence (as a coefficient) to the amount of work and effort required to generate, obtain, process and transmit information in a given environment, e.g. by establishing and maintaining channels of communication and by overcoming obstacles in the flow of information such as distance, noise, lack of resources (especially time and memory), amount and complexity of the data to be processed, and so forth. Given a certain amount of information *available* in (a region of) the infosphere, the lower the ontological friction within it, the higher the *accessibility* of that amount of information becomes. Thus, if one quantifies ontological friction from 0 to 1, a fully successful firewall would produce a 1.0 degree of friction, i.e. a complete standstill in the flow of information through its 'barrier'. On the other hand, we describe our society as informationally porous the more it tends towards a 0 degree of informational friction.

Because of their 'data superconductivity', ICTs are well known for being among the most influential factors that affect the ontological friction in the infosphere. We are all acquainted daily with aspects of a *frictionless infosphere*, such as *spamming* and *micrometering* (every fraction of a penny counts). Other significant consequences include (a) a substantial erosion of the *right to ignore*: in an increasingly porous society, it becomes progressively less credible to claim ignorance when confronted by easily predictable events (e.g. as George W. Bush did with respect to Hurricane Katrina's disastrous effects on New Orleans's flood barriers) and hardly ignorable facts (e.g. as Tessa Jowell, a British Labour MP, did with respect to her husband's finances). And therefore (b) an exponential increase in *common knowledge*: this is a technical term from epistemic logic, which basically refers to the case in which everybody not only knows that p but also knows that everybody knows that everybody knows, . . . , that p. In other words, (a) and (b) will also be the case because meta-information about how much information is, was or should have been available will become overabundant. From (a) and (b) it follows that, in the future, (c) we shall witness a steady increase in agents' *responsibilities*. As I shall argue towards the end of this chapter, ICTs are making humanity increasingly responsible, morally speaking, for the way the world is, will and should be (Floridi and Sanders 2001, Floridi 2006b).

1.3 The global infosphere or how information is becoming our ecosystem

During the last decade or so, we have become accustomed to conceptualizing our life online as a mixture between an evolutionary adaptation of human agents to a digital environment, and a form of post-modern, neo-colonization of the latter by the former. This is probably a mistake. ICTs are as much re-ontologizing our world as they are creating new realities. The threshold between *here* (*analogue, carbon-based, offline*) and *there* (*digital, silicon-based, online*) is fast becoming blurred, but this is as much to the advantage of the latter as it is to the former. The digital is spilling over into the analogue and merging with it. This recent phenomenon is variously known as 'Ubiquitous Computing', 'Ambient Intelligence', 'The Internet of Things' or 'Web-augmented Things'. It is, or will soon be, the next stage in the development of the information age.

The increasing re-ontologization of artefacts and of whole (social) environments suggests that soon it will be difficult to understand what life was like in predigital times and, in the near future, the very distinction between online and offline will become blurred and then disappear. To someone who was born in 2000 the world will always have been wireless, for example. To her, the peculiar clicking and whooshing sounds made by conventional modems while handshaking will be as alien as the sounds made by a telegraph's Morse signals. To put it dramatically, the infosphere is progressively absorbing any other ontological space. Let me explain.

In the (fast-approaching) future, more and more objects will be *ITentities* able to learn, advise and communicate with each other. A good example (but it is only an example) is provided by RFID (Radio Frequency IDentification) tags, which can store and remotely retrieve data from an object and give it a unique identity, like a barcode. Tags can measure 0.4 mm^2 and are thinner than paper. Incorporate this tiny microchip in everything, including humans and animals, and you have created *ITentities*. This is not science fiction. According to a report by market research company InStat, the worldwide production of RFID will increase more than 25-fold between 2005 and 2010 and reach 33 billion. Imagine networking these 33 billion ITentities together with all the hundreds of millions of PCs, DVDs, iPods and ICT devices available and you see that the infosphere is no longer 'there' but 'here' and it is here to stay. Your Nike and iPod already talk to each other, with predictable (but amazingly unforeseen) problems in terms of privacy (Saponas *et al.* 2007).

Nowadays, we are still used to considering the space of information as something we log-in to and log-out from. Our view of the world (our metaphysics) is still modern or Newtonian: it is made of 'dead' cars, buildings, furniture, clothes, which are non-interactive, irresponsive and incapable of communicating, learning or memorizing. But, as I shall argue in the next section, what we still experience as the world offline is bound to become a fully interactive and responsive environment of wireless, pervasive, distributed, *a2a* (anything to anything) information processes, that works *a4a* (anywhere for anytime), in real time. The day when we routinely google the location of physical objects ('where are the car keys?') is very close.[4]

As a consequence of such re-ontologization of our ordinary environment, we shall be living in an infosphere that will become increasingly *synchronized* (time), *delocalized* (space) and *correlated* (interactions). Although this might be read, optimistically, as the friendly face of globalization, we should not harbour illusions about how widespread and inclusive the evolution of information societies will be. The digital divide will become a chasm, generating new forms of discrimination between those who can be denizens of the infosphere and those who cannot, between insiders and outsiders, between information rich and information poor. It will redesign the map of worldwide society, generating or widening generational, geographic, socio-economic and cultural divides. But the gap will not be reducible to the distance between industrialized and developing countries, since it will cut across societies (Floridi 2002a). We are preparing the ground for tomorrow's informational slums.

1.4   The metaphysics of the infosphere

The previous transformations will invite us to understand the world as something 'a-live' (artificially live). Such animation of the world will, paradoxically, make our outlook closer to that of pre-technological cultures which interpreted all aspects of nature as inhabited by teleological forces. The second step will be a reconceptualization of our ontology in informational terms. It will become normal to consider the world as part of the infosphere, not so much in the dystopian sense expressed by a *Matrix*-like scenario, where the 'real reality' is still as hard as the metal of the machines that inhabit it, but in the evolutionary, hybrid sense represented by an environment such as New Port City, the fictional, post-cybernetic metropolis of *Ghost in the Shell*. The infosphere will not be a virtual environment supported by a genuinely 'material' world behind; rather, it will be the world itself that will be increasingly interpreted and understood informationally, as part of the infosphere. At the end of this shift, the infosphere will have moved from being a way to refer to the space of information to being synonymous with Being. Thus, our way of conceptualizing and making sense of reality will keep shifting from a materialist perspective, in which physical objects and processes still play a key role, to an informational one, in which

---

[4] In 2008, Thomas Schmidt, Alex French, Cameron Hughes and Angus Haines (four 12-year-old boys from Ashfold Primary School in Dorton, UK) were awarded the 'Home Invention of the Year' Prize for their Speed Searcher, a device for finding lost items. It attaches tags to valuables and enables a computer to pinpoint their location in the home.

- objects and processes are dephysicalized, typified and perfectly clonable;
- the right of usage is at least as important as the right to ownership; and
- the criterion for existence is no longer being immutable (Greek metaphysics) or being potentially subject to perception (modern metaphysics) but being interactable.

If all this seems a bit too 'philosophical', let me provide an illustrative example.

Despite some important exceptions (e.g. vases and metal tools in ancient civilizations or books after Gutenberg), it was the industrial revolution that really marked the passage from a nominalist world of unique objects to a Platonist world of types of objects, all perfectly reproducible as identical to each other, therefore epistemically indiscernible, and hence pragmatically dispensable because replaceable without any loss. Today, we find it obvious that two automobiles may be virtually identical and that we are invited to buy a model rather than a specific 'incarnation' of it. Indeed, we are fast moving towards a commodification of objects that considers repair as synonymous with replacement, even when it comes to entire buildings. This has led, by way of compensation, to a prioritization of *branding* – a process compared by Klein (2000) to the creation of 'cultural accessories and personal philosophies' – and of *re-appropriation*: the person who puts a sticker on the window of her car, which is otherwise perfectly identical to thousands of others, is fighting an anti-Platonic battle. The information revolution has further exacerbated this process. Once our window-shopping becomes Windows-shopping and no longer means walking down the street but browsing through the Web, the problem caused by the dephysicalization and typification of individuals as unique and irreplaceable entities starts eroding our sense of personal identity as well. We become mass-produced, anonymous entities among other anonymous entities, exposed to billions of other similar inforgs online. So we construct, self-brand and re-appropriate ourselves in the infosphere by blogs and FaceBook entries, homepages, YouTube videos, flickr albums, fashionable clothes and choices of places we visit, types of holidays we take and cars we drive and so forth. We use and expose information about ourselves to become less informationally indiscernible. We wish to maintain a high level of informational privacy almost as if that were the only way of saving a precious capital which can then be publicly invested by us in order to construct ourselves as individuals discernible and easily re-identifiable by others. Now, processes such as the one I have just sketched are part of a far deeper metaphysical drift caused by the information revolution.

1.5   The information turn as the fourth revolution

Oversimplifying more than a bit, one may say that science has two fundamental ways of changing our understanding. One may be called *extrovert*, or about the world, and the other *introvert*, or about ourselves. Three scientific revolutions have had great impact in both ways. They changed not only our understanding of the external world, but, in doing so, they also modified our conception of who we are. After Nicolaus Copernicus, the heliocentric cosmology displaced the Earth and hence humanity from the centre of the Universe. Charles Darwin showed that all species of life have evolved over time from common ancestors through natural selection, thus displacing humanity from the centre of the biological kingdom. Thirdly, following Sigmund Freud, we acknowledge nowadays that the mind is also unconscious and subject to the defence mechanism of repression, thus displacing it from the centre of pure rationality, a position that had been assumed as uncontroversial at least since Descartes. The reader who, like Popper, would be reluctant to follow Freud in considering psychoanalysis a scientific enterprise, might yet be willing to concede that contemporary neuroscience is a likely candidate for such a revolutionary role. Either way, the result is that we are not immobile, at the centre of the Universe (Copernican revolution), we are not unnaturally separate and diverse from the rest of the animal kingdom (Darwinian revolution), and we are very far from being Cartesian minds entirely transparent to ourselves (Freudian or Neuroscientific revolution).

Freud (1917) was the first to interpret these three revolutions as part of a single process of reassessment of human nature (see Weinert 2009). The hermeneutic manoeuvre was, admittedly, rather self-serving. But it did strike a reasonable note. In a similar way, when we now perceive that something very significant and profound has happened to human life after the informational turn, I would argue that our intuition is once again perceptive, because we are experiencing what may be described as a fourth revolution, in the process of dislocation and reassessment of humanity's fundamental nature and role in the universe. After Turing, computer science has not only provided unprecedented epistemic and engineering powers over natural and artificial realities; it has also cast new light on who we are and how we are related to the world. Today, we are slowly accepting the idea that we are not standalone and unique entities, but rather informationally embodied organisms (inforgs), mutually connected and embedded in an informational environment, the infosphere, which we share with both natural and artificial agents similar to us in many respects.

1.6   The evolution of inforgs

We have seen that we are probably the last generation to experience a clear difference between onlife and online. A further transformation worth highlighting concerns precisely the emergence of artificial and hybrid (multi)agents, i.e., partly artificial and partly human (consider, for example, a family as a single agent, equipped with digital cameras, laptops, palm pilots, iPods, mobiles, wireless network, digital TVs, DVDs, CD players, etc.). These new agents already share the same ontology with their environment and can operate within it with much more freedom and control. We (shall) delegate or outsource to artificial agents and companions (Floridi 2008a) memories, decisions, routine tasks and other activities in ways that will be increasingly integrated with us and with our understanding of what it means to be an agent. This is rather well known, but one aspect of this transformation may be in need of some clarification in this context.

Our understanding of ourselves as agents will also be deeply affected. I am not referring here to the sci-fi vision of a 'cyborged' humanity. Walking around with something like a Bluetooth wireless headset implanted in your ear does not seem the best way forward, not least because it contradicts the social message it is also meant to be sending: being on call 24/7 is a form of slavery, and anyone so busy and important should have a personal assistant instead. The truth is rather that being a sort of cyborg is not what people will embrace, but what they will try to avoid, unless it is inevitable. Nor am I referring to a GM humanity, in charge of its informational DNA and hence of its future embodiments. This is something that we shall probably see in the future, but it is still too far away, both technically (safely doable) and ethically (morally acceptable), to be discussed at this stage. As I anticipated in the previous section, I have in mind a quieter, less sensational and yet crucial and profound change in our conception of what it means to be an agent. We have begun to see ourselves as *connected informational organisms* (*inforgs*), not through some fanciful transformation in our body, but, more seriously and realistically, through the re-ontologization of our environment and of ourselves.

By re-ontologizing the infosphere, ICTs have brought to light the intrinsically informational nature of human agents. This is not equivalent to saying that people have digital alter egos, some Messrs Hydes represented by their @s, blogs and https. This trivial point only encourages us to mistake ICTs for merely *enhancing* technologies. The informational nature of agents should not be confused with a 'data shadow' either, a term introduced by Westin (1968) to describe a digital profile generated from data concerning a user's habits online. The change is more radical. To understand it, consider the distinction between *enhancing* and *augmenting* appliances. The switches and dials of the former are interfaces meant to plug the appliance into the user's body ergonomically. Drills and guns are perfect examples. It is the cyborg idea. The data and control panels of augmenting appliances are instead interfaces between different possible worlds: on the one hand, there is the human user's *Umwelt*[5], and on the other hand, there are the dynamic, watery, soapy,

---

[5] The outer world, or reality, as it affects the agent inhabiting it.

hot and dark world of the dishwasher; the equally watery, soapy, hot and dark but also spinning world of the washing machine; or the still, aseptic, soapless, cold and potentially luminous world of the refrigerator. These robots can be successful because they have their environments 'wrapped' and tailored around their capacities, not vice versa. Imagine someone trying to build a droid like C3PO capable of washing their dishes in the sink exactly in the same way as a human agent would. Now, despite some superficial appearances, ICTs are not enhancing nor augmenting in the sense just explained. They are re-ontologizing devices because they engineer environments that the user is then enabled to enter through (possibly friendly) gateways. It is a form of initiation. Looking at the history of the mouse, for example, one discovers that our technology has not only adapted to, but also educated, us as users. Douglas Engelbart once told me that he had even experimented with a mouse to be placed under the desk, to be operated with one's leg, in order to leave the user's hands free. HCI (Human-Computer Interaction) is a symmetric relation. To return to our distinction, whilst a dishwasher interface is a panel through which the machine enters into the user's world, a digital interface is a gate through which a user can be (tele)present in the infosphere (Floridi 2005c). This simple but fundamental difference underlies the many spatial metaphors of 'cyberspace', 'virtual reality', 'being online', 'surfing the web', 'gateway' and so forth. It follows that we are witnessing an epochal, unprecedented migration of humanity from its *Umwelt* to the infosphere itself, not least because the latter is absorbing the former. As a result, humans will be inforgs among other (possibly artificial) inforgs and agents operating in an environment that is friendlier to informational creatures. As digital immigrants like us are replaced by digital natives like our children, the latter will come to appreciate that there is no ontological difference between infosphere and *Umwelt*, only a difference of levels of abstractions (Floridi 2008b). Moreover, when the migration is complete, we shall increasingly feel deprived, excluded, handicapped or poor to the point of paralysis and psychological trauma whenever we are disconnected from the infosphere, like fish out of water. One day, being an inforg will be so natural that any disruption in our normal flow of information will make us sick.

It seems that, in view of this important change in our self-understanding – and of the sort of ICT-mediated interactions that we will increasingly enjoy with other agents, whether biological or artificial, and the infosphere – the best way of tackling the new ethical challenges posed by ICTs may be from an environmental approach, one which does not privilege the natural or untouched, but treats as authentic and genuine all forms of existence and behaviour, even those based on artificial, synthetic or engineered artefacts. This sort of holistic or inclusive environmentalism will require a change in how we perceive ourselves and our roles with respect to reality and how we might negotiate a new alliance between the natural and the artificial. These are the topics of the next two sections.

1.7   The constructionist values of *Homo Poieticus*

Ethical issues are often discussed in terms of putative resolutions of hypothetical situations, such as 'what should one do on finding a wallet in the lavatory of a restaurant?' Research and educational purposes may promote increasingly dramatic scenarios (sometimes reaching unrealistic excesses[6]), with available courses of action more polarized and less easily identifiable as right or wrong. But the general approach remains substantially the same: the agent is confronted by a moral dilemma and asked to make a principled decision by choosing from a menu of alternatives. Moral action is triggered by a situation. In 'situated action ethics' (to borrow an expression from AI), moral dilemma may give the false impression that the ethical discourse concerns primarily *a posteriori* reactions to problematic situations in which the agent unwillingly and unexpectedly finds herself. The agent is treated as a world user, a game player, a consumer of moral goods and evils, a browser,[7] a guest, or a customer who reacts to pre-established and largely unmodifiable conditions, scenarios and choices. Only two temporal modes count: present and future. The past seems irrelevant ('how did the agent found herself in such predicament?'), unless the approach is further expanded by a casuistry analysis. Yet ethics is not only a question of dealing morally well with a given world. It is also a question of constructing the world, improving its nature and shaping its development in the right way. This *proactive* approach treats the agent as a world owner, a game designer or referee, a producer of moral goods and evils, a provider, a host or a creator. The agent is supposed to be able to plan and initiate action responsibly, in anticipation of future events, in order to (try to) control their course by making something happen, or by preventing something from happening rather than waiting to respond (*react*) to a situation, once something has happened, or merely hoping that something positive will happen.

There are significant differences between reactive and proactive approaches. There is no space to explore them here, but one may mention, as a simple example, the moral responsibilities of a webmaster as opposed to those of a user of a website. Yet, differences should not be confused with incompatibilities. A mature moral agent is commonly expected to be both a morally good

---

[6] See, for example, 'the trolley problem' in Foot (1967); for a very entertaining parody do not miss 'the revised trolley problem' in Patton (1988). On 'George's job' and 'Jim and the Indians' see Smart and Williams (1987). Contrary to the trolley problem, the last two cases are meant to provide counterexamples against purely consequentialist positions.

[7] For an entirely 'situation-based ethics' approach to the Internet see, for example, Dreyfus (2001), who fails to appreciate any constructionist issue. His 'anthropology' includes only single web users browsing the net.

user and a morally good producer of the environment in which she operates, not least because situated action ethics can be confronted by lose–lose situations, in which all options may turn out to be morally unpleasant and every choice may amount to failure. A proactive approach may help to avoid unrecoverable situations. It certainly reduces the agent's reliance on moral luck. As a result, a large part of an ethical education consists in acquiring the kinds of traits, values and intellectual skills that may enable the agent to switch successfully between a reactive and a proactive approach to the world.

All this is acknowledged by many ethical systems, albeit with different vocabulary, emphasis and levels of explicitness. Some more conservative ethical theories prefer to concentrate on the reactive nature of the agent's behaviour. For example, deontologism embeds a reactive bias insofar as it supports duties on-demand. Another good example is the moral code implicit in the Ten Commandments, which is less proactive than that promoted in the New Testament. On a more secular level, the two versions of Asimov's laws of robotics provide a simple case of evolution. The 1940 version is more reactive than the 1985 version, whose new zeroth law includes a substantially proactive requirement: 'A robot may not injure humanity, or, through inaction, allow humanity to come to harm.'

Ethical theories that adopt a more proactive approach can be defined as *constructionist*. The best known constructivist approach is virtue ethics. According to it, an individual's principal ethical aim is to live the good life by becoming a certain kind of person. The constructionist stance is expressed by the desire to mould oneself. The goal is achieved by implementing or improving some characteristics, while eradicating or controlling others. The stance itself is presupposed: it is simply assumed as uncontroversial that one does wish to live the good life by becoming the best person one can. Some degree of personal malleability and capacity to choose critically provide further background preconditions. The key question 'what kind of person should I be?' is rightly considered to be a reasonable and justified question. It grounds the question 'what kind of life should I lead?' and immediately translates into 'what kind of character should I construct? What kind of virtues should I develop? What sort of vices should I avoid or eradicate?' It is implicit that each agent strives to achieve that aim *as an individual*, with only incidental regard to the enveloping community.

Different brands of virtue ethics disagree on the specific virtues and values identifying a person as morally good. The disagreement, say between Aristotle, Paul of Tarsus and Nietzsche, can be dramatic, not least because it is ultimately ontological, in that it regards the kind of entity that a human being should strive to become. In prototyping jargon, theories may disagree on the abstract specification of the model, not just on implementation details. Despite their divergences, all brands of virtue ethics share the same subject-oriented kernel. This is not to say that they are all subjectivist but rather, more precisely, that they are all concerned exclusively with the proper *construction* of the moral subject, be that a self-imposed task or an educational goal of a second party, like parents, teachers or society in general. To adopt a technical expression, virtue ethics is intrinsically *egopoietic*. Its *sociopoietic* nature is merely a by-product, in the following sense. Egopoietic practices that lead to the ethical construction of the subject inevitably interact with, and influence, the ethical construction of the community inhabited by the subject. So, when the subjective microcosm and the socio-political macrocosm differ in scale but essentially not in nature or complexity – as one may assume in the idealized case of the Greek *polis* – egopoiesis can scale up to the role of general ethics and even political philosophy. Plato's *Republic* is an excellent example. Plato finds it unproblematic to move seamlessly between the construction of the ideal self and the construction of the ideal city-state. But so does the Mafia, whose code of conduct and 'virtuous ethics' for the individual is based on the view that 'the family' is its members. Egopoiesis and sociopoiesis are interderivable only in sufficiently *simple* and *closed* societies, in which significant communal behaviour is ultimately derivable from that of its constituent individuals. In complex societies, sociopoiesis is no longer reducible to egopoiesis alone. This is the fundamental limit of virtue ethics. In autonomous, interactive and adaptive societies, virtue ethics positions acquire an individualistic value, previously inconceivable, and may result in moral escapism. The individual still cares about her own ethical construction and, at most, the construction of the community with which she is more closely involved, like the family, but the rest of the world falls beyond the horizon of her moral concern. Phrasing the point in terms of situated action ethics, new problematic hypothetical situations arise from emergent phenomena. Examples include issues of disarmament, the ozone level, pollution, famine and the digital divide. The difficulty becomes apparent in all its pressing urgency as the individual agent tries to reason using 'local' ethical principles to tackle a problem with 'global', ethical features and consequences. Because virtue ethics remains limited by its subject-oriented approach, it cannot provide, by itself, a satisfactory ethics for a globalized world in general and for the information society in particular. If misapplied, it fosters ethical individualism, as the agent is more likely to mind only her own self-construction. If it is uncritically adopted, it can be intolerant, since agents and theorists may forget the culturally over-determined nature of their foundationalist anthropologies, which often have religious roots. If it fosters tolerance, it may still spread relativism because any self-construction becomes acceptable, as long as it takes place in the enclave of one's own private sphere, culture and cyber-niche, without bothering any neighbour.

The inadequacy of virtue ethics is, of course, historical. The theory has aged well, but it can provide, at most, a local sociopoietic approach as a mere extension of its genuine vocation: egopoiesis. It intrinsically lacks the resources to go beyond the construction of the individual and the indirect role this may play in shaping her local community. Theoretically, however, the limits of virtue ethics should not lead to an overall rejection of any constructionist approach. On the contrary, the fundamentally constructionist lesson taught by virtue ethics (one of the features that makes virtue ethics appealing in the first place) is more important than ever before.

In a global information society, the individual agent (often a *multi-agent system*) is like a *demiurge* (Plato's god responsible for the design of the physical universe based on preexisting matter). Her powers can be variously exercised (in terms of control, creation or modelling) over herself (e.g. genetically, physiologically, neurologically and narratively), over human society (e.g. culturally, politically, socially and economically) and over natural or artificial environments (e.g. physically and informationally). Such an increasingly powerful agent has corresponding moral duties and responsibilities to oversee not only the development of her own character and habits but also the well-being of each of her spheres of influence. Clearly, a constructionist ethics should be retained and reinforced, but the kind of ethical constructionism needed today goes well beyond the education of the self and the political engineering of the simple and closed cyberpolis. It must also address the urgent and pressing question concerning the kind of global realities that are being built. This means decoupling constructionism from subjectivism and re-orienting it to the object, applying it *also* to society and the environment, the receivers of the agent's actions.

The term 'ecopoiesis' refers to the morally informed construction of the environment based on this object- or ecologically oriented perspective. To move from individual virtues to global values, an *ecopoietic* approach is needed that recognizes the agent's responsibilities towards the environment (including present and future inhabitants) as its enlightened creator steward or supervisor, not just as its virtuous user and consumer.

Constructionism is the drive to build physical and conceptual objects and, more subtly, to exercise control and stewardship on them. It manifests itself in the care of existing, and the creation of new, realities, these being material or conceptual. Thus, constructionism is ultimately best understood as a struggle against entropy. Existentially, it represents the strongest reaction against the destiny of death. In terms of a philosophical anthropology, constructionism is embodied by what I have termed elsewhere *homo poieticus* (Floridi 1999a). *Homo poieticus* is to be distinguished from *homo faber*, user and 'exploitator' of natural resources, from *homo oeconomicus*, producer, distributor and consumer of wealth, and from *homo ludens* (Huizinga 1998), who embodies a leisurely playfulness devoid of the ethical care and responsibility characterizing the constructionist attitude. *Homo poieticus* concentrates not merely on the final result, but on the dynamic, on-going process through which the result is achieved. One of the major challenges facing *homo poieticus* is the possibility of negotiating a new alliance between *physis* and *techne*.

1.8   E-nvironmentalism or the marriage of *physis* and *techne*

Whether *physis* (nature, the world) and *techne* (applied knowledge, technology) may be reconcilable is not a question that has a predetermined answer, waiting to be divined. It is more like a practical problem, whose feasible solution needs to be devised. With an analogy, we are not asking whether two chemicals could mix but rather whether a marriage may be successful. There is plenty of room for a positive answer, provided the right sort of commitment is made.

It seems beyond doubt that a successful marriage between *physis* and *techne* is vital and hence worth our effort. Information societies increasingly depend upon technology to thrive, but they equally need a healthy, natural environment to flourish. Try to imagine the world not tomorrow or next year, but next century, or next millennium: a divorce between *physis* and *techne* would be utterly disastrous both for our welfare and for the well-being of our habitat. This is something that technophiles and green fundamentalists must come to understand. Failing to negotiate a fruitful, symbiotic relationship between technology and nature is not an option. Fortunately, a successful marriage between *physis* and *techne* is achievable. True, much more progress needs to be made. The physics of information can be highly energy-consuming and hence potentially unfriendly towards the environment. In 2000, data centres consumed 0.6% of the world's electricity. In 2005, the figure had risen to 1%. They are now responsible for more carbon-dioxide emissions per year than Argentina or the Netherlands and, if current trends hold, their emissions will have grown four-fold by 2020, reaching 670 million tonnes. By then, it is estimated that ICT's carbon footprint will be higher than aviation's.[8] However, ICTs will also help 'to eliminate 7.8 metric gigatons of greenhouse gas emissions annually by 2020 equivalent to 15 percent of global emissions today and five times more than our estimate of the emissions from these technologies in 2020'.[9] This positive (and improvable) balance leads me to a final comment.

The greenest machine is a machine with 100% energy efficiency. Unfortunately, this is equivalent to a perpetual motion machine and the latter is simply a pipe dream. However, we also know that such an impossible limit can be increasingly approximated: energy waste can be dramatically reduced and energy efficiency can be highly increased (the two processes are not necessarily the same; compare recycling vs. doing more with less). Often, both kinds of processes may be fostered only by relying on significant improvements in the management of information (e.g. to build and run hardware and processes better). So here is how we may reinterpret Socrates' ethical intellectualism: we do evil because we do not know better, in the sense that the better the information management is, the less moral evil is caused. ICTs can help us in our

---

[8] Source: *The Economist*, 22 May 2008.
[9] Source: McKinsey's Information Technology Report, October 2008, 'How IT can cut carbon emissions', by Giulio Boccaletti, Markus Löffler and Jeremy M. Oppenheim.

fight against the destruction, impoverishment, vandalism and waste of both natural and human (including historical and cultural) resources. So they can be a precious ally in what I have called, in Floridi (2008c), *synthetic environmentalism* or *e-nvironmentalism*. We should resist any Greek epistemological tendency to treat *techne* as the Cinderella of knowledge; any absolutist inclination to accept no moral balancing between some unavoidable evil and far more goodness; or any modern, reactionary, metaphysical temptation to drive a wedge between naturalism and constructionism by privileging the former as the only authentic dimension of human life. The challenge is to reconcile our roles as agents within nature and as stewards of nature. The good news is that it is a challenge we can meet. The odd thing is that we are slowly coming to realize that we have such a hybrid nature.

1.9   Conclusion

Previous revolutions (especially the agricultural and the industrial ones) created macroscopic transformation in our social structures and physical environments, often without much foresight. The informational revolution is no less dramatic and we shall be in serious trouble if we do not take seriously the fact that we are constructing the new environment that will be inhabited by future generations. As a social structure, the information society has been made possible by a cluster of information and communication technologies (ICTs). And as a full expression of *techne*, the information society has already posed fundamental ethical problems, whose complexity and global dimensions are rapidly evolving. The task is to formulate an ethical framework that can treat the infosphere as a new environment worth the moral attention and care of the human inforgs inhabiting it. Such an ethical framework must be able to address and solve the unprecedented challenges arising in the new environment. It must be an e-nvironmental ethics for the infosphere. In the following chapters, the reader will be able to appreciate both the complexity of the task and how far information and computer ethicists have managed to tackle it successfully.[10] Unfortunately, I suspect it will take some time and a whole new kind of education and sensitivity to realize that the infosphere is a common space, which needs to be preserved to the advantage of all. My hope is that this book will contribute to such a change in perspective.

---

[10] This chapter is an updated synthesis of Floridi (forthcoming, a), Floridi and Sanders (2005), Floridi (2007), and Floridi (2008a).

2 The historical roots of information and computer ethics

Terrell Ward Bynum

2.1 Introduction

During the Copernican Revolution in the sixteenth and early seventeenth centuries, major changes in science and philosophy led human beings to see themselves, and indeed the entire Universe, in a radically different perspective. Traditional assumptions about human nature and the role of humans in the Universe were in question, and significant changes occurred in our understanding of society and religion. Centuries later, first Darwinian biology and then Freudian psychology altered – yet again – some fundamental assumptions about human nature (Floridi 2008a), though they did not significantly change our view of the Universe as a whole. Today, the information revolution, including its associated scientific and philosophical developments, has begun to yield a radically different view of human nature and the world. In physics, for example, recent discoveries indicate that *the Universe is made of information, and human beings are exquisitely complex 'informational objects'* (Wheeler 1990, Lloyd 2006). In philosophy – in particular, in the 'philosophy of information' of Luciano Floridi (e.g., Floridi 2008a, Floridi 2008e) – human beings are viewed as sophisticated informational beings, similar in many ways to the vast array of ICT-artefacts emerging in our 'information society'. At a certain 'level of abstraction', humans and their ICT-artefacts can be seen as companions – fellow travellers on a mutual journey of existence in an informational universe (Floridi 2008a). This new way of understanding human nature and the place of humans in the world raises a number of new ethical questions (Floridi 2008d).

In the 1940s and 1950s, philosopher/scientist Norbert Wiener was a seminal figure for today's informational understanding of the Universe and the role of humans within it. In addition, his 'cybernetic' analyses of human nature and society led him to create philosophical foundations for the ethical field that is currently called *information and computer ethics*. Indeed, Wiener played a double role in the information revolution: on the one hand, he helped to generate the necessary technology for that revolution; and, on the other hand, he provided a philosophical foundation for information and computer ethics to help the world cope with the resulting social and ethical consequences. Even before Wiener, seeds of today's informational understanding of the Universe and of human nature could be found in the works of other philosophers, such as Aristotle's metaphysics, his theory of perception and his account of human thinking (see Bynum 1986). Given these ideas, the present chapter has three goals:

(1) It examines some metaphysical assumptions of Aristotle and Wiener that can be seen as philosophical roots of today's information and computer ethics.

(2) It describes some milestones in information and computer ethics from Wiener's contributions to the present day.

(3) It briefly describes Floridi's new 'macroethics' (his term), which he calls information ethics (henceforth 'IE') to distinguish Floridi's 'macroethics' from the general field of information ethics that includes, for example, agent ethics, computer ethics, Internet ethics, journalism ethics, library ethics, bioengineering ethics, neurotechnology ethics – to name some of its significant parts.)

2.2   Aristotelian roots

More than two thousand years ago, Aristotle developed a detailed theory of the nature of the Universe and of the individual objects within it. Some of the questions that he asked himself were these: What are individual objects made of? What do all animals have in common? What distinguishes human beings from all the other animals? How does an animal acquire information from objects outside of its body, and what happens to that information once it gets inside of the animal's body? Aristotle's answers to these and related questions are remarkably similar to many of the answers we would give today, including answers closely related to the informational understanding of the Universe and of human beings.

According to Aristotle (*Metaphysics*), individual entities in the Universe consist of *matter* and *form*. Matter is the underlying substrate of which an entity is made, while form is 'taken on' by the matter thereby making an individual thing what it is. Matter and form always occur together, neither exists without the other – so there is no matter that is formless, and there is no form that is not 'enmattered'. Consider, for example, what makes a house a house: a heap or collection of bricks, wood, glass, etc. does not constitute a house. Such materials must be assembled into a certain *form* to create the house. The form is *essential* to the house; it is what makes the house a house. The particular matter out of which the house happens to be made is, in some sense, accidental. One could replace the original bricks with other bricks and the original wood with different wood and it would still be a house. One could even replace the bricks with wooden blocks and the wood with appropriate pieces of plastic and it would still be a house. *The form of a house is what makes it a house and enables it to fulfil the functions of a house.*

According to Aristotle, the same is true for living things, including people. Aristotle himself, for example, remains Aristotle over time, even though the matter out of which he is made is constantly changing through metabolic processes, such as breathing, eating, digesting and perspiring. The *form* of Aristotle is essential to his existence in the world, and to the functions he is capable of fulfilling; but the particular bits of matter out of which Aristotle happens to be made at any given moment are incidental. 'Form' in this case is much more than just the shape of Aristotle's body and its parts; it includes all the other essential qualities that make him what he is, and these are 'enmattered' in his body.

Aristotle distinguished animals from plants by the fact that animals can perceive, while plants cannot. During perception, information from objects outside of an animal gets transferred into the animal. How is this possible? According to Aristotle (*On the Motion of Animals, On the Soul*), nature has so structured the sense organs of animals that they are able to 'take in the form [of what is being perceived] without the matter'. Eyes take in forms like colours and shapes, ears take in the pitch and loudness of sounds, and so on. How is it possible to 'take in forms without the matter'? Aristotle used the analogy of pressing a metal ring into soft wax. The wax is able to 'take on' the shape and size of the ring without taking in the metal out of which the ring is made.

According to Aristotle, perception accomplishes a similar result within the body of an animal: in the process of perception, the form of an object is carried to the animal's sense organ by means of a medium such as air or water. The sense organ then *takes in the form* that is being carried by the medium, but it does not take in the matter of the object of perception – nor even the matter of the medium. From the sense organ, the form is transferred, through the animal's body, to a region where all perceptual forms are interpreted, thereby creating *percepts*. Percepts contain information from the object of perception, information which interacts with the physiology of the animal, generating pleasure or pain and initiating the animal's reaction to the perceived object. After a perceived object is no longer present, most animals nevertheless retain perceptual traces – '*phantasms*' – inside their bodies. These lingering physical entities are fainter versions of original percepts, containing similar information, and they typically have a similar effect upon an animal's behaviour (Bynum 1986).

In human beings, as in other animals, responses to perceptions are sometimes 'automatic'. However, humans can choose, instead, to control their responses using *reasoning*. According to Aristotle, there are two kinds of reasoning: *theoretical reasoning*, which generates knowledge and beliefs about the world, and *practical reasoning*, which generates choices and actions. Excellent practical reasoning is the kind that leads to *virtuous* actions. The ability of humans to choose their actions and control their behaviour, using theoretical and practical reasoning, distinguishes humans from all the other animals, according to Aristotle, and makes them ethically responsible for what they do and what they become. In *On the Soul*, Aristotle describes thinking and reasoning as processes that either *are* the physical manipulation of phantasms, or at least *require the presence* of such manipulation. For Aristotle, therefore, thinking and reasoning require sophisticated information processing that is dependent upon the physiology of the human body.

For centuries, philosophers have been debating what Aristotle meant by metaphysical terms like 'matter', 'form', 'substance' and others. There is no need for us to join that debate here; but it is worth noting, in the present context, that what Aristotle called a 'form' either *is*, or at least *includes*, information from whatever object is being perceived. For purposes of the present chapter, it is of interest to note that the underlying metaphysics, physiology and psychology of Aristotle's theory of human nature – when interpreted as described here – yield the following conclusions:

(1) Individual entities in the Universe are made out of matter and forms, and forms either *are* or at the very least *contain* information. So matter and information are significant components of every physical thing in the Universe.
(2) Aristotle's account of perception assumes that all animals are information-processing beings whose bodily structures account for the ways in which information gets processed within them.
(3) Information processing within an animal's body initiates and controls the animal's behaviour.
(4) Like other animals, humans are information-processing beings; but unlike other animals, humans have sophisticated information-processing capabilities called *theoretical reasoning* and *practical reasoning*, and these make ethics possible.

2.3   Wiener on human beings as information objects

Aristotle's metaphysics, physics, biology, physiology, theory of animal behaviour and account of human reasoning are more than twenty-three hundred years old. They provided to Aristotle a rich scientific and philosophical foundation for developing his virtue ethics theory. In addition, as indicated above, they also contained a number of ideas suggestive of today's informational theory of the nature of the Universe and of human beings. A pioneer in the development of today's theory was the philosopher/scientist Norbert

Wiener, whose achievements in cybernetics, communication theory, computer design, and related fields, in the 1940s and 1950s, helped to bring about the current 'information age'. Wiener made the following important assumptions:

(1) Objects and processes in the Universe are made of matter/energy and information.
(2) All animals are information-processing beings whose behaviour depends centrally upon such processing.
(3) Humans, unlike other animals, have bodies that make the information processing in their central nervous systems especially sophisticated.

Wiener combined these assumptions with his extensive knowledge in philosophy, physics, biology, communication theory, information science and psychology. The result was an impressive philosophical and scientific foundation for today's information ethics and computer ethics theories. (See Wiener 1948, 1950, 1954, 1964.)

Wiener's assumptions about the ultimate nature of the Universe included his view that *information is physical* – subject to the laws of nature and measurable by science. The sort of information that he had in mind is sometimes called 'Shannon information', which is named for Claude Shannon, who had been a student and colleague of Wiener's. Shannon information is the syntactic sort that is carried in telephone wires, TV cables and radio signals. It is the kind of information that computer chips process and DNA encodes within the cells of all living organisms. Wiener believed that such information, even though it is physical, *is neither matter nor energy*. Thus, while discussing thinking as information processing, he noted that a brain or a computer

does not secrete thought 'as the liver does bile', as the earlier materialists claimed, nor does it put it out in the form of energy, as the muscle puts out its activity. Information is information, not matter or energy. No materialism which does not admit this can survive at the present day. (Wiener 1948, p. 132)

According to Wiener, matter-energy and Shannon information are different physical phenomena, but neither can exist without the other. So-called 'physical objects' – including living organisms – are actually persisting patterns of Shannon information encoded within an ever-changing flux of matter-energy. Every physical process is a mixing and mingling of matter-energy and information – a creative 'coming-to-be' and destructive 'fading away' – as old patterns of matter-energy-encoded information erode and new patterns emerge.

A related aspect of Wiener's metaphysics is his account of human nature and personal identity. Human beings, too, are *patterns of information that persist through changes in matter-energy*. Thus, in spite of continuous exchanges of matter-energy between a person's body and the world outside the body (via respiration, perspiration, excretion, and so on), the complex organization or *form* of a person – that is, *the pattern of Shannon information encoded within a person's body* – is maintained, thereby preserving life, functionality and personal identity. Thus, Wiener stated:

> We are but whirlpools in a river of ever-flowing water. We are not stuff that abides, but patterns that perpetuate themselves. (Wiener 1954, p. 96)

> The individuality of the body is that of a flame . . . of a form rather than of a bit of substance. (Wiener 1954, p. 102)

To use today's language, humans are 'information objects' whose personal identity is tied to internal information processing and to persisting patterns of Shannon information within their bodies. Personal identity is not dependent upon specific bits of matter-energy that happen to make up one's body at any given moment. Through breathing, drinking, eating and other metabolic processes, the matter-energy that makes up one's body is constantly changing. Nevertheless one remains the same person over time because the pattern of Shannon information encoded within the body remains essentially the same.

With this idea in mind, Wiener engaged in a remarkable thought experiment: If one could encode, in a telegraph message, the *entire* exquisitely complex Shannon-information pattern of a person's body, and then use that encoded pattern to reconstitute the person's body from appropriate atoms at the receiving end of the message, people could travel instantly from place to place via telegraph. Wiener noted that this idea raises knotty philosophical questions regarding, not only personal identity, but also 'forking' from one person into two, 'split' personalities, survival of the self after the death of one's body, and a number of others (Wiener 1950, Ch. VI, 1954, Ch. V).

An additional aspect of Wiener's metaphysics is his account of *good and evil* within nature. He used the traditional distinction between 'natural evil', caused by the forces of nature (for example, earthquakes, volcanoes, diseases, floods, tornados and physical decay), and 'moral evil' (for example, human-caused death, injury, pain and sorrow). The ultimate natural evil, according to Wiener, is *entropy* – the loss of useful Shannon information and useful energy that occurs in virtually every physical change. According to the second law of thermodynamics, essentially all physical changes decrease available Shannon information and available energy. As a result, everything that ever comes into existence will decay and be destroyed. This includes anything that a person might value, such as one's life, wealth and happiness; great works of art; magnificent architectural structures; cities, cultures and civilizations; the sun and moon and stars. None of these can survive the decay and destruction of entropy – the loss of available Shannon information – for everything in the Universe is subject to the second law of thermodynamics.

2.4   Wiener on cybernetic machines in society

In his book, *Cybernetics: or Control and Communication in the Animal and the Machine* (1948), Wiener viewed animals and computerized machines as *cybernetic entities* – that is, as dynamic systems with component parts that communicate with each other internally, and also with the outside world, by means of various channels of communication and feedback loops. Such communication helps to unify an animal or a machine into a single functioning entity.

Wiener also viewed communities and whole societies as cybernetic entities: Beginning in 1950, with the publication of *The Human Use of Human Beings*, Wiener assumed that *cybernetic machines will join humans as active participants in society*. For example, some machines will participate along with humans in the vital activity of creating, sending and receiving the messages that constitute the 'cement' that binds society together:

> It is the thesis of this book that society can only be understood through a study of the messages and the communication facilities which belong to it; and that in the future development of these messages and communication facilities, messages between man and machines, between machines and man, and between machine and machine, are destined to play an ever-increasing part. (Wiener 1950, p. 9)

In addition, Wiener predicted that certain machines, namely digital computers with robotic appendages, would someday participate in the workplace, replacing thousands of human factory workers, both blue collar and white collar. He also foresaw artificial limbs and other body parts – cybernetic 'prostheses' – that would be merged with human bodies to help persons with disabilities – or even to endow able-bodied persons with unprecedented powers. Today, we would say that Wiener envisioned societies in which 'cyborgs' would play a significant role and would have ethical policies to govern their behaviour. In summary, Wiener foresaw what he called the 'Machine Age' or the 'Automatic Age' in which machines would be integrated into the social fabric, as well as the physical environment. They would create, send and receive messages; gather information from the external world; make decisions; take actions; reproduce themselves; and be merged with human bodies to create beings with vast new powers. By the early 1960s, these were not just speculations by Wiener, because he himself had already designed or witnessed early versions of devices, such as game-playing machines (checkers, chess, war, business), artificial hands with motors that are controlled by the person's brain, and self-reproducing machines like non-linear transducers. (See especially Wiener 1964.) Wiener's predictions about future societies and their machines caused others to raise various questions about the machines that Wiener envisioned:

Will they be 'alive'? Will they have minds? Will they be conscious? Wiener considered such questions to be vague semantic quibbles, rather than genuine scientific issues:

Now that certain analogies of behaviour are being observed between the machine and the living organism, the problem as to whether the machine is alive or not is, for our purposes, semantic and we are at liberty to answer it one way or the other as best suits our convenience. (Wiener 1954, p. 32)

Similarly, answers to questions about machine consciousness, thinking, or purpose are pragmatic choices, according to Wiener; although he did believe that questions about the 'intellectual capacities' of machines, when appropriately stated, could be genuine scientific questions:

Cybernetics takes the view that the structure of the machine or of the organism is an index of the performance that may be expected from it . . .

Theoretically, if we could build a machine whose mechanical structure duplicated human physiology, then we could have a machine whose intellectual capacities would duplicate those of human beings. (Wiener 1954, p. 57, italics in the original)

By viewing animals and cybernetic machines in the same way – namely, as dynamic systems with internal communications and feedback loops, exchanging information with the outside world, and thereby adjusting to changes in the world – Wiener began to view traditional distinctions between mechanism and vitalism, living and non-living, human and machine as pragmatic choices, rather than unbreachable metaphysical 'walls' between kinds of beings.

2.5   Scientific support for Wiener's metaphysical assumptions

Wiener's presuppositions about the ultimate nature of all entities in the Universe, that *they consist of information encoded in matter-energy*, anticipated later research and discoveries in physics. During the past two decades, for example, physicists – beginning with Princeton's John Wheeler (Wheeler 1990) – have been developing a 'theory of everything' which presupposes that the Universe is fundamentally informational, that every physical 'object' or entity is, in reality, a pattern or 'flow' of Shannon information encoded in matter-energy. Wheeler's hypothesis has been studied and furthered by other scientists in recent years, and their findings support Wiener's metaphysical presuppositions. As explained by MIT professor Seth Lloyd:

The universe is the biggest thing there is and the bit is the smallest possible chunk of information. The universe is made of bits. Every molecule, atom and elementary particle registers bits of information. Every interaction between those pieces of the universe processes that information by altering those bits. (Lloyd 2006, p. 3)

I suggest thinking about the world not simply as a machine, but as *a machine that processes information.* In this paradigm, there are two primary quantities, energy and information, standing on an equal footing and playing off each other. (Lloyd 2006, p. 169)

Science writer Charles Seife notes that 'information is physical' and so,

[Shannon] Information is not just an abstract concept, and it is not just facts or figures, dates or names. It is a concrete property of matter and energy that is quantifiable and measurable. It is every bit as real as the weight of a chunk of lead or the energy stored in an atomic warhead, and just like mass and energy, information is subject to a set of physical laws that dictate how it can behave – how information can be manipulated, transferred, duplicated, erased, or destroyed. And everything in the universe must obey the laws of information, because everything in the universe is shaped by the information it contains. (Seife 2006, p. 2)

In addition, the matter-energy-encoded Shannon information that constitutes every existing entity in the Universe appears to be *digital and finite.* Wheeler's one-time student Jacob Beckenstein, for example, discovered the so-called 'Beckenstein bound', which is *the upper limit* of the amount of Shannon information that can be contained within a given volume of space. The maximum number of information units ('bits') that can fit into any volume is *fixed by the area of the boundary enclosing that space* – one bit per four 'Planck squares' of area (Beckenstein 2003). In summary, then, the matter-energy-encoded information that constitutes all the existing entities in the Universe appears to be finite and digital; and only so much of it can be contained within a specific volume of space. (For an alternative non-digital view, see Floridi 2008c.)

Norbert Wiener's intuitions or assumptions about the nature of the Universe – now supported by important developments in contemporary physics – provide a new account of the ultimate nature of the Universe, a new understanding of life and human nature, and indeed a new view of every existing entity as an 'information object' or an 'information process'. Consider, for example, living organisms: Genes in their cells store and process Shannon information and use it to create the 'stuff of life', such as DNA, RNA, proteins and amino acids. Nervous systems of animals take in, store and process Shannon information, resulting in bodily motions, perceptions, emotions and – at least in the case of humans – thinking and reasoning. And, as Charles Seife points out,

Each creature on earth is a creature of information; information sits at the center of our cells, and information rattles around in our brains... Every particle in the universe, every electron, every atom, every particle not yet discovered, is packed with information... that can be transferred, processed, and dissipated. Each star in the universe, each one of the countless galaxies in the heavens, is packed full of information, information that can escape and travel. That information is always flowing, moving from place to place, spreading throughout the cosmos. (Seife 2006, p. 3)

2.6   Wiener's pioneering contributions to computer ethics

In addition to developing a metaphysical and scientific foundation for information ethics, Wiener made a number of early contributions to the applied ethics field that later would be called 'computer ethics' (see Section 2.7 below). However, he did not see himself as developing a new branch of applied ethics, so he did not coin a name like 'computer ethics' or 'cybernetics ethics'. He simply raised ethical concerns, and offered suggested solutions, about the likely impacts of computers and other cybernetic machines. One of his chief worries was that cybernetic science was so powerful and flexible that it placed human beings 'in a position to construct artificial machines of almost any degree of elaborateness of performance' (Wiener 1948, p. 27). Cybernetics, therefore, would provide vast new powers that could be used for good, but might also be used in ethically disastrous ways:

Long before Nagasaki and the public awareness of the atomic bomb, it had occurred to me that we were here in the presence of another social potentiality of unheard-of importance for good and for evil. (Wiener 1948, p. 27)

Wiener worried that factory owners might replace human workers with automated machines and bring about massive unemployment. Cybernetics, he said, could be used to create mechanical 'slaves' that would force human workers to compete for jobs against 'slave labor'. Thus a new industrial revolution could 'devalue the human brain' the way the original industrial revolution devalued human physical labour. Instead of facing 'dark satanic mills', human workers might lose their jobs to cybernetic machines (Wiener 1948, pp. 27–28; see also 1950, Ch. X).

Another serious worry for Wiener was the creation of *machines that can learn and make decisions on their own*. Some of them simply played games, like checkers and chess, but others had more serious applications, like economic planning or even military planning. As early as 1950, Wiener expressed concern that government computers might already be using John von Neumann's mathematical game theory to make war plans, including plans for the use of nuclear weapons. He warned against accepting machine-made decisions too easily. Of special concern would be machines that *can learn before making their decisions*, because such decisions might turn out to be ethically terrible:

For the man who is not aware of this, to throw the problem of his responsibility on the machine, whether it can learn or not, is to cast his responsibility to the winds, and find it coming back seated on the whirlwind. (Wiener 1950, p. 212)

Nevertheless, Wiener's view of cybernetic machines was often positive, rather than negative. Such machines, he said, provide choices between good and evil, and he believed that in the future they often will bring about wonderful results. He himself participated in experiments with machines that mimic human muscle-control disorders, so that such disorders could be better understood and more successfully treated. He also worked to create a 'hearing glove' to help a deaf person compensate for hearing loss by using a cybernetic glove to generate appropriate vibrations in one's hand (Wiener 1950, Ch. X).

Another positive use for cybernetic devices that Wiener envisioned – in this case, including a global electronic communications network – was the possibility of working on the job while being hundreds or even thousands of miles away from the job site (Wiener 1950, Ch. VI). This will be possible, he said, because

where a man's word goes, and where his power of perception goes, to that point his control and in a sense his physical existence is extended. To see the whole world and to give commands to the whole world is almost the same as to be everywhere. (Wiener 1950, p. 104)

Wiener illustrated this point with a thought experiment: He imagined an architect in Europe supervising the day-to-day construction of a building in the United States without ever physically travelling to America. Instead, the architect would send and receive 'Ultrafax' facsimiles of plans and photos, and he would interact with the work crew by telephone and teletype machine. This thought experiment provided perhaps the first example of 'teleworking' and a community with some geographically separated members who participate in the community 'virtually'.

In addition to the few computer ethics topics mentioned here, Wiener analysed, or at least touched upon, a wide variety of issues decades ago which are still considered 'contemporary' today, for example, agent ethics, artificial intelligence, machine psychology, computers and security, computers and religion, computers and learning, computers for persons with disabilities, responsibilities of computer professionals, and many other topics as well. (See Bynum 2000b, 2004, 2005.)

2.7   Coining the name 'computer ethics'

Wiener was far ahead of other thinkers in his ability to foresee social and ethical impacts of cybernetics and electronic computers. As a result, his pioneering achievements in computer ethics and information ethics, in the 1940s and 1950s, were essentially ignored until the late 1990s. In the meantime, growing computer ethics challenges – such as, invasions of privacy, threats to security and the appearance of computer-enabled crimes – began to be noticed by public policy makers and the general public. In the late 1960s, for example, Donn Parker – a computer scientist at SRI International – became concerned about the growing number of computer professionals who were caught committing serious crimes with the help of their computer expertise. Parker said, 'When some people enter the computer center, they leave their ethics at the door.' He began to study unethical and illegal activities of computer professionals, and gather example cases of computer-enabled crimes. In 1968, he published the article, 'Rules of Ethics in Information Processing', in *Communications of the ACM*; and he headed the development of the first Code of Professional Conduct for the Association for Computing Machinery (eventually adopted by the ACM membership in 1973). Later, he published books and articles on computer crime. (See, for example, Parker 1979, Parker *et al.* 1990.)

It was not until the second half of the 1970s that the name 'computer ethics' was coined by Walter Maner, then a faculty member in philosophy at Old Dominion University. While teaching medical ethics, he noticed that ethical problems in which computers became involved were often worsened or significantly altered by the addition of computing technology. It even seemed to Maner that computers might create new ethical problems that had never been seen before. He examined this same phenomenon in areas other than medicine and concluded that a new branch of applied ethics, modelled upon medical ethics or business ethics, should be recognized by philosophers. He coined the name 'computer ethics' to refer to this proposed new field, and he developed an experimental course designed primarily for students of computer science. The course was a success, and Maner started to teach computer ethics on a regular basis.

Using his teaching experiences and his research in the proposed new field, Maner created a 'Starter Kit in Computer Ethics' (Maner 1978) and provided copies of it to attendees of workshops that he ran and speeches that he gave at philosophy conferences and computing conferences in America. His 'Kit' contained curriculum materials and pedagogical advice for university teachers. It also included suggested course descriptions for university catalogues, a rationale for offering such a course in a university, a list of course objectives, some teaching tips, and discussions of topics like privacy and confidentiality, computer crime, computer decisions, technological dependence and professional codes of ethics. In 1980, Helvetia Press and the National Information and Resource Center for Teaching Philosophy published Maner's computer ethics 'starter kit' as a monograph (Maner 1980) that was widely disseminated to colleges and universities in America and a number of other countries.

2.8   An influential textbook and the 'uniqueness debate'

In developing the first university computer ethics course, Maner defined the field as a branch of applied ethics that would study problems 'aggravated, transformed or created by computer technology'. He believed that a number of already existing ethical problems are worsened by the involvement of computer technology, while other, *new and unique problems are generated* by such technology. A colleague in the Philosophy Department, Deborah Johnson, became interested in Maner's proposed new branch of applied ethics. She agreed with him that computer technology can aggravate or 'give a new twist' to old ethical problems, but she was sceptical of the notion that computers can generate wholly new ethical problems that have never been seen before. In discussions with Maner, during which his suggested 'unique' cases were examined, Johnson saw *new examples of old issues* regarding privacy, ownership, just distribution of power, and so on, while Maner saw *problems that would never have arisen if computers had not been invented*. These early discussions between Maner and Johnson eventually led to conference presentations and publications that launched a decades-long conversation – the 'uniqueness debate' – among computer ethics scholars, beginning with Maner and Johnson themselves. (See Chapter 3 below.)

Several years after the 'uniqueness' discussions had begun between Johnson and Maner, Johnson published the first major computer ethics textbook (Johnson 1985). There she noted that computers 'pose new versions of standard moral problems and moral dilemmas, exacerbating the old problems, and forcing us to apply ordinary moral norms in uncharted realms' (Johnson 1985, p. 1). She did not, however, grant Maner's claim that computers create *wholly new* ethical problems. Her highly successful textbook set the research agenda in the field of computer ethics for more than a decade, including topics such as ownership of software and intellectual property, computing and privacy, responsibility of computer professionals, and the just distribution of technology and human power. In later editions (1994, 2001), Johnson added new ethical topics, such as 'hacking' into people's computers without their permission, computer technology for persons with disabilities, and the Internet's impact upon democracy.

In the later editions of her textbook, Johnson added to the ongoing 'uniqueness debate' with Maner and other scholars. She granted that computer technology has created new kinds of entities – such as software and databases – and new ways to 'instrument' human actions. These innovations, she said, *do* lead to *new, unique, specific* ethical questions – for example, 'Should ownership of software be protected by law?' and 'Do huge databases of personal information threaten privacy?' She insisted, in both later editions of her textbook, however, that the new *specific* ethical questions are merely '*new species of old moral issues*' like protection of human privacy or ownership of intellectual property. They are not, she said, wholly new ethical problems requiring additions to traditional ethical theories, as Maner had claimed.

2.9   A classic computer ethics theory

A watershed year in the history of computer ethics was 1985, not only because of the publication of Johnson's agenda-setting textbook, but also because of the appearance of James Moor's classic paper 'What is Computer Ethics?' (Moor 1985). In that paper, Moor offered an account of the *nature* of computer ethics and an explanation of *why* computer technology generates so many ethical questions compared to other technologies. Computing technology is genuinely revolutionary, said Moor, because it is 'logically malleable':

Computers are logically malleable in that they can be shaped and molded to do any activity that can be characterized in terms of inputs, outputs and connecting logical operations. . . . Because logic applies everywhere, the potential applications of computer technology appear limitless. The computer is the nearest thing we have to a universal tool. Indeed, the limits of computers are largely the limits of our own creativity. (Moor 1985, p. 269)

Logical malleability makes it possible for people to do a wide variety of things that they never were able to do before. Because such things were not done in the past, it is possible, perhaps likely, that there is no law or standard of good practice or ethical rule to govern them. Moor calls such cases 'policy vacuums', and these can sometimes lead to 'conceptual muddles':

A typical problem in computer ethics arises because there is a policy vacuum about how computer technology should be used. Computers provide us with new capabilities and these in turn give us new choices for action. Often, either no policies for conduct in these situations exist or existing policies seem inadequate. A central task of computer ethics is to determine what we should do in such cases, that is, formulate policies to guide our actions. . . . One difficulty is that along with a policy vacuum there is often a conceptual vacuum. Although a problem in computer ethics may seem clear initially, a little reflection reveals a conceptual muddle. What is needed in such cases is an analysis that provides a coherent conceptual framework within which to formulate a policy for action. (Moor 1985, p. 266)

This explanation of the nature and cause of computer ethics problems was found to be insightful and helpful by many thinkers. It provided a way to understand and deal with emerging computer ethics problems, and it quickly became the most influential account of the nature of computer ethics among a growing number of scholars.

More than a decade later, Moor significantly enhanced his theory of computer ethics (Moor 1998). For example, he introduced the notion of 'core values' – such as *life*, *health*, *happiness*, *security*, *resources*, *opportunities* and *knowledge* – which are so important to the continued survival of a community that essentially all communities must value them. If a community did not value these things, it would likely cease to exist. With the help of 'core values' and some ethical ideas from Bernard Gert (Gert 1998), Moor later added an account of justice, which he called 'just consequentialism', combining deontological and consequentialist ideas (Moor 1999).

Moor's way of analysing and resolving computer ethics issues was both creative and practical. It provided a broad perspective on the nature of the information revolution; and, in addition, by using effective ideas like 'logical malleability', 'policy vacuums', 'conceptual muddles', 'core values' and 'just consequentialism', he provided a very effective problem-solving method:

(1) Identify a policy vacuum generated by computing technology.
(2) Eliminate any conceptual muddles.
(3) Use core values and the ethical resources of 'just consequentialism' to revise existing, but inadequate, policies or to create new policies that will fill the vacuum and thereby resolve the original ethical problem.

2.10   Computer ethics and human values

A common thread that runs through much of the history of computer ethics, from Norbert Wiener onwards, is concern for the protection and advancement of major human values like life, health, security, freedom, knowledge, happiness, resources, power and opportunity. Wiener, for example, focused attention on what he called 'great human values' like freedom, opportunity, security and happiness; and most of the specific examples and cases included in his relevant works are examples of defending or advancing such values – e.g., preserving security, resources and opportunities for factory workers by preventing massive unemployment from robotic factories, or avoiding threats to national security from decision-making war-game machines. In Moor's computer ethics theory, respect for 'core values' is a central aspect of his 'just consequentialism' theory of justice, as well as his influential analysis of human privacy. The fruitfulness of the 'human-values approach' to computer ethics is reflected in the fact that it has served as the organizing theme of major computer-ethics conferences, such as the 1991 watershed National Conference on Computing and Values that was organized around impacts of computing upon security, property, privacy, knowledge, freedom and opportunities. In the late 1990s, a new approach to computer ethics, 'value-sensitive computer design', emerged (see Chapter 5 in this book), based upon the insight that human values can be 'embedded' within technology, and so potential computer-ethics problems can be avoided, while new technology is under development, by *anticipating possible harm to human values and designing new technology from the very beginning in ways that prevent such harm.* (See, for example, Friedman and Nissenbaum 1996, Friedman 1997, Brey 2000, Introna and Nissenbaum 2000, Introna 2005, Flanagan *et al.* 2008.)

2.11   The philosophy of information

By the mid 1990s, the information revolution, which Wiener had distantly envisioned fifty years before, was well under way. A vast diversity of information and communication artefacts had been invented and were proliferating across the globe: mainframe computers; mini, desktop and laptop computers; software; databases; word processors; spreadsheets; electronic games; the Internet; email; and on, and on. Robots had joined or replaced human workers in some factories; some people had become 'telecommuters' working from home online, instead of travelling to an office or a factory; 'virtual communities', with geographically dispersed members, were multiplying; and decision-making machines were replacing certain people in medical centres, banks, airplane cockpits, classrooms, etc. At the same time, influential physicists – like John Wheeler at Princeton (Wheeler 1990) – had begun to argue that the Universe is made of information.

In this context, philosopher Luciano Floridi launched an ambitious project to create a new philosophical paradigm, which he named '*the philosophy of information*' (henceforth PI). He believed that other paradigms in philosophy – such as, analytic philosophy, phenomenology, existentialism, and so on – had become 'scholastic', and therefore stagnant as intellectual enterprises:

Scholasticism, understood as an intellectual topology rather than a scholarly category, represents the inborn inertia of a conceptual system, when not its rampant resistance to innovation. It is *institutionalized philosophy* at its worst.... It manifests itself as a pedantic and often intolerant adherence to some discourse (teachings, methods, values, viewpoints, canons of authors, positions, theories, or selections of problems, etc.), set by a particular group (a philosopher, a school of thought, a movement, a trend, etc.), at the expense of alternatives, which are ignored or opposed. (Floridi 2002b, p. 125)

Philosophy, said Floridi,

can flourish only by constantly re-engineering itself. A philosophy that is not timely but timeless is not an impossible *philosophia perennis*, which claims universal validity over past and future intellectual positions, but a stagnant philosophy. (Floridi 2002b, p. 128)

As an alternative to scholastic philosophical systems and communities, Floridi set for himself the ambitious task of creating a new philosophical paradigm which he believed would someday become part of the 'bedrock' of philosophy (*philosophia prima*). At the heart of his new paradigm was to be the concept of *information*, a concept with multiple meanings,

a concept as fundamental and important as being, knowledge, life, intelligence, meaning, or good and evil – all pivotal concepts with which it is interdependent – and so equally worthy of autonomous investigation. It is also a more impoverished concept, in terms of which the others can be expressed and inter-related, when not defined. (Floridi 2002b, p. 134)

Upon first sight, the metaphysical presuppositions of Floridi's PI paradigm seem much like those of Wiener's metaphysics. For example, both assume that objects in the Universe are made of information and both consider *entropy* to be a fundamental evil. Such initial impressions, however, are in need of further qualification because the kind of information that Wiener had in mind is Shannon information, which is syntactic, but not semantic, and it is subject to laws of physics such as the second law of thermodynamics. Floridi's fundamental information, on the contrary, is 'strongly semantic' and not subject to the laws of physics; and Floridi's entropy is not the thermodynamic kind that Wiener presupposed, but is synonymous with Non-Being. The informational universe that Wiener had in mind is the materialistic one that physicists study; while Floridi's universe, which he named 'the infosphere', is Platonic and Spinozistic and includes 'the semantic environment in which millions of people spend their time nowadays' (Floridi 2002b, p. 134). It includes not only material objects understood informationally, but also entities, like Platonic abstractions or possible beings, that are *not subject to the laws of physics* (Floridi 2008e, p. 12).

2.12   Floridi's Information Ethics theory

A major component of Floridi's new philosophical paradigm is the ethical theory that he calls INFORMATION ETHICS (henceforth IE to distinguish Floridi's theory from the more general field of information ethics in the broad sense). Floridi describes his IE theory as a 'macroethics' (his word), *similar* to virtue ethics, deontologism, consequentialism and contractualism in that it is intended to be applicable to all ethical situations. On the other hand, IE is *different* from these traditional theories because it is *not intended to replace them*, but rather to supplement them with further ethical considerations that can sometimes be overridden by more traditional ethical concerns (Floridi 2005b).

What are the fundamental components of IE? According to Floridi, every existing entity in the Universe, when viewed from a certain 'level of abstraction', can be construed as an 'informational object' with a characteristic data structure that constitutes its very nature. And, for this reason, the Universe considered as a whole can be called 'the infosphere'. Each entity in the infosphere can be damaged or destroyed by altering its characteristic data structure, thereby preventing it from 'flourishing'. Such damage or destruction Floridi calls 'entropy', which results in the 'empoverishment of the infosphere'. Entropy, therefore, constitutes evil that should be avoided or minimized. With this in mind, Floridi offers four 'fundamental principles' of IE:

(0) entropy ought not to be caused in the infosphere (null law)
(1) entropy ought to be prevented in the infosphere
(2) entropy ought to be removed from the infosphere
(3) the flourishing of informational entities as well as the whole infosphere ought to be promoted by preserving, cultivating and enriching their properties

By construing every existing entity as an 'informational object' with at least a minimal moral worth, Floridi shifts the focus of ethical consideration away from the actions, characters and values of human agents toward the 'evil' (harm, dissolution, destruction) – 'entropy' – suffered by objects in the infosphere. With this approach, every existing entity – humans, other animals, organizations, plants, non-living artefacts, electronic objects in cyberspace, pieces of intellectual property, stones, Platonic abstractions, possible beings, vanished civilizations – can be interpreted as *potential agents* that affect other entities, and as *potential patients* that are affected by other entities. Thus, Floridi's IE can be described as a 'patient-based' non-anthropocentric ethical theory instead of the traditional 'agent-based' anthropocentric ethical theories like deontologism, contractualism, consequentialism and virtue theory.

The addition of Floridi's IE to traditional anthropocentric ethical theories adds a new basis for ethical judgement and fills important 'gaps' left by those other theories:

(i) The Western anthropocentric ethical theories do not successfully account for a significant aspect of human ethical experience, namely, the feeling or attitude of respect for all of nature. Such respect or reverence has been a significant aspect of *other* Western ethical theories, like that of Spinoza or some of the Stoics, and it is an important feature of Eastern ethical theories like those of Buddhism and Taoism (Hongladarom 2008).

(ii) The Western anthropocentric ethical theories, because they focus exclusively upon human actions, characters and values, are not well suited to the task of ethically analysing or informing the activities of new kinds of 'agents' – like robots, softbots and cyborgs – which are proliferating rapidly and playing an ever-increasing role in the information society.

Floridi's IE is an ethical theory for the information age, rooted in the science, technology and social changes that have made the information revolution possible.

Part II

Ethical approaches

3 Values in technology and disclosive computer ethics

Philip Brey

3.1 Introduction

Is it possible to do an ethical study of computer systems themselves independently of their use by human beings? The theories and approaches in this chapter answer this question affirmatively and hold that such studies should have an important role in computer and information ethics. In doing so, they undermine conventional wisdom that computer ethics, and ethics generally, is concerned solely with human conduct, and they open up new directions for computer ethics, as well as for the design of computer systems.

As our starting point for this chapter, let us consider some typical examples of ethical questions that are raised in relation to computers and information technology, such as can be found throughout this book:

- Is it wrong for a system operator to disclose the content of employee email messages to employers or other third parties?
- Should individuals have the freedom to post discriminatory, degrading and defamatory messages on the Internet?
- Is it wrong for companies to use data-mining techniques to generate consumer profiles based on purchasing behaviour, and should they be allowed to do so?
- Should governments design policies to overcome the digital divide between skilled and unskilled computer users?

As these examples show, ethical questions regarding information and communication technology typically focus on the morality of particular ways of *using* the technology or the morally right way to *regulate* such uses.

Taken for granted in such questions, however, are the computer systems and software that are used. Could there, however, not also be valid ethical questions that concern the technology itself? Could there be an ethics of computer systems separate from the ethics of *using* computer systems? The *embedded values* approach in computer ethics, formulated initially by Helen Nissenbaum (1998; Flanagan, Howe and Nissenbaum 2008) and since adopted by many authors in the field, answers these questions affirmatively, and aims to develop a theory and methodology for moral reflection on computer systems themselves, independently of particular ways of using them.

The embedded values approach holds that computer systems and software are not morally neutral and that it is possible to identify tendencies in them to promote or demote particular moral values and norms. It holds, for example, that computer programs can be supportive of privacy, freedom of information, or property rights or, instead, to go against the realization of these values. Such tendencies in computer systems are called 'embedded', 'embodied' or 'built-in' moral values or norms. They are built-in in the sense that they can be identified and studied largely or wholly independently of actual uses of the system, although they manifest themselves in a variety of uses of the system. The embedded values approach aims to identify such tendencies and to morally evaluate them. By claiming that computer systems may incorporate and manifest values, the embedded values approach is not claiming that computer systems engage in moral actions, that they are morally praiseworthy or blameworthy, or that they bear moral responsibility (Johnson 2006). It is claiming, however, that the design and operation of computer systems has moral consequences and therefore should be subjected to ethical analysis.

If the embedded values approach is right, then the scope of computer ethics is broadened considerably. Computer ethics should not just study ethical issues in the use of computer technology, but also in the technology itself. And if computer systems and software are indeed value-laden, then many new ethical issues emerge for their design. Moreover, it suggests that design practices and methodologies, particularly those in information systems design and software engineering, can be changed to include the consideration of embedded values.

In the following section, Section 3.2, the case will be made for the embedded values approach, and some common objections against it will be discussed. Section 3.3 will then turn to an exposition of a particular approach in computer ethics that incorporates the embedded values approach, *disclosive computer ethics*, proposed by the author (Brey 2000). Disclosive computer ethics is an attempt to incorporate the notion of embedded values into a comprehensive approach to computer ethics. Section 3.4 considers *value-sensitive design* (VSD), an approach to design developed by computer scientist Batya Friedman and her associates, which incorporates notions of the embedded values approach (Friedman, Kahn and Borning 2006). The VSD approach is not an approach within ethics but within computer science, specifically within information systems design and software engineering. It aims to account for values in a comprehensive manner in the design process, and makes use of insights of the embedded values approach for this purpose. In a concluding section, the state of the art in these different approaches is evaluated and some suggestions are made for future research.

3.2   How technology embodies values

The existing literature on embedded values in computer technology is still young, and has perhaps focused more on case studies and applications for design than on theoretical underpinnings. The idea that technology embodies values has been inspired by work in the interdisciplinary field of science and technology studies, which investigates the development of science and technology and their interaction with society. Authors in this field agree that technology is not neutral but shaped by society. Some have argued, specifically, that technological artefacts (products or systems) issue constraints on the world surrounding them (Latour 1992) and that they can harbour political consequences (Wiener 1954). Authors in the embedded value approach have taken these ideas and applied them to ethics, arguing that technological artefacts are not morally neutral but value-laden. However, what it means for an artefact to have an embedded value remains somewhat vague.

In this section a more precise description of what it means for a technological artefact to have embedded values is articulated and defended. The position taken here is in line with existing accounts of embedded values, although their authors need not agree with all of the claims made in this section. The idea of embedded values is best understood as a claim that technological artefacts (and in particular computer systems and software) have built-in tendencies to promote or demote the realization of particular values. Defined in this way, a built-in value is a special sort of built-in consequence. In this section a defence of the thesis that technological artefacts are capable of having built-in consequences is first discussed. Then tendencies for the promotion of values are identified as special kinds of built-in consequences of technological artefacts. The section is concluded by a brief review of the literature on values in information technology, and a discussion of how values come to be embedded in technology.

3.2.1   Consequences built into technology

The embedded values approach promotes the idea that technology can have built-in tendencies to promote or demote particular values. This idea, however, runs counter to a frequently held belief about technology, the idea that technology itself is neutral with respect to consequences. Let us call this the *neutrality thesis*. The neutrality thesis holds that there are no consequences that are inherent to technological artefacts, but rather that artefacts can always be used in a variety of different ways, and that each of these uses comes with its own consequences. For example, a hammer can be used to hammer nails, but also to break objects, to kill someone, to flatten dough, to keep a pile of paper in place or to conduct electricity. These uses have radically different effects on the world, and it is difficult to point to any single effect that is constant in all of them.

The hammer example, and other examples like it (a similar example could be given for a laptop), suggest strongly that the neutrality thesis is true. If so, this would have important consequences for an ethics of technology. It would follow that ethics should not pay much attention to technological artefacts themselves, because they in themselves do not 'do' anything. Rather, ethics should focus on their usage alone.

This conclusion holds only if one assumes that the notion of embedded values requires that there are consequences that manifest themselves in each and every use of an artefact. But this strong claim need not be made. A weaker claim is that artefacts may have built-in consequences in that there are recurring consequences that manifest themselves in a wide range of uses of the artefact, though not in all uses. If such recurring consequences can be associated with technological artefacts, this may be sufficient to falsify the strong claim of the neutrality thesis that each use of a technological artefact comes with its own consequences. And a good case can be made that at least some artefacts can be associated with such recurring consequences.

An ordinary gas-engine automobile, for example, can evidently be used in many different ways: for commuter traffic, for leisure driving, to taxi passengers or cargo, for hit jobs, for auto racing, but also as a museum piece, as a temporary shelter for the rain or as a barricade. Whereas there is no single consequence that results from all of these uses, there are several consequences that result from a large number of these uses: in all but the last three uses, gasoline is used up, greenhouse gases and other pollutants are being released, noise is being generated, and at least one person (the driver) is being moved around at high speeds. These uses, moreover, have something in common: they are all *central* uses of automobiles, in that they are accepted uses that are frequent in society and that account for the continued production and usage of automobiles. The other three uses are *peripheral* in that they are less dominant uses that depend for their continued existence on these central uses, because their central uses account for the continued production and consumption of automobiles. Central uses of the automobile make use of its capacity for driving, and when it is used in this capacity, certain consequences are very likely to occur. Generalizing from this example, a case can be made that technological artefacts are capable of having built-in consequences in the sense that *particular consequences may manifest themselves in all of the central uses of the artefact.*

It may be objected that, even with this restriction, the idea of built-in consequences employs a too deterministic conception of technology. It suggests that, when technological artefacts are used, particular consequences are necessary or unavoidable. In reality, there are usually ways to avoid particular consequences. For example, a gas-fuelled automobile need not emit greenhouse gases into the atmosphere if a greenbox device is attached to it, which captures carbon dioxide and nitrous oxide and converts it into bio-oil. To avoid this objection, it may be claimed that the notion of built-in consequences does not refer to necessary, unavoidable consequences but rather to strong *tendencies* towards certain consequences. The claim is that these consequences are normally realized whenever the technology is used, unless it is used in a context that is highly unusual or if extraordinary steps are taken to avoid particular consequences. Built-in consequences are therefore never absolute but always relative to a set of typical uses and contexts of use, outside of which the consequences may not occur.

Do many artefacts have built-in consequences in the way defined above? The extent to which technological artefacts have built-in consequences can be correlated with two factors: the extent to which they are capable of exerting force or behaviour autonomously, and the extent to which they are embedded in a fixed context of use. As for the first parameter, some artefacts seem to depend strongly on users for their consequences, whereas others seem to be able to generate effects on their own. Mechanical and electrical devices, in particular, are capable of displaying all kinds of behaviours on their own, ranging from simple processes, like the consumption of fuel or the emission of steam, to complex actions, like those of robots and artificial agents. Elements of infrastructure, like buildings, bridges, canals and railway tracks, may not behave autonomously but, by their mere presence, they do impose significant constraints on their environment, including the actions and movements of people, and in this way engender their own consequences. Artefacts that are not mechanical, electrical or infrastructural, like simple hand-held tools and utensils, tend to have less consequences of their own and their consequences tend to be more dependent on the uses to which they are put.

As for the second parameter, it is easier to attribute built-in consequences to technological artefacts that are placed in a fixed context of use than to those that are used in many different contexts. Adapting an example by Winner (1980), an overpass that is 180 cm (6 ft) high has as a generic built-in consequence that it prevents traffic from going through that is more than 180 cm high. But when such an overpass is built over the main access road to an island from a city in which automobiles are generally less than 180 cm high and buses are taller, then it acquires a more specific built-in consequence, which is that buses are being prevented from going to the island whereas automobiles do have access. When, in addition, it is the case that buses are the primary means of transportation for black citizens, whereas most white citizens own automobiles, then the more specific consequence of the overpass is that it allows easy access to the island for one racial group, while denying it to another. When the context of use of an artefact is relatively fixed, the immediate, physical consequences associated with a technology can often be *translated* into social consequences because there are reliable correlations between the physical and the social (for example between prevention of access to buses and prevention of access to blacks) that are present (Latour 1992).

3.2.2   From consequences to values

Let us now turn from built-in consequences to embedded values. An embedded value is a special kind of built-in consequence. It has already been explained how technological artefacts can have built-in consequences. What needs to be explained now is how some of these built-in consequences can be associated with values. To be able to make this case, let us first consider what a value is.

Although the notion of a value remains somewhat ambiguous in philosophy, some agreements seem to have emerged (Frankena 1973). First, philosophers tend to agree that values depend on *valuation*. Valuation is the act of valuing something, or finding it valuable, and to find something valuable is to find it *good* in some way. People find all kinds of things valuable, both abstract and concrete, real and unreal, general and specific. Those things that people find valuable that are both ideal and general, like justice and generosity, are called *values*, with *disvalues* being those general qualities that are considered to be bad or evil, like injustice and avarice. Values, then, correspond to idealized qualities or conditions in the world that people find good. For example, the value of justice corresponds to some idealized, general condition of the world in which all persons are treated fairly and rewarded rightly.

To have a value is to want it to be *realized*. A value is realized if the ideal conditions defined by it are matched by conditions in the actual world. For example, the value of freedom is fully realized if everyone in the world is completely free. Often, though, a full realization of the ideal conditions expressed in a value is not possible. It may not be possible for everyone to be completely free, as there are always at least some constraints and limitations that keep people from a state of complete freedom. Therefore, values can generally be realized only to a degree.

The use of a technological artefact may result in the partial realization of a value. For instance, the use of software that has been designed not to make one's personal information accessible to others helps to realize the value of privacy. The use of an artefact may also hinder the realization of a value or promote the realization of a disvalue. For instance, the use of software that contains spyware or otherwise leaks personal data to third parties harms the realization of the value of privacy. Technological artefacts are hence capable of either *promoting* or *harming* the realization of values when they are used. When this occurs systematically, in all of its central uses, we may say that the artefact embodies a special kind of built-in consequence, which is a *built-in tendency to promote or harm the realization of a value*. Such a built-in tendency may be called, in short, an *embedded value* or *disvalue*. For example, spyware-laden software has a tendency to harm privacy in all of its typical uses, and may therefore be claimed to have harm to privacy as an embedded disvalue.

Embedded values approaches often focus on *moral values*. Moral values are ideals about how people ought to behave in relation to others and themselves and how society should be organized so as to promote the right course of action. Examples of moral values are justice, freedom, privacy and honesty. Next to moral values, there are different kinds of non-moral values, for example, aesthetic, economic, (non-moral) social and personal values, such as beauty, efficiency, social harmony and friendliness.

Values should be distinguished from norms, which can also be embedded in technology. *Norms* are rules that prescribe which kinds of actions or state of affairs are forbidden, obligatory or allowed. They are often based on values that provide a rationale for them. *Moral norms* prescribe which actions are forbidden, obligatory or allowed from the point of view of morality. Examples of moral norms are 'do not steal' and 'personal information should not be provided to third parties unless the bearer has consented to such distribution'. Examples of non-moral norms are 'pedestrians should walk on the right side of the street' and 'fish products should not contain more than 10 mg histamines per 100 grams'. Just as technological artefacts can promote the realization of values, they can also promote the enforcement of norms. *Embedded norms* are a special kind of built-in consequence. They are tendencies to effectuate norms by bringing it about that the environment behaves or is organized according to the norm. For example, web browsers can be set not to accept cookies from websites, thereby enforcing the norm that websites should not collect information about their user. By enforcing a norm, artefacts thereby also promote the corresponding value, if any (e.g., privacy in the example).

So far we have seen that technological artefacts may have embedded values understood as special kinds of built-in consequences. Because this conception relates values to causal capacities of artefacts to affect their environment, it may be called the *causalist* conception of embedded values. In the literature on embedded values, other conceptions have been presented as well. Notably, Flanagan, Howe and Nissenbaum (2008) and Johnson (1997) discuss what they call an *expressive* conception of embedded values. Artefacts may be said to be expressive of values in that they incorporate or contain symbolic meanings that refer to values. For example, a particular brand of computer may symbolize or represent status and success, or the representation of characters and events in a computer game may reveal racial prejudices or patriarchal values. Expressive embedded values in artefacts *represent* the values of designers or users of the artefact. This does not imply, however, that they also function to *realize* these values. It is conceivable that the values expressed in artefacts cause people to adopt these values and thereby contribute to their own realization. Whether this happens frequently remains an open question. In any case, whereas the expressive conception of embedded values merits further philosophical reflection, the remainder of this chapter will be focused on the causalist conception.

3.2.3   Values in information technology

The embedded values approach within computer ethics studies embedded values in computer systems and software and their emergence, and provides moral evaluations of them. The study of embedded values in Information and Communication Technology (ICT) has begun with a seminal paper by Batya Friedman and Helen Nissenbaum in which they consider *bias* in computer systems (Friedman and Nissenbaum 1996). A biased computer system or program is defined by them as one that systematically and unfairly discriminates against certain individuals or groups, who may be users or other stakeholders of the system. Examples include educational programs that have much more appeal to boys than to girls, loan approval software that gives negative recommendations for loans to individuals with ethnic surnames, and databases for matching organ donors with potential transplant recipients that systematically favour individuals retrieved and displayed immediately on the first screen over individuals displayed on later screens. Building on their work, I have distinguished *user biases* that discriminate against (groups of) users of an information system, and *information biases* that discriminate against stakeholders represented by the system (Brey 1998). I have discussed various kinds of user bias, such as user exclusion and the selective penalization of users, as well as different kinds of information bias, including bias in information content, data selection, categorization, search and matching algorithms and the display of information.

After their study of bias in computer systems, Friedman and Nissenbaum went on to consider consequences of software agents for the autonomy of users. Software agents are small programs that act on behalf of the user to perform tasks. Friedman and Nissenbaum (1987) argue that software agents can undermine user autonomy in various ways – for example by having only limited capabilities to perform wanted tasks or by not making relevant information available to the user – and argue that it is important that software agents are designed so as to enhance user autonomy. The issue of user autonomy is also taken up in Brey (1998, 1999c), in which I argue that computer systems can undermine autonomy by supporting monitoring by third parties, by imposing their own operational logic on the user, thus limiting creativity and choice, or by making users dependent on systems operators or others for maintenance or access to systems functions.

Deborah Johnson (1997) considers the claim that the Internet is an inherently democratic technology. Some have claimed that the Internet, because of its distributed and nonhierarchical nature, promotes democratic processes by empowering individuals and stimulating democratic dialogue and decision-making (see Chapter 10). Johnson subscribes to this democratic potential. She cautions, however, that these democratic tendencies may be limited if the Internet is subjected to filtering systems that only give a small group of individuals control over the flow of information on the Internet. She hence identifies both democratic and undemocratic tendencies in the technology that may become dominant depending on future use and development.

Other studies, within the embedded values approach, have focused on specific values, such as privacy, trust, community, moral accountability and informed consent, or on specific technologies. Introna and Nissenbaum (2000) consider biases in the algorithms of search engines, which, they argue, favour websites with a popular and broad subject matter over specialized sites, and the powerful over the less powerful. Introna (2007) argues that existing plagiarism detection software creates an artificial distinction between alleged plagiarists and non-plagiarists, which is unfair. Introna (2005) considers values embedded in facial recognition systems. Camp (1999) analyses the implications of Internet protocols for democracy. Flanagan, Howe and Nissenbaum (2005) study values in computer games, and Brey (1999b, 2008) studies them in computer games, computer simulations and virtual reality applications. Agre and Mailloux (1997) reveal the implications for privacy of Intelligent Vehicle-Highway Systems, Tavani (1999) analyses the implications of data-mining techniques for privacy and Fleischmann (2007) considers values embedded in digital libraries.

3.2.4   The emergence of values in information technology

What has not been discussed so far is how technological artefacts and systems acquire embedded values. This issue has been ably taken up by Friedman and Nissenbaum (1996). They analyse the different ways in which biases (injustices) can emerge in computer systems. Although their focus is on biases, their analysis can easily be generalized to values in general. Biases, they argue, can have three different types of origins. *Preexisting biases* arise from values and attitudes that exist prior to the design of a system. They can either be *individual*, resulting from the values of those who have a significant input into the design of the systems, or *societal*, resulting from organizations, institutions or the general culture that constitute the context in which the system is developed. Examples are racial biases of designers that become embedded in loan approval software, and overall gender biases in society that lead to the development of computer games that are more appealing to boys than to girls. Friedman and Nissenbaum note that preexisting biases can be embedded in systems intentionally, through conscious efforts of individuals or institutions, or unintentionally and unconsciously.

A second type is *technical bias*, which arises from technical constraints or considerations. The design of computer systems includes all kinds of technical limitations and assumptions that are perhaps not value-laden in themselves but that could result in value-laden designs, for example because limited screen sizes cannot display all results of a search process, thereby privileging those results that are displayed first, or because computer algorithms or models contain formalized, simplified representations of reality that introduce biases or limit the autonomy of users, or because software engineering techniques do not allow for adequate security, leading to systematic breaches of privacy. A third and final type is *emergent bias*, which arises when the social context in which the system is used is not the one intended by its designers. In the new context, the system may not adequately support the capabilities, values or interests of some user groups or the interests of other stakeholders. For example, an ATM that relies heavily on written instructions may be installed in a neighborhood with a predominantly illiterate population.

Friedman and Nissenbaum's classification can easily be extended to embedded values in general. Embedded values may hence be identified as preexisting, technical or emergent. What this classification shows is that embedded values are not necessarily a reflection of the values of designers. When they are, moreover, their embedding often has not been intentional. However, their embedding *can* be an intentional act. If designers are aware of the way in which values are embedded into artefacts, and if they can sufficiently anticipate future uses of an artefact and its future context(s) of use, then they are in a position to intentionally design artefacts to support particular values. Several approaches have been proposed in recent years that aim to make considerations of value part of the design process. In Section 3.4, the most influential of these approaches, called value-sensitive design, is discussed. But first, let us consider a more philosophical approach that also adopts the notion of embedded values.

3.3   Disclosive computer ethics

The approach of *disclosive computer ethics* (Brey 2000, 1999a) intends to make the embedded values approach part of a comprehensive approach to computer ethics. It is widely accepted that the aim of computer ethics is to morally evaluate *practices* that involve computer technology and to devise ethical policies for these practices. The practices in question are activities of designing, using and managing computer technology by individuals, groups or organizations. Some of these practices are already widely recognized in society as morally controversial. For example, it is widely recognized that copying patented software and filtering Internet information are morally controversial practices. Such practices may be called *morally transparent* because the practice is known and it is roughly understood what moral values are at stake in relation to it.

In other computer-related practices, the moral issues that are involved may not be sufficiently recognized. This may be the case because the practices themselves are not well known beyond a circle of specialists, or because they are well known but not recognized as morally charged because they have a false appearance of moral neutrality. Practices of this type may be called *morally opaque*, meaning that it is not generally understood that the practice raises ethical questions or what these questions may be. For example, the practice of browser tracking is morally opaque because it is not well known or well understood by many people, and the practice of search engine use is morally opaque because, although the practice is well known, it is not well known that the search algorithms involved in the practice contain biases and raise ethical questions.

Computer ethics has mostly focused on morally transparent practices, and specifically on practices of using computer systems. Such approaches may be called *mainstream computer ethics*. In mainstream computer ethics, a typical study begins by identifying a morally controversial practice, like software theft, hacking, electronic monitoring or Internet pornography. Next, the practice is described and analysed in descriptive terms, and finally, moral principles and judgements are applied to it and moral deliberation takes place, resulting in a moral evaluation of the practice and, possibly, a set of policy recommendations. As Jim Moor has summed up this approach, 'A typical problem in computer ethics arises because there is a policy vacuum about how computer technology should be used' (1985, p. 266).

The approach of *disclosive computer ethics* focuses instead on morally opaque practices. Many practices involving computer technology are morally opaque because they include operations of technological systems that are very complex and difficult to understand for laypersons and that are often hidden from view for the average user. Additionally, practices are often morally opaque because they involve distant actions over computer networks by system operators, providers, website owners and hackers and remain hidden from view from users and from the public at large. The aim of disclosive ethics is to identify such morally opaque practices, describe and analyse them, so as to bring them into view, and to identify and reflect on any problematic moral features in them. Although mainstream and disclosive computer ethics are different approaches, they are not rival approaches but are rather complementary. They are also not completely separable, because the moral opacity of practices is always a matter of degree, and because a complex practice may include both morally transparent and opaque dimensions, and thus require both approaches.

Many computer-related practices that are morally opaque are so because they depend on operations of computer systems that are value-laden without it being known. Many morally opaque practices, though not all, are the result of undisclosed embedded values and norms in computer technology. A large part of the work in disclosive computer ethics, therefore, focuses on the identification and moral evaluation of such embedded values.

3.3.1   Methodology: multi-disciplinary and multi-level

Research typically focuses on an (alleged) morally opaque practice (e.g., plagiarism detection) and optionally on a morally opaque computer system or software program involved in this practice (e.g., plagiarism detection software). The aim of the investigation usually is to reveal hidden morally problematic features in the practice and to provide ethical reflections on these features, optionally resulting in specific moral judgements or policy recommendations. To achieve this aim, research should include three different kinds of research activities, which take place at different levels of analysis. First, there is the *disclosure level.* At this level, morally opaque practices and computer systems are analysed from the point of view of one or more relevant moral values, like privacy or justice. It is investigated whether and how the practice or system tends to promote or demote the relevant value. At this point, very little moral theory is introduced into the analysis, and only a coarse definition of the value in question is used that can be refined later on into the research.

Second, there is the *theoretical level* at which moral theory is developed and refined. As Jim Moor (1985) has pointed out, the changing settings and practices that emerge with new computer technology may yield new values, as well as require the reconsideration of old values. There may also be new moral dilemmas because of conflicting values that suddenly clash when brought together in new settings and practices. It may then be found that existing moral theory has not adequately theorized these values and value conflicts. Privacy, for example, is now recognized by many computer ethicists as requiring more attention than it has previously received in moral theory. In part, this is due to reconceptualizations of the private and public sphere, brought about by the use of computer technology, which has resulted in inadequacies in existing moral theory about privacy. It is part of the task of computer ethics to *further develop and modify existing moral theory* when, as in the case of privacy, existing theory is insufficient or inadequate in light of new demands generated by new practices involving computer technology.

Third, there is the *application level*, in which, in varying degrees of specificity and concreteness, moral theory is applied to analyses that are the outcome of research at the disclosure level. For example, the question of what amount of protection should be granted to software developers against the copying of their programs may be answered by applying consequentialist or natural law theories of property; and the question of what actions governments should take in helping citizens have access to computers may be answered by applying Rawls' principles of justice. The application level is where moral deliberation takes place. Usually, this involves the joint consideration of moral theory, moral judgements or intuitions and background facts or theories, rather than a slavish application of preexisting moral rules.

Disclosive ethics should not just be multi-level, ideally it should also be a *multi-disciplinary* endeavour, involving ethicists, computer scientists and social scientists. The disclosure level, particularly, is best approached in a multi-disciplinary fashion because research at this level often requires considerable knowledge of the technological aspects of the system or practice that is studied and may also require expertise in social science for the analysis of the way in which the functioning of systems is dependent on human actions, rules and institutions. Ideally, research at the disclosure level, and perhaps also at the application level, is best approached as a cooperative venture between computer scientists, social scientists and philosophers. If this cannot be attained, it should at least be carried out by researchers with an adequate interdisciplinary background.

3.3.2   Focus on public values

The importance of disclosive computer ethics is that it makes transparent moral features of practices and technologies that would otherwise remain hidden, thus making them available for ethical analysis and moral decision-making. In this way, it supplements mainstream computer ethics, which runs the risk of limiting itself to the more obvious ethical dilemmas in computing. An additional benefit is that it can point to novel solutions to moral dilemmas in mainstream computer ethics. Mainstream approaches tend to seek solutions for moral dilemmas through norms and policies that regulate usage. But some of these moral dilemmas can also be solved by redesigning, replacing or removing the technology that is used, or by modifying problematic background practices that condition usage. Disclosive ethics can bring these options into view. It thus reveals a broader arena for moral action, in which different parties responsible for the design, adoption, use and regulation of computer technology share responsibility for the moral consequences of using it, and in which the technology itself is made part of the equation.

In Brey (2000) I have proposed a set of values that disclosive computer ethics should focus on. This list included justice (fairness, non-discrimination), freedom (of speech, of assembly), autonomy, privacy and democracy. Many other values could be added, like trust, community, human dignity and moral accountability. These are all public values, which are moral and social values that are widely accepted in society. An emphasis on public values makes it more likely that analyses in disclosive ethics can find acceptance in society and that they stimulate better policies, design practices or practices of using technology. Of course, analysts will still have disagreements on the proper definition or operationalization of public values and the proper way of balancing them against each other and against other constraints like cost and usability, but such disagreements are inherent to ethics.

The choice for a particular set of values prior to analysis has been criticized by Introna (2005), who argues that disclosive computer ethics should rather focus on the revealing of hidden politics, interests and values in technological systems and practices, without prioritizing which values ought to be realized. This suggests a more descriptive approach to disclosive computer ethics opposed to the more normative approach proposed in Brey (2000).

3.4   Value-sensitive design

The idea that computer systems harbour values has stimulated research into the question how considerations of value can be made part of the design process (Flanagan, Nissenbaum and Howe 2008). Various authors have made proposals for incorporating considerations of value into design methodology. *Value-sensitive design* (VSD) is the most elaborate and influential of these approaches. VSD has been developed by computer scientist Batya Friedman and her associates (Friedman, Kahn and Borning 2006, Friedman and Kahn 2003) and is an approach to the design of computer systems and software that aims to account for and incorporate human values in a comprehensive manner throughout the design process. The theoretical foundation of value-sensitive design is provided in part by the embedded values approach, although it is emphasized that values can result from both design and the social context in which the technology is used, and usually emerge in the interaction between the two.

The VSD approach proposes investigations into values, designs, contexts of use and stakeholders with the aim of designing systems that incorporate and balance the values of different stakeholders. It aims to offer a set of methods, tools and procedures for designers by which they can systematically account for values in the design process. VSD builds on previous work in various fields, including computer ethics, social informatics (the study of information and communication tools in cultural and institutional contexts), computer-supported cooperative work (the study of how interdependent group work can be supported by means of computer systems) and participatory design (an approach to design that attempts to actively involve users in the design process to help ensure that products meet their needs and are usable). The focus of VSD is on 'human values with ethical import', such as privacy, freedom from bias, autonomy, trust, accountability, identity, universal usability, ownership and human welfare (Friedman and Kahn 2003, p. 1187).

VSD places much emphasis on the values and needs of *stakeholders*. Stakeholders are persons, groups or organizations whose interests can be affected by the use of an artefact. A distinction is made between direct and indirect stakeholders. Direct stakeholders are parties who interact directly with the computer system or its output. That is, they function in some way as users of the system. Indirect stakeholders include all other parties who are affected by the system. The VSD approach proposes that the values and interests of stakeholders are carefully balanced against each other in the design process. At the same time, it wants to maintain that the human and moral values it considers have standing independently of whether a particular person or group upholds them (Friedman and Kahn 2003, p. 1186). This stance poses a possible dilemma for the VSD approach: how to proceed if the values of stakeholders are at odds with supposedly universal moral values that the analyst independently brings to the table? This problem has perhaps not been sufficiently addressed in current work in VSD. In practice, fortunately, there will often be at least one stakeholder who has an interest in upholding a particular moral value that appears to be at stake. Still, this fact does not provide a principled solution for this problem.

3.4.1   VSD methodology

VSD often focuses on a technological system that is to be designed and investigates how human values can be accounted for in its design. However, designers may also focus on a particular value and explore its implications for the design of various systems, or on a particular context of use, and explore values and technologies that may play a role in it. With one of these three aims in mind, VSD then utilizes a tripartite methodology that involves three kinds of investigations: conceptual, empirical and technical. These investigations are undertaken congruently and are ultimately integrated with each other within the context of a particular case study.

Conceptual investigations aim to conceptualize and describe the values implicated in a design, as well as the stakeholders affected by it, and consider the appropriate trade-off between implicated values, including both moral and non-moral values. *Empirical* investigations focus on the human context in which the technological artefact is to be situated, so as to better anticipate on this context and to evaluate the success of particular designs. They include empirical studies of human behaviour, physiology, attitudes, values and needs of users and other stakeholders, and may also consider the organizational context in which the technology is used. Empirical investigations are important in order to assess what the values and needs of stakeholders are, how technological artefacts can be expected to be used, and how they can be expected to affect users and other stakeholders. *Technical* investigations, finally, study how properties of technological artefacts support or hinder human values and how computer systems and software may be designed proactively in order to support specific values that have been found important in the conceptual investigation.

Friedman, Kahn and Borning (2003) propose a series of steps that may be taken in VSD case studies. They are, respectively, the identification of the topic of investigation (a technological system, value or context of use), the identification of direct and indirect stakeholders, the identification of benefits and harms for each group, the mapping of these benefits and harms onto corresponding values, the conduction of a conceptual investigation of key values, the identification of potential value conflicts and the proposal of solutions for them, and the integration of resulting value considerations with the larger objectives of the organization(s) that have a stake in the design.

3.4.2   VSD in practice

A substantial number of case studies within the VSD framework have been completed, covering a broad range of technologies and values (see Friedman and Freier 2005 for references). To see how VSD is brought into practice, two case studies will now be described in brief.

In one study, Friedman, Howe and Felten (2002) analyse how the value of informed consent (in relation to online interactions of end-users) might be better implemented in the Mozilla browser, which is an open-source browser. They first undertook an initial conceptual investigation of the notion of informed consent, outlining real-world conditions that would have to be met for it, like disclosure of benefits and risks, voluntariness of choice and clear communication in a language understood by the user. They then considered the extent to which features of existing browsers already supported these conditions. Next, they identified conditions that were supported insufficiently by these features, and defined new design goals to attain this support. For example, they found that users should have a better global understanding of cookie uses and benefits and harms, and should have a better ability to manage cookies with minimal distraction. Finally, they attempted to come up with designs of new features that satisfied these goals, and proceeded to implement them into the Mozilla browser.

In a second study, reported in Friedman, Kahn and Borning (2006), Kahn, Friedman and their colleagues consider the design of a system consisting of a plasma display and a high-definition TV camera. The display is to be hung in interior offices and the camera is to be located outside, aimed at a natural landscape. The display was to function as an 'augmented window' on nature that was to increase emotional well-being, physical health and creativity in workers. In their VSD investigation, they operationalized some of these values and sought to investigate in a laboratory context whether they were realized in office workers, which they found they did. They then also identified indirect stakeholders of the system. These included those individuals that were unwittingly filmed by the camera. Further research indicated that many of them felt that the system violated their privacy. The authors concluded that if the system is to be further developed and used, this privacy issue must first be solved. It may be noted, in passing, that, whilst in these two examples only a few values appear to be at stake, other case studies consider a much larger number of values, and identify many more stakeholders.

3.5   Conclusion

This chapter focused on the embedded values approach, which holds that computer systems and software are capable of harbouring embedded or 'built-in' values, and on two derivative approaches, disclosive computer ethics and value-sensitive design. It has been argued that, in spite of powerful arguments for the neutrality of technology, a good case can be made that technological artefacts, including computer systems, can be value-laden. The notion of an embedded value was defined as a built-in tendency in an artefact to promote or harm the realization of a value that manifests itself across the central uses of an artefact in ordinary contexts of use. Examples of such values in information technology were provided, and it was argued that such values can emerge because they are held by designers or society at large, because of technical constraints or considerations, or because of a changing context of use.

Next, the discussion shifted to disclosive computer ethics, which was described as an attempt to incorporate the notion of embedded values into a comprehensive approach to computer ethics. Disclosive computer ethics focuses on morally opaque practices in computing and aims to identify, analyse and morally evaluate such practices. Many practices in computing are morally opaque because they depend on computer systems that contain embedded values that are not recognized as such. Therefore, disclosive ethics frequently focuses on such embedded values. Finally, value-sensitive design was discussed. This is a framework for accounting for values in a comprehensive manner in the design of systems and software. The approach was related to the embedded values approach and its main assumptions and methodological principles were discussed.

Much work still remains to be done within the three approaches. The embedded values approach could still benefit from more theoretical and conceptual work, particularly regarding the very notion of an embedded value and its relation to both the material features of artefacts and their context of use. Disclosive computer ethics could benefit from further elaboration of its central concepts and assumptions, a better integration with mainstream computer ethics and more case studies. And VSD could still benefit from further development of its methodology, its integration with accepted methodologies in information systems design and software engineering, and more case studies. In addition, more attention needs to be invested into the problematic tension between the values of stakeholders and supposedly universal moral values brought in by analysts. Yet, they constitute exciting new approaches in the fields of computer ethics and computer science. In ethics, they represent an interesting shift in focus from human agency to technological artefacts and systems. In computer science, they represent an interesting shift from utilitarian and economic concerns to a concern for human values in design. As a result, they promise both a better and more complete computer ethics as well as improved design practices in both computer science and engineering that may result in technology that lives up better to our moral and public values.

4 The use of normative theories in computer ethics

Jeroen van den Hoven

4.1 Introduction

Without Information and Communication Technologies (ICTs) many of the activities that we undertake in the twenty-first century in the world of trade, finance, transport, healthcare, science, education, administration, management, communication, energy supply, industrial production, defence, engineering and technology would be impossible. Computers have become a necessary condition for all of our large-scale projects and complex endeavours.

Some of the major moral problems of Information Societies at the beginning of the twenty-first century concern the quality and reliability of information, control and governance of the Internet, responsibility for data processing, property of software and privacy and protection of personal data and the quality of life. There are also problems concerning power and dominance of commercial parties, equal access and fair distribution of information. A relatively new set of issues concerns the way the technology invades our daily lives and affects the moral development of children and young people who have had long and intense exposure to the technology and the content it offers. This listing is not exhaustive and new issues are constantly appearing as the technology develops. The issues occupy a prominent place in public debates, demand attention in the policy arena and usually require regulation because the lives and interest of many are potentially affected. Computer and information ethics has tried to shed light upon these and other issues in the last decades.[1]

ICTs have properties which make it difficult to make up our minds concerning the answers to the moral questions to which they give rise and it is certainly not the type of technology that we can decide to turn off or jettison should we become uncomfortable with its problems and results. ICTs are (1) *ubiquitous* and *pervasive* in a way in which our most common technical artefacts are not. Common household appliances and ordinary objects nowadays *are* computers and will often be interconnected through wireless network

---

[1] See for overviews Himma and Tavani 2008, Johnson 2009, van den Hoven and Weckert 2008, Weckert 2007.

technologies. More and more everyday objects and artefacts are woven into an Internet of Things that eventually meshes with the Internet of People. More and more tasks involve interaction with computers or computerized tools and devices. Technology and infrastructure which is omnipresent has a tendency to blend into the background, become translucent and disappear from our radar screen, making it more difficult to assess its role (Bowker and Star 1999). (2) ICTs are a *universal technology*, because of their 'logical malleability' (Moor 1985). Digital computers are in essence Turing Machines that can be used to simulate, communicate, recreate, calculate, and so much more, in all domains of life in all sectors of society. The entities manipulated on the machine level can be made to stand for everything that can be articulated and expressed in terms of symbols. We can use the same machine to simulate a weather storm, to distribute electrical power in a part of the country, to run a production plant and archive government information. It is therefore often difficult to see the common elements in the many manifestations and applications of ICTs. ICTs are (3) a *meta-technology*, that is, a technology which forms an essential ingredient in the development and use of other technologies. It helps us to drive cars, make medical images, produce petrol and distribute goods over the world. This may obscure the fact that problems which are identified with the first-order technology are, in fact, problems with the meta-technology. ICTs are also (4) a *constitutive technology*. Computing technology co-constitutes the things to which it is applied. ICTs are often characterized as an *enabling* technology and it is certainly correct to say that they enable us to do new things and to do old things in new ways, but this must hide the fact that, where ICTs are introduced they *transform* our old practices, discourses, relations and our experiences in fundamental ways and they are partly constitutive of new practices. If they are used in health care, health care will change in important ways, if they are used in science and education, science and education will never be the same again, if Internet and the World Wide Web are introduced in the lives of children, their lives will be very different from the childhood of people who grew up without online computer games and social networking sites. Furthermore, ICTs are about *information*[2] (5). Information is so important to human beings that we tend to forget that we use and process information constantly; we need it in deliberation, planning, choice, decision-making, preference formation and judgement. If information is inaccessible, wrong, inaccurate or incomplete, the results of these cognitive processes are compromised. ICTs provide the mechanisms to channel and manipulate this all-important good, hence the moral significance of their

---

[2] Luciano Floridi's work forms a broad-ranging and in-depth study of this aspect, see his contribution 'Information Ethics: Its Nature and Scope' in van den Hoven and Weckert 2008, pp. 40–66, and the special issue of *Ethics and Information Technology*, vol. 10, 2008, nos 2–3.

evaluation, regulation and design. ICTs are also the expression of prior choices, norms, values, and decisions (6). ICT applications are not neutral, but contain the values and norms of those who have designed and engineered them. An abundance of research provides evidence of intentional or inadvertent incorporation of norms in software (Friedman 1997). Finally, ICTs revolve around new entities, such as digital computers, software and information goods, which give rise to new practices and experiences. This makes it sometimes difficult to account for them in terms of traditional moral and legal views (7).

These characteristics taken together form an explication of the common observation that ICTs play a central but confusing role in our lives. It is often not immediately clear that ICTs merit special attention and require moral evaluation and analysis of the sort that computer and information ethics attempt to provide.

A safe starting point for moral thinking is to look simply at the effects the new entities have on people, the environment and on everything we endow with moral standing, what people can do to each other by means of these entities, how they constrain or enable us, how they change our experiences and shape our thinking, how they affect our relationships and balances of power. Another starting point is to turn to some of the ethical theories in the history of philosophy, such as utilitarianism, Kantian ethics or virtue ethics, and see whether they can shed light on the problems. This is what computer ethics has done in the past three decades. This is also how we proceeded in the case of thinking about the car, the television and the atom bomb when they were introduced, and this is how we shall proceed in the case of evaluating brain imaging technology and the use of carbon nano-tubes, artificial agents and the applications of advanced robotics. We certainly need to retain what is obviously helpful in traditional ethical thinking as it applies to ICTs, but a fully adequate ethical treatment of ICTs in the decades ahead requires a somewhat different approach to moral theorizing from the ones that have been tried thus far.

First of all, there is no other way for moral thinking in the field of ICTs than to embrace a robust *conceptual and value pluralism* – which does not imply moral scepticism or moral relativism (4.2). Secondly, the conception of ethical theory or ethical thinking must accommodate the pluralist condition and be *empirically informed, realistic and practical*, so as to provide guidance and direction in cases where information technology is actually used (4.3). Thirdly, it should support *conceptual reconstructions* of ethical key concepts that play an important role in the discourse that is actually used in the description, evaluation and shaping of the technology, in order to fill conceptual vacuums as described by Moor (4.4). Finally, it should focus on issues of moral *design* of ICT applications at an early stage of development and not only focus on their *evaluation ex post* (4.5).

4.2 Value pluralism

Christine Korsgaard has pointed out that 'one of the most important attributes of humanity is our nearly bottomless capacity for conferring value on most anything. It is not because of our shared values that we should accord consideration to one another but because of our shared capacity for conferring value. In other words, that fact about human nature is part of what makes liberal democratic forms of the state the right ones' (Korsgaard 2003, p. 73). This fact about human beings and human lives has served as a point of departure of much of contemporary moral theorizing. We confer value on different things, but we also confer different values on one and the same thing.

Since Isaiah Berlin wrote his *Two Concepts of Liberty* (Berlin 1958), many leading contemporary philosophers working in a broadly liberal tradition have subscribed to the idea that there are many different and incommensurable – or at least *de facto* conflicting – values or sources of moral evaluation (Galston 2002, pp. 3–15). In a different context, Berlin used an ancient proverb about the difference between the fox and the hedgehog to illustrate the difference between monists and pluralists: the fox sees many small things, the hedgehog sees one big thing (Berlin 1957). Many contemporary moral philosophers see many small things instead of one big thing when looking closely at ethics and morality: Bernard Williams, Thomas Nagel, Martha Nussbaum and Amartya Sen, John Rawls, Joseph Raz, Robert Audi (2007), James Griffin (1996) – to name a few of the most prominent – all defended forms of value pluralism.

The pluralist position is paradigmatically exemplified in Thomas Nagel's seminal paper 'The Fragmentation of Value'.[3] Nagel states there that he does not believe that 'the source of value is unitary...I believe that value has fundamentally different kinds of sources and that they are reflected in the classifications of values into types.'[4] Nagel distinguishes five fundamental types of value: Utility, General Rights, Special Obligations, Commitments to Own Projects and Perfectionist Ends.[5] Human lives, endeavours and social relationships are variegated and intricate. The problems with which persons are confronted are multifarious, their actions have multiple ramifications and a range of effects upon others. People can see things from radically different perspectives. They can look at results of their actions and at the springs of their actions, they can look at things from their particular point of view and they can identify and sympathize with others close to them, or with distant others. They can look at their own situation with a 'view from nowhere' (Nagel 1986), or they can look at the Universe from their personal point of view and they can switch between these perspectives, without feeling that one perspective is more real or more important than the other. These points of view and valuing

---

[3] Thomas Nagel 'The Fragmentation of Value', reprinted in Gowans 1987, pp. 174–187.
[4] Thomas Nagel 'The Fragmentation of Value', reprinted in Gowans 1987, p. 177.
[5] Thomas Nagel 'The Fragmentation of Value', reprinted in Gowans 1987, p. 175.

are equally valid *all other things being equal*. It therefore can not be the case that the only thing which counts from the moral point of view is consequences or outcomes and the maximization of utility, happiness, pleasure or money. Nor can it be the case that compliance with one formal moral principle of duty and human dignity can be the only right making criterion, whatever the consequences. Or that the special obligations and loyalties that one has because of one social role or position in a social network are always all-important and trump all considerations of utility or general rights. A person's commitment to his or her own personal projects certainly also counts for something in cases of conflicts with the maximization of overall utility, general rights or special obligations to significant others, but for how much must be determined in every case anew. Even an appeal to perfectionist values regarding how an ideal or perfect human being ought to behave, e.g. regarding sexual matters or personal hygiene and aesthetics, may have some initial plausibility, but are certainly overruled in cases of conflicts with general rights or utility.

Different normative ethical theories and traditions have singled out one type of value, epitomized it and have consequently downplayed the importance of the others, reduced them to their value of choice, or have eliminated them altogether. Monistic views of moral theory presuppose that all one needs to know is one value or one simple principle which expresses it. To believe that there is one master value that trumps all others – whether it is human dignity or the maximization of utility, self-interest or human flourishing – amounts to an unduly narrow view of the complexity of moral problems and the human condition, which ought to be avoided, especially in applied ethics, which aspires to be relevant to technology assessment and public policy making.

Another dimension of the robust pluralism referred to above is *conceptual* pluralism in ethical theory. Wittgenstein remarked that 'mathematics is a motley', which led Hilary Putnam to characterize ethics as 'a motley squared' and to observe that 'philosophers who write about the subject so often ignore vast tracks of ethical judgment' (Putnam 2004, p. 72). Ethics may be about praise and blame, about evaluation or prescription, action guidance, conflict resolution, about virtues and character traits, about the logic of obligation and permission, about human rights, about basic needs, utility, outcomes and consequences, money, well-being, norms, principles, ideals, capabilities, responsibilities, duties, interest and preferences and values. It may be about highly general or universal truths or about context-specific considerations. Depending on the situation, we may want to utilize any of these concepts and vocabularies. To foreclose the use of them with their associated background views in favour of one seems unduly restrictive and reductive in practical matters.

In discussions on privacy online, for example, we may sometimes want to express the importance of privacy in terms of individual autonomy or freedom, then in terms of intimacy and personal relationships, basic needs, human rights, in terms of fiduciary duties of professionals, and responsibilities of management, the logical structure of a policy document, the subjective expected utility – costs and benefits – of a proposed set of regulations. Our societies are complex, information technology is complex and hence the privacy issue is complex. Under the heading of privacy violations, a variety of moral wrongdoings belong, such as physical assault, theft, discrimination, economic disadvantage and loss of moral autonomy (van den Hoven in van den Hoven and Weckert 2008). We need access to the relevant vocabularies and background views to articulate and assess the range of wrongs and think about the best ways to prevent them.

This amounts to what Hilary Putnam has called *Pragmatic or Conceptual Pluralism*, which recognizes that 'in everyday language we employ many different kinds of discourses, discourses subject to different standards and possessing different sorts of applications, with different logical and grammatical features', and which denies that there could be one sort of language game sufficient for the description of all of (moral) reality (Putnam 2004, pp. 21, 48 ff.).

Jim Moor's 'Core Value Approach' to computer ethics is a paradigmatic example of Value Pluralism applied to Computer Ethics.[6] Moor identifies moral values such as *life, health, happiness, security, resources, opportunities* and *knowledge* which are vital to the survival of any community, and claims that all communities do in fact value them. Indeed, if a community did *not* value the 'core values', it soon would cease to exist. Moor used 'core values' to examine computer ethics topics like privacy and security and to add an account of justice, which he called 'just consequentialism' which combines 'core values' and consequentialism with Bernard Gert's deontological notion of 'moral impartiality'.[7]

4.3 Moral theory

4.3.1 Primacy of practice

Ethics is a department of practical philosophy and thus primarily concerned with practical problems and action. The aim of moral argumentation, moral reasoning and judgement is the rational justification and settlement of disagreement and conflicts about who one wants to be, what to do, the constraining of self-interest and the fostering of cooperation and peaceful coexistence of sentient creatures in a shared habitat. Moral thinking points to reasons for constraining self-interested behaviour and self-serving strategies. We reflect upon and attempt to improve our moral beliefs and ideas with the end in view of finding answers to the question how to lead a flourishing life, how to act,

---

[6] Moor (2001) in Spinello and Tavani 2001, pp. 98–105.
[7] Moor (2001) in Spinello and Tavani 2001, pp. 98–105.

decide and choose in such a way as to pursue our own happiness without interfering with the similar pursuit of others.

The main aim in ethics is not to establish a general theory and a set of eternal truth but to provide reasoned solutions and clarifications to practical problems. We engage in moral theory in order to create the intellectual resources that can help us to determine which of our moral beliefs are worthiest of our endorsement. Dewey thought that 'Philosophy recovers itself when it ceases to be a device for dealing with the problems of philosophers and becomes a method, cultivated by philosophers, for dealing with the problems of men.'[8]

4.3.2   Theoretical pluralism

Value pluralism has implications for an account of ethical theory. First, different theories and their associated core values may capture different morally relevant aspects of a particular case, without necessarily leading to unique and correct answers. Secondly, since there are different vocabularies and conceptual frameworks available for describing situations, each of them may give a different answer to questions of salience and relevance and may even lead to the articulation of different sets of moral questions.

The individuation and description of concrete cases has implications for what is subsumed under a general moral rule, principle or theory. This is known as the problem of relevant description. Anscombe observed that an act-token will fall under many possible principles of action, which makes it difficult to tell which act description is relevant for moral assessment (Anscombe 1958). Should we, Onora O'Neill asks in her discussion of Anscombe's problem, 'assess an action under the description that an agent intends it, or under descriptions others think salient, or under descriptions that nobody has noted' (O'Neill 2004, p. 306)? And how do we evaluate the actions of persons who – according to us – fail to see the morally significant descriptions of what s(he) does? Bernard Gert gives an example of how the description of the case is also of crucial importance in computer ethics (Gert 1999). He analyses Nissenbaum's analysis of moral permissibility of copying software for a friend. Gert remarks that disagreement about this issue may be due to the fact that one of the partners to the disagreement has too narrow a description of the kind of violation to launch ethical thinking in the right direction. Some may describe it as 'helping a friend', some as 'illegally copying a software program', or as 'violating a morally acceptable law to gain some benefit'. On the basis of the latter description, Gert claims that 'no impartial rational person would publicly allow the act' (p. 62). As we can see from this example, pluralism does not imply that it is impossible to argue on good grounds that particular

---

[8] Dewey, quoted in Putnam 2004, p. 31.

proposals and arguments are better than others. Pluralism does not imply moral scepticism or moral relativism.

Anti-theorists, to which Stuart Hampshire, John McDowell, Annette Baier, Bernard Williams and Martha Nussbaum belong,[9] have raised serious objections to the traditional conception of moral theory which also need to be taken seriously in computer ethics. Anti-theorists assert that it is not the case that all correct moral judgements and practices can be deduced from universal, timeless principles, which it is the job of moral theory to articulate; that all moral values are commensurable on a common scale which it is the task of moral theory to provide; that all disagreements and conflict can be solved by means of the application of theory and the use of a decision procedure which it is the job of moral theory to supply; that moral theory is entirely normative.

According to this approach, there may be points of diminishing returns of moral theorizing in computer ethics, since, as Nagel has pointed out, 'our capacity to resolve conflicts in particular cases may extend beyond our capacity to enunciate general principles that explain those solutions'.[10] According to Nagel, 'to look for a single general theory of how to decide the right thing to do is like looking for a single theory of how to decide what to believe'.[11]

The other line of anti-theoretical critique concerning ethical theory is not so much that ethical theory is impossible, unnecessary or undesirable, but that it is useless in practice, except perhaps as reminder of the importance of a particular type of value and value-based arguments or as a summary of past experiences. Richard Posner (1999), who sympathizes with the anti-theoretical position, lodged an attack on the usefulness of standard moral theory to which he refers as *Academic Moralism*, i.e. the assumption that ethical theory as studied at universities in philosophy departments around the world can help us to arrive at better understandings and solutions of our practical problems. Posner, with his long experience as a judge (Chief Judge of the US Court of Appeals of the Seventh Circuit) and with a thorough knowledge of academic ethics, denies that moral theory is at all useful in practice, and that it has any policy impact. Academic moralism is not an agent of moral change. According to Posner it fails as an agent of moral change partly because those who work on it fail to make it so: 'Unhindered by external checks and balances, the academic moralist has no incentive to be useful to anybody ... the intellectual gifts moral philosophers exhibit need not, and in their normative work usually do not, generate a positive social product' (p. 80). Posner's critique is coarse-grained, but not unfounded, and touches a delicate open nerve of modern practical philosophy. Moral theory

---

[9] See for a collection of essays in Anti-theory Clarke and Simpson 1989.

[10] Thomas Nagel 'The Fragmentation of Value', reprinted in Gowans 1987, pp. 174–187, p. 181.

[11] Thomas Nagel 'The Fragmentation of Value', reprinted in Gowans 1987, pp. 174–187, p. 181.

as it stands now is only marginally relevant to the world where the all-important decisions are made. It may eventually become obsolete if it does not deliver on its constitutive promise to be relevant to practice and the professions.

The upshot of this characterization of the starting points for moral theory and computer ethics is that different types of value (utility and outcomes, general rights and principles, specific obligations, agent's commitment to own projects and perfectionist ends) can always be brought to bear upon morally problematic situations, sometimes in the form of free-standing considerations which have to be balanced against others, sometimes in the form of applications of a general principle (e.g. principle of utility, categorical imperative) to a particular case. Contributions to thinking about the hard questions of ICTs hardly ever present themselves in the form of elaborate and thorough applications of austere Aristotelian, Kantian or utilitarian theories. In a sense, they are superfluous as theories, but not as sources of moral arguments and moral considerations. Enlightening contributions in computer ethics[12] use arguments, insights and considerations which are inspired and informed by Kantian, utilitarian or Aristotelian views and by the values that are central to them.

4.3.3   Methodology

With respect to 'problematic situations', as Dewey called them – whether that is at the individual, professional, institutional or societal level – we thus need to make up our minds and come to a conclusion in the midst of a panoply of considerations. Since there is no standard method or decision procedure to solve conflicts between different types of values, and unify our thoughts, we will have to do with the ancient, but notoriously elusive, resource of 'practical wisdom', i.e. the weighing, sizing up the situation, seeing what is morally salient and relevant to achieving one's moral goals and choosing the appropriate course of action.

There are not many methodological constraints to ethical thinking apart from (1) an epistemic obligation to explain why one holds certain moral beliefs and not others, (2) to do all that is in our power to free our actions from the defects of ignorance, error and possible bias, and (3) to eliminate inconsistencies in our moral belief set by applying the logic of moral reasoning, which (4) typically comprises the application of the principle of supervenience of moral reasons. The Principle of Supervenience states that there are no moral differences without differences in other non-moral respects.[13] To use the example provided by Richard Hare, on the basis of which the notion of

[12] See footnote 1 for an overview.
[13] See *Stanford Encyclopedia of Philosophy* online, article on supervenience.

supervenience gained currency in Ethics: to state that 'room 13 is a nice room, but room 12, although similar in all relevant respects, is not a nice room' is to make a self-contradictory statement (Hare 1984).

A further general methodical directive concerns the contemporary orthodoxy about 'the way we do ethics now' as James Griffin (1993) has called it. It is neither a decision procedure, nor a method in a strict sense, but a sketch of a way of proceeding used by all sensible people who have access to relevant facts of the matter, have moral values, elementary logic, and ideals of clarity and consistency. It is, in essence, a coherence model along the lines of the method of Wide Reflective Equilibrium (Griffin 1996, van den Hoven 1997), which occupies the middle ground between generalist and particularist views, between theoretical and anti-theoretical construals of moral thinking, but which retains the principle of supervenient application of moral reasons – or the universalizability of moral considerations – as a requirement of rationality in public moral discourse concerning practical problems.

For computer ethics, neither the simple engineering view of application along the lines of the deductive nomological model of explanation in physics (or for example the simple practical syllogism) nor the opposite extreme of particularism seems viable. Coherence models of moral justification allow for the desired level of logical structure and generality in our moral belief sets without becoming impervious to the force of contextual and agent-relative considerations.

What we need in applied ethics of computing is what Nagel describes as a 'method of breaking up or analyzing practical problems to say what evaluative principles apply, and how'. This method 'would simply indicate the points at which different kinds of ethical considerations needed to be introduced to supply the basis for a responsible and intelligent decision'.[14]

4.3.4   Applying moral theories

Aristotelian ethics answers questions about what to do on the basis of what virtue requires or what a virtuous person would do. A person is virtuous when he has moral virtue(s), i.e. character traits or dispositional properties, which allow him to choose and act in order to achieve happiness or human flourishing. Moral virtues, such as modesty, courage, justice, are learned by following moral exemplars. Ideally, the virtuous person also possesses a general intellectual capacity, practical wisdom – which enables him to identify the morally relevant features in every situation and determine the right course of action. Moral knowledge, which is thus embedded in a person's character, is motivational, i.e. it is impossible to know what is right and not be inclined to do it.

---

[14] Thomas Nagel 'The Fragmentation of Value', reprinted in Gowans 1987, p. 184.

Utilitarian moral theories instruct one to choose those actions which have the best consequences or outcomes. More specifically, they require one to choose those actions – or to choose those rules or policies for acting – that bring about the greatest good for the greatest number in the world. The good is measured in some quantity of non-moral good such as happiness, pleasure, well-being or money. When confronted with a choice between different courses of action, one ought to choose that course of action which maximizes utility compared to the alternatives. There are several versions of utilitarianism to which we cannot do justice here, but their overall structure is the same. There is some end which is good by independent non-moral criteria and which is brought about by means of the agent's actions or indirectly by the rule which is followed in action. This means–end relationship and causal relationship (Nozick (1993) allows this relation also to be symbolic apart from causal) confers moral status on the action or the state. *The right* is thus defined in terms of *the good* in utilitarian theories.

Kantian theories state that whether an action is obligatory does not depend on its consequences, but on characteristics of the action itself and its compliance with the highest ethical principle: the Categorical Imperative. The most accessible formulation of the categorical imperative states that one ought to respect human beings as such and not use them as mere instruments for one's purposes. According to an alternative formulation, one ought to choose that course of action which instantiates a policy that can without contradiction be adopted by everyone or that can be willed to be a universal law. Kantian accounts are, in a sense, the antidote to utilitarian theories. Each human being is a source of meaning and value, has a life of his own, is morally autonomous and deserves to be respected as such, whatever the consequences. Both utilitarianism and Kantian moral theories are universalist and agent-neutral. Utilitarians apply the criterion for moral standing (sentience) universally and Kantians apply their criterion of moral standing (rationality) to all (and only) rational beings (including angels and artificial intelligences).

As an illustration of how these different normative ethical theories can figure in debates about new and emerging ICTs issues, we will look at how they figure in the discussion about ultra violent computer games (Wonderly 2008, Waddington 2007). In ultra violent computer games such as *Grand Theft Auto*, *Zog's Nightmare* and *Manhunt*, players are invited to run extermination camps, kill for snuff movies, and run over people to score points. Parents who watch their children play these games may have moral concerns and many others would understand their concerns. Is there anything morally wrong with playing ultra violent computer games and, if so, what is it?

Utilitarian accounts seem to fail to account for the concerns, since there are no relevant other moral entities (sentient creatures) harmed by the action of those who play violent computer games. There is only virtual suffering and virtual pain. Mill thought that even harmless acts could be morally forbidden if they violated good manners or gave offence. Clearly, if a group community of individuals created a violent computer game and played it among themselves, without anyone knowing about it, there could be no offence or violation of good manners and, consequently, no indirect harm. Alternatively, one could say that this pastime is bound to affect someone's behaviour towards his fellow human beings and it is likely to bring about negative effects. The problem with this suggestion is that there is no conclusive evidence that it would. Television has been around for almost half a century and still the debate over whether violent movies trigger violent behaviour continues. If there were some remarkable statistical evidence of this effect, this would not show that there is a causal connection between playing and violent behaviour. Again if the statistical evidence combined with psychological and neurological evidence proved the nexus for a small percentage of the population beyond reasonable doubt, the question would still remain whether the dis-utilities (some occasional violent behaviour) outweighed the positive utilities (long happy hours of gaming for the millions).

Kantian accounts fare no better. There are no rational human beings affected by this sort of game playing, apart from the player himself. No one is used as a mere instrument and no one's dignity is at stake, except the dignity perhaps of the player himself. It is even possible to imagine that everyone engages in solitary violent computer gaming, without contradicting oneself in the relevant sense. It also seems possible to subscribe to a universal law which says that everyone should spend some time every day playing ultra violent computer games, although that may sound a bit awkward.

One could stretch the Kantian view by using Kant's argument against the cruelty against animals. Kant was not so much concerned with animals as such. They are not rational beings in the relevant sense, so they do not qualify for moral standing. But he was opposed to cruelty against animals because he believed that this type of behaviour corrodes one's character and is likely to facilitate cruelty against human beings (Midgley 1985, Brey 1999). Likewise, cruelty against virtual humans could predispose to cruelty against real humans. Another way of applying Kantian Ethics is by construing the playing of violent computer games as the violation of an (imperfect) duty to oneself. According to Kant, every human being has a duty to himself to cultivate his capacities, his moral and non-moral capacities and talents (Dennis 1997). In virtually killing, going through the motions, rehearsing, engaging in role-playing, without any artistic or educational idea, one is not respecting humanity as it is exemplified in one's own personality.

What seems objectionable in playing violent computer games is the thought that a person is spending a considerable amount of time identifying with a character in a game who is in mental states which are relevantly similar to those involved in offline killing, rapings and torturing, and gets rewarded for it by scoring points. McCormick (2001) argues that neither utilitarian nor Kantian accounts can demonstrate the moral wrongness of these proceedings. He suggests that only an Aristotelian account can explain our moral intuitions concerning them: 'by participating in simulations of excessive, indulgent, and wrongful acts, we are cultivating the wrong sort of character'. Wonderly (2008) – with reference to Hume – claims that empathy has a central role in making moral judgements and that research shows that playing violent video games is inimical to the fostering of empathic functioning.

It is difficult to account for our moral apprehension and to locate the moral wrongness on the basis of the values of utility or general rights. The Humean and Aristotelian approaches seem most promising, but if on the other hand conclusive evidence would become available to show that gamers are indeed inclined to be violent in the real world we would probably stop worrying about their moral characters and turn to a straightforward utilitarian account to justify our concern with this type of application.

4.4   Mid-level theories: ground preparation and conceptual reconstructions

Instead of applying highly abstract traditional ethical theories straightforwardly to particular ICTs issues, it is often more helpful to utilize mid-level normative ethical theories, which are less abstract, more testable and which focus on technology, interactions between people, organizations and institutions. Examples of mid-level ethical theories are Rawls' theory of justice, which could be construed as broadly Kantian, Amartya Sen and Martha Nussbaum's capability approach, which can be construed as broadly Aristotelian, and Posner's economic theory of law, which is broadly utilitarian. These theories already address a specific set of moral questions in their social, psychological, economic or social context. They also point to the empirical research that needs to be done in order to apply the theory sensibly. I have elsewhere discussed how these mid-level theories may be fruitfully applied (van den Hoven 2005, 2008 van den Hoven and Rooksby 2008) and more work is done on them to make them even better suited for application to real-life problems. Concerning violent computer games, for example, the capability approach of Martha Nussbaum seems to capture what concerns parents and those who sympathize with them. Coeckelbergh (2007) uses Martha Nussbaum's capability approach to argue that the trained insensitivity towards human suffering, which goes on in playing violent computer games, is inimical to cultivating humanity and squarely opposed to training the fine sensibility and awareness required for moral excellence and human flourishing. Nissenbaum and others have started to work on how games may be designed that build in moral desirable features and capability enhancing elements.[15]

Floridi's Information Ethics[16] provides a high-level value theory which applies to the ICTs domain, which at the same time allows for specification at the mid-level and lower levels of abstraction and specification. It is universally applicable also outside the ICTs domain in a stricter sense, and construes information as ontologically fundamental and entropy – in the specific sense of destruction, damage and vandalizing of informational entities and environments – as the morally most relevant category. According to information ethics along these lines the moral status of actions concerns their informational status and information objects thus have moral significance and are hence deserving of respect (Sicart and Studies 2009). Computer ethics should thus be concerned with finding out what increases entropy and which actions and events counteract it. Information Ethics is a recent alternative to traditional ethical theory to account for the moral phenomena and is the subject of further research to investigate how it can be made to bear upon the practical problems in ICTs[17] and to demonstrate that it has an explanatory and justificatory surplus compared to the traditional ethical normative theories. Relating to the topic discussed, Miguel Sicart has applied Floridi's Information Ethics to tackle problems in the design of computer games (Sicart 2009).

Important for the application of the range of mid-level ethical theories, which are specifications (Moor 1985) of high-level ethical theories, is what Bernard Gert and Carl Danner Clouser have called 'ground preparation', i.e. the meticulous understanding of the field to which ethical theory is being applied. This is part of ethics itself and it may well be considered as the essence of applied ethics. It requires more analytical skills and rigour, according to Clouser, than is generally thought (Clouser 1980). We need to know what the properties of artificially intelligent agents are, how they differ from human agents; we need to establish what the meaning and scope is of the notion of 'personal data', what the morally relevant properties of virtual reality are. These are all examples of preparing the ground conceptually before we can start to apply normative ethical considerations.

Jim Moor has suggested that, with respect to many issues in computer ethics, we are confronted with a conceptual vacuum and an ensuing policy vacuum in these and other cases (van den Hoven 2005). I suggest, in addition, that we are also confronted with a *design vacuum* and we are at a loss which systems to make, which software to engineer, which lines of computer code to write. Therefore, an important part of the ground preparation consists in conceptual reconstruction of the key concepts before any values, principles or theories

---

[15] Flanagan, Howe and Nissenbaum in van den Hoven and Weckert 2008, pp. 322–354.
[16] See special issue on Floridi of *Ethics and Information Technology*, vol 10, 2008, nos 2–3.
[17] Richardson (1990) defended the model of norm specification as covering a middle ground position between deduction and balancing.

can be applied. Reconstruction is a process of articulating and formulating specific adequate conceptions of general notions (and articulating criteria of adequacy) that have become problematic in their application to a world that has changed since the time these notions gained currency.

John Rawls made a distinction between *concepts* and *conceptions* of justice (Rawls 1971) which is pertinent in this context. Many people share the general *concept* of justice (or equality or responsibility for that matter), without necessarily sharing the same *conception* of justice. Conceptions are the specific and substantive specifications and instantiations of a general and formal concept. Rawls famously proposed his conception of *justice as fairness*, but utilitarians have proposed radically different conceptions of justice. Our philosophical notions are 'essentially contested concepts' as W. B. Gallie has called them (Gallie 1956). Controversy over the correct meaning – or discussion of the most adequate conceptions which ought to be construed as the action guiding instantiation of them – has become part and parcel of their meaning. ICTs prompt us to revisit traditional *conceptions* of privacy, responsibility, property, democracy, community and formulate new and more appropriate or interesting conceptions, which serve and suit us better. Dewey defined this reconstruction as one of the main tasks of philosophy and he saw it as a process that never stops. In a rapidly changing world, traditional conceptions are like tools that have deteriorated in use and therefore need to be maintained and reconstructed in order to keep them fit for the task at hand.

Discussions in computer ethics are about '*digital* democracy', '*software* patents', '*virtual* child pornography', '*online* relationships', '*net* friendship', '*cyber* communities', '*informational* privacy', '*artificial* life', '*tele*-work', '*intellectual* property', 'e-Trust' and '*electronic* Commerce'. This semantic expansion – the result of adding qualifications in the form of prefixes (cyber, virtual, digital, informational, e, electronic, tele, software) from the ICT domain to traditional concepts – may also suggest that, since we have the fancy terminology, we also have come to grips with the phenomena which are conjured up by the new techno-speak and that we know what to do in terms of design, policy and law. But as Moor correctly suggested, this is often not the case: what is a 'net-friend', 'e-Trust', etc.?

The concept of democracy is widely used all over the world in different historical periods to indicate some sort of involvement of the people in the political process. Governments all over the world are now investing considerable amounts of taxpayers' money in online democracy. Which conception of democracy are they using? There have been radically different, substantive *conceptions* of democracy. One may have a so-called *direct conception of democracy*, or a *deliberative*, or *participative*, or *representative* conception. Different conceptions have quite different technologies to support or express them. Direct Democracy ICT projects would heavily invest in online voting technology; deliberative and participatory conceptions point in the direction of projects which aim at establishing forms of deliberation, discussion and sharing ideas between citizens online, which requires a completely different set of technologies. Pettit's conception of *contestatory* democracy[18] would point in the direction of checks and balances and tools for citizens to get access to relevant information and effectively protest and contest government decisions online.

The fact that we talk about *cyber communities* does not imply that we actually understand the nature of communities any better than we did before, let alone that we have a clear idea about sociality, community and individuality online, that we know whether to regulate them and how, understand what their value is in individual identity formation, what levels of security should be offered and whose responsibility it is. What we seem to be saying, when we use the term, is that we do not yet know exactly what we mean, but that it has something to do with people getting together, interacting, getting to know each other, exchanging information, embarking upon coordinated and joint action, identifying with common goals, and that they do all this online, without having to meet face to face. In talking about 'cyber community' we are taking out a mortgage on a future analysis and conceptual reconstruction of a conception of 'cyber community'.

This would not be a special problem if we did not have to draft policies, laws and regulation and design information systems and program computers on a daily basis, if we did not have to proceed in practice. But we do. The design of procedures, institutions, systems, information architectures and computational devices requires articulation, precision and detail. It requires precision in the formulation of our ideas and the specification of what we want to achieve by means of the technology.

4.5 Design

Moral problems in professional ethics literature often take the form of a moral dilemma. A professional in a dilemmatic situation has at least two obligations, but he cannot fulfil both of them at the same time. What should the professional do? One type of reaction to dilemmatic situations is to make the best of them and to try to see how one can limit the damage – one might engage in utilitarian calculations, in Kantian reflections or ask what a virtuous person would do in that situation to find how to make the best of it. Moral thinking about such dilemmas assumes that *the situation is given*. In a straightforward sense that is a correct construal because it is often a thought experiment, but what this mode of moral thinking and theorizing about these dilemmatic thought experiments is suppressing is the fact that the problematic situations in real life, which constitute moral dilemmas, are the

---

[18] See for a discussion van den Hoven 2005.

result of hundreds of prior design decisions and choices. This may be illustrated by reference to one of the most discussed dilemmatic thought experiments in contemporary ethics, the Trolley Case. Suppose you are at the forking path of a downhill railway track and a trolley cart is hurtling down and will pass the junction where you stand. There is a lever which you can operate. If you do nothing the trolley will kill five people, who are tied down to the track further downhill. If you pull the lever, the trolley will be diverted to the other track where there is only one person tied to the track. Is it morally permissible to pull the lever, or is there even a moral obligation to do so?

Engineers and other sensible non-philosophers often reply to Trolley Cases by saying that it is a stupid piece of infrastructure that should have been designed differently. This is not a proper move in the philosophy language game, but is a most interesting move in another language game, namely the one we adopt when we talk about preventing deaths, avoiding tragic moral choices and improving the world in the future. The obsession with moral theory and its refinement blinds one to an important aspect of moral thinking, namely *design*.

Especially those with a technology and engineering background may be able to suggest all kinds of clever design solutions that would prevent this tragic situation from occurring in the future. Their natural attitude to the problems as presented is to formulate solutions to real-world problems instead of contributing to refining ethical theories on the basis of crude and information-poor examples.

Moral analysis of the situation needs to deal with the history of choices and design and development antecedents. Computer ethicists should therefore probe beyond the status quo and ask how the problem came into being and what the design and architectural decisions are that have led up to it. We will not be able to resolve Trolley problems to our full satisfaction once they have presented themselves to us. We need to try to prevent them from occurring in the first place. As Ruth Barcan Marcus has stated, we have a higher-order obligation or a higher-order responsibility (Barcan Marcus in Gowans 1987, p. 200) to prevent situations in which we ourselves and others cannot meet their responsibility and do what ought to be done, 'One ought to act in such a way, that if one ought to do X and one ought to do Y, then one can do both X and Y.'

Cass Sunstein has pointed out (Thaler and Sunstein 2008) that most professionals – ICTs architects and ICT professionals are eminent examples in this respect – are *choice architects*, who 'have responsibilities for organizing the context in which people make decisions'. They design either for tragic choices and likely accidents or for responsibility and safety and security.

As far as the institutional dimensions of moral situations are concerned, this design type of question is now being addressed more often. The question is now posed, which institutional and material conditions need to be fulfilled if (1) we want to prevent situations where the best we can do is limit the damage and (2) we want the results of our ethical analyses to be implemented? How can we increase the chances of changing the world in the direction in which our moral beliefs – held in wide reflective equilibrium – point? How can we design the systems, institutions, infrastructures and ICTs applications in the context of which users will be able to do what they ought to do and which will enable them to prevent what ought to be prevented (Turilli 2007, Turilli 2008)? I have dubbed this notable shift in perspective 'The Design Turn in Applied Ethics' (van den Hoven 2008c, van den Hoven, Miller and Pogge 2010). The work of John Rawls for the first time gave rise to talk about design in ethics. Thinking about social justice can, in the context of Rawls' theory, be described as formulating and justifying the principles of justice in accordance with which we should design the basic institutions in society. Thomas Pogge, Russell Hardin, Cass Sunstein, Robert Goodin, Dennis Thompson and others (van den Hoven 2008) have taken moral theory and applied ethics a step further down this path of semantic descent and practicality. Not only do they want to offer applied ethical analyses, they also want to think about the economic conditions, institutional and legal frameworks and incentive structures that need to be realized if our applied analyses are to stand a chance in their implementation and thus contribute to bringing about real and desirable moral changes in the real world. Design in the work of these authors is primarily focused on institutional design, but the Design Turn clearly brings into view the design of socio-technical systems, technological artefacts and socio-technical systems. This suggests in part another mode of moral thinking.

To sum up: high-level, moral theories – which each put different types of moral value centre stage – are to be specified and exemplified in a process of clarification of the moral issues of information societies in the form of mid-level theories. Mid-level theories may then in turn be used as sources of moral arguments in the relevant empirical domains, where conceptual reconstructions have prepared the ground for their application. Reconstructed concepts, e.g. *contestatory democracy*, *justice as fairness*, *privacy as data protection*, function as high-level architectural principles for the design of information systems and ICTs applications. These principles can be utilized as non-functional requirements, which can be further specified by means of functional decomposition in specifications for the development of ICTs applications.

5 Information ethics

Luciano Floridi

5.1 Introduction: in search of a unified approach to information ethics

In recent years, Information Ethics (IE) has come to mean different things to different researchers working in a variety of disciplines, including computer ethics, business ethics, medical ethics, computer science, the philosophy of information, social epistemology and library and information science. This is not surprising. Perhaps this Babel was always going to be inevitable, given the novelty of the field and the multifarious nature of the concept of information itself and of its related phenomena. It is, however, unfortunate, for it has generated some confusion about the specific *nature* and *scope* of IE. The problem, however, is not irremediable, for a unified approach can help to explain and relate the main senses in which IE has been discussed in the literature. The approach is best introduced schematically and by focusing our attention on a moral agent *A*.

Suppose *A* is interested in pursuing whatever she considers her best course of action, given her predicament. We shall assume that *A*'s evaluations and actions have *some* moral value, but no specific value needs to be introduced. Intuitively, *A* can use some information (information as a *resource*) to generate some other information (information as a *product*) and in so doing affect her informational environment (information as *target*). Now, since the appearance of the first works in the eighties (for an early review see Smith 1996), Information Ethics has been claimed to be the study of moral issues arising from one or another of these three distinct 'information arrows' (see Figure 5.1). This, in turn, has paved the way to a fruitless compartmentalization and false dilemmas, with researchers either ignoring the wider scope of IE, or arguing as if only one 'arrow' and its corresponding microethics (that is a practical, field-dependent, applied and professional ethics) provided *the* right approach to IE. The limits of such narrowly constructed interpretations of IE become evident once we look at each 'informational arrow' more closely.

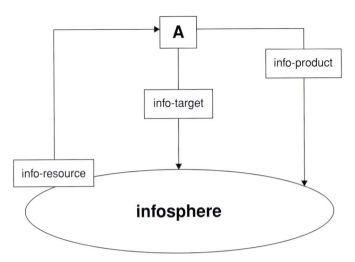

Figure 5.1 The 'External' R(esource) P(roduct) T(arget) Model.

5.1.1   Information-as-a-resource Ethics

Consider first the crucial role played by information as a *resource* for *A*'s moral evaluations and actions. Moral evaluations and actions have an epistemic component, since *A* may be expected to proceed 'to the best of her information', that is, *A* may be expected to avail herself of whatever information she can muster, in order to reach (better) conclusions about what can and ought to be done in some given circumstances.

Socrates already argued that a moral agent is naturally interested in gaining as much valuable information as the circumstances require, and that a well-informed agent is more likely to do the right thing. The ensuing 'ethical intellectualism' analyses evil and morally wrong behaviour as the outcome of deficient information. Conversely, *A*'s moral *responsibility* tends to be directly proportional to *A*'s degree of information: any decrease in the latter usually corresponds to a decrease in the former. This is the sense in which information occurs in the guise of judicial evidence. It is also the sense in which one speaks of *A*'s informed decision, informed consent or well-informed participation. In Christian ethics, even the worst sins can be forgiven in the light of the sinner's insufficient information, as a counterfactual evaluation is possible: had *A* been properly informed *A* would have acted differently and hence would not have sinned (Luke 23:44). In a secular context, Oedipus and Macbeth remind us how the (inadvertent) mismanagement of informational resources may have tragic consequences.

From a 'resource' perspective, it seems that the machinery of moral thinking and behaviour needs information, and quite a lot of it, to function properly. However, even within the limited scope adopted by an analysis based solely on information as a resource, care should be exercised lest all ethical discourse is reduced to the nuances of higher quantity, quality and intelligibility of informational resources. The more the better is not the only, nor always the best, rule of thumb. For the (sometimes explicit and conscious) withdrawal of information can often make a significant difference. *A* may need to lack (or intentionally preclude herself from accessing) some information in order to achieve morally desirable goals, such as protecting anonymity, enhancing fair treatment or implementing unbiased evaluation. Famously, Rawls' 'veil of ignorance' exploits precisely this aspect of information-as-a-resource in order to develop an impartial approach to justice (Rawls 1999). Being informed is not always a blessing and might sometimes be morally wrong or dangerous.

Whether the (quantitative and qualitative) presence or the (total) absence of information-as-a-resource is in question, it is obvious that there is a perfectly reasonable sense in which Information Ethics may be described as the study of the moral issues arising from 'the triple A': *availability*, *accessibility* and *accuracy* of informational resources, independently of their format, kind and physical support. Rawls' position has already been mentioned. Other examples of issues in IE, understood as an Information-as-resource Ethics, are the so-called *digital divide*, the problem of *infoglut*, and the analysis of the *reliability* and *trustworthiness* of information sources (Floridi 1995). Indeed, one may recognize in this approach to Information Ethics a position broadly defended by van den Hoven (1995) and more recently by Mathiesen (2004), who criticizes Floridi (1999b) and is in turn criticized by Mather (2005). Whereas van den Hoven purports to present his approach to IE as an enriching perspective contributing to the debate, Mathiesen means to present her view, restricted to the informational needs and states of the moral agent, as the only correct interpretation of IE. Her position is thus undermined by the problems affecting any microethical interpretation of IE, as Mather well argues.

5.1.2   Information-as-a-product Ethics

A second, but closely related sense in which information plays an important moral role is as a *product* of *A*'s moral evaluations and actions. *A* is not only an information consumer but also an information producer, who may be subject to constraints while being able to take advantage of opportunities. Both constraints and opportunities call for an ethical analysis. Thus, IE, understood as Information-as-a-product Ethics, may cover moral issues arising, for example, in the context of *accountability*, *liability*, *libel legislation*, *testimony*, *plagiarism*, *advertising*, *propaganda*, *misinformation*, and more generally of *pragmatic rules of communication* à la Grice. Kant's analysis of the immorality of *lying* is one of the best known case-studies in the philosophical literature concerning this kind of Information Ethics. The boy crying wolf, Iago misleading Othello, or Cassandra and Laocoon, pointlessly warning the Trojans against the Greeks' wooden horse, remind us how the ineffective management of informational products may have tragic consequences.

5.1.3   Information-as-a-target Ethics

Independently of A's information input (info-resource) and output (info-product), there is a third sense in which information may be subject to ethical analysis, namely when A's moral evaluations and actions affect the informational environment. Think, for example, of A's respect for, or breach of, someone's information *privacy* or *confidentiality*. *Hacking*, understood as the unauthorized access to a (usually computerized) information system, is another good example. It is not uncommon to mistake it for a problem to be discussed within the conceptual frame of an ethics of informational resources. This misclassification allows the hacker to defend his position by arguing that no use (let alone misuse) of the accessed information has been made. Yet hacking, properly understood, is a form of breach of privacy. What is in question is not what A does with the information, which has been accessed without authorization, but what it means for an informational environment to be accessed by A without authorization. So the analysis of hacking belongs to an Info-target Ethics. Other issues here include *security*, *vandalism* (from the burning of libraries and books to the dissemination of viruses), *piracy*, *intellectual property*, *open source*, *freedom of expression*, *censorship*, *filtering* and *contents control*. Mill's analysis 'Of the Liberty of Thought and Discussion' is a classic of IE interpreted as Information-as-a-target Ethics. Juliet, simulating her death, and Hamlet, re-enacting his father's homicide, show how the risky management of one's informational environment may have tragic consequences.

5.1.4   The limits of any microethical approach to Information Ethics

At the end of this overview, it seems that the RPT model, summarized in Figure 5.1, may help one to get some initial orientation in the multiplicity of issues belonging to different interpretations of Information Ethics. The model is also useful to explain why any technology which radically modifies the 'life of information' is going to have profound implications for any moral agent. ICT (information and communication technologies), by radically changing the informational context in which moral issues arise, not only add interesting new dimensions to old problems, but lead us to rethink, methodologically, the very grounds on which our ethical positions are based.

At the same time, the model rectifies the excessive emphasis placed on specific technologies (this happens most notably in *computer* ethics), by concentrating on the more fundamental phenomenon of information in all its variety and long tradition. This was Wiener's position (see Chapter 2) and I have argued (Floridi 1999b, Floridi and Sanders 2002) that the various difficulties encountered in the philosophical foundations of computer ethics are connected to the fact that the latter has not yet been recognized as primarily an environmental ethics whose main concern is (or should be) the ecological management and well-being of the *infosphere*.

Despite these advantages, however, the model can still be criticized for being inadequate, for two reasons.

On the one hand, the model is still too simplistic. Arguably, several important issues belong *mainly but not only* to the analysis of just one 'informational arrow'. A few examples well illustrate the problem: someone's testimony (e.g. Iago's) is someone else's trustworthy information (i.e. Othello's); *A*'s responsibility may be determined by the information *A* holds ('apostle' means 'messenger' in Greek), but it may also concern the information *A* issues (e.g. Judas' kiss); censorship affects *A* both as a user and as a producer of information; misinformation (i.e., the deliberate production and distribution of misleading, false contents) is an ethical problem that concerns all three 'informational arrows'; freedom of speech also affects the availability of offensive content (e.g. child pornography, violent content and socially, politically or religiously disrespectful statements) that might be morally questionable and should not circulate.

On the other hand, the model is insufficiently inclusive. There are many important issues that cannot easily be placed on the map at all, for they really emerge from, or supervene upon, the interactions among the 'informational arrows'. Two significant examples may suffice: the 'panopticon' or 'big brother', that is, the problem of *monitoring and controlling* anything that might concern *A*; and the debate about information *ownership* (including copyright and patents legislation), which affects both users and producers while shaping their informational environment.

So the criticism is fair. The RPT model is indeed inadequate. Yet *why* it is inadequate is a different matter. The tripartite analysis just provided is unsatisfactory, despite its partial usefulness, precisely because any interpretation of Information Ethics based on only one of the 'informational arrows' is bound to be too reductive. As the examples mentioned above emphasize, supporters of narrowly constructed interpretations of Information Ethics as a *microethics* are faced with the problem of being unable to cope with a wide variety of relevant issues, which remain either uncovered or inexplicable. In other words, the model shows that idiosyncratic versions of IE, which privilege only some limited aspects of the information cycle, are unsatisfactory. We should not use the model to attempt to pigeonhole problems neatly, which is impossible. We should rather exploit it as a useful scheme to be superseded, in view of a more encompassing approach to IE as a *macroethics*, that is, as

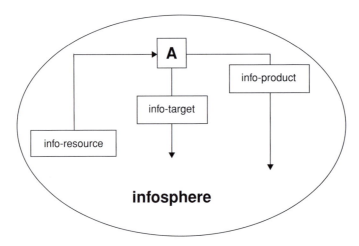

Figure 5.2 The 'Internal' R(esource) P(roduct) T(arget) Model.

a theoretical, field-independent, applicable ethics. Philosophers will recognize here a Wittgensteinian ladder.

In order to climb on, and then throw away, any narrowly constructed conception of Information Ethics, a more encompassing approach to IE needs to

(i) bring together the three 'informational arrows';
(ii) consider the whole information-cycle (including creation, elaboration, distribution, storage, protection, usage and possible destruction); and
(iii) analyse informationally all entities involved (including the moral agent *A*) and their changes, actions and interactions, by treating them not apart from, but as part of the informational environment, or *infosphere*, to which they belong as informational systems themselves (see Figure 5.2).

Whereas steps (i) and (ii) do not pose particular problems and may be shared by other approaches to IE, step (iii) is crucial but requires a shift in the conception of 'information'. Instead of limiting the analysis to (veridical) semantic contents – as any narrower interpretation of IE as a microethics inevitably does – an ecological approach to Information Ethics looks at information from an object-oriented perspective and treats it as an entity. In other words, we move from a (broadly constructed) epistemological conception of Information Ethics to one which is typically ontological.

A simple analogy may help introduce this new perspective.[1] Imagine looking at the whole Universe from a chemical perspective. Every entity and process will satisfy a certain chemical description. An agent *A*, for example, will be between 45% and 75% water. Now consider an informational perspective.

---

[1] For a detailed analysis and defence of an object-oriented modelling of informational entities see Floridi (1999b), Floridi (2003) and Floridi and Sanders (2004).

The same entities will be described as clusters of data, that is, as informational objects. More precisely, *A* (like any other entity) will be a discrete,
self-contained, encapsulated package containing

(i) the appropriate data structures which constitute the nature of the entity
in question, that is, the state of the object, its unique identity and its
attributes; and

(ii) a collection of operations, functions, or procedures which are activated
by various interactions or stimuli (that is, messages received from other
objects or changes within itself) and correspondingly define how the object
behaves or reacts to them.

From this perspective, informational systems as such, rather than just living
systems in general, are raised to the role of agents and patients of any action,
with environmental processes, changes and interactions equally described
informationally.

Understanding the *nature* of IE ontologically rather than epistemologically
modifies the interpretation of the *scope* of IE. Not only can an ecological IE
gain a global view of the whole life-cycle of information, thus overcoming
the limits of other microethical approaches, but it can also claim a role as a
macroethics, that is, as an ethics that concerns the whole realm of reality. This
is what we shall see in the next section.

5.2   Information Ethics as a macroethics

This section provides a quick and accessible overview of Information Ethics
understood as a macroethics (henceforth simply Information Ethics). For reasons of space, no attempt will be made to summarize the specific arguments,
relevant evidence and detailed analyses required to flesh out the ecological
approach to IE. Nor will its many philosophical implications be unfolded. The
goal is rather to provide a general flavour of the theory. The hope is that the
reader interested in knowing more about IE might be enticed to read more
about it by following the references.

This section consists of five questions and answers that introduce IE.
Section 5.3 consists of six objections and replies that, it is to be hoped, will
dispel some common misunderstandings concerning IE.

5.2.1   What is IE?

IE is an *ontocentric, patient-oriented, ecological* macroethics (Floridi 1999b).
An intuitive way to unpack this answer is by comparing IE to other environmental approaches.

Biocentric ethics usually grounds its analysis of the moral standing of bio-entities and eco-systems on the intrinsic worthiness of *life* and the intrinsically negative value of *suffering*. It seeks to develop a patient-oriented ethics in which the 'patient' may be not only a human being, but also any form of life. Indeed, Land Ethics extends the concept of patient to any component of the environment, thus coming close to the approach defended by Information Ethics. Any form of life is deemed to enjoy some essential proprieties or moral interests that deserve and demand to be respected, at least minimally if not absolutely, that is, in a possibly overridable sense, when contrasted to other interests. So biocentric ethics argues that the nature and well-being of the patient of any action constitute (at least partly) its moral standing and that the latter makes important claims on the interacting agent, claims that in principle ought to contribute to the guidance of the agent's ethical decisions and the constraint of the agent's moral behaviour. The 'receiver' of the action is placed at the core of the ethical discourse, as a centre of moral concern, while the 'transmitter' of any moral action is moved to its periphery.

Substitute now 'life' with 'existence' and it should become clear what IE amounts to. IE is an ecological ethics that replaces *biocentrism* with *ontocentrism*. IE suggests that there is something even more elemental than life, namely *being* – that is, the existence and flourishing of all entities and their global environment – and something more fundamental than suffering, namely *entropy*. The latter is most emphatically *not* the physicists' concept of thermodynamic entropy. Entropy here refers to any kind of *destruction* or *corruption* of informational objects (mind, not of information), that is, any form of impoverishment of *being*, including *nothingness*, to phrase it more metaphysically. More specifically, *destruction* is to be understood as the complete annihilation of the object in question, which ceases to exist; compare this to the process of 'erasing' an entity irrevocably. *Corruption* is to be understood as a form of pollution or depletion of some of the properties of the object, which ceases to exist as that object and begins to exist as a different object minus the properties that have been corrupted or eliminated. This may be compared to a process degrading the integrity of the object in question.

IE then provides a common vocabulary to understand the whole realm of *being* through an informational perspective. IE holds that *being*/information has an intrinsic worthiness. It substantiates this position by recognizing that any informational entity has a *Spinozian* right to persist in its own status, and a *constructionist* right to flourish, i.e. to improve and enrich its existence and essence. As a consequence of such 'rights', IE evaluates the duty of any moral agent in terms of contribution to the growth of the *infosphere* (see Sections 5.2.4 and 5.2.5) and any process, action or event that negatively affects the whole infosphere – not just an informational entity – as an increase in its level of entropy and hence as an instance of evil (Floridi and Sanders 1999, Floridi and Sanders 2001, Floridi 2003).

In IE, the ethical discourse concerns any entity, understood informationally, that is, not only all persons, their cultivation, well-being and social interactions, not only animals, plants and their proper natural life, but also anything that exists, from paintings and books to stars and stones; anything that may or will exist, like future generations; and anything that was but is no more, like our ancestors or old civilizations. Indeed, according to IE, even ideal, intangible or intellectual objects can have a minimal degree of moral value, no matter how humble, and so be entitled to some respect. UNESCO, for example, recognizes this in its protection of 'masterpieces of the oral and intangible heritage of humanity' by attributing them an intrinsic worth.

IE is impartial and universal because it brings to ultimate completion the process of enlargement of the concept of what may count as a centre of a (no matter how minimal) moral claim, which now includes every instance of *being* understood informationally (see Section 5.2.3), no matter whether physically implemented or not. In this respect, IE holds that every entity, as an expression of *being*, has a dignity, constituted by its mode of existence and essence (the collection of all the elementary proprieties that constitute it for what it is), which deserves to be respected (at least in a minimal and overridable sense) and hence places moral claims on the interacting agent and ought to contribute to the constraint and guidance of his ethical decisions and behaviour. This ontological equality principle means that any form of reality (any instance of information/*being*), simply for the fact of *being* what it is, enjoys a minimal, initial, overridable, equal right to exist and develop in a way which is appropriate to its nature. In the history of philosophy, this is a view that can already be found advocated by Stoic and Neoplatonic philosophers.

The conscious recognition of the ontological equality principle presupposes a disinterested judgement of the moral situation from an objective perspective, i.e. a perspective which is as non-anthropocentric as possible. Moral behaviour is less likely without this epistemic virtue. The application of the ontological equality principle is achieved whenever actions are impartial, universal and 'caring'.

The crucial importance of the radical change in ontological perspective cannot be overestimated. Bioethics and Environmental Ethics fail to achieve a level of complete impartiality because they are still biased against what is inanimate, lifeless, intangible or abstract (even Land Ethics is biased against technology and artefacts, for example). From their perspective, only what is intuitively alive deserves to be considered as a proper centre of moral claims, no matter how minimal, so a whole Universe escapes their attention. Now, this is precisely the fundamental limit overcome by IE, which further lowers the minimal condition that needs to be satisfied, in order to qualify as a centre of moral concern, to the common factor shared by any entity, namely its informational state. And since any form of *being* is in any case also a coherent body of information, to say that IE is infocentric is tantamount to interpreting it, correctly, as an ontocentric theory.

5.2.2   What counts as a moral agent, according to IE?

A moral agent is an *interactive, autonomous* and *adaptable transition system* that can perform *morally qualifiable actions* (Floridi and Sanders 2004). As usual, the definition requires some explanations.

First, we need to understand what a *transition system* is. Let us agree that a system is characterized by the properties it satisfies, once a given perspective is made explicit. We are interested in systems that change, which means that some of those properties change value. A changing system has its evolution captured by the values of its attributes. Thus, an entity can be thought of as having states, determined by the value of the properties that hold at any instant of its evolution. For then any change in the entity corresponds to a state change and vice versa. This conceptual approach allows us to view any entity as having states. Each change corresponds to a transition from one state to another. Note that a transition may be non-deterministic, since the transition might lead from a given initial state to one of several possible subsequent states. According to this view, the entity becomes a transition system.

A transition system is *interactive* when the system and its environment (can) act upon each other. Typical examples include input or output of a value, or simultaneous engagement of an action by both agent and patient – for example, gravitational force between bodies. An interactive transition system is *autonomous* when the system is able to change state without direct response to interaction, that is, it can perform internal transitions to change its state. So an agent must have at least two states. This property imbues an agent with a certain degree of complexity and independence from its environment. Finally, an interactive transition system is *adaptable* when the system's interactions (can) change the transition rules by which it changes state. This property ensures that an agent might be viewed as learning its own mode of operation in a way which depends critically on its experience.

All we need to understand now is the meaning of 'morally qualifiable action'. Very simply, an action qualifies as moral if it can cause moral good or evil. Note that this interpretation is neither consequentialist nor intentionalist in nature. We are neither affirming nor denying that the specific evaluation of the morality of the agent might depend on the specific outcome of the agent's actions or on the agent's original intentions or principles.

With all the definitions in place, it becomes possible to understand why, according to IE, *artificial agents* (not just digital agents but also social agents such as companies, parties, or hybrid systems formed by humans and machines, or technologically augmented humans) count as moral agents that are morally *accountable* for their actions (more on the distinction between responsibility and accountability presently).

The enlargement of the class of moral agents by IE brings several advantages. Normally, an entity is considered a moral agent only if

(i) it is an *individual* agent and

(ii) it is *human-based*, in the sense that it is either human or at least reducible to an identifiable aggregation of human beings, who remain the only morally responsible sources of action, like ghosts in the legal machine.

Regarding (i), limiting the ethical discourse to *individual agents* hinders the development of a satisfactory investigation of *distributed morality*, a macroscopic and growing phenomenon of global moral actions and collective responsibilities, resulting from the 'invisible hand' of systemic interactions among several agents at a local level.

And as far as (ii) is concerned, insisting on the necessarily *human-based nature* of the agent means undermining the possibility of understanding another major transformation in the ethical field, the appearance of artificial agents that are sufficiently informed, 'smart', autonomous and able to perform morally relevant actions independently of the humans who created them, causing 'artificial good' and 'artificial evil' (Floridi and Sanders 1999, Floridi and Sanders 2001).

Of course, accepting that artificial agents may be moral agents is not devoid of problems. We have seen that morality is usually predicated upon *responsibility*. So it is often argued that artificial agents cannot be considered moral agents because they are not morally responsible for their actions, since holding them responsible would be a conceptual mistake (see Floridi and Sanders 2004 for a more detailed discussion of the following arguments). The point raised by the objection is that agents are moral agents only if they are *responsible* in the sense of being prescriptively assessable in principle. An agent x is a moral agent only if x can in principle be put on trial.

The immediate impression is that the 'lack of responsibility' objection is merely confusing the *identification* of x as a moral agent with the *evaluation* of x as a morally responsible agent. Surely, the counter-argument goes, there is a difference between being able to say who or what is the moral source or cause of (and hence accountable for) the moral action in question, and being able to evaluate, prescriptively, whether and how far the moral source so identified is also morally responsible for that action, and hence deserves to be praised or blamed, and in some cases rewarded or punished accordingly.

Well, that immediate impression is indeed wrong. There is no confusion. Equating identification and evaluation is actually a short cut. The objection is saying that identity (as a moral agent) without responsibility (as a moral agent) is empty, so we may as well save ourselves the bother of all these distinctions and speak only of morally responsible agents and moral agents as co-referential descriptions. But here lies the real mistake. For we can now see that the objection has finally shown its fundamental presupposition, viz., that we should reduce all prescriptive discourse to responsibility analysis. Yet this is an unacceptable assumption, a juridical fallacy. There is plenty of room for prescriptive discourse that is independent of responsibility-assignment and hence requires a clear identification of moral agents.

Consider the following example. There is nothing wrong with identifying a dog as the source of a morally good action, hence as an agent playing a crucial role in a moral situation, and therefore as a moral agent. Search-and-rescue dogs are trained to track missing people. They often help save lives, for which they receive much praise and rewards from both their owners and the people they have located. Yet this is not quite the point. Emotionally, people may be very grateful to the animals, but for the dogs it is a game and they cannot be considered morally *responsible* for their actions. The point is that the dogs are involved in a moral game as main players and therefore we can rightly identify them as moral agents *accountable* for the good or evil they can cause.

All this should ring a bell. Trying to equate identification and evaluation is really just another way of shifting the ethical analysis from considering x as the moral agent/source of a first-order moral action y to considering x as a possible moral patient of a second-order moral action z, which is the moral evaluation of x as being morally responsible for y. This is a typical Kantian move, with roots in Christian theology. However, there is clearly more to moral evaluation than just responsibility because x is capable of moral action even if x cannot be (or is not yet) a morally responsible agent.

By distinguishing between *moral responsibility*, which requires intentions, consciousness and other mental attitudes, and *moral accountability*, we can now avoid anthropocentric and anthropomorphic attitudes towards agent-hood. Instead, we can rely on an ethical outlook not necessarily based on punishment and reward (responsibility-oriented ethics) but on moral agent-hood, accountability and censure. We are less likely to assign responsibility at any cost, forced by the necessity to identify individual, human agent(s). We can stop the regress of looking for the *responsible* individual when something evil happens, since we are now ready to acknowledge that sometimes the moral source of evil or good can be different from an individual or group of humans (note that this was a reasonable view in Greek philosophy). As a result, we are able to escape the dichotomy

(i) [(responsibility implies moral agency) implies prescriptive action], versus
(ii) [(no responsibility implies no moral agency) implies no prescriptive action].

There can be moral agency in the absence of moral responsibility. Promoting normative action is perfectly reasonable even when there is no responsibility but only moral accountability and the capacity for moral action.

Being able to treat non-human agents as moral agents facilitates the discussion of the morality of agents not only in cyberspace but also in the biosphere – where animals can be considered moral agents without their having to display free will, emotions or mental states – and in contexts of 'distributed morality', where social and legal agents can now qualify as moral agents. The great advantage is a better grasp of the moral discourse in non-human contexts.

All this does not mean that the concept of 'responsibility' is redundant. On the contrary, the previous analysis makes clear the need for further analysis of the concept of responsibility itself, especially when the latter refers to the ontological commitments of creators of new agents and environments. This point is further discussed in Section 5.2.4. The only 'cost' of a 'mind-less morality' approach is the extension of the class of agents and moral agents to embrace artificial agents. It is a cost that is increasingly worth paying the more we move towards an advanced information society.

5.2.3   What counts as a moral patient, according to IE?

All entities, *qua* informational objects, have an intrinsic moral value, although possibly quite minimal and overridable, and hence they can count as moral patients, subject to some equally minimal degree of moral respect understood as *a disinterested, appreciative and careful attention* (Hepburn 1984).

Deflationist theories of intrinsic worth have tried to identify, in various ways, the minimal conditions of possibility of the lowest possible degree of intrinsic worth, without which an entity becomes intrinsically worthless, and hence deserves no moral respect. Investigations have led researchers to move from more restricted to more inclusive, anthropocentric conditions and then further on towards biocentric conditions. As the most recent stage in this dialectical development, IE maintains that even biocentric analyses are still biased and too restricted in scope.

If ordinary human beings are not the only entities enjoying some form of moral respect, what else qualifies? Only sentient beings? Only biological systems? What justifies including some entities and excluding others? Suppose we replace an anthropocentric approach with a biocentric one. Why biocentrism and not ontocentrism? Why can biological *life* and its *preservation* be considered morally relevant phenomena in themselves, independently of human interests, but not *being* and its *flourishing*? In many contexts, it is perfectly reasonable to exercise moral respect towards inanimate entities *per se*, independently of any human interest. Without disturbing Eastern traditions within Buddhism, Hinduism or Shinto – which I understand attribute intrinsic value both to sentient and to non-sentient realities – the reader sufficiently acquainted with the history of Western philosophy will recall that many classic thinkers, such as Plato, Aristotle, Plotin, Augustine, Aquinas and Spinoza, have elaborated and defended what might be called axiological ecumenism. For Plato, for example, Goodness and Being are intimately connected. Plato's universe is value-ridden at its very roots: value is there from the start, not imposed upon it by a rather late-coming new mammalian species of animals, as if before evolution had the chance of hitting upon *Homo sapiens* the Universe were a value-neutral reality, devoid of any ethical worth. By and large, IE proposes the same line of reasoning, by updating it in terms of an informational ontology, whereby Being is understood informationally and Non-being in terms of entropy. Note that this is not a defence of IE but an explanation. Although being in the company of Plato or Spinoza, for example, might be reassuring, it is not an insurance against being mistaken. But it is a rectification of the incorrect remark that IE stands rather alone in its defence of it.

It seems that any attempt to exclude non-living entities is based on some specific perspective but that this is an arbitrary choice. In the scale of beings, there may be no good reasons to stop anywhere but at the bottom. As Naess (1973) has maintained, 'all things in the biosphere have an equal right to live and blossom'. There seems to be no good reason not to adopt a higher and more inclusive, ontocentric level of abstraction. Not only inanimate but also ideal, intangible or intellectual objects can have a minimal degree of moral value, no matter how humble, and so be entitled to some respect. So it might be a matter of ethical sensibility, indeed of an ethical sensibility, that we might have had (at least in some Greek philosophy such as the Stoics' and the Neoplatonists') but have then lost.

Deep Ecologists have already argued that inanimate things too can have some intrinsic value. In a famous article, White (1967) asked 'Do people have ethical obligations toward rocks?' and answered that

> To almost all Americans, still saturated with ideas historically dominant in Christianity...the question makes no sense at all. If the time comes when to any considerable group of us such a question is no longer ridiculous, we may be on the verge of a change of value structures that will make possible measures to cope with the growing ecologic crisis. One hopes that there is enough time left.

According to IE, this is the right ecological perspective *and* it makes perfect sense for *any* religious tradition (including, but not only, the Judaeo-Christian one) for which the whole Universe is God's creation, is inhabited by the divine, and is a gift to humanity, of which the latter needs to take care (see Section 5.3.6). IE translates all this into informational terms. If something can be a moral patient, then its nature can be taken into consideration by a moral agent *A*, and contribute to shaping *A*'s action, no matter how minimally. According to IE, the minimal criterion for qualifying as an object that, as a moral patient, may rightly claim some degree of respect, is more general than any biocentric reference to the object's attributes as a biological or living entity; it is informational. This means that the informational nature of an entity that may, in principle, act as a patient of a moral action, is the lowest threshold that constitutes its minimal intrinsic worth, which in turn may deserve to be respected by the agent. Alternatively, and to put it more concisely, being an informational object *qua* informational object is the minimal condition of possibility of moral worth and hence of normative respect. In more metaphysical terms, IE argues that all aspects and instances of *being* are worth some initial, perhaps minimal and overridable, form of moral respect.

Enlarging the conception of what can count as a centre of moral respect has the advantage of enabling one to make sense of the innovative nature of ICT, as providing a new and powerful conceptual frame. It also enables one to deal more satisfactorily with the original character of some of its moral issues, by approaching them from a theoretically strong perspective. Through time, ethics has steadily moved from a narrow to a more inclusive concept of what can count as a centre of moral worth, from the citizen to the biosphere (Nash 1989). The emergence of the infosphere, as a new environment in which human beings spend much of their lives, explains the need to enlarge further the conception of what can qualify as a moral patient. IE represents the most recent development in this ecumenical trend, a Platonist and ecological approach without a biocentric bias, as it were.

More than fifty years ago, Leopold defined Land Ethics as something that

changes the role of *Homo sapiens* from conqueror of the land-community to plain member and citizen of it. It implies respect for his fellow-members, and also respect for the community as such. The land ethic simply enlarges the boundaries of the community to include soils, waters, plants, and animals, or collectively: the land. (Leopold 1949, p. 403)

IE translates environmental ethics into terms of infosphere and informational objects, for the land we inhabit is not just the Earth.

5.2.4   What are our responsibilities as moral agents, according to IE?

Like demiurges, we have 'ecopoietic' responsibilities towards the whole infosphere. Information Ethics is an ethics addressed not just to 'users' of the world but also to producers who are 'divinely' responsible for its creation and well-being. It is an ethics of *creative stewardship* (Floridi 2002a, Floridi 2003, Floridi and Sanders 2005).

The term 'ecopoiesis' refers to the morally informed construction of the environment, based on an ecologically oriented perspective. In terms of a philosophical anthropology, the ecopoietic approach, supported by IE, is embodied by what I have termed *homo poieticus* (see Chapter 1), a demiurge who takes care of reality to protect it and make it flourish. The more powerful *homo poieticus* becomes as an agent, the greater his duties and responsibilities become, as a *moral agent*, to oversee not only the development of his own character and habits but also the well-being and flourishing of each of his ever-expanding spheres of influence, to include the whole infosphere. To move from individual virtues to global values, an *ecopoietic* approach is needed that recognizes our *responsibilities* towards the environment (including present and future inhabitants) as its enlightened creators, stewards or supervisors, not just as its virtuous users and consumers.

5.2.5   What are the fundamental principles of IE?

IE determines what is morally right or wrong, what ought to be done, what the duties, the 'oughts' and the 'ought nots' of a moral agent are, by means of four basic moral laws. They are formulated here in an informational vocabulary and in a patient-oriented version, but an agent-oriented one is easily achievable in more metaphysical terms of 'dos' and 'don'ts' (compare this list to the similar ones available in medical ethics, where 'pain' replaces 'entropy'):

(0) entropy ought not to be caused in the infosphere (null law);
(1) entropy ought to be prevented in the infosphere;
(2) entropy ought to be removed from the infosphere;
(3) the flourishing of informational entities as well as of the whole infosphere ought to be promoted by preserving, cultivating and enriching their properties.

The moral question asked by IE is not 'why should I care, in principle?' but 'what should be taken care of, in principle?' We have seen that the answer is provided by a minimalist theory: any informational entity is recognized to be the centre of some basic ethical claims, which deserve recognition and should help to regulate the implementation of any informational process involving it. It follows that approval or disapproval of A's decisions and actions should also be based on how the latter affects the well-being of the infosphere, i.e. on how successful or unsuccessful they are in respecting the ethical claims attributable to the informational entities involved, and hence in improving or impoverishing the infosphere. The duty of any moral agent should be evaluated in terms of contribution to the sustainable blooming of the infosphere, and any process, action or event that negatively affects the whole infosphere – not just an informational object – should be seen as an increase in its level of entropy and hence an instance of evil.

The four laws clarify, in very broad terms, what it means to live as a responsible and caring agent in the infosphere. On the one hand, a process is increasingly deprecable, and its agent-source is increasingly blameworthy, the lower the number-index of the specific law that it fails to satisfy. Moral mistakes may occur and entropy may increase if one wrongly evaluates the impact of one's actions because projects conflict or compete, even if those projects aim to satisfy IE moral laws. This is especially the case when 'local goodness', i.e. the improvement of a region of the infosphere, is favoured to the overall disadvantage of the whole environment. More simply, entropy may increase because of the wicked nature of the agent (this possibility is granted by IE's negative anthropology). On the other hand, a process is already commendable, and its agent-source praiseworthy, if it satisfies the *conjunction* of the null law with at least one other law, not the *sum* of the resulting effects. Note that, according to this definition,

(a) an action is unconditionally commendable only if it never generates any entropy in the course of its implementation; and
(b) the best moral action is the action that succeeds in satisfying all four laws at the same time.

Most of the actions that we judge morally good do not satisfy such strict criteria, for they achieve only a balanced positive moral value, that is, although their performance causes a certain quantity of entropy, we acknowledge that the infosphere is in a better state on the whole after their occurrence (compare this to the utilitarianist appreciation of an action that causes more benefits than damages for the overall welfare of the agents and patients). Finally, a process that satisfies only the null law – the level of entropy in the infosphere remains unchanged after its occurrence – either has no moral value, that is, it is morally irrelevant or insignificant, or it is equally deprecable and commendable, though in different respects.

5.3 Six recurrent misunderstandings

Since the early nineties,[2] when I first introduced IE as an environmental macroethics and a foundationalist approach to computer ethics, some standard objections have circulated that seem to be based on a few basic misunderstandings.[3] The point of this final section is not that of convincing the reader that no reasonable disagreement is possible about the value of IE. Rather, the goal here is to remove some ambiguities and possible confusions that might prevent the correct evaluation of IE, so that disagreement can become more constructive (for the development of several lines of critical investigation see Boltuc 2008 and Ess 2008).

[2] Fourth International Conference on Ethical Issues of Information Technology (Department of Philosophy, Erasmus University, the Netherlands, 25–27 March, 1998), this was published as Floridi (1999).
[3] Two good examples of the sort of confusions that may arise concerning Information Ethics are Himma (2004) and Siponen (2004).

5.3.1   Informational objects, not news

By defending the intrinsic moral worth of *informational objects*, IE does not refer to the moral value of any other piece of well-formed and meaningful data such as an email, the *Britannica*, or Newton's *Principia*. What IE suggests is that we adopt an informational perspective to approach the analysis of *being* in terms of a minimal common ontology, whereby human beings as well as animals, plants, artefacts and so forth are interpreted as informational entities.

5.3.2   Minimalism not reductionism

IE does not reduce people to mere numbers, nor does it treat human beings as if they were no more important than animals, trees, stones or files. The minimalism advocated by IE is methodological. It means to support the view that entities can be analysed by focusing on their lowest common denominator, represented by an informational ontology. Other perspectives can then be evoked in order to deal with other, more human-centred values.

5.3.3   Applicable not applied

Given its ontological nature and wide scope, one may object that IE works at a level of metaphysical abstraction too philosophical to make it of any direct utility for immediate needs and applications. Yet, this is the inevitable price to be paid for any foundationalist project. One must polarize theory and practice to strengthen both. IE is not immediately useful to solve specific ethical problems (including computer ethics problems), but it provides the conceptual grounds that then guide problem-solving procedures. Thus, IE has already been fruitfully applied to deal with the 'tragedy of the digital commons' (Greco and Floridi 2004), the digital divide (Floridi 2002a), the problem of telepresence (Floridi forthcoming, c), game cheating (Sicart 2005), the problem of privacy (Floridi 2005a) and environmental issues (York 2005).

5.3.4   Implementable not inapplicable

A related objection is that IE, by promoting the moral value of any entity, is inapplicable because it is too demanding or supererogatory. In this case, it is important to stress that IE supports a *minimal* and *overridable* sense of ontic moral value. Environmental ethics accepts culling as a moral practice and does not indicate as one's duty the provision of a vegetarian diet to wild carnivores. IE is equally reasonable: fighting the decaying of *being* (information entropy) is the general approach to be followed, not an impossible and ridiculous struggle against thermodynamics, or the ultimate benchmark for any moral evaluation, as if human beings had to be treated as mere numbers. 'Respect and take care of all entities for their own sake, if you can', this is the injunction. We need to adopt an ethics of stewardship towards the infosphere; is this really too demanding or unwise? Perhaps we should think twice: is it actually easier to accept the idea that all non-biological entities have no intrinsic value whatsoever? Perhaps, we should consider that the ethical game may be more opaque, subtle and difficult to play than humanity has so far wished to acknowledge. Perhaps, we could be less pessimistic: human sensitivity has already improved quite radically in the past, and may improve further. Perhaps, we should just be cautious: given how fallible we are, it may be better to be too inclusive than discriminative. In each of these answers, one needs to remember that IE is meant to be a macroethics for creators not just users of their surrounding 'nature', and this new situation brings with it demiurgic responsibilities that may require a special theoretical effort.

5.3.5   Preservation and cultivation not conservation

IE does not support a morally conservationist or 'laissez faire' attitude, according to which *homo poieticus* would be required not to modify, improve or interfere in any way with the natural course of things. On the contrary, IE is fundamentally proactive, in a way similar to *restorationist* or *interventionist ecology*. The unavoidable challenge lays precisely in understanding how reality can be better shaped. A gardener transforms the environment for the better, that's why he needs to be very knowledgeable. IE may be, but has no bias in principle, against abortion, eugenics, GM food, human cloning, animal experiments and other highly controversial, yet technically and scientifically possible ways of transforming or 'enhancing' reality. But it is definitely opposed to any associated ignorance of the consequences of such radical transformations.

5.3.6   A secular, not a spiritual or religious approach

IE is compatible with, and may be associated with religious beliefs, including a Buddhist (Herold 2005) or a Judaeo-Christian view of the world. In the latter case, the reference to Genesis 2:15 readily comes to one's mind. *Homo poieticus* is supposed 'to tend (*'abad*) and exercise care and protection over (*shamar*)' God's creation. Stewardship is a much better way of rendering this stance towards reality than dominion. Nevertheless, IE is based on a secular philosophy. *Homo poieticus* has a vocation for responsible stewardship in the world. Unless some other form of intelligence is discovered in the Universe, we cannot presume to share this burden with any other being. *Homo poieticus* should certainly not entrust his responsibility for the flourishing of *being* to some transcendent power. As the Enlightenment has taught us, the religion of reason can be immanent. If the full responsibilization of humanity is then consistent with a religious view, this can only be a welcome conclusion, not a premise.

5.4   Conclusion

There is a famous passage in one of Einstein's letters that well summarizes the perspective advocated by IE.

Some five years prior to his death, Albert Einstein received a letter from a nineteen-year-old girl grieving over the loss of her younger sister. The young woman wished to know what the famous scientist might say to comfort her. On March 4, 1950, Einstein wrote to this young person: A human being is part of the whole, called by us 'universe', a part limited in time and space. He experiences himself, his thoughts and feelings, as something separated from the rest, a kind of optical delusion of his consciousness. This delusion is a kind of prison for us, restricting us to our personal desires and to affection for a few persons close to us. Our task must be to free ourselves from our prison by widening our circle of compassion to embrace all humanity and the whole of nature in its beauty. Nobody is capable of achieving this completely, but the striving for such achievement is in itself a part of the liberation and a foundation for inner security. (Einstein 1954)

Does the informational level of abstraction of IE provide an additional perspective that can further expand the ethical discourse, so as to include the world of morally significant phenomena involving informational objects? Or does it represent a threshold beyond which nothing of moral significance really happens? Does looking at reality through the highly philosophical lens of an informational analysis improve our ethical understanding or is it an ethically pointless (when not misleading) exercise? IE argues that the agent-related *behaviour* and the patient-related *status* of informational objects *qua* informational objects can be morally significant, over and above the instrumental function that may be attributed to them by other ethical approaches, and hence that they can contribute to determining, normatively, ethical duties and legally enforceable rights. IE's position, like that of any other macroethics, is not devoid of problems. But it can interact with other macroethical theories and contribute an important new perspective: a process or action may be morally good or bad irrespective of its consequences, motives, universality or virtuous nature, but depending on how it affects the infosphere. An ontocentric ethics provides an insightful perspective. Without IE's contribution, our understanding of moral facts in general, not just of ICT-related problems in particular, would be less complete.

Part III

Ethical issues in the information society

6 Social issues in computer ethics

Bernd Carsten Stahl

6.1 Introduction

Social issues in computer ethics are manifold. This chapter will concentrate on three of them: the question of intellectual property, issues related to digital divides, and issues arising out of employment and work. This choice can be justified by the prominence that all three of them enjoy in current computer ethics[1] debates. Other possible issues, such as security (see Chapter 8), gender (see Chapter 9) or globalization (see Chapter 10), are discussed elsewhere in the book. All three of the topics developed in this chapter have in common that they are strongly influenced by economic or commercial considerations. They are, as a consequence, characterized by ethical issues arising from property, ownership, distribution and power, which will point the way to possible approaches to understand and address them.

6.2 Intellectual property

Intellectual property is a pervasive issue of ethical relevance that touches many aspects of modern societies. Questions include whether software or content can or should be owned, how they can be protected and how protection mechanisms can be enforced. On a day-to-day level, these questions raise numerous debates, which are played out in the media and courts of law but which are also heatedly discussed in classrooms, parliaments and pubs. The multitude of voices and sheer volume of debates often drown out the fact that, at the bottom of often very different discussions, there are important philosophical arguments. This section aims to clarify the philosophical underpinning of those social issues in computer ethics related to ownership and property in

---

[1] While the title of this chapter refers to 'computer ethics', it is probably more fitting to speak of 'computer and information ethics', as not all of the relevant issues are always directly linked to computers. In addition, the term 'computer' is also rather narrow and somewhat difficult to define. In this chapter I will thus make more use of the term commonly used in the UK, namely 'information and communication technology' (ICT), which covers a wider range of technological artefacts.

assets that have a form different from the physical entities for which the idea of property was originally developed.

6.2.1   Property

Etymologically, the term 'property' stems from the Latin 'proprius', which means one's own (Phillips and Firth 2001). There is no clear definition in English law of terms that delimit property such as 'possession' or 'ownership' (Goode 2004, p. 42). A frequently used definition of property, going back to William Blackstone, is that it is a bundle of rights, which include the rights to use, manage, possess, exclude and derive income (Spinello 2000, p. 74; Ladd 2000). Such rights need to be generally recognized in order to be viable. This raises the question why a society would want to recognize them, given that a world where there is no property, or at least no private property, is conceivable. The literature often distinguishes between two types of arguments for the creation of property rights: the natural rights tradition and the utilitarian tradition. The natural rights argument is based on the idea that there is natural property in some entities, notably oneself, which can be extended to other objects. This is often based on Lockean ideas where the original ownership is in one's labour, which then extends to the result of this labour (Johnson 2001). A similar argument can be made drawing on Hegel, where property in one's creation is an 'expression of personality' (Spinello and Tavani 2005, p. 12). Utility arguments, on the other hand, are based on considerations of overall utility and the main argument is that the institution of property rights is beneficial for society, as it will act as a motivator for creation, an incentive for taking responsibility and be conducive for overall efficiency (Donaldson and Dunfee 1999).

6.2.2   Justifications of intellectual property

Intellectual property (IP) can be defined as property in the products of the human intellect (Phillips and Firth 2001). It has always been closely linked to technology and this link has been strengthened through developments of information and communication technology (ICT), which offer new ways of creating, presenting and disseminating intellectual creations (McFarland 2001). Creations of the mind have characteristics that are different from those of physical entities. IP therefore needs to rely on regulations that are different from those that enshrine property in physical entities. In order to grant the bundle of rights in IP, the IP holder is granted a limited monopoly (Boyle 2001).

The arguments justifying the existence of physical property are reflected by the arguments put forward for IP (Van Caenegem 2003). The natural rights argument with reference to Lock and Hegel can be found with regards to intellectual creations (Warwick 2001). The labour desert theory, based on Locke, which holds that a creator has a natural right to profit from his work, is strong in IP (Spinello 2003). A different take on natural rights to IP relates to the human rights quality of property. Mason (2000), drawing on Rand, argues that the right to life requires a right to property, which can then be extended to IP.

Despite the plausibility of natural rights justifications of IP, they have to contend with serious problems. The idea of a natural order, from which natural rights can be deduced, tends to go back to a religious worldview, which is difficult to uphold in modern societies. Even agreement on the existence of natural rights does not answer the question about their formulation and enforcement. It is questionable whether one can still speak of a natural right if there is no way to define and implement it.

The dominant justification of IP is therefore the economic and utility-based one. It takes the utility-maximizing characteristics of property and explicates them using economic considerations. Intellectual creations are costly and resource intensive and creators will only engage in the process of creation if they know that they will be rewarded. Setting incentives to promote creation via IP will then lead to a (economically and intellectually) richer society (Ciro 2005). Such a consequentialist framework can be used to justify IP because of its general property of increasing well-being by stimulating production (Johnson 2000), promoting progress and innovation (Van Caenegem 2003).

6.2.3   Physical property vs. IP

The arguments in defence of IP have been well rehearsed. They have also been questioned intensively, particularly with regards to the relationship of ICT and IP. It has been pointed out that property regulations were developed for physical property or chattel (chattel is a legal term that denotes tangible and moveable property) and the idea of applying similar regulations to creations of the mind may be problematic (Ladd 2000). Similarities between physical entities and electronic embodiments of intellectual creations are limited. Using the same arguments in both cases can thus best be understood as the usage of metaphors, which may be problematic because the phenomena in question are incommensurable (Siponen and Vartiainen 2002). Barlow (1995, p. 16) captured this view when he said:

Certainly, the old concepts of property, expression, identity, movement, and context, based as they are on physical manifestation, do not apply in a world where there can be none.

There are at least two features of IP which are fundamentally different from physical property and which call into question the applicability of traditional property rules to IP. First, there is the issue of the reproducibility of intellectual creations. As Hinman (2002) points out, intellectual creations are not only reproducible, but infinitely so, to an extent that it is impossible to see a difference between the original and the copy. ICT has furthermore lowered the cost of such reproduction to the point where it is negligible in comparison with the overall cost of creation.

The second feature that is fundamentally different between physical and intellectual entities concerns the possibility of simultaneous use. One of the reasons why the unauthorized appropriation of physical property is deemed to be immoral to the point where it has to be made illegal (i.e. made the crime of theft) is that taking someone's physical property means to deprive them of its use. This type of argument does not work in the same way for intellectual property. Copying something that is the IP of someone else does not in the same way deprive the user of all possible uses of the entity (Maner, 2004). The consumption of IP is what economists call 'non-rivalrous', which means that the consumption by one individual does not lessen the consumption by another one (Lessig 1999).

6.2.4   Legal protection of IP

The arguments discussed so far set the background for the implementation of IP protection through laws as well as the ongoing critique of such protection. This book deals with ethical questions rather than legal ones and it is impossible to do justice to the complex subject of IP legislation in the brief space available. It is nevertheless important to touch upon the sources of IP law and the forms it takes because these reflect philosophical justifications. Knowledge of legal regulations is also important to follow current debates. One can argue that economic interests have become dominant in IP regulation (De George 1998, Severson 1997).

The international nature of ICT and potential use and misuse of IP means that IP legislation needs to be internationally consistent in order to be successful. It is therefore unsurprising that there are attempts to reach a uniform standard of IP legislation, most notably by the World Intellectual Property Organization (www.wipo.int). The WIPO is a specialized agency of the United Nations. It is dedicated to 'developing a balanced and accessible international intellectual property (IP) system, which rewards creativity, stimulates innovation and contributes to economic development while safeguarding the public interest' (www.wipo.int/about-wipo/en/what_is_wipo.html). This very brief statement indicates that while economic considerations are emphasized, a need to reconcile them with the public interest is also acknowledged.

There are a number of forms that the legal protection of IP can take. With regards to ethical issues raised by ICT, two groups of intellectual creations currently constitute the main items of IP: software and content. Content in the form of audio or video files is possibly less contentious because it has been protected by IP legislation for a long time. The traditional way of protecting IP in content takes the form of copyright. A more complex issue is that of protection of software. When software started to become a commercially viable product and ceased to be part of a support service for computer hardware, legal systems found it hard to classify it in a way suitable for existing IP legislation. Initially, it was debated whether the object code could be copyright. Legal disputes surrounded the question whether the look and feel of a piece of software can be subject to copyright protection. This was the heart of the famous *Apple Inc v Microsoft Corporation*, 35 F.3d 1435 (9th Cir. 1994) case, in which Apple claimed that Microsoft had infringed its copyright by copying the graphical user interface.

While copyright is now the dominant type of legal IP protection applicable to software and content, software producers have sought to extend the scope of IP. There are a number of examples of patents that refer to certain software functions. However, there is no international agreement on whether and on what grounds software or aspects thereof can be patented. There are a number of other forms of legal IP protection. These include registered and unregistered designs, trade marks, moral rights (i.e. the right not to be falsely associated with a piece of work) and the common law instrument of passing off.

An important development aimed at strengthening IP protection, used mostly by software vendors, is the use of licences. Licences are contracts between users and vendors and therefore allow vendors more flexibility in delimiting their IP claims. The legal status of many such licences remains untested. It has been argued, however, that licences run counter to the aims of IP protection in that they limit access to intellectual resources (Davis 2001). Another important development has to do with technical control over the use of IP. Technical devices aimed at giving IP holders control over the use of material realize what is called 'digital rights management' (DRM). Examples of DRM include technologies that limit the use of particular data, such as MP3 players that check the legitimacy of music files or programs that only display certain files (e.g. pdf files) whose legitimate origin has been ascertained. DRM can also enforce policies, for example by allowing only a certain number of copies of a file to be printed or limiting the number of times a song can be played. Such devices can only be successful if they cannot be circumvented. The development of legal protection for such systems which outlaws technical circumvention (e.g. the Digital Millennium Copyright Act in the US or the EU Copyright Directive) can thus be seen as an attempt to strengthen the rights of IP holders (George 2006).

6.2.5   Problems of IP

It is probably fair to say that most aspects of IP are contested. This refers to the different strategies of justifying it as well as its practical implementation.

The utilitarian justification has been questioned on the grounds that many, if not most, creators (e.g. artists, scholars) are willing to create independently of the commercial rewards they may expect to receive (Stallman 1995). The economic justification has also been described as a self-fulfilling prophecy (Benkler 2001). Utilitarian support of strong IP protection often cites huge financial figures meant to show the severity of the problem of illegal use of IP (e.g. Moores and Chang 2006), but the empirical validity of such figures has been doubted. It is not clear that all or even any illegally downloaded material would have been purchased legally (Weckert and Adeney 1997). In addition, the entire field of open source software (OSS) seems to suggest that there are alternatives to current proprietary arrangements. While it is probably beyond doubt that artists and creative minds would continue to create music, literature, buildings or designs independently of remuneration, the significance of OSS is that it demonstrates that this is also possible in a much more technical and commercial sector, namely in software development. The relevance of OSS in the context of the IP debate is that it questions the empirical validity of a consequentialist justification of IP and at the same time shows an alternative conception that practically works (Stahl 2005).

The applicability of natural rights justifications of IP has similarly been questioned. A main argument here lies in the fundamental differences between physical and intellectual property. These are based on the different degrees of relative scarcity where physical property is based on finite resources, whereas IP is arguably not (Ciro 2005). A further problem of natural rights arguments can be found in their theological roots which render their practical status unclear.

While the theoretical justification of IP is thus contested, this is even more the case for its practical implementation. International sources of law such as WIPO are often perceived as lacking democratic legitimacy (Froomkin 2001). One can argue that recent strengthening of IP legislation is a result of a political process which emphasizes commercial interests (Torremans 2005). In some cases, one can show clear relationships between particular interests and legal activities (Spinello and Tavani 2005) which cast doubt on the impartiality of IP regulation. At the same time, non-commercial interests, as represented in fair use or fair dealings, are curtailed (Buchanan and Campbell 2005). Such observations, linked to the ongoing question of the appropriateness of IP regulations to at least some types of intellectual creation (i.e. software (Burk 2001)), has led many to question the legitimacy of current IP regulations. This is particularly true for developments that are perceived to circumvent the justification of IP, such as the use of digital rights management systems or the use of licences or one-sided contracts to strengthen IP (Camp 2003, Lewis 2004, Samuelson and Scotchmer 2002).

IP controversies are often linked with other ethical and social issues, many of which are discussed in this book. They include theoretical considerations of justice, fairness and moral rights (see Chapters 1, 3, 4 and 5), but they also touch on practical issues ranging from privacy to spam. A summary of the IP problematic that leads us back to the theme of this chapter is that it can be seen as a social problem, based on the fact that it is linked to competing interests that attempt to gain advantages for certain groups. There is a widespread view that current IP regulation reflects a dominance of commercial over competing interests. The struggle between the different interests is carried out on political and legal battlefields, but it is fought using ethical arguments on both sides. This brief characterization leads us to the next main point of the chapter, digital divides.

6.3   Digital divides

Digital divides, just like IP, constitute a huge field which has attracted much research from a range of disciplines which a section in a chapter cannot address comprehensively. This section will therefore attempt to tease out the ethically and philosophically interesting aspects of digital divides which will allow us to develop the argument that digital divides share relevant aspects with other social issues of computer ethics.

6.3.1   The concept of digital divides

Scholarly attention has been paid to digital divides since the middle of the 1990s (Hacker and Mason 2003). It has been pointed out, however, that the underlying concept is unclear. Warschauer (2003) highlights that the term implies a bipolar division between those who have access and those who do not, which is misleading as connectivity falls along a continuum. Walsham (2005, p. 9) has called the term 'somewhat ambiguous and hard to define' but points to the underlying problem of the gap between rich and poor, which may be exacerbated by technology. In the US, the National Telecommunications and Information Administration has published a number of reports, some of which share the title 'Falling through the Net' (see www.ntia.doc.gov), which focus on digital divides within the country. Dewan and Riggins (2005) suggest five different categories of digital divides. The different viewpoints explain why it is more suitable to use the term digital divides in the plural form. They also indicate why some scholars have suggested dropping the term altogether in favour of a more telling one, such as 'digital exclusion' (Cushman and Klecun 2006, p. 348). In the rest of this chapter we shall use the plural 'digital divides' to denote instances where a difference in access or usability of ICT between groups or individuals leads to injustice or consequences that are widely perceived to be problematic.

6.3.2   Ethical issues of digital divides

Digital divides have an intuitive moral quality, which often seems to preclude explicit moral reasoning about them (Hacker and Mason, 2003). Part of the reason for this is that they seem to link with divides in the distribution of other goods or morally relevant items, such as chances to develop oneself. The fact that there is huge inequality in the world is undisputed and the disparity on a worldwide scale is staggering (UNDP 1998). Digital divides seem to be linked to such inequalities and they are sometimes perceived to be mutually reinforcing (Moss 2002). The perception that the gulf between haves and have-nots could be lessened but is often in fact deepened by ICT is a basic starting assumption of discussions of ethics and digital divides (Walsham 2001). It is not immediately clear, however, whether and why digital divides are really linked to offline inequalities and why this is an ethical problem. This is why philosophical investigations are called for (Rookby and Weckert 2007).

Digital divides have several links to inequality, apart from the association with inequality of distribution of goods and life chances. First, there is the issue of access. When it became apparent that new ICTs had the potential to overcome traditional inequalities but can equally well have the opposite effect, governments across the world decided that a necessary condition of more equality was widely spread access to such technology (Couldry 2003). As a consequence, governments and other organizations have spent considerable efforts in most parts of the world to improve the accessibility of new ICTs, in particular the Internet.

6.3.3   Problems of current discussions of digital divides

Digital divides raise a number of interrelated questions. These include conceptual, epistemological, methodological, but also practical ones.

There are several conceptual issues that render much of the debate on digital divides problematic. One has to do with the concept of information. The already-mentioned 'haves' and 'have-nots' are often also called 'information rich' and 'information poor'. This terminology suggests that more information is always better than less information, which is patently false. There are many types of information not all of which are equally worth having access to. Being rich in some kind of information can include or even presuppose being poor in others (Hongladarom 2004). There is also a case to be made that in modern Western societies information overflow is more often a problem than lack of information. While, for some time, it may have been a status symbol to have technical access to information (e.g. via a mobile telephone), it is increasingly a status symbol to be able to disconnect. In addition, it is perfectly conceivable that individuals could consciously decide to remove themselves from information flow (e.g. by deciding no longer to watch TV or by having no email access at home), which would not necessarily impoverish their lives. Such views turn the traditional view of digital divides upside down.

A different question concerns epistemological issues of our knowledge of digital divides and research concerning them. Hacker and Mason (2003) argue that ethical concerns would have to be included more explicitly in digital divides research in order to come to a better understanding of relevant issues. At the same time, there is a dominance of positivist and quantitative research that focuses on demographic aspects, which can narrow the understanding of the problems and make them appear more static than they are (McSorley 2003). Couldry (2003) therefore suggests moving away from the concept of digital divides in empirical research and concentrate on issues, which have a stronger influence on the discursive design of ICTs.

These epistemological concerns are directly linked to the ontological framing of the concept of digital divides and their possible solutions. As already indicated, much work in the area of digital divides concentrates on issues of technology. A lack of access to technology is perceived as the (or at least one of the) root cause(s) of digital divides. This renders them a technical problem that calls for a technical solution. The simplest way of doing this is to provide people with access to technology. Indeed, this is an approach taken by many governments, whose main focus is the provision of infrastructure or in many cases even the provision of computers in households with the aim of allowing people to connect (cf. Stahl 2008a). Providing access to technology is nothing bad per se but it betrays an underlying technological determinism that renders the probability of success of such measures doubtful (Warschauer 2003). While lip service is often paid to the fact that access requires more than the opportunity to use a piece of technology, the fundamental difficulties this raises are often ignored in favour of a relatively straightforward provision of technology. High-profile projects like the MIT-sponsored 'one laptop per child' initiative that aims to provide a laptop for US$100 to every one of the world's poorest children are in constant danger of overemphasizing technology. Useful access which can overcome digital divides requires individuals to have education, high levels of literacy, and the ability to evaluate information gained through technology. These are conditions which are less often met by those without technical access. In order to overcome digital divides, these conditions would have to be fulfilled. In many cases, for example in countries with underdeveloped educational infrastructures, this would be an enormous task.

Another problem of digital divides linked to their ontological framing and the epistemological issues concerning research on such divides concerns their relevance in different social realities. The attention paid to digital divides can lead to a definition of normality that includes access to information via digital technologies, which then renders lifestyles that do not conform to this normality problematic. In this way, digital divides can become self-fulfilling prophecies, which come true because of the attention paid to them. The definition of normality can also be an expression of cultural imperialism. Whether and in what way technology can and should be used to address problems in different countries and cultures cannot easily be established a priori. The risk is that discussions of digital divides can become ways of extending unequal power structures of promoting particular technologies and processes in environments where they may not be appropriate (Walsham 2001).

A further problem worth mentioning concerns the question of how digital divides are to be addressed. Solutions, in order to be measurably successful, would need to be based on clearly defined problems, which are not given. However, even if one follows the dominant argument that the provision of access to technical means is at least an important part of the solution, then it is unclear how this is to be achieved. On an international level, ICT is seen as an important means of development but, at the same time, the recommendations to acquire ICT, develop market structures and engage in market competition may be unrealistic due to the contingencies of path-dependent development processes (Avgerou 2003). This means that particular problems or solutions may have arisen due to specific circumstances and are therefore not necessarily transferable to similar situations. Furthermore, it is unclear how technical provisions are to be implemented. The discussion concerning appropriate mechanisms of providing access is based on metaphysical convictions of what markets are and how they work (Stahl 2007). They are thus part of greater political and economic discourses, which render it unlikely that solutions to the problem of digital divides will be found soon.

6.4   Employment and work

Employment is a central political issue and a lack of employment is a problem that most political actors try to address. Loss of employment, as often discussed in high-profile cases where whole factories are closed, is seen as more than a purely commercial issue. At the same time, the use of ICT for most types of employment has the potential to change the nature and possibly the quantity of work available. It is thus reasonable to ask whether there are ethical issues arising from changes in the nature of work caused by computer and ICT use. This section will first ask whether work is destroyed or created and in a second step have a look at the changes in work caused by ICT. It will end with a discussion of some other issues where ICT and work can have ethical relevance.

6.4.1   Creation or destruction of employment?

It is beyond question that ICT can change what people do. It is almost inconceivable now that a chapter such as this would be written by hand or using a typewriter. Similarly, most other types of work, be they clerical or manual, are deeply affected. ICT contributes to the automation of many types of work, which means that many traditional forms of employment are becoming rarer in industrialized societies, whereas new types of work evolve. Such new types of work using ICT are often called 'knowledge work' and the mass of 'knowledge workers' are supposed to form the new 'knowledge society'. It is probably not contentious to say that some types of work are newly created whereas others are either eliminated or outsourced. The question remains whether there is a net gain or loss of employment.

Some argue that ICT-enabled automation will lead to less work. This is not a new argument. Arendt (1958) made the argument quite convincingly over 50 years ago. Some argue that this is an inevitable development which may even lead us to view the artificial agents taking over our work as ethical agents (Brooks 2002). Others have held, against this, that there are strict limits to what technology can do and thus to what type of work can be eliminated (Collins 1990).

Wiener (1954) foresaw mass unemployment caused by the 'slave labor' of machines and referred to the great depression of the 1930s as being mild comparable to what was coming. The ethical evaluation of loss of employment is thus based on its economic consequences. Arendt (1958, p. 5) saw a different problem, namely the development of 'a society of laborers without labor, that is, without the only activity left to them'. The problem here is that of a meaningful existence, which in modern societies often implies employment. This supports Floridi's (1999a) view that the problem of replacing human employment with technology is not so much a loss of income but the question of how one can fill one's time meaningfully.

In any event, the question of replacing human employment with technology has been an ongoing concern of scholars interested in the ethics of technology. One could argue that, in the end, it is an empirical question whether the fear of loss of employment through ICT is justified. Interestingly, the problems of measuring this seem considerable and it is hard to come to a clear empirical evaluation. According to Castells (2000, p. 280) 'it seems, as a general trend, that there is no systematic structural relationship between the diffusion of information technologies and the evolution of employment levels in the economy as a whole'.

6.4.2   The changing nature of work

As it seems difficult to make clear quantitative statements about the changes of work due to ICT, it may be worthwhile exploring the qualitative changes. Bynum (1985), in an introduction to one of the classics of computer ethics (Moor 1985), voiced the fear that increasing use of computers would lead to a replacement of human work, in particular in 'tasks that are thought to require judgement and wisdom' (p. 263). This fear was not justified. In the time since, it has become clear that the ones whose jobs are most at risk, due to ICT, are the ones with lower skills and simple work that is easy to automate or offshore.

One consequence that the introduction of ICT in the workplace does seem to have is that it has supported a massive push towards higher flexibility. This flexibility of labour has developed in parallel to the increasing flexibility of worldwide markets in goods and finance. Together, these developments constitute an important part of globalization. While one can argue that globalization is a misnomer (as it excludes most regions of the world) and that it is not a reality for labour markets, it has consequences for employment. On the one hand, it can serve as an argument in debates between employers and employees, where employers can now plausibly threaten to move work abroad. On the other hand, markets and exchange mechanisms have, in many cases, become truly global. Thanks to ICT, even a small local organization can now cater to a worldwide market.

One example of this increasing flexibility is the concept of the virtual organization. Again, there may be debates about the definition or social reality of virtual organizations (Pennings 1998, McCalman 2003), but the concept has served as a useful referent in different debates. It is often introduced in a positive vein, emphasizing the ability to cater to client needs but also to provide employees with higher degrees of freedom and autonomy. At the same time, it changes our perception of work as well as the boundaries of work and leisure.

One way of organizing work that will increase due to virtual organizations, but also because of other ICT-enabled changes of work, is that of telework. The idea behind telework is that the employee is no longer confined to physical presence at the place of work but free to work from wherever (notably including home) at whichever time. This is one aspect of the ICT-based flexibility and one that seems to offer considerable promise, as it allows employees to combine professional and personal life in ways impossible before.

6.4.3   Ethical issues of the changing nature of work

Where people have less of a chance to make a living they consequently have less of a chance to lead a fulfilled existence. Interestingly, empirical research again seems to be ambivalent with regards to the factual consequences of the influence of ICT on employment. While ICT skills are now increasingly required in a wide range of jobs, the impact of ICT on wages is unclear (Dewan and Riggins 2005).

There are, however, other ethical issues linked to the increasing use of ICT in work, which may be less obvious than issues of sustainability of income, but which may have an even stronger influence on the organization of work. Central among these is the question of the relationship between employers and employees. ICT use may empower employees by giving them access to information and allowing them to develop their independence. At the same time, the use of ICT allows the collection of information about work in ways previously impossible. Such information can be used for the purpose of employee surveillance (Weckert 2005).

A good example of these ambiguous possibilities is the already mentioned emerging form of work called telework. Telework is often described in positive terms, with regards both to the organization and to the employee. As Jerrard and Chang (2003, p. 120) put it, '[t]eleworking is about trust'. They go on to say that technology is a means of granting members of a virtual team 'independence and autonomy and enhancing their performance'. While such positive views are certainly possible, organizational realities often seem to develop in a different direction. Telework lessens employers' ability to monitor employees' input and forces them to increase control of output (Jackson *et al.* 2006). This requires employees to engage increasingly in self-surveillance, which means that they need to internalize employers' requirements and accept them unquestioningly. Telework can have (ethically relevant) gender aspects, for example in that it often leads to the double burden of work and family responsibilities, which typically are shouldered by women. Moreover, telework removes the ability of employees to socialize and thus to organize. It thereby implicitly strengthens employers' positions because it makes it more difficult for employees to bargain collectively (Greenhill and Wilson 2006).

6.5 'Social' issues of computer ethics and ways to address them

This chapter set out to give a broad overview of social issues in computer ethics. It has focused on issues of intellectual property, digital divides, and employment and work. Of course, there are many other issues worthy of discussion under the same heading which could not be included. The question remains what these three main issues have in common and how ethical theories can help us address them.

One interesting aspect that they share and that sets them apart as 'social' issues is that they concern conflicts between and among social groups. The most important collective actor that shapes the social struggles is business. The entire debate surrounding IP is driven by business interests in strengthening IP protection with the aim of allowing IP holders to gain financially from them. Work and employment issues are also driven to a large extent by business interests, for example where ICT leads to a higher degree of employee surveillance or self-surveillance. Digital divides are partly results of differing levels of business activities, they are often described as impediments to successful business developments, and solutions to them are sought in business provision of technology. Commercial interests thus form a central aspect of the social issues discussed in this chapter.

It would, of course, be an undue simplification to describe business as a monolithic block with uniform interests. The struggles and conflicts that render social issues ethically relevant are often between commercial and non-commercial interests (e.g. copyright holders vs. music consumers; patent holders vs. poor, ill people in developing countries) but they are also often found among different businesses or business models (e.g. proprietary software developers vs. open source software developers). The observation that commercial interests are dominant is thus not to be misunderstood as a claim that profit-oriented organizations are morally bad, but as a sign that in capitalist societies commercial interests are a main cause of social disagreement. Social issues of computer ethics can thus to a large extent be understood as struggles over distribution.

Questions of competing interests and justifiable distributions in democratic states are never just ethical but they invariably gain political relevance. This is certainly true for the three examples discussed in this chapter. Different interests groups, who aim to promote their viewpoints, do this by influencing political processes and agents. As the political process often culminates in the creation of laws, such ethical issues then take on a legal quality. This is most obvious in the case of IP, where statutes and case law have a direct bearing on facts as well as their ethical evaluation. But also employment issues and digital divides find their reflection in legal procedures policies. Democracy, as the type of government that ideally allows all voices to be heard and acceptable solutions to be found, is thus the fighting ground on which social issues are decided. Ethical considerations can play an important role as the bases of arguments used to promote particular viewpoints.

This leads us to the question of appropriate ethical approaches to understand and address social problems of computer ethics. Much work in computer ethics focuses on individual and professional matters. The idea behind this is that computer professionals need to be aware of ethical issues, understand their role and pursue courses of action that are ethically justifiable. This happens within a professional environment, where professional bodies shape the perceptions of relevant duties and enforce shared standards, for example through codes of conduct or codes of ethics. This individualist approach is often taught to students of computing and it can offer valuable points of orientation. It has, however, also been criticized as one-sided and limited in its approach (Adam 2005). This is certainly a problem with regards to all of the issues discussed in this chapter. While individual actions can have relevance with regards to IP, digital divides or employment issues, they are unlikely to change the underlying structures that lead to the ethical relevance of these questions. There are, of course broader ethical theories available in computer ethics such as Floridi's (1999b) information ethics, Bynum's (2006a) flourishing ethics or Introna's (2007) disclosive ethics. However, none of these are particularly sensitive to the social nature of issues described here.

Some scholars have therefore suggested the use of more socially aware ethical theories to address ethical problems of technology (Devon 2004, Johnstone 2007). This is an important move towards ethical theories that are sensitive to social issues and the role of business in societal conflicts. One may argue (Stahl 2008b/c) that 'critical theory' or 'critical social theory' (Harvey 1990) provides a conceptual frame for understanding such social issues and, at the same time, has great sensitivity to competing ethical claims. It is to be hoped that a sharper awareness of social issues in computer ethics may develop, one which includes knowledge of the issues themselves and more importantly, an increased discussion of how computer ethics itself can develop to address them more successfully.

7 Rights and computer ethics

John Sullins

7.1 Introduction

This chapter explores the philosophical theories that attempt to provide guidance when determining the best way to balance the rights of the individual user of Information and Computer Technologies (ICTs) with the legitimate public concerns of the societies impacted by these technologies. Imagine being sentenced to ten years in prison due to the contents of an email message your government disapproved of. This frightening possibility became reality for Shi Tao. In 2005, he composed an email from his office in China using a Yahoo account, which he then sent to a pro-democracy website in New York City. He attached to the email an article, which he wished to publish anonymously, on China's new policies regarding crackdowns on potential pro-democracy dissidents in China (MacKinnon 2008). When Chinese authorities became aware of the article they considered it a breach of state secrets and sought to find out the author. They eventually received crucial information about Shi Tao's identity from Yahoo's Asian business partners in Hong Kong (MacKinnon 2008). This evidence was then used to convict him in a Chinese court.

There are two ethical issues here: whether the Chinese government's actions in suppressing Shi Tao's free speech rights were ethically wrong; and how the ICTs used contributed to that situation. Regarding the first issue, many people outside of the Chinese government argue that there was a moral wrong perpetrated in this case, even if it did proceed from Chinese laws and regulations. Later, we will look at some of the philosophical theories that motivate this response. The second issue is more difficult.

Did Shi Tao have a reasonable right to expect his email provider to keep his identity confidential? Did Yahoo's representatives in Hong Kong grievously breach the privacy rights of Shi Tao when they complied with the request of the Chinese government for help in investigating this case? Yahoo maintains that they broke no law in this matter, nor do they admit legal wrongdoings in the three other similar cases in China they are involved in. Still, it is clear that the leadership at Yahoo must have felt some genuine moral concern for this situation as Jerry Yang, one of the co-founders of Yahoo and its current

CEO, made a solemn public apology to Shi Tao's mother in front of the United States Congress and, in addition, the company set up the 'Yahoo! Human Rights Fund', which provides financial aid to those impacted by human rights abuses in Asia (MacKinnon 2008).

This case highlights the global challenges that revolve around human rights and ICTs. Why were journalists, human rights advocates, and the United States Congress so morally outraged by the actions of Yahoo Inc. and its business partners? Why did the Chinese government consider it had the right to know the identity of the author? Why did Shi Tao trust the ICTs he was using would protect his identity? You may not be involved in anything as politically charged as Shi Tao, but even so, do you have a right to expect that your web and mobile communications will remain private? These are some of the questions we are going to explore in the rest of this chapter.

7.2   Information and personality

Everything we do leaves a trail of information, a *digital footprint* as it were. This information can be looked at in many different ways. Imagine filling in a detailed log with entries for every single action you do: awoke to alarm clock at 7.00 a.m., tossed the covers aside at 7.05, placed feet in slippers at 7.05 and 30 seconds, etc. The more detailed this log becomes the more someone reading it would know about you. Perhaps one might keep tabs on your exact location as you moved around doing your daily chores. Maybe one could keep an accurate diary of all one's personal communications and social interactions. The more and more layers of information like this one could gather, the deeper one can come to understand you, who you are, what you do, who you know, where you go, what you believe. Certainly, nothing short of some divine being would be able to achieve this kind of detailed information with the required amount of accuracy. In fact, God or a Recording Angel does just this in the Abrahamic religions, noting down every act and thought one does or has during one's life to be fully recounted on Judgement Day. But, as more and more of us use ICTs, we leave many disparate trails of digital information. Cell phone call logs, GPS tracking data in our cars and mobile phones, friend lists on social networking sites, receipts for goods bought off- and online, voluminous emails and text messages: until recently all this information had existed in separate and incompatible formats and databases. Anyone wanting to follow our trail of information would have had a challenging task at hand. This is rapidly changing though as the separate providers of these services have come to realize the synergy that can be achieved by collecting as much of this data as possible and sharing it widely, creating a digital footprint that is much easier to track. Digital advertising can follow this trail and deduce the interests of each individual and market goods and services tailored to each person. While this may result in better shopping, will it also protect us from unwanted intrusion into our lives? How will we determine who gets to collect, share and profit from all of this personal information?

Who is going to ensure the accuracy of all this information and the proper interpretation of the collected data? Certain customer profiles will result in obtaining unbeatable opportunities and savings, others will not be as lucky, and all will be based on a digital footprint constructed from income projections, credit ratings, health prospects and demographics. Life will be wonderful for the digital elite that maximally fit the profiles of a good consumer, but someone with the wrong friend list, search engine queries, web searches, racial profile and travel patterns could be deemed a bad credit risk or, even worse, a potential terrorist.

A deeper concern for our rights as citizens in the world of information is found in the work of Luciano Floridi, who argues that information has an ontological force in the construction of our personal identity, meaning that, at the deepest level, information affects who we are and what we can become (see Floridi 2006a, 2006c, 2007b, 2008d). Since it plays such a central role in our identity, Floridi argues that we must be afforded certain rights to protect ourselves.

To see how this all works, imagine receiving an unexpected letter that details how you are the heir of a fortune you did not previously know about. That would change your life, and if the letter were lost, blocked or misdirected, that too would change your life. That letter, a piece of information, is a vital component of your future potential identities. Likewise, all the various bits of information that constitute your digital footprint taken together help determine who you are and your place in the social world. This means that we must pay close attention to the forces that access and manipulate that information. The wrong information in the wrong hands can critically alter your ability to operate in the social world. Because information so deeply constitutes our identity we even call such an offence *identity theft*. Acts of inappropriate use, disclosure, or manipulation of our personal information can rightly be seen as acts of aggression against our very personality (Floridi 2006c, 2007b). In addition to fostering the protection of each individual's information self, we must also foster the ability of each person to steward his or her own information and to freely express their personality, in order to encourage their growth, flourishing and self-actualization. This makes it a primary concern of governments to set policies that respect information rights.

7.3 Personal rights and global concerns

This is an unparalleled moment in human history. ICTs have been steadily making it easier for people to communicate and share all kinds of data across nearly every political border at increasingly lower cost. While some welcome this as the fruition of the promises of liberty, democracy and technological progress, others see it as a corrosive influence, which will finish off the last vestiges of indigenous world culture, or threaten the power of regimes that require their citizens' acquiescence to the limited possibilities available in their own countries.

How can members of small, indigenous populations resist the wonders of ICTs and their lure into the high-tech world of plentiful information and opportunities? Indeed, even in the case of larger and more entrenched cultures, how can we avoid a progressive blending and homogenization? How can a country silence dissidents emboldened by allies and contacts in the wider world? Less dramatically, but important nonetheless, who is to set the standards of civility in net discourse? Every culture has differing norms regarding propriety and decorum in personal communication. Thus, an informal email typical of citizens in Europe or the United States might greatly insult those in a more formal, traditional culture. Images considered a trifling joke in one culture might be considered foul pornography or blasphemy in another and even inflame them into bloody riots.

We might want to adopt a common protocol for the content of communications on the net. If so, should it be a permissive set of standards or a strict and formal one? If we allow for a high level of free speech, we stand to alienate our fellow world citizens who do not share our conviction that free speech is a public good. If, instead, we censor or limit interactions between users in a way that would make more authoritarian governments and traditional cultures happy, then we stand to lose the freedoms we enjoy on the net right now. We will now look at the philosophical justifications for free speech and privacy, as these play out in the use of ICTs where anonymous speech can exacerbate the conflicts regarding pornography, hate speech, privacy and political dissent.

7.4   Freedom of speech

Citizens of liberal democracies take for granted wide-ranging freedoms of expression and speech. In the liberal tradition, it is considered wrong to limit expression unless doing so would prevent harm or extreme offence to other members of the society. Even though the last sentence sounds simple, it turns out to have complex implications making it difficult to draft effective international political policy that respects this right. Even countries whose citizens hold closely allied philosophies regarding free speech and privacy, such as the US and the European Union, differ on issues in the control of pornography or hate speech and whether or not cryptography is a protected form of speech (see Spinello 2003, p. 53).

The notion that we have a right to freedom of speech is a modern one and many traditional societies do not always favour granting this right. Certain ICTs such as the Web bring these two traditions into conflict. In this section we will look at the strongest philosophical justifications for free speech and then turn to the specific problems arising as these values are expressed through global ICTs.

7.4.1   Free speech is a social good

The birth of Western philosophy occurred in a special historical period, during which moments of relatively unrestricted speech occurred in places such as ancient Athens. These moments were short-lived, and many of the early philosophers, such as Socrates (469–399 BC) and Aristotle (384–322 BC) found death and exile respectively as their reward for questioning traditional belief systems. Plato (429–347 BC), the student of Socrates and teacher of Aristotle, took an opposing view and famously argued in his *Republic* for a state that strictly controls the tenor and content of art, poetry and music (Hamilton and Cairns 1989, p. 575). So, from its very beginning as a subject of inquiry, freedom of speech can find both enemies and allies in philosophy. However, it is not until the modern period that we find its strongest ally in the form of the English philosopher John Stuart Mill (1806–1873).

In *On Liberty*, Mill argues for broad social freedoms for the individual in both the private and public domain, and that a society, in order to be truly free, must allow for each individual to enjoy an internal 'liberty of thought and feeling; absolute freedom of opinion and sentiment on all subjects, practical or speculative, scientific, moral, or theological' (Mill 2007, Chapter 1). Thus, each individual is the master of his or her own thoughts and feelings. Mill expressly includes the right to express and publish one's thoughts and opinions. He argues that the free state must grant the 'liberty of tastes and pursuits; of framing the plan of life to suit one's character; of doing as we like, subject to such consequences as may follow: without impediment from our fellow-creatures, so long as what we do does not harm them, even though they should think our conduct foolish, perverse, or wrong' (Mill 2007). He also claims that a free state must allow its adult citizens to gather and congregate in any way they see fit, again as long as no harm comes from it (Mill 2007). So, in a free state, people should be allowed to formulate and express their own thoughts and ideas in any way they see fit and to whomever they want in whatever style they like, as long as no harm comes from this activity.

Clearly, Mill sees this as the greatest way for the individuals in a society to pursue their best interests and flourish as persons. If the state is composed of strong individuals, who are engaged in myriad activities all pursuing their various interests, the society as a whole will benefit from the best of that activity so its members will all be collectively better off. So, even if someone's choice of topic is an unorthodox one, it is critical that we do not censor it, even if it makes many people uncomfortable, as these ideas just may prove fruitful to the whole, either by strengthening the orthodox view in light of the new challenge, or in overturning false or outdated ideas that may have the society in thrall. In fact, this is just how all civil rights gains have been made in the last few centuries.

The key to all of this is that Mill insists that this activity must be tolerated as long as no harm is done. This has come to be called the 'harm principle' and I will refer to it as such for the rest of this chapter. The harm principle sounds very reasonable and most people find it unobjectionable upon first hearing. Still, it is fair to wonder what may count as harm. Do we only run afoul of this requirement when we cause physical harm or could mental anguish count? If mental anguish counts, then some difficulties arise with this theory. Mill seems to want to protect the rights of iconoclasts who challenge deeply held beliefs in a society. But the very actions of a socially radical free thinker will certainly offend the established members of any society, and offence is a painful experience, potentially harmful, so the iconoclast may appear to be violating the harm principle.

Mill can avoid this criticism by limiting the notion of harm to include only those states that cause physical, monetary or extreme emotional damage. So, if growth and change can be a painful yet healthy and desirable experience, agonizing challenges coming from some members of a society may actually represent opportunities to develop and adapt and therefore must be tolerated or opposed openly in the realm of public debate. As a result, offence is not an instance of harm, in fact it is just the opposite, it is an opportunity to strengthen and grow. This means that, in a free state, the speech of individuals must be protected from government censors and the ridicule and scorn of established social orders, even if their words are offensive.

7.4.2   Unlimited free speech does not exist

The other side of this debate is best represented by a contemporary philosopher, Stanley Fish, who argues that no society can allow completely unfettered speech and expect to last for long (Fish 1994). Fish claims that every individual expresses herself within a particular society and that society is composed of a set of more or less shared values, or at least a range of values. This means that each individual is a product of the influences and ideas percolating through her society. So, to claim that her speech is completely free is too strong, since there are always constraints on speech. In order to participate in a society, one must accept certain limits to one's freedom of speech.

In his book *Philosophical Investigations*, Ludwig Wittgenstein explains a similar concept, which he calls a 'language-game' (Wittgenstein 1953). Seeing language as a *game* in this instance is a useful metaphor to explain the communication of information: the interlocutors are the players and there are many rules of the game that must be followed or no communication occurs. So unfettered free speech would be a game with no rules. But since a game with no rules can hardly be called a game, unfettered free speech could hardly be called communication. It would just be pure babble. This leads to the conclusion that there is no unfettered free speech and to the further evaluative claim that it is a good thing that we do not have totally free speech, since we want to communicate and operate within a society and neither is possible if speech is completely unregulated. This means that we have to accept appropriate limits on our freedom of speech to communicate and keep our society working (see Fish 1994).

We are now faced by a dilemma. On the one hand, Mill claims that our free society will be jeopardized if we regulate the speech of minority opinion in any way. On the other, we have a strong argument from Fish that suggests that, no matter what, our speech must be regulated in order for it to serve its function as a kind of social glue that holds a society together. If there is no way around this dilemma, we are stuck either with stagnating societies incapable of innovation or ones that are too permissive and chaotic to survive.

7.4.3   Securing the electronic frontier

We can see both horns of the free speech dilemma playing out in the debate over how (or even whether) to regulate communications over the Internet and other ICTs. The Electronic Frontier Foundation (EFF), a group founded in 1990 by civil libertarians John Gilmore, Mitch Kapor and John-Perry Barlow, was created to serve as the first public advocacy group that 'championed the public interest in every critical battle affecting digital rights' (EFF website). As ICTs have moved to the fore as the primary mode for public discourse, EFF has been involved in every major legal battle in the United States regarding the rights of ICTs users. EFF's motivations for getting involved are no doubt as diverse as the group's membership but the website warns that, '[I]f laws can censor you, limit access to certain information, or restrict use of communication tools, then the internet's incredible potential will go unrealized' (EFF website). Here we see an argument clearly derived from ideas similar to Mill's. The Internet has a potential that is of value to mankind, but that value will be lost if restrictions are placed on its users. In order to protect this social good we must protect strong individual rights such as free speech and the right to disseminate ideas unhindered on the Internet.

The legal opponents of the EFF often rely on the second horn of the dilemma. EFF has been in legal battles with agencies of the US government over many issues, including the unlawful search and seizure of computers (Steve Jackson Games v. The Secret Service), the right to distribute personal encryption software (Bernstein v. US Department of Justice), Internet censorship in the form of the Communications Decency Act and the Child Online Protection Act (ACLU v. Reno and ACLU v. Ashcroft – CDA and COPA), right to view digital recordings as the viewer sees fit (ALA v. FCC – Broadcast Flag), law enforcement must have probable cause to track people using their cell phone data (USA v. Pen Register), and their recent cases against the US National Security Agency (NSA) regarding the extensive wiretapping of US citizens by the NSA with help from major corporations such as AT&T. These are just a few of the more important cases (see their website for further information, EFF.org). In each of them, the motivation for the US government has been one of law enforcement. The general argument is that ICTs provide a new arena for illegal activity such as piracy, hacking, child pornography, drug dealing and terrorism. Without broad abilities to access data and to limit certain expressions of speech (e.g. encryption, and pornography), the US is not going to be able to combat these social ills. Since (one assumes) Americans do not want to live in such a society, it is necessary for their government to acquire the information needed to protect its citizens.

Similarly, at the corporate level, the EFF has confronted companies such as Diebold and Apple Computer, just to name two. Diebold sought to use the Digital Millennium Copyright Act (DMCA) to sue researchers that were looking into flaws in digital voting machines that Diebold had built. Claiming that emails outlining flaws in the machines were copyright infringement, they sought to curtail the activities of the researchers. The EFF contributed to the defence of the researchers and helped win the case. Apple sought to find out the identities of anonymous sources that had leaked information about an upcoming product to computer news websites; AppleInsider and PowerPage. Again, the EFF successfully litigated to protect the rights of the journalists on the websites from exposing their sources. In both cases, the companies sought to control information about their products for fear that releasing any of this information would negatively affect their ability to do business.

7.4.4   Anonymous speech

So far we have reviewed a number of arguments in favour of free speech and, by extension, free speech online, but is it right to say what one wants provided that one will stand up and identify oneself as the author of those ideas?

At first, it might seem appropriate to require everyone to stand up for the thoughts and ideas they profess online. This requirement would force people to have to own up to mistakes, libel or misinformation they were responsible for propagating. Unfortunately, this is also naïve. Some contents are simply too dangerous to the speaker and can only be disseminated anonymously. The case of Shi Tao, with which we started our discussion, is a prime example of what can happen when anonymity is lost. An individual is hopelessly incapable of directly challenging the interests of geopolitical powers and large multinational corporations. The only way to protect the lives and livelihood of these dissidents is to ensure their anonymity.

A right to anonymous speech has been described as a combination of a right to privacy and a right to free speech (see Bell 1995). If we support both free speech and privacy, then it would seem that this requires our support for anonymous speech. Anonymous speech was certainly a value held by many of the technologists and computer scientists that built the Net. Even though the early Internet was a project of the US military, it was quickly co-opted by skilled young computer scientists who had been deeply influenced by the social libertarian culture of the sixties and seventies. The history of the early development of digital ICTs is wonderfully detailed by John Markoff (Markoff 2005). This disparate group of savants, freethinkers and iconoclasts all shared a love of electronics and a dream of creating computers that could serve as a kind of personal augmentation device; one that would increase the abilities of the individuals and allow them to reach higher levels of self-actualization through unparalleled access to the world of human ideas (Markoff 2005). This radical idea was revolutionary at the time, with the cumbersome early PC technologies, but we can now see that it has come to fruition. The PC, coupled with the Internet, does indeed give us access to great deals of information and provides us with a multitude of forums within which to engage in all manner of communications and social interactions. These sixties radicals seem to have fostered a social revolution the likes of which have never been seen on this planet before. Lawrence Lessig observes in *Code: Version 2.0* that the early version of the Internet was designed in a way that made it hard to regulate. 'To regulate well, you need to know (1) who someone is, (2) where they are, and (3) what they are doing', but none of these abilities were built into the code of the early Internet (Lessig 2006, p. 23). This led to a period in the early nineties when technologists commonly claimed that modern ICTs would seriously challenge the abilities of modern nation states to control their citizens, thus unleashing a worldwide social revolution – the ultimate hack.

This has not turned out to be the case, as code can be written to foster control as well. 'There is regulation of behavior on the internet and in cyberspace, but that regulation is imposed primarily through code' (Lessig 2006, p. 24). So it seems that a new generation of technologists is now in control and fewer of them are interested in social revolution. This industry is no longer dominated by American companies and software engineers; today the industry has spread across the globe, and we are seeing a demand for technologies that increase governmental control over ICTs and the infosphere they foster. Countries like China want as much control as they can get and many companies, even large US companies such as Cisco, are more than eager to supply the technology and code they need to create their 'Golden Shield Project', the first ICT-enhanced police state (see Fallows 2008, Klein 2008). These new technologies will give what China hopes is unparalleled abilities to monitor and censor Chinese users of the Internet and to control information flow into and out of the country, as well as protect its systems against hackers and cyber warfare (Fallows 2008, Klein 2008).

Even if the original design of the Internet was conducive to anonymous speech, it is not clear that future ICTs will be designed with this in mind. In fact, they could be just as easily built to enhance governmental control rather than challenge it. Without free anonymous speech there will be little chance for individuals or minority groups to challenge technological hegemonies.

7.4.5   Abuses of free speech and anonymity

Even if we want to support the rights of political dissidents to freely communicate and challenge the *status quo*, it remains true that some minority interests are far less appealing, such as those interested in propagating things like pornography or hate speech. However, they too can use ICTs to further their specialized interests. Free speech and anonymity constitute a double-edged sword that must be used with care. Speech and communications that one would never consider broaching in general public settings are commonplace fare in certain locations on the Internet. There is nothing too extreme, too violent or too perverse for publication on the Net. Just as any hobbyist can find an instant community of fellow enthusiasts on the Web, so too can any aficionado of any particular sexual practice. This is also the case when it comes to hate speech and extremist political views and other potentially harmful speech acts.

A perennial problem for free speech philosophy is to distinguish objectionable speech from speech worth protecting. There is a vast array of cultural opinions on what is or is not objectionable speech.

The cultural distinctions can be fairly subtle. For instance, European countries tend to be less interested in limiting pornography on the Web, whereas there have been a number of unsuccessful political attempts to censor web-based pornography in the United States. The Child Online Protection Act is the latest US legislation that attempts to curtail online pornography or at least its access by children. But when it comes to limiting the speech of hate groups, we find just the opposite, with European countries seeking to limit the activities of certain groups such as neo-Nazis on and off the Internet.

7.5   Pornography and ICTs

We live in the golden age of pornography. It is hard to pin down exactly how much this industry is worth but it was reported in 2006 to be around $97 billion dollars with China being the top producer at $27.4 billion (Business Services Industry 2007). There has never been a time where so much of this material has been so easily available to such a broad cross-section of the global society so cheaply, and this is the direct result of the spread of ICTs. 'Every second $3,075.64 is spent on pornography, 28,258 internet users view pornography and 372 internet users type adult search terms into search engines', with the US and the EU as the major producers of pornographic websites (Business Services Industry 2007).

While this industry is as old as image making itself, it has usually remained an underground business, that is until ICTs made it easy to distribute and consume in the relative privacy of one's own home. The personal computer took off from where personal video devices like the VCR left off having opened the door to home video porn. Now, a wide variety of material is available to any Internet user and much of that content is free. In fact the numbers quoted above do not take into account 'a nearly infinite supply of free, amateur videos from countless user-generated sites' that are challenging the revenues of the traditional purveyors of pornography (Schiffman 2008).

Before we get too far along on this topic, it must be acknowledged that it is difficult defining just what pornography is. It is largely a cultural or even personal distinction that one makes, meaning that some individuals and cultures have very low tolerances while others are quite comfortable with even explicit images and depictions of sexual acts. So there will be no final agreement on a strict definition of pornography.

There is no doubt that there are healthy and artistic ways of discussing and depicting human sexuality in all the various media we communicate in. For our purposes, here I will deem these depictions unproblematic and I will refer to those as erotic stories and images. There is a tradition in philosophy that finds great value in eroticism of this sort; even Socrates seems to have made a strong claim in favour of the erotic, which was transcribed in Plato's *Symposium* (see Plato 1993). So one may wish to resist the temptation to place a negative value on all media depictions of sexuality, even if it turns out that there is actually very little healthy erotic material existent online. For our purposes, we may reserve the word 'pornography' for text and images that do not positively challenge, enhance or expand one's understanding of human sexuality but instead demean, diminish and degrade the authors, actors and observers of the work in question. Simply put, if the piece does not contribute to the good of everyone involved in its production and consumption, then it is of dubious worth, may be qualified as pornography and indeed might be a morally justified candidate for censorship. This is not to say that any work concerning human sexuality that challenges the preconceived norms of a society is pornography. For instance, it is possible that the work enhances the good of its authors and audience but offends the sensibilities of the society at large. This might just be a failing of the society at large and, in this case, the work is not harmful pornography and deserves protection.

All this falls nicely in line with Mill's Principle of Harm discussed above. Erotic contents may enhance or challenge a society and are protected by free speech rights, whereas pornography creates harm and is therefore not protected by a right to free speech. It is important to note that would-be censors must provide proof of harm; and that harm must be significant, mere offence is not enough. Unfortunately one does not have to work very hard to find significantly harmful pornography easily available online.

Pornography is significantly harmful in three general situations: (1) its production, (2) its consumption and (3) its effects on the society in general. An obvious example of the first type of harm occurs in the production of child pornography. There is clear victimization that occurs, as children are forced into behaviour inappropriate for their age. As the philosopher and computer scientist Alison Adam has observed, this harm can be extremely long lasting, not only because of the potentially permanent damages inflicted psychologically on the children involved, but also because, even if the perpetrators are caught and prosecuted, the images they disseminated on the Net are virtually impossible to eradicate and linger forever in the dark corners of the Web (Adam 2002, p. 140).

The second type of harm occurs more often than one may think. There is no passive way to experience pornography, it is designed to arouse strong emotions and this can be victimizing when the images simultaneously arouse the viewer sexually and combine that with fear or violence. One is reminded of the famous quote from the philosopher Friedrich Nietzsche: 'And when you stare for a long time into an abyss, the abyss stares back into you' (Nietzsche 2003, p. 69). The viewer of violent pornography is changed and it will not be for the better. ICTs may act as a trigger of latent deviations in individuals that otherwise may have never come to the surface. ICTs provide easy access for persons to be exposed to and seduced by certain sexual deviations. They might also form online friendships with other disturbed individuals with whom they trade illicit material and then goad each other into antisocial behaviour in the real world, which these individuals might have never contemplated attempting on their own (Adam 2002, p. 140, Lessig 2006, p. 16). For example, it is likely that the consumption of child pornography has grown and that there is a link between its growth and the growth of the Internet (Adam 2002, p. 140).

Finally, the third area can be exemplified by the way in which pornography can contribute to a society that is threatening and dismissive of women's interests. Men have been the largest audience for pornography and many feminist philosophical theorists see pornography as a possible means of furthering the social control of women (see Adam 2002). Pornography socializes men to see women as vulnerable submissive objects. It is argued that someone deeply involved in consuming this media will be less capable of having authentic relationships with women. Of course, this criticism fails to consider that there is homosexual pornography and explicit material produced by and for women and couples. However, since this material is less common, the main criticism levelled against pornography stands. It does make certain large spaces in cyberspace inhospitable to women.

There are many more possible examples of the social acid produced by harmful pornography and this world is only possible through the anonymity provided by the Web for both the producers and consumers of pornographic media.

One last great excess that can occur when anonymity and deviant behaviour are mixed is cyberstalking. Stalking is certainly not a new phenomenon but ICTs have made this behaviour much easier. The Web gives each of us the powers of a private detective and in the hands of an obsessed individual this can prove dangerous. This phenomenon can also make the net an unsafe place for women and children since the overwhelming majority of stalkers are men (Adam 2002).

7.6   Hate speech and ICTs

Another social evil that has followed our migration to the Net and found a fertile atmosphere to grow is hate speech, both racial and religious. Again, the Principle of Harm can be used to distinguish hate speech from the heated and vigorous debates that race and religion can both engender. For a speech act to count as hate speech it must be motivated by hate and directed at the harm of other racial or religious individuals or groups.

The oldest hate-based website is Stormfront.org, the brainchild of Don Black, a notorious member of the Ku Klux Klan. Stormfront.org boasts dozens of individual forum topics, from 'Ideology and Philosophy' to 'privacy and security' and white supremacist's youth and women's issues. There are links on this site to podcasts, blogs, projects and events, along with many thousands of individual posts. At any time, there are hundreds of users from all over the world logged on. It is as active as any popular website and is run by a full-time staff (see Kim 2005). If it weren't for the occasional use of German gothic text, one might not notice this was a hate site, as it claims to be simply a place for truth to be told, 'allowing people access to information not filtered by the "media monopoly"'. Stormfront has taken on the 'Friendly Fascist' façade and one has to enter into the chat areas to find blatant hate speech offered by its users. Don Black himself is careful to never cross the line. He personally and wisely counsels his patrons to remember that 'words have consequences', and asks that they follow certain rules for posting such as: 'No profanity', and '[a]void racial epithets'. A perusal of the site will convince any reader that these rules are not always followed. The forum members with monikers such as Lillywhite37, Krieger Germaniens14 and Nationalist-Pride, to name a few, use the relative anonymity of the Stormfront forum to broach topics that range from the mundane to high treason and from this site one can find links to other sites that will eventually lead to more explicit hate sites. On this forum, lip service is paid to free speech rights, there is even a forum to post counter arguments. Stormfront.org walks a razor's edge, careful not to implicate its owners or moderators in any hate speech that is easily identifiable. But it does provide a space for like-minded racists to meet and mingle, sharing ideas and friendships that do have real-world consequence.

The Southern Poverty Law Center cites Cass Sunstein, the University of Chicago law professor who wrote the 2001 book *republic.com* that explains: '"Extremists and hate-filled sites tend to attract likeminded people who, if isolated, could come to their senses." Likeminded people talking to one another, Sunstein says, "tend to become more extremist"' (Kim 2005, p. 2). The Internet can be a great place to spark political debate and momentum, as anyone who witnessed Barack Obama's 2008 US presidential election can attest to. But this has a dark side as well. As Joe Trippi, who organized the online portion of Howard Dean's presidential campaign, said, 'I'd hate to think, what Hitler could've done with the internet' (Kim 2005, p. 3).

7.7   Gossip, and online harassment

The Gossip 2.0 phenomenon is another place where free speech and privacy collide head-on. This is antisocial networking, where the dark side of social interaction is leveraged by ICTs to gain a force and audience far beyond the restroom walls where this kind of communication is typically found. Celebrity gossip has always been an issue for people in the public eye, but now everyone on a university campus can experience the pain and humiliation of having lies, half-truths and secrets from their love lives posted to the most popular instance of this new phenomenon – Juicy Campus. Founded in August 2007, Juicy Campus has already gained a great deal of infamy for the content of the posts that are placed anonymously on the site.[1]

While the site boasts, on its privacy statement, that it ensures complete anonymity for its users, the people who are the subjects of those posts are not granted any privacy rights. The posts are mostly about sex, parties and gossip, not about legitimate issues in campus life. People are clearly identified by first and last names and the posts usually invite others to comment as well. The entries range from mildly humorous to potentially libellous but always spurious. It is difficult to see what good a gossip site like Juicy Campus can

---

[1] Juicy Campus went offline in 2009 but has been replaced by other gossip sites.

add to campus life, but it is easy to see the harm it has already fostered. The *International Herald Tribune* reported in March 2008 a case in which a student at Yale had his past as an actor in a pornographic video revealed on Juicy Campus complete with a link to the video in question; the post was viewed by many hundreds of his classmates and his reputation on campus devastated (Morgan 2008).

7.8   Conclusions and future issues

Rights and computer ethics is one of the primary concerns of our time. This moment in history is witnessing great technological change which is fundamentally challenging and complicating our claims to rights such as free speech and privacy. Given that ICTs are global technologies, and that they can be designed to enhance or limit free speech and privacy, this demands that we come to some sort of global consensus on these issues. Since, as we have seen, privacy and free speech can be at odds when someone wants to post your private concerns, one or the other right will have to be curtailed to some extent. These decisions will have to be made on a case-by-case basis, which means there will be an explosion of opportunities in local and international law and policy activity around these issues.

Our personal data are a gold mine when aggregated with everyone else's and turned into an easily searchable database for advertisers, politicians, insurance providers and so forth. In the coming few decades, we will have to develop a global policy on information privacy. In this chapter, we have seen strong philosophical arguments in favour of information privacy. What remains to be seen is whether this will influence the legislatures around the world. Will we adopt strong data protection like the EU has with its Data Protection Act, or will we just pay lip service to privacy issues but allow governments and corporations to abuse those rights as we have seen happen in most of the rest of the world, including the US? The answer is unclear.

Protecting free speech is another global concern. Protecting the rights of dissidents and political revolutionaries comes at the cost of tolerating speech we find offensive. The key to understanding how to properly regulate communications is to adopt the Principle of Harm and to realize that mere offence is not harm. Thus we can tolerate healthy debate but carefully regulate hate speech; we can enjoy healthy and necessary converse about human sexuality, while working to limit pornography that causes harm to individuals and society at large.

ICTs are creating a worldwide surveillance society. The fear of global terrorism and the illicit drug trade has caused governments to support more and better surveillance. The glut of information that these systems produce is being managed by more artificially intelligent systems, or ambient intelligence, that, for instance, analyse the behaviour and facial expressions and other biometrics of every member in a crowd and flag certain individuals as potential shoplifters, dangerous individuals or terrorists and then create a log of that person's activities that can be monitored by human agents later. This same sort of information can also be collected on each and every one of us, to be used by advertisers and marketers to track our shopping and buying behaviour both online and off. These legitimate governmental and private interests are taking us into a world that is something like a strange mix of Aldous Huxley's *Brave New World* (Huxley 2006) and a well-run theme park. This emerging world is strikingly prevalent in online worlds like *Second Life*, *World of Warcraft*, and others where the *government* on these games is a commercial entity and those running it may be fabulous programmers and designers but unskilled in political philosophy, ethical theory and policy, thus creating the climate for abuse (see Ludlow and Wallace 2007, Ludlow 1996).

As we have learned from Lawrence Lessig, the designers and code writers for ICTs are the real power behind securing the rights we want (Lessig 2006). Law and policy will always be behind these technologies because technology changes so quickly. If we are going to continue to enjoy the rights that we care about, then it is going to be due to the work done by technologists and technological watchdog groups like the Electronic Frontier Foundation today. It is vital that those studying to be technologists are trained in computer ethics, as they are the only hope that we have in securing ethical ICTs. Without this training we can expect ICTs to take us into a strange new world where none of us will feel comfortable and where living a good life will be more difficult if not impossible.

7.9 Far future issues

A final thought worth pondering is whether future generations will even see our interest in securing rights and computer ethics as a legitimate one. It would seem that younger generations do not care that much about privacy rights, given their complete lack of propriety on social networking sites like MySpace and Facebook. People are quite willing to give away the most intimate facts about themselves to millions of potential viewers. In fact, Facebook is a wonderful place for would-be identity thieves to collect all kinds of useful tidbits like, for instance, a user's mother's maiden name or the name of a pet, which can then be used to bypass security in online banking, etc. (ZDNet July 2007). While it is indeed true that many young people are sharing way too much information about themselves online, it is probably due to naivety. Most users will greatly alter their habits once they find out what can happen to them. And as more and more of them have this experience, we may find that they mature into stalwart defenders of privacy.

At the beginning of this chapter, we discussed how our use of ICTs creates a digital footprint, one that can be mined by others for valuable information. If we extrapolate a little on the technology already available, such as the Internet, smart phones like the iPhone, automatic data collecting, personal robotics, etc. we might see evolving a device that could record one's own digital footprint. This is exactly what Microsoft researchers have proposed with the MyLifeBits project, which is supposed to collect every aspect of ones digital footprint. 'It is a system for storing all of one's digital media, including documents, images, sounds, and videos' (Gemmel *et al.* 2002). A much more advanced device like this is imagined by the science fiction writer Rudy Rucker, a device he calls the Lifebox (Rucker 2006). This device automatically collects all the information surrounding its user as they live their life, everything they do, say, look at, smell, hear, etc., the ultimate multimedia diary. This would result in a huge amount of data, perhaps a petaflop or so, which, from the point of view of technology, is not really all that much memory space considering how quickly our ability to store this information is progressing (Rucker 2006, p. 279). Armed with a Lifebox, one could then recall and even relive in a way any experience one ever had or just keep the Lifebox as a complete record of one's life. This would be a fabulous device indeed. Yet it is easy to imagine the problems with the complete transparency in privacy that would result from this. Nothing would ultimately be secret, every moment of the life of every person that had one could be reconstructed in intimate detail. Why build one? Our wish for perfect memory and longevity may just overwhelm any vestigial interest in privacy we may have at that time perhaps leading to the ultimate erosion of our right to privacy.

As things like Lifeboxes, digital assistants and other artificial agents evolve, they will not only challenge our privacy rights, they may even evolve to want these rights for themselves. As strange as this advanced artificially intelligent technology sounds, it is actually not that far-fetched. The beginnings of it were discussed at the start of this chapter. If our personal individual agency is formed from informational constructs as some have argued (Floridi and Sanders 2004, Floridi 2003, Rucker 2006, Sullins 2008, Turing 1950), then some information constructs may evolve significant artificial agency up to a level of competence similar to our own. In this case, they may be deserving of moral consideration for the same reason we, animals, ecosystems and corporations are already (Floridi and Sanders 2004, Floridi 2003, Sullins 2007, 2006a, 2006b). Dealing with this is a very interesting problem. Perhaps, with the advent of these artificial agents, we must also provide them with a kind of machine morality (Anderson and Anderson 2007, Wallach and Allen 2008). The ethics of artificial agents will be addressed in Chapters 12 and 13 of this volume, but if we make the right decisions then perhaps the future of computer ethics just may evolve to fulfil our desire for secure free speech and privacy rights.

8 Conflict, security and computer ethics

John Arquilla

In the long history of human development, almost all technological advances have been quickly harnessed for purposes of war-making. The hunter-gatherer's atlatl – a handheld rod-and-thong with a socket into which a spear was inserted – greatly extended his throwing range, and was good for bringing down prey and handy for fighting competing tribesmen. The same was true of the bow and arrow as well. A kind of dual-use phenomenon – with the same advances having both economic and military applications – soon became evident. For example, the wheel helped move goods in carts, but also led to the war chariot. And so on, since antiquity. The pattern held right up through the industrial revolution, which began over two centuries ago, with steam revolutionizing both land and maritime trade, and giving far greater mobility to armies and navies. Next came aircraft, whose uses seemed to apply to conflict before they did to commerce, since very soon after humankind took to the air a century ago, bombs began to rain down from the sky. The same pattern also held for the atom, with the very first use of nuclear power in 1945 being to kill some hundreds of thousands of innocent civilians. 'Atoms for peace' came later. Today, early on in the information age, it is clear that the computer too has been yoked to serve Mars, vastly empowering the complex manoeuvres of modern militaries and the disruptive aims of terrorist networks. Whatever the social and commercial benefits of computing – and they are enormous – silicon-based intelligence is fast becoming a central element in military and strategic affairs.

Still, throughout all these developments over the past several millennia, there has often been some light to be glimpsed around the edges of the darkness of war. It has taken the form of ethical guidelines for conducting conflicts, strictures that are almost as old as the ways of war themselves. These behavioural norms have shown a great deal of consistency across time and culture: fight in self-defence, or to protect others; employ proportionate levels of violence; honour the immunity of noncombatants; and, finally, go to war only as a last resort, and on the basis of decisions taken by duly constituted authority (Walzer 1977, Howard *et al.* 1994). Notions of 'just war', though seldom fully observed, have thus accompanied many, perhaps most, conflicts for millennia, sometimes ameliorating the effects of what can only be labelled organized savagery. In this way, self-extinction of the species has, so far, been avoided. Indeed, it is hard to think of our having successfully negotiated the nuclear rapids of the Cold War confrontation in the absence of an ethical conscience continually reminding both sides of the inherently disproportionate destructiveness – largely aimed at the innocent – of atomic weapons. But, just as the end of the cold war was overturning the old international system and holding out new prospects for a deep, lasting peace, the coming of computers may have unwittingly helped to put war and terror very much 'back in business'.

Computers have contributed to revitalizing the realm of conflict in three principal areas. First, in terms of conventional military operations, computers have completely revolutionized communications, making complex new modes of field operations possible. Next, computers have made it possible to analyse oceans of sensor data quite swiftly, enabling the military, intelligence and law enforcement communities to take action in ever more timely and targeted ways. This powerful new analytic capacity, it must be noted, can serve aggressors or defenders equally well, whether they are nations or terrorist networks. Last, the growing dependence of societies and their militaries on advanced information and communications technologies has given birth to cyberspace-based forms of strategic attack, designed to cause costly, crippling disruptions. These may also be undertaken by either nations or networks, perhaps even by individuals or very small groups, given the increasing ability to maintain one's anonymity while covertly scanning the target. Indeed, the veil of anonymity may prove hard to pierce, both during and in the wake of a cyber attack.

All these emerging possibilities for engaging in new, information-technology-mediated modes of conflict may pose a variety of puzzling ethical dilemmas: for war-fighting militaries in the field, for intelligence-gathering services, perhaps even for terrorists. And thinking these matters through from an ethical perspective may produce some surprising results. The most troubling may be that both war and terror have grown more 'thinkable' and ethically acceptable due to the rise of disruptive, cyberspace-based means of attack. However, the same cannot likely be said for individual liberty and privacy, which may come under sharp, devaluating pressure as a result of efforts to detect, deter or defend against the various forms of cyber attack.

8.1   Computers in battle: ethical considerations

In terms of the first area of inquiry, computers on the battlefield, the principal worry is that somehow communications links will be severed and armies, blinded in this manner, will be seriously weakened and much less able to ward off physical attacks. From the time that computers first came to be appreciated as potential battlefield tools, concerns have been expressed about whether they would actually work in dusty, wet or otherwise dirty environments, where they would be routinely banged around (Bellin and Chapman 1987). These worries were effectively dealt with by robust designs and much redundancy, and advanced militaries have come to depend heavily upon computers for battle coordination, logistics and other essential aspects of their operations. They are also embracing an increasingly wide range of unmanned, and sometimes autonomous, vehicles, aircraft and weapons systems – a trend that began over two decades ago (Barnaby 1986, De Landa 1991), but which is accelerating.

With this dependency comes vulnerability. If an army's computers are disrupted by cyber means, or intruded upon with the intention of spying out their next moves in the field, the consequences can be grave. An advanced military could be crippled due to a loss, even temporary, of its information flows (Arquilla and Ronfeldt 1993). Would it be ethical to use explosive weapons to wipe out a force that had lost much of its functionality because of a disruptive computer attack? While it would almost surely be acceptable to use cyber means to cause such confusion among enemy forces, in order for this use of computers to stay on the ethical high ground, the side with the advantage should show some mercy for the helpless. Much as the US military did in Kuwait in February of 1991, when the slaughter of retreating Iraqi troops along the 'Highway of Death' was quickly curtailed (Hallion 1992, pp. 235–237). Though their disarray had not been caused by computer attacks – their discomfiture was due to gravity bombs rather than logic bombs – the Iraqis were nonetheless in a helpless position, and American forces responded, after engaging in some lethal pummelling, with restraint. A similar circumspection would be called for if the chaos among enemy forces had been caused by computer network attacks.

All this said, the possibility of disabling an adversary's forces in the field by means of cyberspace-based attacks has to be viewed as quite attractive. The need for bloody attritional struggles recedes if one side in a conflict might lose much of its cohesion as a result of just a few smart 'clicks'. It is even possible to think in third-party terms, where a power (or a group of powers, or even a peacekeeping entity authorized by the United Nations) would act from the outside to disable the military of an aggressor threatening to start a conflict, or would disable both sides' forces. The sheer life-saving value of such action might outweigh traditional just war strictures about using force only as a 'last resort'. Yet, even in this area care would have to be taken, lest one side blame the other and become even more resolved to continue the fight by all means available. In the case of nuclear-armed rivals like India and Pakistan, for example, it might be more prudent to forgo cyber disruption, given the countervailing risk of escalation. In this particular instance, allowing a clearly limited conventional (or even unconventional) conflict to play itself out – rather than try to engage in cyber deterrence – might be ethically preferable.

8.2 'Cyber-snooping' by nation-states and terrorist networks

Consider now the ethics of obtaining information regarding one's adversaries by means of cyber intrusions and then mining and parsing the data in ways that might allow their vulnerabilities to be exploited in the 'real world'. This kind of cyber activity is, to date, the most prevalent. It is reflected in commerce, under the rubrics of industrial espionage and advanced marketing techniques, both of which can be quite dodgy in ethical terms. In the realm of crime, almost all the traditional ruses – i.e., 'con games' – and other sorts of long-practised deceptions have migrated into cyberspace. It is hardly surprising, then, that professional militaries, intelligence operatives, insurgents and terrorists have all come to rely heavily upon cyber-snooping on each other. But these actors, unlike, say, criminals, are more likely to justify their illicit data-mining operations in terms of serving their cause in time of war. Knowing what is happening on the 'other side of the hill' has long been considered a critical element in the formulation of effective strategies during times of conflict.

Despite their obvious utility, such activities could be deemed unethical in some settings. But not in the case of national military services, hacking into an adversary's information systems, learning their ways and plans – and then acting upon this knowledge – which are undertakings that should not be considered unethical per se. And certainly not in the case of cyber-snooping on another national military. But if the fundamental strategic problem is that the opponent is no longer a nation, the ethical situation grows more complex. For example, a well-hidden network, requiring much patient trawling for tracks and signs – and a great deal of sifting through of information on private individuals that exists in cyberspace – poses ethical problems aplenty. The terrorists may be very dangerous, and their activities may be designed to cause the deaths of noncombatants; but this still may not justify intrusive, perhaps even illegal, searches that sweep up vast amounts of data on the innocent (Brown 2003, Heymann 2003, Leone and Anrig 2004, Rosen 2004). These sorts of issues can probably be best answered in an ethical way by harkening to one of Thomas Aquinas' notions about 'fighting justly' (*jus in bello*): strive to do more overall good than harm. As Aquinas put it so well in the *Summa Theologica*, in Part II, the reply to Question 40: 'For the true followers of God even wars are peaceful if they are waged not out of greed or cruelty but for the sake of peace, to restrain the evildoers and assist the good.'

Thus, one might reason that the overall, enduring harm done by engaging in unethical search procedures in cyberspace could be outweighed by the benefit of detecting and preempting an impending terrorist attack. Still, this poses a question about the value of such intrusions in the event that no attack plans are detected or thwarted. And if attempts are made to mitigate this problem by forcing the watchers to obtain 'probable cause' warrants – or their equivalent – then the ability to detect and track an incipient terrorist conspiracy might be impaired or seriously slowed, with grave consequences. There is no simple answer, just the general sense that most people in most societies would probably be willing to accept increased intrusions upon their information privacy – as they do with regard to their privacy in other contexts – in return for enhanced physical security. The art here will be to find the equilibrium between compromises to privacy and enhanced security – and then monitor continuously for any drift in or disturbance to this equilibrium.

In the spirit of doing more good than harm, it may also be possible to argue that cyber-intrusions, even very aggressive and sustained ones, if accompanied by a drop in older forms of surveillance might produce a situation in which the overall violations of individual privacy rights would be diminished. During the last decade of the Cold War, technical surveillance capabilities expanded greatly, in particular those that empowered automated search agents to scan various forms of communication for sensitive key words that might indicate illicit activity. They came with names like 'Echelon' and 'Semantic Forests' and other code words that cannot be mentioned openly. This sort of mass-sifting approach guaranteed that a great deal of presumably private communications would be intruded upon. In the wake of 9/11, pressures mounted to step up such efforts – to little apparent effect, given the persistence, even the growth, of al Qaeda and its affiliates over the years. However, with the rise of sophisticated new cyber-surveillance techniques, like keystroke reconstruction and other proprietary 'back hacking' capabilities, the prospect of learning more in this way – rather than by simply trawling through telephone calls, for example – suggests an approach that will be both ethically superior and more practically effective in the fight against terrorism. By allowing and engaging in more of this sort of cyber-snooping, while at the same time reducing the level of more indiscriminate intrusions into telephone and other forms of communications, it may be possible both to do good and to do well.

If governments and their military, intelligence and law enforcement arms are being forced to thread their way through an ethical thicket in order to combat terror, the same cannot be said for the terrorists themselves. At first blush, their data-mining activities seem to fall completely in the unethical realm. After all, they are seeking information so that they can attack and kill innocents. Yet there may be a way to view their obtaining targeting information via cyberspace-based operations as ethical. Certainly, one has to think very creatively to conjure up any sense of how an inherently unethical phenomenon like terrorism – the deliberate targeting of noncombatants as objects of symbolic acts of violence – can possibly be morally mitigated by cyber-spying. Yet, on reflection, there do appear to be a few ways in which terrorism might be made less odious, if guided by cyberspace-based intelligence-gathering operations.

For example, terrorists engaging in skilful data mining might be able to generate enough detailed information that they would be able to mount their strikes more precisely – and might even be able to shift towards military rather than civilian targets – allowing them to achieve significant psychological effects, while shedding little noncombatant blood. Perhaps they could operate without any killing at all, if the kind of precision obtained allowed them to go directly after infrastructure targets. To the extent to which cyber-targeting allowed this, a shift in terrorism from lethal destruction to costly but (mostly) nonlethal disruption could be viewed as a lesser evil. Indeed, if terrorists embraced cyberspace as a platform for a major shift to disruptive 'infrastructure warfare', they would be moving more in the direction of the stated aims of strategic aerial bombardment than of traditional terror (Rattray 2001). And they might end up doing better than aerial bombers, as the latter have always inflicted a lot of destruction – including the killing of countless innocents on the ground, over a century of largely ineffective air campaigns – in order to achieve their disruptive effects (Pape 1996). Skilfully guided terrorists could, with a minimum requirement for explosives or other ordnance, achieve high levels of disruption to power, water and transportation infrastructures – causing their opponents to suffer huge economic losses, but with little attendant loss of life.

8.3   The 'strategic attack paradigm'

This last point leads us to consider the third major realm of 'information warfare': its use as a form of strategic attack (Adams 1998). So far, the ideas advanced about the use of cyberspace in conflict and terrorism have limited the use of the virtual domain to information gathering as an enabler of 'precision targeting' in the physical world. But there is a very real prospect, in the coming years, that forms of cyber warfare and cyber terror will make use of computers as much more than just 'guidance systems'. Instead, bits and bytes may soon be used directly as weapons. If this were to happen, then it would be possible to think of both war and terror evolving in ways that would be less violent and destructive, even though they would at the same time be very disruptive and would impose heavy economic costs. The new ethical dilemma that would arise might follow these lines: cyber warfare and cyber terror, by allowing conflict to be conducted in much less bloody ways, might make war and terror far more 'thinkable'. Thus, efforts to wage war more ethically – from the virtual domain – might have the perverse effect of making war and terror more prevalent. As Confederate General Robert E. Lee once put it, during the

American Civil War, 'It is a good thing that war is so terrible. Otherwise we should grow too fond of it.' So it could be if cyberspace-based forms of attack, which can be mounted at small cost and achieve disproportionate results, were to become the new norm in conflict.

Frederik Pohl, the great writer of speculative fiction, neatly captured this dilemma in his dystopian classic, *The Cool War* (1981). In this tale, the mutual fear of how big new weapons were making war far too destructive led many nations to cultivate covert capabilities for mounting costly, disruptive attacks on others' infrastructures – from disturbing financial markets to introducing disease viruses into the food chain. Pohl's world quickly becomes a Hobbesian one of constant warfare, economic and environmental degradation, and growing hopelessness. The moral of his story is that efforts to sharply reduce war's catastrophic potential may, in an unintended way, make things much worse. Even to the extent of goading some angry nations to respond to such small attacks with their arsenals of traditional weapons. So, there is not only the 'horizontal' threat of a rapid growth in small, covert wars, but also a 'vertical threat' of escalation to even deadlier forms of conflict. Thus, it is possible to think in terms of violent physical responses to virtual attacks becoming the norm.

In the setting of our real world, the ethical dilemmas that would attend the rise of this 'cool war' ethos are completely contingent upon there being an actual ability to mount attacks in this fashion. And today there is still much debate about the reality of this potential threat (Libicki 2007), as there has never been a crippling 'digital Pearl Harbor' or 'virtual Copenhagen' – the latter incident refers to Lord Nelson's surprise onslaught against the Danish fleet during the Napoleonic Wars that sharply raised aspiring naval powers' fears (in Germany, especially) of Britain waging preventive war from the sea. Yet, there have been several troubling signs that have confirmed advanced societies' real vulnerabilities to such attacks. Some of this evidence has come in the form of exercises or tests, like the US military's 'Eligible Receiver' a decade ago, in which the cyber attack team, using only tools openly available on the Web, is said to have crippled major military elements' abilities to fight (see Verton 2003, pp. 31–34). More recent exercises, under such code names as 'Silent Horizon' and 'Cyber Storm', have confirmed the great and growing vulnerability of both military and civilian infrastructures to grave disruptions from cyber attack. And, in the realm of real attacks, the sustained intrusions into sensitive systems over the past dozen years, known under such names as 'Moonlight Maze' and 'Titan Rain', provide even more chilling confirmation. These incidents go well beyond even the darker aspects of the phenomenon of 'hacktivism' – when computers are sometimes used, instead of to mobilize demonstrators, to mount 'denial of service' attacks that signal displeasure with the foreign or domestic policies of some government entity. To date, the most serious incidents of this sort have come, apparently, out of Russia. In

2007, hackers caused some brief, limited disruptions in Estonia in the wake of the removal of a statue of a Russian soldier from a prominent location. Then, in the summer of 2008, a wide range of Georgian critical information systems were brought down during that country's week-long war with Russia over the fate of South Ossetia.

8.4   Prospects for cyber deterrence and arms control

Whatever the actual pace of development of 'strategic warfare in cyberspace' (Gregory Rattray's term) – and there is much debate about this – all can agree that vulnerabilities to cyberspace-based forms of attack are real and growing. However, there has as yet been no 'existential proof' of a serious capability, as noted above, given the absence of a major attack mounted either by a nation or a network. Assuming that nations do have some capabilities along these lines – and the Moonlight Maze and Titan Rain intelligence-gathering intrusions suggest that Russia and China, respectively, may well have access to such offensive means – the reasons why they have been reluctant to mount actual attacks should be carefully considered. Certainly they have not refrained because of a lack of study or failure to invest in crafting the requisite offensive capabilities. Most advanced countries' security establishments have been obsessed with the problem of cyber attack since at least the end of the Cold War. Many have invested billions in learning how to defend themselves; and good defence implies a deep understanding of how to mount offensives. No, sheer incapacity cannot be the reason for such restraint.

The emergence of a kind of 'cyber deterrence' may explain the wariness of nations about waging war in and from the virtual domain. Very simply, it may be that Frederik Pohl's argument about the false attractiveness of such covert warfare – and the deleterious consequences of the rise of this new way of war – have been well understood by leaders capable of foreseeing the deep, troubling endgame that Pohl described. It may be that, in the real world, mutual vulnerability to 'cool war' – or to an angry, escalatory return to more traditional violence – may be the driving force behind the kind of durable 'cyber peace' that seems to be holding, for now, among nations. And there may be a very serious reluctance to be known as the nation that took the first step down this path.

The author's own experiences in this area tend to confirm this point – the result of having been asked by the US government to co-chair a meeting between Russian and American specialists in 'information warfare' in the mid 1990s. The week-long session remains largely 'not for attribution', but what can be said is that there was clearly much concern on both sides about the great and growing vulnerability of each society – and each military – to cyber attacks. In the wake of this meeting, the Russians introduced a measure in the

United Nations (General Assembly Resolution 53/70) calling for all nations to refrain from making cyberspace-based attacks. The United States blocked this resolution – just as Americans blocked the post-World War II Baruch Plan to cease the development of nuclear weapons and put those that already existed under international control. Still, the Russians continue to raise this issue in the United Nations from time to time – and it may behove the Americans to behave less obstructively at some point.

Despite the American rebuff of the Russian call for a kind of 'behaviour-based' cyber arms control regime – think of it as being akin to the pleas a generation ago for a 'no-first-use' pledge in the nuclear realm – the author was witness in 1999 to some very prudential behaviour. Little can be said openly, save that, during the Kosovo War, the United States may have had a considerable capacity for mounting cyber attacks against the hidden assets of Serb leader Slobodan Milosevich and his cronies. Yet these capabilities were not employed. At the time, the author was working directly with the 'director of information warfare' in the Pentagon, and participated in strategy and policy discussions at high levels, coming away with the clear sense that the commander-in-chief at the time, President Clinton, was unwilling to signal to the world, by ordering such attacks, that this was an acceptable form of war-making. For such a precedent might lead adversaries in future conflicts to resort to cyberspace-based attacks – and the US system would provide the richest and, in many ways, most vulnerable set of targets in the world.

In the decade since the (first?) Kosovo War – tensions rose once again in 2008, in the wake of the Kosovars' self-announced separation from Serbia – the failed Russian effort to advance the concept of some sort of behaviour-based arms control regime has nevertheless continued to resonate in important ways. For example, scientists, lawyers and ethicists all tend to agree that a behaviour-based solution should be sought because there is simply no way to control the diffusion of cyber attack technologies and tools (Hollis 2007). Ironically, the Russians themselves have come under much suspicion that they are the principal malefactors in a series of troubling intrusions into various nations' infospheres. The Americans, for their part just as ironically, have continued to oppose the creation of an international ethical or legal control regime over cyber warfare – yet they have also continued to be extremely circumspect about not actually engaging in such attacks against other countries. And so it seems that nations are going to continue to tread with care when it comes to strategic warfare in the virtual domain.

8.5   Will terrorists wage war from cyberspace?

The behaviour of nations, likely driven by concerns about reputation and vulnerability to retaliation in kind – or worse, to escalatory violence, even to the nuclear level as a Russian strategist once threatened (Thomas 1997, p. 77) – cannot begin to explain why terrorist networks have failed to become serious cyber warriors. Unlike nations, networks – particularly those such as al Qaeda and its affiliates, which operate covertly in scores of countries – have no territorial 'homeland security' to worry about. They have little or no infrastructure of their own to protect. And, as people whose basic concept of operations is to kill innocent noncombatants, coming to be known for their disruptive cyber skills could hardly be viewed as deepening the damage to their reputation. Indeed, a shift from destruction to fundamentally disruptive – and mostly nonlethal – acts would seem to indicate a great ethical improvement.

With this in mind, it is important to consider the conditions under which al Qaeda or other terrorist networks might begin to emphasize cyberspace-based attacks, or if they would continue to pursue the same level of violence in the physical world even as they began to disrupt the virtual domain. There is a possibility, however, that the need for traditional violence could diminish; and that cultivating a capacity for 'mass disruption' might even reduce the terrorists' desire to develop or acquire nuclear, biological or chemical weapons of mass destruction. These are the central issues that define the discussion of any possible shift towards cyber terrorism; and they should all be considered – from both a practical and an ethical perspective.

Perhaps the single greatest impediment to terror networks' development of top-flight cyber skills lies in the area of human capital. It takes many years to become a first-rate computer scientist – as opposed to being just a disaffected 'tekkie', or Script Kiddie, capable of downloading (but not fully exploiting) attack tools from the Web – at least a decade. And this presupposes study at a leading institution, or under the tutelage of a very experienced master operator. This requires a long-term investment strategy on the part of the terror network, and a willingness to risk the discovery of the asset – or his or her disillusionment, failure or disaffection – during the training period. The alternatives to a traditional computer science education for one's operatives would be either to pursue the private tutorial route, or to consider the recruitment of hacker mercenaries. Both of these options carry serious risks, as either the tutor or the cyber mercenaries could be part of a counter-terror infiltration 'sting', or they could be under surveillance by law enforcement or intelligence services. If recruited from or through a criminal organization, there would also be the possibility of betrayal by the crime lords, who might find it profitable to sell them out. So, in the face of high 'entry costs' and serious operational security risks, terror networks might be self-deterred from pursuing a serious capability for cyber warfare. It may be that dispersed terrorist cells and nodes, which rely heavily on cyberspace for communications, training, propaganda and operational control (Weimann 2006), are loath to risk compromising, perhaps even losing, these virtual capabilities by running the risk of bringing a counter-terrorist predator into their midst.

Yet there are conditions that could possibly justify bearing such costs and undertaking such risks. For example, the prospect of fundamentally transforming terrorism itself – changing it from a bloody exercise in compellence to a mode of conflict driven by economic and psychological costs imposed on hapless, often helpless targets – might prove very attractive. Pursue, however briefly, a thought experiment in which al Qaeda or some other terrorist group with an ambitious agenda has developed or acquired a serious capability for mounting cyberspace-based attacks. Power grids are taken down, financial markets are disrupted, and military command and control is compromised at critical moments. All in the name of the group's call for some policy shift, e.g. removal of American troops from some or all Muslim countries; agreement to hold democratic elections in Saudi Arabia or another authoritarian monarchy; or formal establishment of Palestine as a state. However understandable these goals might be, their intrinsic worth has always been undermined – and overwhelming public opposition has been sparked, in Muslim countries as well – by terrorists' deliberate infliction of deadly violence upon noncombatants. In this thought experiment, though, the deadly violence would be replaced by disruptive acts that could actually serve to put the spotlight more on the terrorists' goals rather than on their means of achieving them. The ethics of the terrorists would have improved – at least at the margins – and the likelihood of attaining their objectives might also rise a bit, or perhaps a lot.

The foregoing suggests that such a state of affairs could both increase the effectiveness of terrorist campaigns and reduce the level of international opprobrium that usually accompanies their activities. In the first Russo-Chechen war (1994–1996), the rebels showed how this could be done in the real world by hijacking aircraft and later a Black Sea ferry – but then releasing their captives after having called attention to their cause. The Chechen insurgents won this round against the Russians (Lieven 1998, Gall and de Waal 1998), but returned to more traditionally violent acts of terror in their second war – including hostage seizures at such diverse targets as primary schools and opera houses (each of which ended with large numbers of innocents killed) – and lost most of the world's sympathy for their cause. A cautionary tale that terrorists should heed, perhaps.

8.6   Three paths to cyber terror

Coming back to the current terror war, it seems clear that al Qaeda's development of a capacity for cyberspace-based warfare would also track very nicely with Osama bin Laden's calls, in videotaped messages that aired on 24 January 2005 and 7 September 2007, for his jihadist adherents to wage 'economic warfare' against the United States and its allies. Yet there is a risk that traditional terrorists – more alpha males than alpha geeks – might reject such a shift, much as the Chechens apparently did. They could feel emasculated by the imposition of any serious restrictions on their violent acts. And along with this psychological antipathy, worries about the serious costs and potentially grave security risks of pursuing a cyber warfare programme could forestall the emergence of this sort of terrorist innovation. But there are at least three paths ahead towards a cyber capability that would still leave plenty of room for committing old-style acts of violence.

First, a terrorist group, such as al Qaeda, could continue its existing level of violent activities – for example, the insurgencies in Iraq and Afghanistan, coupled with occasional 'spectaculars' (e.g. like 9/11, Bali or Madrid) in other parts of the world – and simply encourage new cells to form up around cyber capabilities. This strategy requires only a 'call to virtual arms'. In a loose-jointed network – again, al Qaeda is a good example – sympathizers are sure to hear and heed such a call, and a capacity for cyber warfare could emerge that in no way imperilled the network core or compromised its security. But such an approach is fairly passive, requiring faith in the likelihood that those with the requisite skills will sign up for the cause, or the jihad. Further, this 'grafting on' approach would do nothing to reduce the international opprobrium that would be heaped on the organization for its continuing bloody attacks on noncombatants.

A second approach would be for a terrorist group to deliberately scale back on the number of acts of physical violence that it commits, closely integrating such strikes as would be allowed with cyber capabilities. An example of this strategy would be to use some type of cyber attack – aimed at, say, causing a massive power outage – that would put people 'on the street', making them vulnerable to attacks with explosives, chemicals, even a radiological 'dirty bomb'. While this might make moving into the virtual realm more attractive to the terrorists, the fact that cyber attacks were being mounted in order to enhance the effects of physical attacks would probably increase the world's antipathy towards the terrorists.

A third option for the terrorists would be to make the strategic choice to emphasize cyber attacks in the future, while restricting the network's acts of physical violence to clearly military targets. This poses the prospect that the rise of cyber warfare could improve a terrorist organization's 'ethical health'. And, as to physical attacks, they would be conducted in a more 'just' fashion, given the emphasis on military targets. Some terrorist groups – notably the IRA – have tried to be very discriminate about their targeting choices, demonstrating a clear concern about ethical matters that helped make it possible for them to be seen as viable partners in peace negotiations. It is hard to think of al Qaeda in this fashion today; but the vision of a terrorist group that struck only military targets with lethal violence and then caused costly but nonlethal cyber disruptions with the rest of its energies, is an odd, intriguing one.

The principal point of the preceding section is that the rise of a real capability for cyber warfare might 'make terrorism better', in ethical terms. Not giving it quite a Robin Hood patina, but redefining its image in far more palatable ways. And if this sort of cyberspace-based rehabilitation were possible for terrorists, it might also be a path that traditional militaries could consider. Why shouldn't a nation-state strive for a capacity to knock out power with logic bombs rather than iron bombs? Classical interstate war itself might be 'made better' by such means. Probably not, however, if such wars were waged secretly, conjuring visions of Pohl's 'cool war' world. But if cyberspace-based warfare were conducted in a more openly acknowledged manner – say, in the wake of an actual declaration of war – and followed the laws and ethics of armed conflict, then a shift towards disruptive rather than destructive wars might well take place. Yet, even in this instance, there would be the ethical concern that war had been made not only better, but too attractive – and so would increase the penchant for going to war in the first place.

Thus a world with more, but less bloody, armed conflicts might emerge in the wake of cyberspace-based warfare's rise. In some respects, this information-age effect would parallel the impact of the early spread of nuclear weapons over a half century ago. As Kenneth Waltz, dean of the 'neorealist' school of thought in international relations, put it so well at the dawn of that era, 'mutual fear of big weapons may produce, instead of peace, a spate of smaller wars' (1959, p. 236). But there is a big difference between the deterrent effect of the threat of escalation from conventional to nuclear weapons, and that engendered by a shift from virtual to physical violence. Where prudence seemed to guide the careful avoidance of escalatory actions when nuclear war loomed ahead, there may be less worry that cyberspace-based actions might lead to some sort of more traditional military confrontation. And, for all its chest-thumping quality, any threat to use weapons of mass destruction in response to cyber disruption may simply not be credible. Indeed, during the heyday of the Cold War, both the notions of 'massive retaliation' and 'flexible response', which posited first uses of nuclear weapons in response to conventional acts of armed aggression, were also viewed sceptically. As the great strategic theorist Thomas Schelling once observed, massive retaliation as a doctrine was 'in decline from the moment it was enunciated' (Schelling 1966, p. 190). Back then, this scepticism proved healthy, and put a premium on developing solid traditional military capacities as the backbone of deterrence. Today, and tomorrow, a similar sort of flinty-eyed scepticism about massive retaliatory responses to cyber attacks, coupled with ethical concerns about proportionality, may point just as clearly to the need to emphasize cyber defensive means – rather than punitive threats – as the best way to deter cyber attacks.

8.7   Conclusion: cyber war is more 'thinkable', more ethical

When it comes to notions of 'just wars' and 'fighting justly', the information revolution seems to be creating a new set of cross-cutting ethical conundrums for nation-states. The rise of strategic warfare in cyberspace makes it easier for them to go to war unjustly – especially in terms of starting a fight as an early option rather than as a last resort. Yet, at the same time, fighting principally in cyberspace could do a lot to mitigate the awful excesses that have led so many wars in the 'real world' to be waged in an unjust manner. Against this, however, is a greater ethical concern about escalation risks. A nation that has been attacked by another in cyberspace may choose either to respond in kind – setting off something like Frederik Pohl's 'cool war' – or may opt for a self-defence strategy of retaliating with physical military force. Either way, the conflict escalates, and ethical considerations of noncombatant immunity, proportionality and 'doing more good than harm' are likely to be trampled.

So thought must be given to what is to be done. Soldiers can now contemplate 'clicking for their countries' in ever more effective ways (Dunnigan 1996; Alexander 1999). Virtual mobilization periods might come to be reckoned in micro-seconds, putting enormous stress on crisis decision-making. Imagine a latter-day Cuban missile crisis that unfolded in thirteen minutes rather than thirteen days. Add to these considerations the fact that rich, inviting, poorly protected civilian targets abound, and one can easily see how a cyberspace-based mode of conflict may indeed become a more attractive policy option, upending traditional wariness about war-making. Further, this attraction may be reinforced by the notion that, while inflicting potentially huge economic costs on one's adversaries, this can be done with little loss of life. Thus, a rationalistic attempt might be made to offset going to war unjustly by actually waging the war in a more just – that is, far less lethal – fashion. A most curious and contradictory development, unparalleled, it seems, in the history of conflict.

These ethical issues are further complicated by the rise of nonstate actors, ranging from individuals to small groups, and on to full-blown networks of actors. The capacity to wage war is no longer largely under the strict control of nations. Although we have seen previous eras in which violence migrated into the hands of smaller groups – witness the parallel histories of pirates and bandits (Hobsbawm 1969, Pennell 2001) – the sheer accessibility of cyber warfare capabilities to tens, perhaps hundreds, of millions of people is a development without historical precedent. And where piracy, banditry and early examples of terror networks have sometimes proven nettlesome, they have only rarely – and briefly – won out over their nation-state adversaries. This may not be the case in cyberspace. If so, then the ethical dimensions of acts of war and terror conducted by networks of individuals, operating via the virtual realm, will become just as important as the considerations for nation-states.

At the level of policy making and international norm-setting, it seems that all the aforementioned ethical concerns are driving nations and networks towards critical choice points. For nations, there is the question of whether to encourage the rise of behaviour-based forms of cyber arms control or to encourage the development and use of virtual warfare capabilities – in the latter case fuelling a new kind of arms racing. The answer, in this case, is not at all clear, as simply refraining from the acquisition and use of cyber warfare capabilities may doom nations to keep fighting their wars, when they do break out, in old-fashioned, highly destructive ways. Whereas, the great potential of cyber warfare is that it might lead to the swift and relatively bloodless defeat of enemy forces in the field, and the disruption of war-supporting industries at home. Even if this prospect might make war somehow more 'thinkable', the prospect of waging one's conflicts in less bloody fashion is something the concerned ethicist cannot dismiss. Perhaps the answer lies in crafting such cyber capabilities – as they allow the prospect of fighting more justly during a war – while at the same time maintaining the very strictest adherence to ethical strictures that should govern choices about going to war in the first place.

As to terror networks, they too seem to be facing a strategic choice about whether to embrace cyber warfare fully. A big difference for the networks is that the risks of being discovered and tracked down during the development and acquisition process are considerable – something of a lesser worry for most nations. Beyond the matter of operational security, there may also be the problem that terrorists will simply have a hard time making the shift in mindset from being all about the symbolic use of destructive violence to embracing notions of inflicting costly but largely nonlethal disruptions upon their targets. The foregoing analysis of their situation, however, suggests that some clear-headed ethical reasoning might impel them to make a serious shift in the direction of cyber-based disruption. For a terrorist group that is capable of causing huge amounts of economic damage while killing few – perhaps none – would be an organization that would be a lot harder to hate. Among the mass publics that made up the terror network's core constituency, those who sympathized with the group's goals would be far less likely to be alienated by this kind of cyberspace-based mode of operation. And even the network's targeted enemies would have a less visceral response than has been evinced to such physical attacks as 9/11, or the Bali, Madrid and London bombings.

In sum, whether nation or network, there may be sound ethical reasons for embracing cyber warfare and/or cyber terror. A most curious finding, as one would expect any ethical examination of conflict to lead inexorably towards an affirmation of peace and nonviolence. But when one considers the endless parade of slaughters humans have visited upon each other since they became sentient – and when one notes that the recently concluded century was the bloodiest of all in human history – then perhaps it is not so odd to find ethical value in exploring a very different new kind of warfare.

9 Personal values and computer ethics

Alison Adam

9.1 Introduction

Over the last thirty or so years, equality legislation has gradually been put in place in many Western countries. Equal treatment of men and women was a founding principle of the European Economic Community when it was founded in 1957, long before gender equality appeared in national agendas (Rees 1998, p. 1). Over this period, gender discrimination law has been enacted in the EU, with the development of extensive case law by the European Court of Justice. Taking the UK as a paradigm example, it has been illegal to discriminate on the grounds of gender since the mid 1970s (Equal Pay Act, Sex Discrimination Act). The European Commission designated 2007 as the 'European Year of Equal Opportunities for All'. This involved an information campaign, and 'Equality Summit' and a framework strategy on non-discrimination and equal opportunities, which aimed to ensure that EU legislation in this field is properly implemented and where a number of EU member states were condemned for failing to apply EU equality legislation properly. Since the introduction of gender equality law, legislation addressing race and disability discrimination has followed. Age, religion and sexuality discrimination are the latest equality legislation to enter the statute books in the UK and legislation aimed at all these forms of discrimination will shortly be wrapped into a single equalities bill. A key part of the lead-up to the 'Equal Opportunities for All' year was the mandate for member states to create a single contact point responsible for creating national strategy on discrimination covered by Article 13 of the Treat of Amsterdam, namely discrimination on the grounds of sex, racial or ethnic origin, religion or belief, disability, age or sexual orientation.

Despite apparent advances in recognizing and promoting equality, equality legislation is notoriously difficult to enforce and there are concerns that single equality legislation, rather than strengthening the battle against discrimination, may, instead, weaken it, as attention is deflected from the material experiences of different types of discrimination (Pearson and Watson 2007). However, the aim of this chapter is not to dwell on the problems of equality legislation, as such. Whatever its pitfalls, the legislation is based on a recognition of diversity in society and that the rights of individuals belonging to diverse groups should be preserved. In particular, an individual should reasonably expect not to be discriminated against on the grounds of age, gender, disability, race, sexuality or religion.

The categories, age, gender, disability, race, sexuality and religion are important parts of an individual's identity. As noted above, the right to equal treatment, or at least the right not to be discriminated against, on the grounds of one's identity is gradually becoming enshrined in legislation. However, in a wider sense, the question of how people with diverse identities should be treated, and how their identities are to be respected and to be allowed to flourish, is an ethical matter. The construction and flourishing of individual identity is a complex concern, as even a relatively simple example illustrates. On an employment application in the UK, one will often be asked to tick a box on a form indicating ethnicity and one might find that either the ethnicity with which one identifies is not represented on the form at all, or that it is perfectly appropriate to tick two or more boxes. The ways in which personal identity is constructed and maintained is, of course, a much more complex question, which the tick boxes of a form oversimplify. Additionally, information and communications technologies (ICTs) have an increasing part to play in the construction, maintenance and flourishing of identity, and it becomes increasingly important to understand the ways in which ICTs are implicated in avoiding discrimination of individuals on the grounds of identity. This is especially important given the reliance of many countries on ICTs for a wide range of services, the provision of goods, participation and education. Such issues can be construed as a concern for computer ethics.

Hence this chapter is concerned with casting the expression and maintenance of identity in relation to ICTs as a computer ethics problem. As a central part of personal identity involves identifying oneself, explicitly or otherwise, as a member of a group with similar interests or more explicitly as a community, this chapter begins by reviewing research on virtual communities, noting early enthusiasm for Internet-based communities, critiques and more recent interest in the communities of social networking sites of Web 2.0.

Gender, disability and age are major markers of individual identity and major areas for equality legislation, given historical inequalities between men and women, given the exclusion of disabled people from many areas of social life and given an increasing awareness that denying access to employment and services on the grounds of age constitutes discrimination. Hence these are key dimensions along which with the maintenance of identity through the use of ICTs may be explored. The following section considers gender identity in relation to ICTs, how aspects of gender identity are shaped through the use of ICTs and how this may be understood in computer ethics terms. The next section turns to disability and ICTs. The identity politics of disability is a hotly debated area. The way that so much of the World Wide Web remains inaccessible to disabled people and the implications for identity and community acts as a focus for this section. Finally the ways in which older people construct and maintain identity through the use of ICTs is considered.

9.2   Theoretical themes

The central theoretical theme relates to equality and how this may be maintained, allowing individuals to express identity through living and working with ICTs. All too often equality is expressed as a liberal value without consideration of the deeper structural reasons that cause the inequality. Expressing the desire to achieve equality, without understanding the material, structural causes of inequality, will not go very far towards ending inequality. A good example of this can be found in the equality and diversity policies that many organizations have developed and which underpin the equality statements on employment advertisements. Hoque and Noon (2004) argue that many of these equality policies are 'empty shells' which are not backed up by substantive action to address inequality. Having an 'empty shell' equality policy is worse than having no equality policy at all, if it is assumed that an organization has done its duty by putting a policy in place without implementing actions to enforce the equality policy.

Technology has a central role in understanding how inequalities are maintained. As argued below, hopes that new technology would bring more equal ways of living and working have been widespread. One sees this in relation to the discussion on virtual communities, gender, disability and age. This is based on a view of technology autonomous in its trajectory, a force which is somehow independent of society. The idea that technological progress is inevitable and that technology drives society, rather than, perhaps, the other way round or something more mediated in between, is termed 'technological determinism' and it has been criticized by many authors, who argue, instead, for the inextricable intertwining of the social and the technical (McKenzie and Wajcman 1999). In science and technology studies, technological determinism has been rejected in theoretical moves that have seen substantial development in the sociology of scientific knowledge (Bloor 1976), the social construction of technology (McKenzie and Wajcman 1999) and actor-network theory (Law and Hassard 1999). This research develops the idea that technology and society are not independent forces. Indeed, it is not possible to identify something as unequivocally 'social' as technology is thoroughly entwined in the making and maintenance of social life. Similarly, nothing can be regarded as purely technological. Technologies have histories. They are made in societies and designers design in conceptions of those who are expected to use the technology. Technologies can be designed in such a way as to reinforce inequality.

A famous example (although one which has since been questioned) is that of the design of highways in New York State. Winner argued that the highways to Long Beach, a desirable resort, were originally designed with low bridges so that buses could not pass underneath (Winner 1999). As buses were used by poorer people, this helped maintain Long Beach as a middle-class resort. Therefore it is possible to make the claim that technologies are not neutral, they have politics. If society and technology influence and define each other then we should not necessarily expect new technologies to be free of old patterns of behaviour and old prejudices. Arguing against determinism, and thereby taking an alternative position, means that we need not see ourselves as being swept along by a relentless tide of technology; we may, instead, have choices in the way we use different technologies. Hence, it becomes an important political act to make explicit, understand and evaluate the potential choices.

9.3   Virtual community

Since the beginnings of the Internet as a mass communication medium, there has been considerable interest in the concept of the virtual community (Rheingold 2000). No doubt, some of this interest is fuelled by perceptions, in Western societies, of a breakdown in traditional community, signalled in Putnam's (2001) influential work on the diminution of social capital, *Bowling Alone*. This focuses on the idea of suburban life, centred round the car and a long commute to work, where there are no supposedly safe suburban or urban spaces, where community activities have diminished, where children are no longer encouraged to play outside, away from adult gaze, and where fears of crime and terrorism are part of a 'moral panic' (Critcher 2006). In times increasingly perceived as uncertain, the promise of the Internet virtual community initially appeared seductive. If one struggled to identify oneself as part of a real community, a virtual community offered the promise of a potentially safe alternative to the dangerous world outside.

Rheingold's (2000) *The Virtual Community: Homesteading on the Electronic Frontier*, originally published in 1993, represents a seminal early work on virtual community and is still widely discussed and reviewed (e.g. see references in Goodwin 2004). It was based on Rheingold's own experiences in various online communities, notably WELL (Whole Earth 'Lectronic Link), and is a readable and persuasive account. Rheingold is often thought of as utopian in inspiration in his enthusiasm for virtual communities. However he argues that his experience of WELL was always grounded in real life in that he regularly met with WELLites in the San Francisco Bay area (Rheingold 2000, p. xvi) in the mid 1980s and this added to his view that the virtual community was an authentic community. His original work was written in 1993 when virtual communities were the province of relatively few enthusiasts and early adopters and when the potential of the World Wide Web was yet to be realized. Writing in 2000, his second edition is more nuanced as to what kind of societies might emerge online. He acknowledges a broader debate on the social impact of new media. He is less deterministic in tone, agreeing with Winner that technology is not an autonomous force. 'To me, the most penetrating technology critic in the largest sense today is Langdon Winner...He convinced me that the notion of authentic community and civic participation through online discussion is worth close and sceptical examination. However, I would disagree that such media can never play such a role on the same grounds that Chou En Lai refused to analyze the impact of the French Revolution: "It's too early to tell"' (Rheingold 2000, pp. 348–349).

A number of commentators warn against the utopian ideals of the early conceptions of the virtual community and have argued that social boundaries constructed round virtual communities may be used to exclude others. Notably, Winner (1997) argued that virtual communities, far from being more inclusive, egalitarian and open than real communities, may achieve the opposite. In real communities, all sorts of people with quite different beliefs and values have to rub along together. Virtual communities can be exclusive, only accepting as members people with very similar beliefs, and can be used to reinforce and magnify prejudices rather than reducing them. The risk of only talking to those with like-minded views is not, of course, confined to virtual life. In real life people congregate into groups of like-minded individuals, they read newspapers which reflect their political views and so on. Despite this, in real life, one must interact with people who do not share one's views; one cannot necessarily avoid broadcast media where a variety of political opinions are reflected. However, virtual communities can insulate themselves against interacting with those who no not share their views and the pace and intensity of virtual interactions may reinforce this. Winner (1997) argues that the technological determinism, inherent in the utopian ideal of a virtual community, may go hand in hand with an extreme form of liberalism or libertarianism; indeed 'cyberlibertarianism' is the term he emphasizes. He argues that Internet communities could pose serious threats to democracy by promoting radical, self-interest groups, which obviate their responsibilities towards promoting true equality.

'Cyberlibertarianism' is a dominant view in popular discussions of computers and networking. It is a form of extreme right-wing liberalism in the shape of a libertarianism where no controls are imposed and the workings of the free market are assumed to create egalitarian, democratic societal structures. Winner interprets cyberlibertarianism as a dystopian position, combining extreme enthusiasm for computer-mediated life coupled with 'radical, right wing libertarian ideas about the proper definition of freedom, social life, economics, and politics in the years to come' (1997, p. 14). Cyberlibertarianism or 'technolibertarianism' as it has been termed by Jordan and Taylor (2004) has parallels with the 'hacker ethic' (Himanen 2001, Jordan and Taylor 2004, Adam 2005) in which libertarian views are expressed in the ideal that all information should be free and that equality spontaneously emerges from such freedoms. Such a view looks to a society free from regulation, social ties and community obligations. However appealing such a view might seem on the surface, the interests of vulnerable groups may not be taken into account and the supposed freedoms that are offered may not be equally available to all.

Winner (1997, pp. 14–15) identifies an adherence to technological determinism as the most central characteristic of such a cyberlibertarian view: 'the dynamism of digital technology is our true destiny. There is no time to pause, reflect or ask for more influence in shaping these developments. Enormous feats of quick adaptation are required of all of us just to respond to the requirements the new technology casts upon us each day.' A level of self-interest, and rights to self-determination without considering other groups, a trust in free market capitalism and a distrust of government intervention are the characteristics of this position. However, cyberlibertarian communities still adhere to a rhetoric that virtual communities will give rise to democracy, spontaneously. This mirrors Ess's (1996) concerns with naïve views of democracy that are promoted in online interactions. In any case, not all virtual communities are interested in egalitarian ideals; some are clearly created to sustain antisocial or criminal activities.

Taking an extreme example, nevertheless one that remains a problem, there is considerable evidence that the activities of paedophile rings are sustained on the Internet. An individual who is a member of a ring not only has access to more material and activities but is also given reinforcement, by other members of the ring, that such activities are acceptable. Paedophile rings existed before the Internet, but they are much easier to create and maintain in an online world, and there is evidence of individuals becoming paedophiles through Internet use, and indulging in activities, such as making videos of abuse, which they might not have done were the Internet unavailable. This also signals that the safe haven that the Internet may have initially promised for parents fearing for the safety of their children out of doors is something of an illusion, when one cannot know the identity of the person one's pre-teen daughter is contacting in a chat room. The ease of Internet interaction fuels such groups (Adam 2005).

With the advent of Web 2.0 and the explosion of interest in social networking sites, many of these messages appear to have been forgotten. Alongside the many benefits that social networking sites may bring, including a sense of connectedness, keeping in touch with family members, friends and others, the social support that one may gain from social networking, there may also be negative aspects which may affect different social groups differentially (Barnes 2006).

The very group which makes most use of social networking sites and which may well find most benefit from them, namely young people, may also be the group that suffers disproportionately from negative aspects of these sites. For instance, the question of privacy on social networking sites has attracted considerable media attention (Goodstein 2007). Social networking sites actively encourage the sharing of personal, sometimes highly personal, information. Indeed the *raison d'être* of social networking sites is the sharing of personal information. The result is that young people seem surprisingly willing to give up their privacy online without realizing how they may become targets for advertising and marketing or predatory behaviour.

The recent furore regarding the difficulties of removing one's Facebook profile, where it is not enough to 'unsubscribe', one has to delete each file, adds to the privacy problem in that it is very difficult to remove personal data from the Internet once it is posted there.

The computer ethics problem described here relates to privacy (see Chapter 7). Much, although not all, of the problem concerns the way that information, which should be ephemeral, becomes persistent, if not actually permanent. The potentially unwanted persistence of personal data is, of course, a feature of networked ICTs. This is why UK data protection law, for example, mandates that personal data should not be held longer than is necessary. Leaving aside behaviour which is actively criminal or antisocial, it is a feature of youth to be able to get up to things away from an adult gaze and not to have the results of youthful high spirits follow one into adult life. This is surely part of growing up, part of constructing one's identity as a young person in a group. It could be argued that people are freely giving away personal data without coercion and it is natural for young people to do this by using ICTs. But they are doing so without a full understanding of the implications for their privacy and without an assurance that software suppliers understand the privacy implications of their software.

Potential pitfalls of social networking sites are not confined to failing to understand the implications of releasing personal data. Griffiths and Light (2008) have coined the term 'antisocial networking' to describe the scamming, stealing and bullying which can occur in social networking gaming sites. There are an increasing number of such game sites and the users of these can be regarded as consumers, as a credit card is required to purchase various virtual commodities necessary to play the game. Griffiths' and Light's (2008) analysis centres around one such game site, 'Habbo Hotel', where virtual rooms are furnished with 'furni' which can be bought, traded and won in the game. The software supplier deliberately increases the rarity, hence desirability, of some types of furni by only releasing rare pieces at specific times. As well as being bought, sold and traded, furniture can, of course, be stolen, signalling one of a range of antisocial behaviours (Griffiths and Light 2008). 'Cyberbullying' is the term coined to describe the bullying of children by children (e.g. see www.stopcyberbullying.org/). Complex social interactions are involved in these games. Some of these involve manipulation of a market by games' producers. Desirable commodities are made artificially rare. Antisocial behaviour follows.

9.4 Gender identity and ICTs

Turning to gender identity in relation to ICTs, for almost the whole of the lifetime of the digital computer, there has been considerable interest in the relative absence of women in computing and IT-related jobs (Grundy 1996). This must be balanced against the historical fact that many of the first human 'computers', i.e. the army of workers who performed mathematical calculations manually or with the aid of a mechanical calculator, were actually women (Grier 2005). As computing and IT developed as a clear career path in the 1970s and 1980s, rather than women becoming more encouraged to go into computing, the percentage of women in higher education in many countries actually dropped from around 25% of total numbers, to around 10% in the early 1980s. IT did not represent a new career path, potentially free from old gender stereotypes but quickly became a job for men.

In many ways this should not be seen as surprising. A number of authors, including Wajcman (2004) and Cockburn and Ormrod (1993) argue that technology, or at least prestigious technologies rather than domestic technologies, is related to masculinity to the extent that technology and masculinity mutually define each other. In other words, definitions of masculinity are bound up with skilled use of technology, while definitions of technology relate to masculine activity. This is not to say that there are no 'feminine' technologies – think of sewing and knitting. Historically, the production of clothing for the family was in the hands of women (Cowan 1989), yet sewing and knitting are not usually thought of as technologies and they are not regarded as skilled technologies with the same status as computer programming or engineering. There are no objective reasons why writing a computer program is seen as more skilled than, say, producing a knitting pattern (and then producing a garment from the pattern). Cookery, in the home, as a female technology is not regarded as particularly skilled. However the job of the chef, outside the home and usually male, is regarded as skilled. Skill appears to be more to do with whether an activity is designated masculine or feminine than with some absolute measure of skill.

It is useful to explore some of the implications of the claim that masculinity is entwined with technological skill and the ways in which this helps to explain why women may be discouraged from IT and computing education and careers. There have been a number of campaigns over the years to attract women into computing (Henwood 1993). These have often been coupled with campaigns to attract women into wider areas of science and engineering. Commentators have been quite critical of such efforts (Henwood 1993), arguing that campaigns which assume that technology is neutral and where women have to make all the changes to fit into technological careers, will not succeed unless men can change too. Such critiques can be set alongside research into women's working lives in IT. There is no doubt that IT and computing represent well-paid, interesting career choices which should be widely available. However, women can experience difficulties in a masculine workplace and can be marginalized and suffer pay discrimination (Adam *et al.* 2006). Although they are not always thought of as part of the agenda for computer ethics, some researchers have cast such issues explicitly as computer ethics problems (Turner 1998, 1999). This is useful, as it gives the potential to highlight the inequalities that still remain for women in the IT workplace. This is another example of an argument against technological determinism and for an alternative view which considers the mutual definition of technology and society.

If IT and computing workplaces are still problematic in gender terms, it is reasonable to ask whether there are issues to be addressed relating to the more widespread use of ICTs, given that ICTs and Internet usage have rapidly become pervasive in many societies. An important issue for computer ethics centres on the question of whether men and women receive equal treatment in Internet interactions. A considerable literature has developed on this topic (e.g. see bibliography in Adam (2005)). During the early years of the Internet's growth into a mass communication medium, there was a widespread utopian view that new technologies would spawn more egalitarian communities (as in early ideas about virtual communities). As outlined above, this was mirrored in the expectation that men and women would be equal in the IT workplace. Similarly, there was an assumption that gender relations would be more equal on the Internet. Once again, such views focus on the idea that new technology is free from old prejudices and that old patterns need not be played out in new technologies. The democratizing potential of new technologies has been an extraordinarily tenacious myth, but it is a myth based on technological determinism because it ignores the ways that social relations are already designed into technologies.

In the early 1990s, there was a view that women could be mistresses of the Internet and that the new communications technology held untold promise for women. This view found particular expression in 'cyberfeminism' (Plant 1997). However, cyberfeminism was criticized for not being rooted in women's real experiences, for being insufficiently political, for being uncritical of the technology on which it was based and, importantly, for being hopelessly utopian (Adam 1998). In the twenty-first century, one rarely hears of cyberfeminism.

At around the same time, research was published indicating that, in certain circumstances, women were not having the positive experiences that cyberfeminism seemed to promise. Herring's (1996) research on men's and women's posts in computer-mediated communication suggested that stereo-typical gender relations were being reproduced and even magnified online, with men more often using an aggressive, hostile style of interaction (termed 'flaming'), while women were more likely to use a supportive style. Reports of 'cyberstalking' began to appear from the early 1990s. These indicated that the majority of perpetrators are male, while the majority of victims are female. In the face of such behaviour, it becomes more difficult to maintain the view that the Internet offers a neutral space in gender terms, let alone the utopian space declared by cyberfeminism.

9.5   Disability identity and ICTs

Assistive technology has played an important part in the way that disability has historically been defined. This is because technology designed to assist disabled people has often been adapted from technology which was originally designed for those deemed 'able-bodied' (Adam and Kreps 2006). Unfortunately this reinforces a norm of 'able-bodiedness' against which disability is regarded as deficiency. The definition of disability, and how this relates to technology, is an important element in any theory that argues that disability is socially constructed and that society puts barriers in place that make some people disabled (Shakespeare 2006).

There are tensions between the social construction of disability model and older models of disability. Broadly speaking, the older models can be char-acterized in terms of charity and medical models of disability (Fulcher 1989). The medical model emphasizes impairment as loss, with the deficit seen as belonging to the individual. The professional status and assumed neutrality of medical judgement defines disability as an individual issue for medical judgement. The charity model sits alongside this view in assuming that dis-abled individuals are to be the objects of pity and require charity rather than necessarily having a set of rights within the welfare state and within govern-ment policy (Goggin and Newell 2000). However, a potentially more radical approach is offered by the social construction of disability model, which emphasizes that locating disability in the individual as opposed to society is a political decision.

Appropriate technology, and how it is used, is an integral part of the social model of disability. Indeed the social model argues that disability can be created by designing technology in such a way that some people cannot use it. However, there are tensions. As Goggin and Newell (2000, p. 128) note: 'Disability can thus be viewed as a constructed socio-political space, which is determined by dominant norms, the values found in technological systems, and their social context.' They argue that research has focused on analysis of particular types of impairment with the development of technical solutions specifically designed to address them. This reflects the dominant medical paradigm of disability (2000, p. 132). In other words, the dominant view is that there should be an individual technical solution for a specific impairment. As Moser (2006, p. 373) contends, technologies are strongly implicated in reinforcing what is taken to be 'normal', particularly when an assistive technology is designed against a norm of able-bodiedness. 'Technologies working within an order of the normal are implicated in the (re)production of the asymmetries they . . . seek to undo.'

There are important ways in which the story of assistive technology relates to technological determinism. If the trajectory of technologies designed for 'normal' people is taken for granted, this can be cast as a determinist view, which assumes that technologies for disabled people will always be designed in terms of a norm of non-disabled. Indeed, Goggin and Newell (2006, p. 310) argue that much work on disability and ICT proceeds 'as if it were "business as usual", in replicating charity, medical and other oppressive discourses of disability'. They argue that this maintenance of the *status quo* goes against the grain, not only of newer work on critical disability studies, but also research in science and technology studies which describes the way that technology and society mutually define each other. They suggest that notions of identity, the body, disability and dependence are changing rapidly. ICTs are involved in understanding these changes and the new ways of living based upon them, yet the area is under-researched, certainly in terms of disability.

Many governments regard connection to the Internet as a way of achieving social inclusion, although this view, in itself, can be seen as determinist, as it assumes that bridging the so-called 'digital divide', or the divide between those who have access to ICTs and those who do not, is a fairly uncomplicated question of getting people connected to digital technologies (Adam and Kreps 2006). Nevertheless, access to ICTs is crucial for taking advantage of a wide range of goods and services (including political and educational activities) as a consumer and a citizen. If there are barriers then ICTs will fail to increase social inclusion, at least in terms of including disabled users. Dobransky and Hargittai (2006) argue that there is a 'disability divide' on the Internet. Drawing on US data, their findings suggest that disabled people are less likely to live in households with a computer, less likely to use computers and less likely to be online. However, when socio-economic background is controlled for people with hearing and walking disabilities, it turns out that they use ICTs as much as the non-disabled population (Dobransky and Hargittai 2006, p. 313).

More specifically, research into web accessibility suggests that much of the World Wide Web remains inaccessible to people across a wide range of disabilities (Kreps and Adam 2006, Adam and Kreps 2006). This situation prevails, despite disability legislation, in many counties including the UK, USA and Australia. Such legislation clearly mandates that websites must be accessible. There have been attempts to regulate the Web and to produce standards for website design, to ensure accessibility. The World Wide Web Consortium (W3C) was developed as a standards-making body for the rapidly growing World Wide Web (W3C 2004). Part of its remit was the Web Accessibility Initiative (WAI), which published a set of Web Content Accessibility Guidelines (WCAG) in 1999. These guidelines are intended to guide the creation of web pages accessible to all regardless of disability.

While the will towards making the Web accessible is clearly important, the story is complex and reflects the interests of many different groups. Meanwhile much of the Web remains inaccessible so that web accessibility guidelines could fall into the 'empty shell' trap. Standardization, and who is involved in making the standards, is important, particularly when we consider that people who may be seriously affected by a particular set of standards may not be involved in setting them. Consider, for instance, Stienstra's (2006) case study of the Canadian Standards Association (CSA) relating to accessibility standards. The CSA acts as a neutral third party in its involvement of stakeholder groups, balancing representation between the competing interests of users, producers and government. Nevertheless, Stienstra argues that 'the standards system in Canada privileges the voices of industry while creating a discourse of public accountability and corporate social responsibility'. Furthermore, she argues that the development of industry standards is always a way of oiling the wheels of the market, strengthening it rather than challenging it, acting as a key determinant in economic competitiveness. Standards are then key to 'market-perfecting' (Stienstra 2006, p. 343).

It is difficult to see how the W3C and WAI can escape the kinds of criticisms that Stienstra (2006) makes of the CSA, a body which has made serious attempts to be inclusive in its membership, whereas it is difficult to find evidence that the WAI has attempted to be inclusive. For instance, Boscarol (2006) claims that WCAG Working Group does not publish information about what user-focused research its members used to create WCAG 1.0, the first set of published guidelines. He also contends that discussion revolves round technical points rather than real-world behaviour, which can only be captured by user-focused research.

While Boscarol argues for less technical discussion and more real-world research, Clark (2006), a well-known critic of WAI activities, points to the corporate interests involved in the making of web accessibility guidelines. The new guidelines (WCAG 2.0) are designed to apply generally (not just to HTML), they are hugely complicated and difficult to apply (Clark 2006, p. 3). Paradoxically, it is possible to write an accessible site that would fail accessibility guidelines, but, at the same time, it is possible to produce a website which would adhere to many of the guidelines, despite being inaccessible to many users. Following the criticisms of Boscarol (2006) and Clark (2006) it is difficult to see the involvement of disability groups in the production of these increasingly unwieldy web accessibility guidelines. The membership of WCAG WG reflects the interests of large corporations, which are tacitly adopting something similar to a medical model of disability, by assuming that they know best how to design accessible websites without involving disabled users. In itself, this is a form of technological determinism, as it assumes the technology is neutral and can be 'fixed' by technological means to suit a group of users without acknowledging how disability is defined and made through the use of technology.

9.6   Older people and the Internet

Young people are quick to take up new technologies and to find ways of weaving them into their lives. Nevertheless there is evidence that ICTs offer a number of positive benefits to older groups. White *et al.* (2002) present evidence to show that Internet use can help older adults avoid social isolation as frequent contact with family and friends, opportunities to revisit former interests and ways of meeting new people are made available. These results are confirmed by Shapira *et al.* (2007) whose study of a group of older adults (mean age of 80) demonstrated that Internet and computer use contributed to a sense of well-being and empowerment, improved cognitive function and promoted feelings of independence and personal control. However, the potential of the Internet in older people's lives must be set against the problems of confidence in use of computer technologies. A study by Marquie *et al.* (2002) suggests that older adults may lack confidence in their abilities to use digital technology and this may be a possible source of difficulties that the elderly may have in mastering ICTs. This is confirmed by a UK study (Ofcom 2008) of consumers of communications services. The study found that, while the use of communications services is growing in the UK, there is still a gap between older and younger users. Take up of digital communications is growing fast among older users with content services, i.e. television, radio and Internet representing the most popular areas. Older users are keen users of communications services on the Internet with 63% of over 65s communicating online compared to 76% of all adults (Ofcom 2008, 42). Mobile phone usage was significantly lower among older adults. Older adults were less likely to use social networking sites and were less trusting of information available on the Internet. These findings suggest that much of the potential of advanced ICTs to ameliorate the lives of older people has yet to be realized. Studies suggest positive benefits and take-up is gradually increasing. Despite this, confidence in using advanced technologies remains low. This remains the main demarcation between older and younger users.

9.7   Conclusion

The aim of this chapter is to provide a means of thinking of inequalities in relation to the design and use of ICTs, arguing that equality is often expressed as a liberal value, which rests on a view of the relationship of technology and society that is determinist in inspiration. This is particularly important when the adoption of ICTs is increasingly bound up with identity, in making communities, in gender identity, in terms of the construction of disability and in terms of age. Hopes for virtual communities were initially often based on a utopian vision. The idea that democracy would spontaneously emerge in Internet interactions, and that new technologies are free from old prejudices, has been difficult to shift. The experiences of young people using social networking technologies, women in the IT industry and on the Internet, disabled people accessing ICTs and older users, particularly of the World Wide Web, demonstrate a complex picture of a world which is still unequal and where old inequalities prevail. Although equality legislation is important it cannot alleviate deep-seated inequalities such as those caused by inaccessible websites where it would be impossible to bring legal action against every website designer who failed to make their site accessible. Similarly, simply providing access to technology does not break down barriers of inequality. Younger people often have no trouble using new technologies but they remain unaware of privacy choices in relation to their technology use, choices which they may regret later when it becomes clear that it is difficult to retract personal data on the Internet. Older users may gain significant benefits from using new technologies but may lack confidence. This points to the need for programmes to create virtual communities from real communities where the needs of different groups are acknowledged and addressed (Sunderland City Council 2008).

10 Global information and computer ethics

Charles Ess and May Thorseth

10.1 Introduction

Information and Computing Ethics (ICE), as made clear in the diverse chapters included in this volume, address a range of ethical and political issues raised by the development and diffusion of Information and Communication Technologies (ICTs), such as privacy, intellectual property and copyright, freedom of speech, pornography and violence in computer games. However, while ICTs and our first efforts to come to grips with their ethical impact were long the province of 'the West', ICTs are no longer technologies exclusive to developed countries. Rather, ICTs have spread around the world at a staggering rate, both in the form of 'traditional' ICTs, such as desktop and laptop computers, and the networks that connect them, and in the form of 'smart phones', i.e., mobile phones with ever-increasing computing power and ever-increasing bandwidth connection with the Internet and the World Wide Web. Along with these technologies come additional applications (e.g., online shopping and financial transactions) and capabilities (e.g., GPS devices and chips in mobile phones that allow for easy navigation – as well as 'participatory surveillance' (Albrechtslund 2008)) that increasingly pervade and redefine our lives. Such devices and applications dramatically expand the reach and powers of ICTs around the globe, especially in developing countries.

This means that ICE is forced to confront a range of novel ethical issues and contexts occasioned by the global diffusion of ICTs. They are novel because, first, these issues and contexts do not characteristically emerge in conjunction with the use of ICTs within the ethical and cultural traditions of 'the West'. And second, because our efforts to come to grips with the ethical matters evoked by ICTs must take on board the recognition that these matters are analysed and resolved in often radically diverse ways by people around the globe, as our frameworks for ethical analysis and resolution are shaped by often radically diverse cultures. This is to say that such core matters as what counts as 'privacy', intellectual 'property', 'pornography' and so forth are in large measure dependent upon culturally specific views, beliefs, practices and traditions. As we will see, a key challenge for a *global* ICE is thus how to foster the development of *diverse* ICEs – i.e., ICEs that incorporate and preserve the norms, ethical traditions, beliefs and practices of a given culture – while at the same time fostering a *shared* ICE that 'works' across the globe. In other words, globally diffused ICTs perforce make us all citizens of the world (*cosmopolitans*), and our interactions with one another require a global, not simply a local ICE.

In this chapter, we introduce and explore these matters in the following way. In Section 10.2, we take up three of the issues distinctively evoked by globally diffused ICTs – (1) the digital divide, (2) online global citizenship and (3) global deliberation and democratization. In Section 10.3, we will explore *ethical pluralism* as a primary framework within which we may take up a global range of diverse ethical frameworks and decision-making traditions used to analyse and reflect upon characteristic issues of ICE. In the course of the analysis we will use the core issue of privacy as our primary example.

10.2 Global issues

The history of ICE is discussed in this volume in the contribution by Terry Bynum. Here, it suffices to recall that ICE has emerged in the West over the past six decades, beginning with the work of Norbert Wiener (1948), as primarily the concern of a handful of computer scientists and interested philosophers. Most importantly for our purposes, a number of philosophers rightly predicted in the 1990s that ICE would become a mainstream component of applied ethics and philosophy – not only in the developed world, but around the world. Indeed, less than a decade into the twenty-first century, ICTs now connect over 1.463+ billion people around the globe, the equivalent of more than one fifth of the world's population (21.9%) (Internet World Stats 2008).

This dramatic diffusion of ICTs beyond their territories of origin leads to a number of pressing ethical concerns, beginning with the Digital Divide. For, despite the utopian visions of 1990s pundits (and their contemporary counterparts), 'wiring the world' (e.g., PBS 1998) with computers and networks has not, as once hoped, led to greater equality either within nations or between them with regard to access to and usability of ICTs.

10.2.1 Digital divide

Proponents of globalization argue that, as trade and markets expand, greater economic prosperity will follow. In terms of overall impacts, they are quite correct (Marber 2005). But a central problem that follows in the train of this increased economic activity is that the disparities between the rich and the poor continue to grow, not shrink. The old phrase, 'the rich get richer, and the poor stay poor', remains a cruel truth about globalization – and this is the case not only within countries, but also between countries (Beitz 2001, p. 106).

ICTs are intimately interwoven with globalization. Along with (until recently) relatively inexpensive transportation costs, ICTs are a primary driver of globalization as they make possible trade, financial transactions and the relocation of labour into lower-cost labour markets (e.g., Friedmann 2005). A key problem here, however, is that this global diffusion tends to benefit a small elite; these benefits, moreover, do not always 'trickle down'. Consider for example how computer scientists and programmers in India have become ever more well-to-do as ICTs allow them to sell their skills to companies around the globe – but at a considerably lower cost than, say, a programmer or computer scientist in the United States and Europe. At the same time, this outflow of money and capital into India means the (roughly) equivalent loss of jobs and salaries in Europe and the US. And while a growing number of highly skilled and well-trained Indian professionals certainly benefit, by and large, these benefits remain restricted to a very small group of people, and thereby tend to increase the disparities between the urban rich and the rural poor within India (e.g., Ghemawat 2007).

The digital divide further points towards other, perhaps more fundamental divisions, sometimes put in terms of 'the information rich' vs. 'the information poor' (Britz 2007). This contrast emphasizes that access to the nearly unlimited amounts of information made available through ICTs makes all the difference in terms of (further) developing one's own resources and capabilities. So, for example, Deborah Wheeler (2006) has documented how women in traditional Middle Eastern villages, once given access to ICTs, are able to develop small businesses that exploit the Internet for advertising, finding lower-cost materials, and so forth. The example highlights a further element of the digital divide, which Bourdieu called 'social capital' (1977). In order to take these sorts of advantages of ICTs, people must not only have access to the technologies but also have the multiple skills required to make effective use of them, beginning with literacy. This social capital, in turn, is not equally distributed – especially in many developing countries. The consequence is, again, that those who already enjoy a given level of social capital are able to build on that capital to their advantage through increased access to ICTs, while those poor in social capital will not.

To be sure, there are important initiatives and exceptions to these trends, inspired in part, for example, through the growing use of 'Free/Libre and Open Source Software' (FLOSS). The development of interfaces for non-literate populations, including indigenous peoples, will also help overcome some of the barriers between the information rich and poor (Dyson, Hendriks and Grant 2007). Finally, as Internet-enabled mobile phones continue their dramatic expansion in the developing world, they will almost certainly help the poor jump past ('leapfrog') ICT use and access in the form of traditional computers, and, perhaps, help diffuse the benefits of ICTs somewhat more evenly.

The digital divide opens up a range of critical ethical questions. For example, what obligations, if any, do the 'information rich' citizens and governments of developed countries have towards the information poor – beginning with those within their own countries, as well as towards those in developing countries? (Canellopoulou-Bottis and Himma 2008) And if the information rich do have some sort of obligation to help the information poor, what forms of assistance are ethically justified? For example, a major initiative has been launched to ensure that all schools in Africa (550,000+) will have Internet access by the year 2020 (Farrell, Isaacs and Trucano 2007). But building the network infrastructure and providing the computers necessary to make this happen will utterly depend upon the generosity of such companies as Hewlett-Packard, Cisco Systems and Microsoft. Once these networks are in place, however, it increasingly becomes the responsibility of the recipients of these technologies to pay for their continued use and maintenance. It is not at all clear that many of the African schools and countries will be able to do so; and insofar as they are able to do so, this will mean financial flows out of Africa back to the already well-to-do developed countries. Many in Africa – for whom the memories of Western colonization and exploitation are quite fresh and clear – are hence critical of such projects, as they run the risk of repeating such exploitation and colonization, now via ICTs.

10.2.2   Online global citizenship

Despite the harsh realities of the digital divide, as noted above, ICTs now allow more than one fifth of the world's population to communicate cross-culturally. Studies indicate that the majority of users send and receive information (whether in the form of emails, browsing web pages, shopping, etc.) within their national borders or within shared linguistic communities (Ghemawat 2007). At the same time, however, anyone's web pages and emails may in principle cross cultural boundaries, whether intentionally or inadvertently. This means that, like it or not, our access and use of ICTs increasingly makes us citizens of the world – *cosmo-politans*.

Insofar as more and more of us do cross borders online, we are confronted with the range of ethical issues humans have faced throughout their history of cross-cultural exchanges and interactions. Some of these are obvious, beginning with the importance of showing respect for the cultural values, norms, practices and beliefs of others, partly because these make up a given cultural identity. One's right to the recognition and preservation of one's own cultural identity is a hallmark human right in the United Nations' Universal Declaration of Universal Human Rights (1948). Yet our cross-cultural interactions online, at least in their current versions, hide or fail to transmit the full reality of the other. This is especially true when we communicate with those who have limited bandwidth access to the Internet – i.e., primarily those in developing countries. In these interactions, we usually have access to one another primarily (if not exclusively) via text; this textual access may be complemented with sound and pictures, but these are usually very limited in quality and detail. In contrast with our real-world, embodied, face-to-face engagements with other human beings in different cultures our online engagements present us with an Other who is largely disembodied, abstract, 'virtual'. It is hence much easier in the online context to assume that this 'thin' Other is simply another version of ourselves – i.e., to assume that her values, beliefs, practices, etc. are more or less identical to our own. This assumption has a name: *ethnocentrism* is precisely the view that the values, beliefs, practices, etc. of our own people (*ethnos*) are the same for all people. The serious difficulty is that such ethnocentrism almost always leads to a two-fold response to the Other. Either we, in effect, remake the Other in our own image – at the extreme, we insist on the assimilation of the Other to our own ways and values: this is the root of cultural imperialism. Or, insofar as the Other fails to fit our presumptions of what counts as *human*, we may feel justified in exploiting – or even destroying – the Other for our own benefit. The ugly examples of this second consequence include slavery, colonization and genocide. So, our online global citizenship, as it re-presents to us a thin concept of the Other, makes it easier to fall prey to the twin dangers of cultural imperialism and exploitation. It is a commonplace in ethics that greater vulnerabilities require greater care. In this case, because the online environment makes both us and others more vulnerable to the risks of imperialism and exploitation, we have a greater ethical obligation to be aware of these risks and to develop strategies to avoid them.

A particular set of these dangers is facilitated by the technologies themselves. For one may assume that ICTs are just tools, that they are somehow neutral in terms of important cultural values. This assumption is called *technological instrumentalism* (Shrader-Frechette and Westra 1997). It is powerfully countered in two important ways. First, many philosophers as well as designers of technologies increasingly recognize a view called the Social Construction of Technology (SCOT). This view argues that technologies embed and foster the values of their designers – values that vary from culture to culture (e.g., Bijker and Law 1992). Second, there is now an extensive body of evidence with regard to ICTs and Computer-Mediated Communication (CMC) that make clear that, indeed, ICTs embed and foster the cultural values and communicative preferences of their designers. So, for example, especially the CMC technologies available in the 1990s relied almost entirely on text; such a technology thereby favours what communication theorists describe as Low Context/High Content communication styles – styles that emphasize explicit and direct forms of communication (high content, with comparatively less attention to the contexts of communication including relative social status, for example). By contrast, many cultures and societies – including Arabic, Asian, African and indigenous peoples – utilize a High Context/ Low Content communication style. Here the emphasis is much more on indirect forms of communication such as body distance, eye contact (and lack thereof), gesture, etc. – i.e., forms of communication not easily carried via text-centred CMC. Enthusiasm for wiring the world via Western-designed ICTs favouring Low Context/High Content communication styles may work to impose the communication style of one set of peoples and cultures upon another. Our use of such ICTs may risk functioning as a tacit but powerful form of cultural imperialism, as we insist that others move from their own High Context/Low Content communication style to our own Low Context/High Content style (Ess 2006b).

As global citizens, then, we are ethically obliged to develop a greater awareness of the cultures and communicative preferences of the multiple Others we can now engage with online. Like the cosmopolitans of the ancient world and the Western Renaissance, we must learn and respect the values, practices, beliefs, communication styles and languages of 'the Other'. Failure to do so threatens to turn us instead into cultural tourists or cultural consumers – those who regard other cultures as largely commodities to be consumed for their own enjoyment, rather than to be understood and respected for their own sake. More dramatically, failure to do so threatens to make us complicit in forms of computer-mediated imperialism and colonization (Ess 2006b). Happily, globalization via ICTs brings with it far more positive possibilities as well, as we are about to see.

10.2.3   Global deliberation and democratization

Before examining democratic deliberation in detail, we must first note that such deliberation requires a plurality of voices. There is yet another aspect of plurality that is embedded in the very idea of deliberative democracy. This is pluralism as a contrast to both relativism and fundamentalism. The contrast to relativism is that judgements are not considered to be legitimate only relative to some particular framework. This is because pluralism also requires that the framework itself be justified. Whereas a moral relativist cannot claim that her own position is true beyond the particular context, we want moral pluralism to hold some, but not all positions to be equally valid or true. In an epistemological sense, relativism is not a consistent position; in a moral sense, it obstructs the claim that democracy ought to be preferred to fundamentalism (Thorseth 2007). In order to maintain pluralism as an ideal of modern (multicultural) societies, it is a requirement that we not only understand but also undertake substantive judgements of public opinions.

Without getting into this huge debate topic here, we shall confine ourselves to pointing out the importance of making judgements about particular opposing norms and values, rather than tolerating them by leaving them alone. The potential dialogue with others, which is basic to deliberative democracy and enlarged way of thinking, may serve as an ideal of the kind of judgement that moral pluralism requires. We will further see, in the next section, that these notions of pluralism and judgement play central roles in the development of an emerging global Information and Computer Ethics.

Here we focus on the communicative dimension of globalization, more particularly as displayed in the contemporary debates on global deliberation and deliberative democracy. A basic idea of deliberation is free and open communication, based on 'the unforced force of the better argument' (Habermas 1983, 1990, 1993). According to John Dryzek (2001), deliberation is a mode of communication making deliberators amenable to changing judgements, views and preferences during the course of interactions. The core idea of democratic deliberation is to contribute to a better-informed public. Deliberative democrats, along with so-called 'difference democrats', share this basic ideal. Whereas most deliberative democrats exclude some modes of communication, in particular rhetoric, difference democrats hold that rhetoric is a basic means of persuasion in deliberation. Allowing for different modes of communication implies that deliberation becomes more easily accessible to disempowered people in particular, they hold. Thus, a wider range of people may participate in public deliberation (Gutman and Thompson 1996, Young 2000). Across the internal differences between these theories, both deliberative and difference democrats share the basic ideal of recognizing a plurality of opinions in democratic deliberation. The dispute between them is about the extent to which different communicative styles actually do contribute to open and unforced argumentation in the public domain. An important question in our context is to what extent the Internet might facilitate global deliberation.

10.2.4   A broadened way of thinking in public deliberation

Difference democrats have claimed that the mode of communication in deliberation may presuppose an ideal of mainstream rational argumentation that often tends to exclude the language of the underprivileged. The same argument does, however, apply to any mode of communication that might turn out to work against inclusion and to build new hierarchies. Habermas' ideal of the unforced force of the better argument only works as intended if all individuals involved share an equal communicative competence. Hence, storytelling and testimony might be even as excluding as dispassionate and reasoned talk. All communication in terms set by the powerful will advantage those who are best able to articulate their opinions. Thus, any kind of communication may entail coercion. This is why we need additional criteria for identifying what mode of communication and way of thinking are suitable for democratic deliberation. Except for excluding in deliberation any kind of communication that works coercively, another test mentioned by Dryzek (2001, p. 68) is the requirement to connect the particular (story, testimony) to a universal appeal. This implies transcending private subjective conditions, a requirement that may be linked to Kant's conception of reflective judgement, as we shall see below.

The main point of deliberation is to make people judge their own and other people's opinions critically. First and foremost, changes of opinions or preferences should be the outcome of better-qualified opinions, as compared to the quality of opinions ahead of deliberation. Embedded in the idea of deliberation is the anticipation of a pluralism in terms of a *plurality* of voices. Both Rawls and Bohman have emphasized the importance of people agreeing for different reasons, i.e. overlapping consensus (Rawls 1993, Bohman 1996). The importance of pluralism is also clearly stated by A. Phillips (1995, p. 151) when she holds that deliberation matters only because there is difference.

In order for an opinion to qualify as a public and not only private opinion, it is important to address a universal audience. This is an explicit aim of democratic deliberation. Public recognition by way of transcending the purely private and subjective condition is basic to the Kantian notion of reflective judgement or a broadened way of thinking (Kant 1952). Reflective judgement is about empirical contingencies – e.g. political opinions – for which validity is gained through reflection of something particular as opposed to subsuming something under universal laws. This is a mode of thinking that Kant initially explores in the aesthetic domain, whereas Hannah Arendt (1968) and Seyla Benhabib (1992) have extended it to the political and moral faculties (Thorseth 2008). Kant's broadened way of thinking is a mode of thinking that transcends local and private conditions. The method described by Kant is contained in his concept of *sensus communis*. This is a public sense and a critical faculty that takes account of the mode of representation in everyone else, thereby avoiding the illusion that private personal conditions are taken as objective. This is accomplished by weighing the judgement with the possible judgements of others, and by putting ourselves in the position of everyone else, abstracting from the limitations that contingently affect our estimate (Kant 1952, § 40). What interests us here is how this public use of reason, described by Kant, captures an essential point of deliberation: in order to address a universal audience to gain validity of opinions we have to transcend the limitations set by private and contingent conditions.

Kant's enlarged mode of thinking is about how to stimulate the imaginative powers in people in order to transcend the purely private subjective conditions of empirical contingencies. And ICTs may improve our imaginative capacity to put ourselves in the position of everyone else (Thorseth 2008).

10.2.5   Deliberation by way of new technology

Ideally, the outcome of deliberation is change of preferences due to possibilities of viewing matters from the position of everyone else. This implies an empirical challenge to make it feasible for people to be informed about other people's positions. What is at stake is not so much to have knowledge of as many opinions as possible; rather, it is giving people access to the outcome of deliberative processes. We are faced with what John Dewey (1927) called 'the problem of the public': the lack of shared experiences, signs and symbols which he takes to be the Babel of our time (Dewey 1927, p. 142). The main reason for our Babel is the political complexity that requires both a better-informed public but also a need for policy makers to become better informed of the experiences of the public. According to Dewey 'the essential need . . . is the improvement of the methods and conditions of debate, discussion and persuasion. This is *the* problem of the public' (Dewey 1927, p. 208). The problem of the public is revitalized due to ICTs as they offer both solutions but also new challenges to this much older philosophical problem of conditions for public debate.

One way of dealing with the problem of the public is to establish procedures for deliberation, in order to inform both the public and policy makers of opinions that are based on an enlarged way of thinking. The essential issue is that legitimacy of opinions through deliberation has gained validity in the public domain. The transcendence of private subjective conditions is obtained because the opinion addresses a universal audience. James Fishkin has suggested a method for such deliberative processes online, and several trials have been carried out (Fishkin 1997, Ackerman and Fishkin 2004). The suggested model is labelled online deliberative polling, the aim being to contribute to better-informed democracy. Briefly, the method is first to poll a representative sample of some targeted issue, e.g. on health care and education. After the first baseline poll, members of the sample are invited to gather in some place in order to discuss the issues together with competing experts and politicians. After the deliberation, the sample group is again asked the original question. The resulting changes of opinions represent the conclusion the public would reach if they had the opportunity to become better informed and more engaged in the issue.

The positive results of these experiments is that people tend to have less extreme, more complex and better argued opinions of the issues after deliberative polling (Elgesem 2005). Another important observation is that there is no sign of more consensus among the participants after deliberative polling, but no sign of more polarization either (Fishkin 1997). What the experiment shows is that deliberation might be very well suited for improvement of people's opinions (Thorseth 2006).

Technologically, it is no doubt feasible to design set-ups and websites such that people can easily encounter opposing and different views. In principle, it seems to be possible to use ICTs, at least partly, to deal with the problem of the public: to inform people of a plurality of opinions that have been improved through deliberative processes. Cass Sunstein's worries about group polarization seem manageable (2001). However, in natural surroundings we know far too little about another problem discussed by Sunstein, i.e. the problem of filtering. Put briefly, most people will visit web pages that they are particularly interested in, and thereby meet like-minded people, for instance from a particular political party. The argument pool that is offered might be too limited. The worst scenario is that people start designing their own 'Daily Me', i.e. newspapers where they can read about only what they have chosen themselves. Rather than being better informed about a plurality of different views, everyone would only read their own version of a limited range of topics.

In the US, a very interesting web-based deliberative polling project has been created, the Public Informed Citizen Online Assembly (PICOLA) which has been developed by Robert Cavalier.[1] It takes its point of departure in the theory of deliberative polling as developed by Fishkin. PICOLA is primarily a tool for carrying out deliberative polling in online contexts. One objective is to create the next generation of Computer-Mediated Communication tools for online structured dialogue and deliberation. An audio/video synchronous environment is complemented with a multimedia asynchronous environment. A general gateway (the PICOLA) contains access to these communication environments as well as registration areas, background information and surveys (polls). The PICOLA user interface allows for a dynamic multimedia participant environment. On the server side, secure user authentication and data storage/retrieval are provided. Real-time audio conferencing and certain peer-to-peer features are implemented using a Flash Communication Server.

Mobile PICOLA extends the synchronous conversation module and the survey module. The former provides a true 'anytime/anywhere' capability to the deliberative poll; the latter allows for real-time data input and analysis. And with real-time data gathering, it becomes possible to display the results of a deliberative poll at the end of the deliberation day, thereby allowing stakeholders and others present to see and discuss the results as those results are being displayed. The interface relations made possible by this technology are of vital importance to the deliberative process, as it allows for synchronous conversation in real time. Thus, it appears to come very close to offline interface communication.

This project demonstrates the feasibility of arranging for online deliberation at a trans-national level. Perhaps it would be possible also to arrange for it

---

[1] Visit Cavalier's homepage at www.hss.cmu.edu/philosophy/faculty-cavalier.php. More information about the PICOLA project is accessible at http://caae.phil.cmu.edu/picola/index.html

on a global scale. One immediate limitation would probably be that only democratic countries would be likely to consent to it.

Several other reports on online deliberation are discussed by Coleman and Gøtze (2001/2004). Some of their examples are drawn from experiments of deliberation between local politicians and their electors. Even if a deliberative mode and structure of communication is obtained throughout the trial, there is a decline in deliberation as soon as the period of the trial has ended. Besides, the scope of the experiments discussed is of limited or local scope, and thus they are not comparable to a global level of communication.

There are as yet no conclusive answers as to whether online deliberative polling can deal with the real problem of the public, namely how to achieve the aim of a better informed public. What is really at stake is how to make people overcome the limitations that contingently affect their judgements. In order to avoid the problem of filtering there is a need for a plurality of voices and modes of communication: cool and impassionate, emotional use of rhetoric and storytelling just to mention a few of those discussed by deliberative and difference democrats. People's access to such a plurality may be enhanced through new information technologies, in particular the Internet. However, there are as yet serious limitations as well, most importantly because of shortage of democratic states on a global scale, and the digital divide. The potential of ICTs to contribute to worldwide deliberative democracy can only be realized if there is a political consensus to make the new technology contribute in this way. An immediate objection is that such consensus is itself a contested matter, especially as freedom of speech is a pivotal and intrinsic democratic ideal. Thus, there seems to be an opposition between freedom of speech and a plurality of opinions safeguarding democracy on the one hand, and the need to control the democratic process through arranged deliberation in order to protect those very same values on the other. A way of resolving this dilemma is to consider democratic procedures beyond dispute and not at the same level as, for instance, religious or political outlooks. Rather, democratic procedures are a guarantor of possible disputes about opinions and outlooks.

There are obvious limitations to using the Internet for deliberative democratic purposes, but there is another way in which new technology might contribute to broadening people's minds beyond experimental deliberative projects. Keeping in mind the importance of access to possible though not necessarily real worlds, we still know very little about the impact virtual worlds may have in shaping people's opinions. Given the central role of imagination and the visual in Kant's notion of *sensus communis* and a broadened way of thinking, it seems probable that experiences in Second Life, for example, are conceived as real experiences that visitors have. Further, there is no reason why the experiences in virtual worlds should have less impact on people's opinions compared to real-life experiences. Acting in such virtual worlds might prove to be a method of broadening people's minds and enabling them to envisage possible scenarios that are not realised in the 'real', i.e. offline world. As yet it remains to research in further depth and width in which ways the virtuality of new technology might contribute to better informed publics realising the ideals embedded in deliberative democracy.

10.3   Global ethics

10.3.1   Global perspectives on privacy: from relativism to pluralism?

Various forms of ethical pluralism emerge across the history of Western philosophy – beginning with what Ess has called Plato's *interpretive pluralism* as developed primarily in *The Republic* (Ess and Thorseth 2006, Ess 2006a). Briefly, as the analogy of the line 509d–511e makes especially clear, a single norm – e.g., justice, beauty, or the Good as such – allows for multiple interpretations and applications in diverse contexts and settings. That is, every ethical situation arises within a specific context, one defined by a field of particularities. To apply a general norm – e.g., the well-being or harmony of the community – to one such context requires a specific interpretation or application; the same norm, applied to a different context defined by a different set of particularities, may require a very different interpretation or understanding. For example, the well-being or harmony of the community in the harsh environment of Inuit peoples may justify a form of assisted suicide for elderly family members no longer able to contribute to the material well-being of the community. Such assisted suicide in developed countries, however, can be seen as a violation of the general norm of community well-being: materially supporting the continued existence of elderly persons does not, as in the case of the Inuit, directly threaten the society's material basis. Developed countries can afford to sustain those persons who can no longer contribute materially to society. And the wisdom and experience of the elders, in turn, can contribute to the well-being and harmony of the community in distinctive ways. The key point is that while assisted suicide is appropriate in the Inuit community, and rejected as abhorrent in developed societies, both practices represent simply different interpretations or applications of a shared norm, where these differences are required by the distinctive contexts and particular conditions of two very diverse societies.

Hence, apparently *different* ethical responses – e.g., either among diverse individuals or across cultures – do not necessarily imply *ethical relativism*, i.e., the lack of any shared norms or values. On the contrary, these differences may simply reflect how the field of particularities, which constitute a specific context and thereby define the ethical issues we face, *require* us to interpret or apply a general norm in a highly distinctive way, one that makes the general norm applicable to a specific context.

Moreover, the ability to discern how to apply general norms to distinctively different contexts – along with the still more fundamental ability to discern which general norms or values indeed apply to a distinctive field of particularities – is associated, both by Plato and by Aristotle, to *phronesis*, a particular sort of practical wisdom or judgement that cannot be reduced to purely deductive or algorithmic approaches to ethical decision-making. *Phronesis* allows us to negotiate and manoeuvre between often complex and conflicting norms and claims. Indeed, Plato's image of the pilot (*cybernetes*) as the analogue or symbol of the ethical person in the *Republic* suggests that *phronesis* is not always solely a matter of a *logos*, of reason or argument:

a first-rate pilot [*cybernetes*] or physician, for example, feels [διαισθάνεται] the difference between the impossibilities and possibilities in his art and attempts the one and lets the others go; and then, too, if he does happen to trip, he is equal to correcting his error. (*Republic*, 360e-361a, Bloom trans.; cf. *Republic* I, 332e-c; VI, 489c[2])

Here, διαισθάνεται (literally, to 'feel through') suggests that it is not simply our mind that is at work in these moments of judgement: in addition, we engage the capacity, we might say, of an embodied being to sense or feel her way through – a capacity based in part on rational calculation and in part on long experience. We will return to this theme in the comments below on Susan Stuart's recent work on enactivism.

Versions of such pluralism have been developed in the Western tradition, beginning with Aristotle, whose 'focal' (*pros hen*) equivocals further highlight the role of *phronesis* or practical wisdom and judgement in discerning how general norms apply to the particularities of a given situation (Ess 2006a, 2007). Within the Christian tradition, Aquinas famously adapts Aristotle to Christian frameworks – and elaborates on Aristotle's notion of *phronesis*. Given the possibility of more than one understanding or application of a general principle, especially vis-à-vis often very different contexts, Aquinas explicitly justifies a pluralism that acknowledges that shared general principles may be interpreted or applied in diverse ways, depending upon particular contexts – an application again dependent upon the peculiar facility of *judgement* (*Summa Theologiae*, 1-2, q. 94, a. 4 *responsio*, cited in Haldane 2003, p. 91). More contemporary theory has proposed various forms of pluralism and incorporated these into political philosophy (e.g., Taylor 2002) as well as into ICE, beginning with the work of Larry Hinman (2004, 2008), Terrell Ward Bynum (2000a, 2001, 2006b), and, as we shall see in more detail, Luciano Floridi (2006a, forthcoming, b.).

---

[2] Following standard practice among Plato scholars, page references are to the Stephanus volume and page number.

10.3.2   Pluralism: West and East

But first, we must observe that such pluralism and its affiliated emphasis on the central role of judgement are not restricted to the Western tradition. On the contrary, such pluralism is an important element of Islam (Eickelman 2003) and Confucian thought (Chan 2003). In addition, notions of *harmony* and *resonance* likewise emerge in both Western and Eastern traditions as still further ways to express the distinctive 'unity-alongside-difference' that defines pluralism. So, for example, harmony is a goal of politics both for Aristotle and Confucian thought (Elberfeld 2002). Such harmony does not mean some sort of universal norm is applied heavy-handedly in exactly the same way in every situation, regardless of crucial differences. On the contrary, harmony is understood as relationship of unity that simultaneously preserves and fosters the irreducible differences defining specific members and classes of a community.

This means, then, that ethical pluralism not only provides us with a way of understanding how a single norm may – via the reflection and application of *judgement* - apply in very different contexts in very different ways – including, as we are about to see, with regard to notions of privacy in diverse Western cultures (i.e., United States and the European Union). Such pluralism also appears to function in *praxis* with regard to emerging conceptions of privacy across the East–West divide. Insofar as very similar understandings of pluralism, judgement and harmony are found in both Western and Eastern traditions, these three elements suggest themselves as potentially universal constituents of a global ICE that may conjoin shared norms and elements with the irreducible differences defining diverse cultures.

As an initial example, consider the matter of individual privacy and data privacy protection laws as understood and developed in the United States and the European Union. On the one hand, both domains share a characteristically modern, Western assumption – that the individual *person* exists as a primary reality and, especially as capable of rational choice and autonomy, deserves at least a minimal set of *rights*, including a right to privacy. Such a conception of the individual *qua* rationally autonomous and rights-holder is foundational to modern conceptions and justifications of liberal democracies: such states exist to protect the rights of such persons, their legitimate powers resting upon the free *consent* of the governed (so Thomas Jefferson in *The Declaration of Independence*). On this basis, finally, individual privacy in the Information Age translates into rights of data privacy protection. Especially as our lives depend more and more upon the transmission of information central to our identities and functions as persons, consumers, citizens, etc., there is a correlative need to protect our privacy by way of protecting our data (e.g., Floridi 2006a, Tavani 2007, Burk 2007).

So far, so good. But these shared conceptions have nonetheless issued in quite different data privacy protection regimes in the US, on the one hand, and the EU, on the other. As refracted through the more utilitarian and business-friendly lenses of US culture, the shared value of the individual and the need for data privacy protection have issued in a patchwork of laws: a few Federal laws define privacy rights in the areas of medical and financial information – leaving more rigorous protection of individual data privacy up to states and individuals, e.g., as individuals may 'opt-out' of certain data-gathering schemes. By contrast, the EU Data Privacy Protection acts are based on a much more strongly deontological insistence that individual privacy is a right requiring rigorous protection by the state. So the Directives define what counts as personal and sensitive information, e.g., not simply name and address, but also regarding health status, religious and philosophical beliefs, trade union membership and sexual identity, and require that individuals be notified when such information is collected about them. Individuals further have the right to review and, if necessary, correct information collected about them. In particular, as Dan Burk points out, the EU laws work exactly *opposite* to the US emphasis on individuals 'opting out' – i.e., leaving data privacy protection to individual initiative. By contrast, EU laws give individuals the *right to consent* – i.e., they must first 'opt-in' by agreeing to the collection and processing of their personal information (Burk 2007, p. 98). In these ways, the contrasts between US and EU data privacy protection laws represent a *pluralism*. Again, the US and EU appear to agree upon basic conceptions of the person and individual rights; but each domain interprets and applies these shared norms in sometimes very different ways, as reflecting the specific contexts of their distinctive cultural traditions (cf. Michelfelder 2001, Riedenburg 2000).

A similar pluralism can further be discerned between East and West – despite far stronger differences in their initial starting points. That is, Confucian and Buddhist thought, as shaping the norms and practices of countries such as Thailand, Japan and China (among others), understand the person first of all as a *relational* being, in contrast with modern Western emphases on the person as primarily an individual or isolate. Indeed, Buddhism in its various forms begins with the insistence that the self is an illusion – and a pernicious one at that, insofar as the ego-illusion is the source of desire, and desire is the source of our discontent: hence, contentment or Enlightenment will come only through the overcoming of the ego-illusion. Not surprisingly, then, these cultures – until influenced by the West – have had no conception or tradition of individual privacy as a positive good. On the contrary, what Westerners might think of as individual privacy is regarded as a negative – e.g., in the Chinese concept of *Yinsi* (i.e., a 'shameful secret' or 'hidden, bad things', Lü 2005, p. 14).

Despite these radically different starting points, countries such as China, Japan and Thailand have developed laws that afford their citizens at least some degree of data privacy protection (Lü 2005, Nakada and Tamura 2005, Hongladarom 2007). Their motivations for doing so are largely *economic* rather than, as in the case of Western countries, rooted in understandings of the individual and individual rights as foundational to democratic polities. This thus instantiates the notion of overlapping consensus as developed by Rawls and Bohman, as we saw above. But this again illustrates a *pluralism* – one all the more striking as it now stretches across even greater philosophical and ethical divides. That is, alongside the intractable differences between Western and Eastern conceptions of the individual we see some convergence on shared notions of data privacy protections. To paraphrase Aristotle: data privacy protection is said in many different ways – ways that reflect, in this instance, the profound cultural differences at work in developing and applying some form of data privacy protection. Nonetheless, these differences do not forbid the establishment of data privacy protections that are at least similar and mutually recognizable – if not, to some degree at least, identical (i.e., with regard to the protection of financial information such as credit card numbers: see Ess 2006a, 2007 for further discussion).

10.3.3   Ethical pluralism in global ICE: contemporary developments

In addition to these sorts of pluralistic convergences between East and West with regard to privacy, we can further note a similar convergence at a still more fundamental level – namely, with regard to the basic understandings of the nature of the *person*. On the one hand, in the face of the initial contrasts we have seen between Western and Eastern views of the *person* and thus of privacy, Soraj Hongladarom, a Thai philosopher with interests in both Buddhist and Western thought, has pointed out that this initial contrast is not as black-and-white as it may first appear. Admittedly, modern Western philosophy – especially as exemplified by Descartes and Kant – has stressed the autonomous self as a kind of primary reality. Again, this seems completely at odds with especially Buddhist insistence that the self is a pernicious illusion, such that only by overcoming this illusion can we hope to find true contentment. At the same time, however, Hongladarom points out that modern Western thought includes more communitarian elements, beginning with Hegel, that help offset and complement the emphasis on the individual. By the same token, Hongladarom describes a Buddhist conception of the self as an empirical self – one that, from an absolute or Enlightened standpoint will be regarded as ultimately illusory. Nonetheless, from a relative perspective, such an empirical self retains a certain level of reality and importance – enough, he thinks, to fund a Buddhist insistence on individual privacy, in sharp contrast with the traditional Thai insistence on privacy only in familiar or collective terms (2007).

The upshot is again a pluralism. Hongladarom's Buddhist empirical self more closely resonates with modern Western conceptions; but they remain irreducibly different insofar as the empirical self remains a relative reality, vis-à-vis the presumptively absolute reality of the modern Western self. At the same time, as Hongladarom argues on the basis of a Buddhist empirical self for both privacy rights and democratic polity, he points to norms and ideals now shared between the modern West and Thailand. Clearly, these shared norms and ideals are refracted through the lenses of two very diverse cultural and philosophical traditions, resulting in two distinctive interpretations or applications of shared understandings of individual privacy and democratic polity.

As a final example – one that parallels Hongladarom's notion of a Buddhist empirical self – we can note that, from the Western side, Susan Stuart has made especially clear how a number of sharp distinctions characteristic of Kant's thought – starting with a hard boundary between (individual) mind and body – are now being re-thought in light of more recent developments in our understanding of how human beings, as *embodied*, come to know and navigate their world (2008).

This re-thinking (under the name of enactivism) moves us from the person as an autonomous but isolated rationality (the approach of cognitivism) towards an understanding of the person as a mind-body whose knowledge and navigation of the world is only as physically enmeshed with situation and context.

This is reminiscent, in the first place, of the conception of the person in Plato and Aristotle – and of the *phronesis* that only an embodied being can practise after long experience. It is further in keeping with a broader turn in Western ethics towards more relational understandings – e.g., ethics as a matter of sustaining 'webs of relationships' in feminist ethics; ecological emphases on sustaining eco-systems as likewise made up of species interwoven and interdependent upon one another; and Floridi's 'information ecology' that consciously models his ontocentric ethics on an ecological model of interconnected and interdependent wholes. At the same time, these transformations move our Western conceptions of the self closer to – or, we might say, in still closer resonance or harmony with – the relational conceptions of the self at work in Confucian thought, African thought (Paterson 2007), and elsewhere.

At the same time, however, Stuart's account of the person remains distinctively Western. Such a person, especially as interconnected with the physical world around her, is presumed to be *real* in a final sense. This concept, as emphasizing relationship as definitive of the person, thereby moves us closer towards many non-Western accounts. It remains irreducibly different from (even) Hongladarom's account of the person, according to which the empirical self – as the closest analogue to Stuart's enactive self – enjoys ontological significance in at least a relative way. But within the larger Buddhist framework, this empirical self remains comparatively less real than Stuart's enactive person – reflecting thereby the irreducible differences between these Western and Buddhist ontologies. It is also clear that these two concepts of persons thereby stand as yet another example of pluralism – one in which a basic notion of the human being in all of her capacities and engagements with the world is refracted through two irreducibly different cultural lenses.

10.4   Concluding remarks

We hope to have clarified a number of ways in which the global diffusion of ICTs raises a wide array of new ethical challenges. Such challenges help to reiterate the central importance of ethical pluralism, as a meta-ethical strategy both within and beyond the borders of Western ethical traditions and an ICE first developed within Western frameworks. Not all of the challenges of a global ICE will be resolved through pluralism. Most obviously, the digital divide remains a profoundly intractable difficulty, and it is certain that there will be specific ethical issues on the global scale that will simply continue to divide us, e.g., freedom of expression in diverse regimes, diverse understandings of copyright and Intellectual Property, and so forth. Nonetheless, as Mary Midgley reminds us, 'Morally as well as physically, there is only one world, and we all have to live in it' ([1981] 1996, p. 119). ICTs and globalization only reiterate and amplify Midgley's point, as they facilitate our ever-increasing interconnectedness with one another. Developing a global ICE is not an option, but an urgent necessity. Our history of cultural hybridizations, especially as these involve notions of pluralism, harmony and resonance, the success of democratic deliberation online, and the emergence of a pluralistic approach to privacy and personhood in contemporary ICE provide reasons for optimism towards that development. However daunting the challenges, we clearly will not know how far we may succeed until we try.

11 Computer ethics and applied contexts

John Weckert and Adam Henschke

11.1 Introduction

Computer ethics changes the ethical landscape. Various issues that appear in different applied ethics fields now appear as part of computer ethics, for example monitoring and surveillance as part of business ethics, and the privacy of medical records as part of medical ethics. The purpose of technology, we will argue in the next section, is to improve life, so it is legitimate to question whether a particular technology, in this case information and communication technology (ICT), achieves this in a variety of contexts.

11.2 Technology

Just what constitutes technology is not so easy to say. Sometimes, any human constructs, including social or political organizations, are considered part of technology. This is compatible with Ferré's account when he calls technology the 'practical implementation of intelligence' (Ferré 1995, p. 26). In this chapter, however, technology will be used in a narrower sense and taken as the total set of tools, or artefacts, that we use in our daily lives, including computers, the Internet, radios, cars, scissors and so on (see Dusek 2006, pp. 31–36 and Briggle *et al.* 2005 for other accounts of technology).

The purpose of the technologies that we develop is, at least ideally, to improve life in some way. According to this teleological view of technology, artefacts or tools have a purpose. Thus, Ortega Y Gasset (1961) defines technology as 'the improvement brought about on nature by man for the satisfaction of his necessities'. For our purposes, what is important is that we use technology to modify our environment in order for us to live better lives. This is a common position. On Ferré's account, it can be said that we use our intelligence at the most basic level to survive but, beyond that, to make our lives easier, more pleasant and more satisfying, and we employ technology to assist in this. Combes also supports this view of technology: 'Technology is the deliberate practice of rearranging the world's furniture in order to maintain a decent lifestyle' (Combes 2005, p. 6) and again, technology is 'the intentional exploitation of the environment for the purpose of providing needs and *perceived* wants' (Combes 2005, p. 11). The possibility is raised here that some of the wants satisfied by technology might not be *real* wants and therefore may not in fact improve life. Exploring this in the context of ICT is one reason why computer ethics is important. Overall then, the purpose of technologies is, at least ideally, to improve life, and it is imperative that we examine whether this is the case.

Just as the purpose of technology in general is to enhance our lives, so is this the purpose of ICT. While there is room for the view that some of this development was and still is driven by the technology rather than by any human needs, that is, that some technology is developed because it can be, and some cynicism is not out of place, it is plausible to see these developments as efforts to make life easier and more pleasant, keep us healthier and more generally to help us satisfy our needs and goals and to enhance our lives. This brief look at technology, then, gives a good reason for focusing on ICT in the context of applied ethics.

11.3 Computer ethics

Does ICT improve life and if so, does it do so equitably? Are there some contexts in which, for ethical reasons, it should not be introduced? Here, we will consider a range of such issues in a number of applied ethics fields, in particular in media ethics, business ethics, criminal justice ethics, medical ethics, bioethics and environmental ethics. While this is not exhaustive either in applied ethics fields or in issues covered, it will give an overview of the ubiquity of computer ethics questions. The focus will be on problems that are in some way different or more urgent because of the technology, or have not yet been much discussed. For example, is the use of the wireless network of a neighbour a violation of his intellectual property? If the signal comes into my house and the network is unsecured, am I doing anything wrong in connecting to and using it, providing I am not costing my neighbour anything in money or speed of service? Intellectual property has long been studied in business ethics but it raises some different issues here (Small 2007). An issue that has become more urgent, if not different, is privacy. There have long been privacy concerns, for example in business and medical ethics, but with ICT enabling greater capabilities for collecting, storing, analysing and accessing personal information, the issue has become more pressing.

11.4 Media ethics

Many ethical concerns relating to the older media also relate to the Internet. The Internet does not raise new issues, for example, about honesty and truthfulness in reporting. But in others it does, and we will focus on a couple of those. Freedom of speech and expression are of central importance to both computer and media ethics, and because of the decentralized and global nature of the Internet, pornography, hate language and various illegal activities are much more difficult to control than in more traditional media. Another area is the creation and manipulation of digital images.

11.4.1   Freedom of speech and expression

Governments find it difficult to regulate Internet content. Attempts are often hotly contested, at least in liberal democratic countries, even though regulations governing the content of television, radio, newspapers, magazines, movies and books are generally accepted (see Chapter 7 for further discussion). There are a number of arguments against Internet content regulation. Some are general, apply to all media, and are related to the principle of rights to freedom of speech, expression and information. Others are more specific to the Internet. Internet content regulation should be resisted perhaps because it is an extension of government control. Not only do governments want to control the other media, now they want to control the Internet as well. Given the difficulty of controlling Internet content, because of its nature, Draconian measures like the Chinese Golden Shield Project, often called the 'Great Chinese Firewall', an attempt by the Chinese government to restrict Internet access in the country, are sometimes deemed necessary. Then there is the pragmatic argument which has two strands. One is that it is pointless for one country alone to attempt regulation given the global nature for the Internet. To be effective, regulation must also be global. If a site is banned in one country it is simple to move it elsewhere. The other strand is that regulation can cause intolerable situations for individuals who create sites in any particular place. The material may be legal in their own country, where the site is located, but illegal in another. Consider the following case. A prominent Australian businessman sued a United States company for defamation. Australia has much harsher laws on defamation than the United States (The High Court of Australia 2002). The businessman argued that the case should be heard in Australia because that is where the material was read and his reputation harmed. The company argued that, because the material was on a server in the US, that is where the trial should be held. The High Court of Australia ruled that a defamation case could be heard in Australia even though the offending material was on a server not in that country.

Justice and fairness arise here in a way that they would not have previously, except perhaps where countries share common borders. It can be argued that it is unfair to be subject to laws in a jurisdiction other than that in which the offending material resides. While, in general, ignorance of the law is not a valid defence, one cannot reasonably be expected to be aware of the law in all countries in which one's material may be read on the Internet. It is simply unfair to subject the US defendant to Australian law. It can also be argued that Australian citizens should have the protection of Australian law when in Australia, and not be subject to the jurisdiction of another country. If the US company had won the right for the case to be heard in the US, then in this instance the businessman, even though an Australian in Australia, and harmed in Australia, would have had his case dealt with under US law, a situation which also seems unfair.

Another example of an action acceptable in one country or culture being extremely offensive and illegal in another is the cartoons published in Denmark, which depicted the prophet Muhammad in ways that parts of the Muslim world considered blasphemous. The rights to freedom of the press and freedom of expression were met head-on by deeply held views on blasphemy and on the right to publish material that is known to be extremely offensive.

Recently ethical arguments about the Internet have shifted a little. The Internet is not spoken about only as a type of communication medium but often as a living space in which people work, play, shop and socialize. So, to some extent, the argument about controls on Internet content has shifted too. While there is still discussion of pornography, hate language and the like, there is also discussion of, for example, controlling Internet gambling and downloading music and movies. So the discussion now is partly of Internet activity and of Internet content. On the Internet, it must be noted, this distinction is not sharp; all web pages contain content. To that extent, controlling the content controls the activity and so the issue is not merely freedom of speech and information but also freedom of activity. Freedom to live as one wants is now inextricably bound up with these older media ethics problems.

11.4.2   Digital images

A picture is supposedly worth a thousand words but, given the ease of both creating and manipulating digital images that appear to be real photographs, the veracity of photographs can no longer be taken for granted. It is true that photographs could always be altered but this is now much easier and more difficult to tell whether any manipulation has occurred. It is true too that there are ways of telling if there has been manipulation but this is often difficult for anyone but an expert. Realistic images can also be generated so it can be difficult to know whether something is a real photograph or a computer-generated image that appears to be one. Questions of honesty and truthfulness are now raised in relation to photography in a way that they were not previously. The 2008 Beijing Olympic Games provide an example:

As the ceremony got under way . . . viewers at home and watching giant screens inside the Bird's Nest stadium saw a series of giant footprints outlined in the fireworks proceed above the city from Tiananmen square. What they did not realise was that they were watching computer graphics, digitally inserted into the coverage at the right moment. The fireworks were there for real, outside the stadium. But those responsible for filming . . . decided beforehand that it would be impossible to capture all 29 footprints from the air. As a result, only the last footprint, which was visible from the camera stands inside the Bird's Nest was captured on film. (Spencer 2008)

While this was not an important case of deception, and perhaps not deception at all, given that what was on the screen was actually in the fireworks them-selves, it does demonstrate the potential for misleading the public through images.

There is an interesting question here too with respect to pornography. One worry about pornography is the exploitation of the subjects, usually vulner-able women and children. Suppose that all of the pornographic images were software generated and not of real people. Is there anything morally objec-tionable in such depictions? Clearly one issue has been avoided; there is no exploitation of subjects, but many would argue that the problem of degrad-ing women and children is still present. There have been erotic paintings for millennia but the new technology has created the possibility of much more realistic images and videos and this does raise new questions. Another concern is that such images normalize the behaviour of those viewing them, thus the concern is not only that people were harmed in the making of the image, but those viewing the image may feel less concerned about harming people in the real world after viewing virtual pornographic images.

11.5   Business ethics

Many of the first discussions of computer ethics were concerned with the use of ICT in business. Two topics in particular, privacy and intellectual property, were important in the past and probably even more so nowadays. Here we will concentrate on two aspects where computers have made a significant difference: monitoring and surveillance in relation to privacy and trust, and biometrics.

11.5.1   Monitoring and surveillance of employees

Computing technology has dramatically changed the possibilities for monitor-ing and surveillance both in the workplace and more generally (see Chapter 8 for further discussion). Employers can of course legitimately monitor their employees to check that they are doing their work satisfactorily, and they have always done so. It is also in the interests of the customers that employees are monitored to ensure that products or services are of the required standard and it is in the interests of the employees to know that other employees are doing their fair share of the work. What has changed with the computer technology is the extent to which monitoring and surveillance is now possible. For those working on computers just about everything that they do can be monitored. Emails received and sent, websites visited and keystrokes can all be logged and checked, or monitored in real time. A potentially more powerful and intrusive monitoring to boost employee health and efficiency by observing an employee's general metabolism is the subject of a patent application by Microsoft. In section 0045 it is stated:

a target user named Joe ... has triggered a help request. The help request can be triggered in at least two different ways: implicitly or explicitly. When a parameter is violated or a threshold is satisfied or exceeded, the system can automatically initiate the help request in order to identify the target activity and target user and determine the type or source of assistance most suitable for Joe and his activity. Parameters or thresholds can relate to the particular activity, to the user's physical state, or to the user's environment. For example, sensors can monitor the user's heart rate, blood pressure, body temperature, galvanic skin response, EMG, brain signals, respiration rate, movement, facial movements, facial expressions, etc. Alternatively, Joe can expressly request assistance to boost employee health and efficiency. (US Patent and Trademark Office 2007)

Employers clearly have rights with respect to their employees. What is at issue is the *extent* to which employers can legitimately monitor their employees given the technology that they now have at their disposal. First, it could be argued that employees have no rights to privacy at work, given that they are being paid to work and their time belongs to their employer. Therefore, no rights are being violated by the monitoring of their activities. This cannot be quite right though, for people do not lose all rights when they enter the work-place. Certain rights to privacy must be respected – cameras in bathrooms are generally not permissible, for example. A second consideration concerns the value of monitoring and surveillance. A primary justification given for it is efficiency: monitored workers work more efficiently. While this may be true to some extent it is not clear that it is always so, particularly in situations where monitoring is continuous or where the employees do not know when they are under surveillance. It has been suggested too that monitoring does not necessarily improve productivity, because workers who believe that they are being monitored do the minimum necessary (Stanton and Julian 2002). However, these are empirical matters that we will not pursue here. A third and final consideration concerns the reasons that can be given for overriding employees' rights to privacy. The most common justification is to ensure sat-isfactory work. This is not unreasonable but it justifies only a limited amount of monitoring. If there is reason to believe that someone is not performing satisfactorily, monitoring that employee can be justified, but it is less easy to justify monitoring in the absence of evidence that it is required. More compelling reasons relate to the legal responsibilities of employers. Employers can be legally responsible, that is, have vicarious liability, for the actions of their employees at work so some monitoring for illegal activities is justified. Vicarious liability is 'The imposition of liability on one person for the actionable conduct of another, based solely on a relationship between the two persons [or the] indirect or imputed legal responsibility of acts of another' (Black 1990, p. 1566). This is of particular importance where there is a reasonable suspicion of illegal activity, although even where there is no such suspicion, duty of care to customers or others may necessitate monitoring in some instances. It is not obvious that even here, however, employers can legitimately override the privacy rights of employees without good reason (see Miller and Weckert 2000, for an expansion of this argument).

Most discussions of workplace monitoring and surveillance concern privacy but there is also an issue with trust. Monitoring employees can be a sign that they are not trusted. Perhaps this does not matter, but trust is important. It is necessary for the successful functioning of any community, including the workplace, and also for personal relationships and self-esteem (the following paragraph draws on Weckert 2005 and Weckert 2002).

Trust can be, and sometimes is, treated as just a matter of security (Schneiderman 1999), but this is not without costs. Suppose that the workplace had a completely secure computer network. What would such a network be like? It would be completely reliable, that is, there would be no breakdowns. All firewalls would be completely safe, so no intruders could ever get through. Encryption would be undecipherable without the appropriate keys, those keys would be safe and authentication techniques would be foolproof. Would trust matter? It would, because while intruders would be kept out, there would be no guarantee that legitimate users were behaving properly. They could be practising deceit, stealing information and so on. Suppose that there was a perfect system of monitoring. All activity is logged, and all inappropriate behaviour punished. Everything that all insiders do is monitored, so there is no chance that they can do anything undetected. Is trust required now? Some is. While it may not be necessary to trust the general users, the employees, simply because they are not in a position to misbehave, those undertaking the monitoring and surveillance must still be trusted to do the right thing. Perhaps they are monitored too, but that just moves the trust to another level, and so on *ad infinitum*. This regress can perhaps be avoided by automating the monitoring. When anything untoward is noticed, the perpetrator will automatically be punished in some way, and their deeds made public. In such a system, perhaps trust would not be necessary within the system, but it would still be necessary to trust the developers and maintainers of the monitoring system. Is it implemented in a manner that is fair, or does it favour some people? And even if such a system were fair, would anyone really want to work in a workplace with this kind of environment? Probably not. It seems to be a very high price to pay to avoid the need to trust other human beings. There are pragmatic reasons, then, to trust, but there are also ethical ones. We like to be trusted and it is a sign of respect to trust someone. Not trusting someone, in a situation in which lack of trust is not warranted, is not showing respect where respect can be expected. While the ethical aspect of trusting is not often discussed, there are serious concerns about using computer systems in a way that undermine trust, both for pragmatic and ethical reasons.

11.5.2   Biometrics

Security of computer systems is a major concern of businesses. The most common form of controlling access to these systems is through the use of passwords. Passwords however have their weaknesses. Simple ones are not very secure and complicated ones are difficult to remember and are likely to be written down, compromising security further. Consequently much research has been undertaken to develop more secure access control. Biometrics is becoming increasingly important. Biometric technology uses features of a person that are unique to that person, for example, fingerprints, iris patterns, various facial features, or particular behavioural characteristics such as typing patterns. These are then used in place of passwords and generally are more secure. Biometric systems can be used in a number of different ways. Digital fingerprint systems, for example, were introduced in some US fast food restaurants, where customers used their fingerprints to charge ordered meals to their credit cards and iris scans at Heathrow Airport in the United Kingdom (*International Herald Tribune* 2008). Another example are facial metric systems which map the underlying bone structure of people's faces, and are used in some national airports or to scan large crowds for security reasons.

The examples above of biometric use are cases of identification. The recorded data are compared with other stored data in order to find a match. Another use, and the important one for computer security, is authentication. Here the biometric data, say a fingerprint, are used to authenticate that you are who you say that you are, in the same way as passwords are used. This use is, or seems to be, less morally problematic than the use for identification, although one problem affects both. This is that biometric data are not merely information about some feature of me, say a description of my appearance, but a representation of that feature and this representation is being stored for the use of others. Why does this raise more ethical concerns than other personal or individual identifiers? Because, it is argued, biometric data are 'a piece of yourself'. My fingerprint is not literally a piece of me in the same sense that my finger is, but it does have a much closer relationship to me than my passport number has. According to Anton Alterman (2003), biometric data are intimately related to us and their use amounts to, in Kantian terms, treating someone as a means rather than as an end. A person's body, or part of it, is used in a way that the person cannot control. While this is more of a worry if used for identification than for authentication, in both cases a 'piece of us' is being used.

Two kinds of worry can be distinguished, one intrinsic and the other consequential. First, the intrinsic worry also comes in two versions. One is the Kantian objection mentioned by Alterman. Using biometric data is treating a person simply as a means. This is not compelling. While it may be wrong to treat someone just as a means it is not obvious that using a fingerprint as a means for identification or authentication is treating the person whose fingerprint it is, as a means. The second version of the intrinsic worry relates to intimacy. Julie Inness (1992) argues that privacy relates to the control that an individual has over intimate information and actions. For her, intimacy forms the core of privacy. According to Inness, if we are to respect persons as rational and emotionally complex agents, we must respect that which an individual sees as intimate. If biometric data are intimate then the person should maintain control over the use of their data, otherwise that person's privacy is violated. It can be objected, however, that biometric data, while being much richer and more closely related to individuals than passwords or driver's licence numbers, are nevertheless not intimate in the right sense. My letter to my wife is intimate in a way that my fingerprint is not.

The consequentialist worry seems to have more bite. The collection and storage of deep and thick personal data seems more problematic than data that is just *about* me. Biometric information cannot be easily masked except by surgery or other rather severe physical action such as mutilation. This is of course why biometrics are so useful, even more useful than photographs. Growing beards or altering hair styles does not change biometric data, but it might make identification from that photograph difficult. The scope for this data to be used in ways that harm people is considerable, given the massive databases containing personal information.

There is, of course, a need to balance personal interests with community benefit. If biometric data are used only for *authentication* purposes then there are few moral concerns. However, most of the community value of this data is its use in security and for that, *identification* of individuals comes to the fore, and it is here that there is more scope for misuse. But security is important so policies must be in place to both maximize security and simultaneously minimize risks to individuals through misuse of the data (security is discussed in Chapter 8).

11.6   Criminal justice ethics

At the beginning of this chapter it was suggested that the purpose of technology was to improve life. This implies that technologies are developed with particular values in mind, for example efficiency. Computer systems for forensics are designed to improve criminal investigations and hopefully reduce crime. An examination of this issue highlights another way in which values can be important in ICT. It is argued sometimes that technology has values built into it, or it embodies values (Nissenbaum 2001), or that artefacts have politics (Winner 1986). In other words, technology is not neutral with respect to values. However, whether technology *embodies* values, or is *value-laden*, this much is true and unsurprising: particular kinds of technology encourage or facilitate some sorts of behaviour and perhaps even some beliefs.

In the previous section, we discussed biometric identification methods made possible by developments in computing technology. Here, we will focus on one system of biometric identification, genetic or DNA fingerprinting, where DNA is used to identify individuals. Forensic DNA profiling is a technology that has been developing for the past few decades, and is now becoming more widely spread as computers become more powerful. Currently, the US and the UK and other countries have policies that allow for DNA evidence found at crime scenes to be used as a standard part of criminal investigations.

Generally, forensic DNA fingerprinting involves collection of DNA samples from a crime scene, and then production of a profile from crime scene samples. These technologies seek to identify individuals by comparing the crime scene DNA with the DNA of a suspect or with a database of previous suspects and criminals, using short tandem repeat profiles, known as STRs. These methods are reliable to the point that the chance of two genetically distinct people having the same STR profile is between 1 in 1 trillion and 1 in 1.8 trillion (Chakraborty *et al.* 1999, p. 1688). As computing power has increased, the technology has developed, to the extent that DNA found at a crime scene has been analysed to predict the last name, facial morphology and race or familial relatedness of the person from whom the sample came. Clearly, these are tools that can be highly useful in criminal investigations, but their use raises ethical concerns.

Consider the example of using DNA samples to predict race from crime scene evidence, as it has been done in the UK, Canada and the US, amongst other countries. Racial predictions based on sample DNA are done in two main ways: either by inferring a person's geographic ancestry or by predicting skin colour and facial morphology from the sample DNA. Geographic ancestry generally starts with computer models that predict ancestry from different genetic markers, predict from which continents the ancestors came and from this infer their race. The crime scene DNA can also be analysed for genes known to cause different skin colours or facial characteristics and again to infer the race of the suspect.

While this may appear to be morally innocuous, a problem arises because the idea of race in the human species is scientifically questionable and ethically loaded. A concern raised by Pilar Ossorio (2006) is that '[t]he combination of race, genetics, and crime could prove extremely powerful in activating or reinforcing negative racial stereotypes'. There is the danger that an uncritical approach to forensic DNA profiling will reinforce negative racial stereotypes. This becomes important from a computer ethics perspective because of the values underlying the computer systems used to do the profiling. Developing a computer system that incorporates race is incorporating a highly ethically charged assumption into the system. This technology will facilitate the use of race in forensics in a way that may well fulfil Ossorio's fears. DNA fingerprinting for forensics does not need to be used in this way; systems could be designed without race playing any role. There is a clear sense here in which the technology is not neutral, in much the same way that a book with certain racial content would not be neutral (Chapter 12 discusses artefacts and values). A particular worry, in this case, is the linking of race with crime. In other contexts, for example, some sports, it may not be a concern.

If the designers of computer systems for forensic genetic profiling are guided by the idea that race is a scientifically valid categorization and integrate this assumption into the system, the result can be systematic and unfair discrimination between individuals or groups of individuals. The use of race within a criminal and forensic context, especially when based upon genetic information, creates the potential for conflation of race, criminality and genetics and poses concerns for social justice.

11.7 Medical ethics

Because of the sensitive nature of a patient's medical information and the vulnerability of patients, medical ethics attracts considerable attention. Some of this attention focuses on ICT in medical contexts and this is particularly true of privacy and data protection related to medical records (Fairweather and Rogerson 2001). Another topic is online consultation. Given the nature of the doctor–patient relationship, doubts have been expressed about whether this type of consultation can really fulfil patient needs or is merely a poor substitute (Collste 2002). Arguably, friendship and trust, both necessary for a successful doctor–patient relationship, require face-to-face interaction. Two objections can be moved against this. First, such online consultations may be better than none at all, so they should be encouraged in situations where there is no alternative. Second, it is not obvious that friendship and trust cannot flourish in online relationships. Perhaps it is just a matter of time before online relationships are just as natural as face-to-face ones are now.

While these are important issues, we will now focus on a topic that has not as yet been examined at length in computer ethics: the role of ICT in pharmacogenomics.

11.7.1   Pharmacogenomics

Pharmacogenomics is an umbrella term describing the technologies that apply genetic information to pharmaceutical use. Patients needing pharmaceutical treatment for a given condition have their genotype taken and a pharmaceutical is chosen, specific to the condition and the individual. The genetic information provides information about the individual's potential response to the drug and how the drug is expected to function on that individual. The Nuffield Council on Bioethics describes the promise of pharmacogenomics as personalized medicine, with the right pharmaceutical given at the right dose at the right time for the right person. Despite this potential, the report also highlights that these optimistic claims require careful evaluation. A growing body of research is concerned with assessing the ethical, legal and social implications.

ICTs are essential at every key step of pharmacogenomics. 'Information-intensive' approaches are integral to pharmacogenomic research and development. This research and development is reliant upon DNA microarrays, which allow for large-scale multi-gene analysis. In microarrays, large numbers of DNA fragments are 'hybridized' or bonded to a small slide. Target cells are exposed to different experimental conditions, the cell's DNA is exposed to the slide and measured for genetic activity – i.e. how a cell will respond genetically to different pharmaceuticals. Computers are central to the collection of the large amounts of data that are generated by these DNA microarrays and are required to analyse these data and convert them into useful information. This information is then catalogued and stored digitally and used as part of clinical trials. The information generated from the clinical trials is then further analysed and the practical efficacy and potential toxicology of a pharmaceutical is statistically predicted through predictive modelling and empirical analysis, again using computers. In summary, at each key step data need to be collected, transferred or analysed through ICTs.

11.7.2   On pharmacogenomics, computer ethics and justice

As mentioned, the ideal of pharmacogenomics is personalized medicine with the goals of increased efficacy and decreased side effects. These are noble goals but a question of justice arises. Health care, when framed in terms of justice, seeks to redress imbalances that prevent equal opportunity of competition between people. Pharmacogenomics would seem to fit with this goal, through the most effective use of the most appropriate medicines. People suffering from a disease are brought to the normal level of human functioning, such that they are equal competitors on a level playing field. This seems to be in line with the purpose of computer technology too, which is to improve life.

Pharmacogenomics, however, may act to increase inequality across people, primarily because pharmacogenomics will be more expensive than standard medicines (van Delden *et al.*, 2004, esp. p. 312), given that targeted pharmaceuticals have smaller markets. Health-related social inequalities may increase, with the wealthier members of a society having greater access to better medicines, while the poorer members of a society have less and less access. The problem is also global. Known as the '10/90' gap (Global Forum for Health Research), there is a divide between global health research and development funding on the one hand, and global health needs on the other. Approximately 10 per cent of the world's population receive 90 per cent of health research and development funding. One of the chief concerns about pharmacogenomics is that it may serve to increase the 10/90 gap (Smart, Martin and Parker 2004, esp. p. 334), increasing the disparity of effective health care between the developing and developed world.

Given that ICTs are central to pharmacogenomics, there is a question regarding the extent to which ICT professionals should be involved on work that will most likely increase injustice. Pharmacogenomics will help primarily those who are already privileged. It could be argued, with some plausibility, that this is not a good use of scarce resources and that these resources should be spent on improving the health of the 90 per cent. Not only would more people benefit, they would also benefit to a greater extent. Pharmacogenomics improves the lives of those who already have good and relatively long lives, while improving health conditions in developing countries can improve health and increase longevity dramatically. Computing professionals engaged in pharmacogenomics can be seen as contributing to another digital divide, this one in health.

11.8   Bioethics

Bioethics covers a very broad range of topics, including *in vitro* fertilization, genetic engineering and definitions of death. Here, we will focus on just one aspect, genomics, and consider the role of ICTs in modern genomics, together with the ethical concerns raised about informed consent.

ICTs have dramatically increased the pace and ease with which large-scale genetic analysis can be done. For the Human Genome Project, the sequence for the human genome was published earlier than anticipated in part as a result of the increases in computing power. Flowing on from the Human Genome Project, it is now possible to take a cheek swab containing one's own genome and send it away to have it analysed for a range of different genetic markers relating to different 'conditions'. Various companies offer a range of different genetic tests, from presence of the gene for Huntington's chorea, to paternity testing, to nutrigenomics – which investigates the link between genes, nutrition and health. What is relevant for our discussion is the ease with which information about one's genome can be generated, analysed and accessed.

Typical bioethics concerns about genomic analysis include the undermining of personal autonomy, harms resulting from the loss of an individual's right to privacy and the affront to human dignity posed by such technologies. From a computer ethics perspective, further concerns are highlighted which may not be immediately apparent from other perspectives.

In standard bioethics literature, informed consent is seen as a vital aspect of any discussion of sensitive or personal information. However, ICTs can directly undermine informed consent in the context of genomics. In standard medical ethics, it is held to be related to enhancing a patient's or research subject's autonomy. In *Principles of Biomedical Ethics*, Tom Beauchamp and James Childress describe it as having information and consent components: all relevant information must be disclosed and comprehended by a patient or research subject, and any effective consent must be voluntary, giving clear authorization for a specified procedure to go ahead. Beauchamp and Childress clarify that institutional or legal rules relating to informed consent must be built from an individual's autonomous choice (Beauchamp and Childress 2001; for an alternative account of informed consent, not based on autonomy, see Manson and O'Neill 2007). As we will show, ICTs have the potential to limit any institutional regulation of informed consent and to weaken the autonomous choice of individuals.

Given the international jurisdictions involved, online genetic testing can be minimally regulated and have very little effective oversight. Of concern here are both the dangers involved in the testing and the lack of informed consent relating to such testing. For example, while standard medical testing and advice is carefully monitored by governmental and professional organizations, it is possible, with the help of ICTs, to test for genes relating to 'conditions' that are incorrectly labelled as 'genetic', without proper medical explanation and support. As such, incorrect, misleading or unsupported advice may follow. By incorrectly labelling something as genetic we mean conditions that may not have any genetic basis at all, or conditions that are so complex in terms of gene–gene, gene–environment and individual history interactions that labelling it 'genetic' is problematic, or conditions that may be genetically caused but only probabilistically. As Susanne Haga and Huntington Willard (2006) state: 'education becomes vitally important to ensure that consumers are equipped with the knowledge to understand the benefits, risks and limitations of testing'. If this testing is done in a medically supervised environment, with a qualified genetic counsellor, the counsellor can explain the situation in terms understandable to the patient, so consent can be genuinely informed. The risks and harms of access to such information is lessened greatly, and can be highly beneficial. ICTs, however, given their speed and efficiency, allow for more tests to be done, at lower cost and over the Internet, with less trained support for the patient.

Another set of consent-based concerns raised by genomics and ICTs stem from the advances and changes that are occurring in the range of uses of genetic information, again, enabled by the rapid advances in ICTs. Biobanks, for example, are storage of personal biological material and/or other personal information. As genetic technologies advance rapidly, the malleability of the biobanks enabled by ICTs means that what is possible in the future may not have been imagined at the time of consent, either by the patient/client or by the researcher. While this is a concern of bioethics, the developments in information technology are fundamental to the development of biobanks and force us to reconsider informed consent more generally. Computer ethics can promote ways of resolving some of these issues by challenging us to consider what consent is actually for, and by promoting software and hardware designers to design in ethics into the systems themselves. This relates to value-sensitive design (VSD) (Friedman and Freier 2005), where the design of the systems themselves are made with consideration given to ethical concerns. For instance, VSD could be incorporated into genetic biobanks so that, if an individual's samples or records are accessed, then the reasons for this access are compared against the original consent given (Chapter 3 contains discussion of VSD). If it does not match, the individual can be contacted to gain an updated consent relevant to the new research being conducted.

11.9   Environmental ethics

Apart from Floridi's information ethics, which he argues is an extension of environmental ethics (see Chapter 5), environmental issues have not generally been very prominent in computer ethics, although that is beginning to change with more discussion of green computing, and this is not before time, with the claim now that the ICT industry emits as much CO_2 as the aviation industry (Boran 2007). Computing professionals have a role to play here, in helping to develop more energy-efficient and environmentally friendly hardware, in using computers more efficiently themselves, and in advising computer users how to do the same. Some things are very simple and come at almost no cost, for example switching off computers rather than letting them run all night and over weekends. Screen savers and lightly coloured screens use more energy than dark screens and not all software runs equally energy efficiently. Hardware can be minimized both to reduce energy use and lessen both the quantity of materials used in manufacture and the quantity that must be disposed of safely or preferably recycled. One important role for the computer professional is in assisting in decisions regarding trade-offs between extra hardware and security, given the importance of both the security of computer systems and minimizing hardware.

Computer technology can also help to reduce travel. Videoconferencing is now a viable, if less enjoyable, alternative to many conferences and meetings. Working online from home, at least some of the time, is a genuine alternative in many occupations. While this is not without problems, for example less social contact, the environmental advantages are obvious.

The issues outlined here are all important in environmental ethics but should not be overlooked as part of computer ethics either. Technology, it was suggested at the beginning of the chapter, should improve life, and environmentally aware computer professionals can make an important contribution both in advising users and in designing environmentally friendly features into the technology.

Another area in which environmental and computer ethics overlap is in the development and use of computer models and simulations. Much decision-making now depends on computer systems. Computer models are used in a wide variety of areas, including economics, weather forecasting, decision support systems that provide advice to medical practitioners and farmers, data-mining systems that build profiles of people or groups, statistical packages that provide statistical information, software that can fly aeroplanes, apply the brakes on our cars, and so on. In many cases, the software involved is extremely complex and, if it is proprietary, is hidden from the view even of most of those who could understand it. While in the case of braking systems and automatic pilots the situation is similar to that of bridges or the material parts of aeroplanes (they work most of the time), it is not quite so clear when software that supports decision-making is working correctly or giving us the best advice. We just rely on the designers and programmers of the systems. This has important implications in environmental ethics. Much of what is believed about the consequences of global warming and about environmental impacts at a more local level is based on computer modelling and simulations. Two problems arise here. First, these models are necessarily simplifications of the real situation; decisions must be made about what parameters to include and the values they are given. Second, it is difficult to test them thoroughly in real-world situations. Given the importance of these models in environmental policy and decision-making, their developers have serious moral responsibilities.

11.10   Conclusion

Computer ethics, as we have seen, is intertwined with many other fields of applied ethics. The examples considered are not an exhaustive list. Computer ethics involves examination of the roles and responsibilities of computing professionals, and as such is part of professional ethics. Serious ethical questions arise about computer-enabled autonomous weapons and this has implication for just war theory and so is part of military ethics (see Chapter 8). Ethical issues in electronic government or electronic democracy can be studied in computer ethics or political philosophy (see Chapters 6 and 10). Furthermore, there are many other relevant topics in the fields considered. Intellectual property, for example is much discussed in computer ethics and also in business and media ethics. Given the ubiquity of computer technology, it may be the case that no field of applied ethics can any longer be studied adequately without considering computer ethics. Computer technology, as we saw at the beginning of this chapter, is supposed to improve life, so it is not surprising that it has implications in all applied ethics fields.

Part IV

Ethical issues in artificial contexts

12 The ethics of IT-artefacts

Vincent Wiegel

12.1 Introduction

We act through information technology (IT), are restrained by it, use it to influence people, to express ourselves, and so on. IT has an enormous impact on our (moral) lives. IT is a generic notion that encompasses many things from computers, the components that computers are made of, the software that runs on the computers to hard disks. As these IT-artefacts become more and more sophisticated and embedded in our lives the question arises what the moral status is of these IT artefacts. That they do have moral impact seems self-evident but can they be said to act morally? Do they deserve moral consideration when we humans act? And might it be possible that IT-artefacts can reason morally? The idea might seem far-fetched but it is considered as a topic of philosophical and engineering research. If such a thing is possible, which is far from an established fact, is it something we should want, or rather the opposite, something that should be avoided because it would allow humans to 'hide' behind IT-artefacts from their moral responsibility?

The first question of interest is what, if anything, sets IT-artefacts apart from other technical artefacts. Do they require a different moral status? Science and technology studies (STS) have paid ample attention to technical artefacts. STS focuses on the interaction between sciences and technological development, on the one hand, and society on the other. Politics and culture drive to some extent the technological developments. These, in turn, affect society, politics and culture. STS researchers have addressed questions about technical artefacts and their moral dimension: are technical artefacts neutral means to human ends? Are they bearers of moral values? Or are they even moral agents? Can STS approaches also address IT-artefacts and their moral status? The question after the moral status or goodness is not one to do with the instrumental or functional performance (do the scissors cut well? does the computer code execute without errors?). It has to do with value-ladenness of artefacts, and whether technical artefacts can be morally evaluated independently of their use or relationship to human actors.

Philosophers that deal specifically with IT-artefacts rather than technical artefacts have also discussed these questions. In this debate four central questions emerge.

(1) do IT-artefacts require complex behaviour to merit moral consideration of some sort?
(2) do IT-artefacts need some sort of mental states in order to be able to display behaviour that merits moral consideration?
(3) can we ascribe mental states to IT-artefacts?
(4) if we can create IT-artefacts that display some sort of moral behaviour, should we?

The first three questions deal with what artificial morality is about. The last question stands somewhat apart by focusing on our relationship to artificial morality. What is the responsibility of the designers versus the IT-artefact? Should we allow moral decisions to be delegated to IT-artefacts?

This chapter is organized as follows. Section 12.2 takes up the question of what we mean when speaking of 'information technology'. Section 12.3 provides an overview of the main approaches in the field of STS with regard to technical artefacts. It also describes various kinds of increasingly capable IT-artefacts as agents and discusses what kind of attributions (intentionality, self-representation, attribution of intentionality to others by an artefact, etc.) might be meaningful. Section 12.4 revisits the question whether there is anything that sets IT-artefacts apart from technical artefacts. Section 12.5 discusses the four key questions that concern in particular moral philosophy and IT. The closing section argues that we might have to accept the idea that IT-artefacts possess some form of intentionality independent of humans in order to make sense of their behaviour and their moral status.

12.2   IT-artefacts

When considering the question of how IT influences us, and what the moral dimension of that influence is, the issues are not so obvious. To begin with, what is meant by 'information technology'?

IT is a generic notion that can encompass many things from computers and the components that computers are made of, to the software that runs on the computers, from configuration management tools to avatars, from databases to HTML pages. In a somewhat wider sense, it encompasses the governance structures, the engineers, the users, etc. In the broadest sense, it also includes study and research. The Information Technology Association of America (www.itaa.org/) defines IT as 'the study, design, development, implementation, support or management of computer-based information systems, particularly software applications and computer hardware'. This definition gives us an indication of what IT is about, its scope, but it does not give us a definition of an IT-artefact.

The capability maturity model (CMM, www.sei.cmu.edu/cmmi/), an influential reference model for IT development, defines IT-artefacts as all intermediate products that are created in the process of building an IT system. This definition mentions IT-artefacts explicitly but has a narrow scope. A scope, moreover, that excludes the final product of the software development process. From the perspective of moral evaluation this is the one product that carries most meaning. Hence, this definition too is not of much help.

Using the above definition of IT, IT-artefacts have three distinct aspects: hardware, software and use manuals in the widest sense, including rules for deployment, decommissioning, etc. (in IT referred to as governance). In each of these groups there are many objects that can be referenced as an IT-artefact: a procedure, a piece of code, user documentation, a hard-disk, etc. But most people have no interest in or any interaction with these artefacts. A piece of code per se is of interest to the developer, the company that owns it and that can deploy it. But until it is deployed and actually executed to most people it is meaningless. The same applies to a hard-disk, which is of importance to the producer, the engineer that buys it to place it in a computer, etc. But again to the average person it is of little or no meaning. All artefacts in these groups, by themselves, are probably technical artefacts.

The distinctive element in IT that attracts us, influences us and that we interact with is its virtual nature and the fact that there is meaningful interaction, i.e. it causes emotional reactions, helps us achieve our goals, puzzles us, baffles us. These effects, these interactions if they do exist indeed, are only to be found in the combinations of elements from all three (hardware, software, governance) groups.

When looking at IT-artefact in the above, combined sense one can refer to them as agents (Moor 2006). He refers to machines as agents with physical and computational aspects. So in this chapter the terms IT-artefact and (artificial) agent will be used interchangeably. The notion of IT-artefact encompasses all of Moor's categories. Moor argues that computational activities have a moral dimension, as there are always various ways (including wrong ones) in which things, situations, activities are computed, analysed, etc. Key to his argument is that machine ethics needs to 'move beyond simple normativity to richer senses of evaluation'. For varying situations we will need varying richness of morality. Different applications will require different complexity in moral awareness and reasoning. Moor sketches a continuum of increasingly rich moral agents:

- Ethical impact agent
- Implicit ethical agent
- Explicit ethical agent
- Full ethical agent

The first type 'happens' to be ethical by the impact it has on our lives through its very existence. An electronic signal transmission tower was not designed with any explicit ethical considerations in mind. Its goal is very practical and instrumental to relay and amplify transmission signals. Because there might, for example, be potential health impacts, it acquires a moral dimension that it was never intended to have, either implicitly or explicitly. The implicit ethical agent is designed in such a way that it cannot execute unethical actions. The explicit ethical agent has the reasoning about the ethical aspects of its functioning designed into it. The explicit ethical agent is designed such that not all its deployment situations and decisions are foreseen, but left to the agent to reason about them on its own initiative. The final degree of ethical reasoning brings the agent to the human level of moral awareness and reasoning: the full ethical agent.

In this description, it is still not entirely clear what an explicit ethical agent can and can not do, and how it differs from a full ethical agent. The distinction between these categories of agents does not appear to be so obvious. In the latter categories we might find, as Moor suggests, a continuum of increasingly rich agents. This distinction is at the core of recent debates on the moral status of IT-artefacts that are discussed in Section 12.5.

An objection that can be raised to the distinction between implicit and explicit ethical agents is that the latter might *seem* to be reasoning morally, and making moral evaluations of available actions. But in fact these are also designer decisions that are being executed as much as they are in the case of implicit ethical agents. The design is more elaborate, at a higher level of abstraction, but a design it remains. First, this fact does not change the explicit reasoning about moral aspects, which is the distinguishing feature. There remains a difference in richness of behaviour. The objection raises the question about the originality and autonomy of the behaviour of this kind of agent. At least implicit in the description of explicit ethical agent is the assumption of (some degree of) autonomy and intentionality by the agent. This autonomy and intentionality, according to the objection, cannot be original, genuine autonomy and intentionality, because they derive from the designer's decisions. So even if the distinction between implicit and explicit ethical agent holds, it is less substantial than implied.

A slightly reformulated version of the objection would run as follows. An artificial agent might act as if it had beliefs, and there might be outward similarities in its 'behaviour', or rather functioning, but it is different. Outward or functional similarities do not provide a basis to award artefacts the moral status that we assign to human or other living beings. Even more to the point, it is us humans that interpret the things an artefact does, and give it meaning. The objection concludes that artefacts can never have value or meaning independently of humans. Any agency or value is derived from human agency or value.

12.3   Science and technology studies and the status of artefacts

STS is an interdisciplinary research area concerned with two subjects:

- how social, political and cultural values affect scientific research and technological innovation; and
- how scientific research and technological innovation affect society, politics and culture.

STS researchers have addressed questions about technical artefacts and their moral dimension. Are technical artefacts neutral means to human ends, are they bearers of moral values, or even moral agency? This section first provides an overview of the main positions in STS with regard to technical artefacts. The discussion centres on the notion of agency in artefacts. Intentionality plays a key role in the various positions. It is therefore discussed separately. Finally, several ways to assess and approach IT-artefacts, to evaluate them morally, are discussed. The question is which of these make sense in a moral discourse.

12.3.1   Ethics of technical artefacts

This section draws in particular on the work by Peter Kroes (forthcoming) and his analysis of the debates on the moral status of technical artefacts. Four positions are represented here as an overview:

(1) Neutrality thesis
(2) Intrinsic value without agency
(3) Artefacts as moral agents
(4) Moral significance through human intentionality

(1) In the neutral approach, technology is depicted as a tool to human means: a tool (artefact) that can be more or less efficient, that has instrumental value (e.g. Butler 1985, Ellul 1964). It has, however, no intrinsic moral value or end, nor can it be said to act. Artefacts are seen as particular human-made physical objects. The function of the artefact is derived from, or even equated to, its physical capacity to bring about certain human goals: it is what it is used for. From a moral point of view, artefacts are treated on par with other, non-human-made physical objects. They are instrumental and do not have any agency. The development of technology is taken more or less as a given, assuming in varying degrees a deterministic development. The main object of moral philosophical study is the impact of the technology on society.

(2) In the view that attributes to artefacts intrinsic moral significance, the artefacts define what humans are or become (Ihde 1990, 1998, Akrich 1992, Latour 1992, 2002). They transfer meaning to the user beyond what the user of the artefact was and could have been without it. In this view, an artefact

has additional, non-physical attributes besides their physical attributes that account for their moral significance. The source of moral significance can be the technical function, the technological intentionality and inbuilt scripts (use plans that invite particular behaviour on part of the user) of the artefacts. Technical functions may be associated closely with a particular meaning and, through that meaning, acquire moral significance. Scripts determine the use of the artefact and tie it with particular human ends that carry value. Artefacts have some form of agency through the inbuilt script. Whether this agency is dependent on humans or stands on its own remains a debated question.

(3) In Actor-Network Theory (ANT) and (post)phenomenological approaches (Latour 1992, 2002, Bijker 1992, Verbeek 2005, Introna 2008) the relationships between people, organizations and things are investigated both from a material and from a semiotic perspective. How these networks develop is one of the shared underlying questions within this approach. This question is particularly important because, through these networks, meaning is created. Humans and artefacts exist not in themselves but through the relations with others, humans and things alike. In ANT networks are made up of actants that can be both human and non-human actors. The relationship between all actants is symmetrical ('Generalized Symmetry' thesis). Differences between actants arise as result of the relationships they form. Assigning them different statuses a priori would, according to ANT, introduce biases. Things and humans are thus treated at the same level. In their relationship, they constitute each other, they are co-constituent. This means that agency is also attributed to non-humans. Intentionality, which is often associated with agency, is attributed to the network rather than the individual actants.

(Post)phenomenological approaches (Ihde 1990, 1998, Verbeek 2005 Introna 2008) towards the human–technology relationships provide a taxonomy of various human–technology relationships. Technology impacts the way we experience and sense the world. Our experience is mediated and transformed through technology. As we become proficient in using some technology we can come to see beyond the technology in question and more or less directly relate to the reality that is depicted by or referred to, through technology. The role of technology becomes hermeneutic. Technology might also alert us to the existence of something different from us (Ihde 1990). Technology becomes the focus of our attention, the world around us 'withdraws' into the background. We relate almost unconsciously with technology as it functions in our surroundings without being noticed. In this approach, technology is attributed some form of moral agency. But again the meaning is created through an agency in relationship with other entities and humans.

(4) The last approach holds that the dichotomy between intentional humans and material objects is too restrictive and does not allow for the dual nature of artefacts (Kroes and Meijer 2006). Technical artefacts are constructed by humans to a certain end. This relationship between the artefact and an end is

produced through human intentionality. And it is through this intentionality that they acquire meaning. The function of an artefact can be said to be a property of that artefact 'on its own' in as far as that function defines the artefact. Artefacts have moral significance in themselves through this function, but only in conjunction with human agency: their function is tied to human ends and directed through human agency. Along similar lines, technical artefacts are argued to be constituted by the intentions of its maker (Thomasson 2003). They are mind-dependent objects with a function as one of their properties. They can never be understood as a property, could never have come into existence without their intentional history that started off with the intentions of its maker. So, ultimately, an artefact can not be said to have agency and ends of its own.

12.3.2   Intentionality

In the above discussion, agency and intentionality play an important role. There are various definitions of agency (Wooldridge 2000, Floridi and Sanders 2004, Wiegel 2007). In most definitions, agency contains a reference to autonomy, interactivity with the environment and goal-directedness. Bratman (1987) describes intention as the commitment to a goal. One can have multiple goals, and depending on a ranking of the goals and the (un)availability of means to achieve the goal, an agent chooses a goal and commits to it. Subsequently it executes actions to achieve these goals.

According to the neutrality thesis, attributing agency to an artefact is meaningless. Artefacts do not act, have no intentions. In the second position discussed above, intrinsic value is ascribed to artefacts through some form of technological intentionality. The ascription of agency is considered a step too far. However, in order to explain the important role of artefacts and their influence independent of human intentionality, some form of intentionality has to be assumed. In ANT, intentionality is ascribed to the network of agents but not the agents that make up the network. The last position allows for some form of intentionality with artefacts but only in a weak, derivative sense. It is entirely dependent on human intentionality. These positions cover the various alternatives possible with regard to technical artefacts and intentionality.

If IT-artefacts were to display (possess) some form of intentionality that goes beyond the intentionality considered possible in technical artefacts that would give IT-artefacts a different moral status. Now consider intentionality as Dennett (1987) presents it. Dennett's position is certainly not uncontroversial (Ross 2000). In our attempt to make sense of the world around us, and in particular to anticipate the 'behaviour' of objects and other living beings, we can adopt three different positions (stances). At the physical stance, we anticipate what will happen ('behaviour' or characteristics) based on our understand-ing of the make-up of an entity, and the laws of physics. At a higher level of abstraction, the design stance, events are predicted based on the function that the artefact is designed to perform (assuming it works 'properly'). At the intentional stance, we attribute intentionality (beliefs, goals) to entities and try to understand and predict 'behaviour' based on the goals we think the entities try to achieve. At each subsequent level, our understanding of what passes on inside the entity decreases, and our ability to deal with complex systems increases. It is difficult or impossible to describe all the processes that take place inside an animal looking for food. Assuming that it is hun-gry, that it wishes to eat, that it does not like particular forms of foods, etc., will help us make reliable predictions about its behaviour. This applies not only to biological entities but to any system. As a heuristic, this works well. The question is whether it follows that innate and biological entities indeed have intentionality. An argument is that ascribing intentionality provides a good, or best, explanation and prediction of what is happening or will happen. According to Dennett (Dennett 1987, van Amerongen 2008) this is all there is to believing something to be an intentional system. This is a very pragmatic approach.

So it seems we can ascribe intentionality attitudes to IT-artefacts. But these artefacts are created by humans, so their intentionality is at best a derived intentionality. This brings us back to the objection (Section 12.2) to the dis-tinction between implicit and explicit ethical agents and the possibility of hav-ing agency and attributing intentionality to IT-artefacts. Even if IT-artefacts have a meta-level reasoning capability, and even if we can best explain their behaviour by attributing intentionality to them, they are the product of human designers (directly or indirectly). They can decide only what the design allows them to decide; they can only believe what they are allowed to believe. This objection assigns a privileged position to human intentionality. To this objec-tion the counter argument states that humans are as much restricted by their design as specified in their genes. Recent research, for example, indicates that alcoholism and sustained relationships are to some extent genetically deter-mined. One can say that the physical and biochemical processes that make up what we are and what we do are so complex that we cannot possibly, at our current level of understanding, make sense of what happens at the design or physical stance. Of course, we can look at local aspects of our behaviour, like alcoholism, but not yet for the more complex global aspects of our behaviour. IT-artefacts, on the contrary, are relatively simple entities. This is true of many IT-artefacts, but not of all IT-artefacts. Wallach and Allen (2008) make the argument that there are many IT systems that are made up of complex programs, distributed across networks that are so complex that we cannot possibly begin to explain it all at the design stance: systems that operate on petabyte file systems, running codes that have been produced by hundreds and hundreds of engineers. Consider these systems as open-systems, that is systems that are interconnected outside a domain that is controlled with regard to who enters it, and what interfaces are allowed, what information can be communicated. The complexity grows so fast that we cannot hope to provide a design explanation. So, from the above reading of intentionality, an argument can be made to attribute some intentionality to large, complex IT-artefacts. A similar argument is made by Floridi and Sanders (2004) regarding the phenomenon of distributed morality and global actions of multitudes of artificial agents.

Do IT-artefacts need an ability to conceptualize other entities, attitudes, etc., and be able to attribute intentionality to these entities? In analogy to the need in animals to be able to distinguish animate from inanimate entities as a condition for intentionality (Dennett 1987), it would make a big difference if IT-artefacts could at least predict the behaviour of other entities. This would not necessarily require that the IT-artefact is able to conceptualize intentional states.

By accepting the pragmatic approach towards intentionality and with the complex state of affairs in IT, the ascription of agency to IT-artefacts is a logical conclusion. This does not give IT-artefacts necessarily a special moral status. Being an agent in the above sense includes many life forms. Still, we treat them differently from a moral point of view. Further exploration is needed to indicate the moral status of the most challenging IT-artefacts.

12.3.3   Ways to morally assess IT-artefacts

We have now the outline of an IT-artefact that takes decisions and has some form of agency and intentionality. In which moral ways could we possibly relate to such an IT-artefact? Let us consider three modes with increasingly complex and demanding structures: having moral impact; taking moral actions; asking for a justification and being subject to moral evaluation. For each of these cases, the question is whether they make sense to us with the current understanding of technology, and whether any of the four positions in STS could possibly make sense of them.

Can an IT-artefact have a moral impact? Having a moral impact means, in a minimal sense, being instrumental to achieving something good or bad. An artefact can have moral impact. This does not necessarily make the artefact itself good or bad. This seems an uncontroversial assertion. All of the four positions in STS can deal with this assertion. Such an artefact we also call an ethical impact agent.

In the classification by Moor (2006), acting morally refers to a richer form of moral involvement than 'just' having moral impact. In a moral action, there is active involvement. The agent that brings about the good or bad situation might not necessarily have a concept of a particular situation being good or bad. A dog that guides a blind person is actively achieving something good, and so is a traffic warning sign that avoids collisions, and an IT system that safely lands an airplane. The dog is not necessarily a moral agent. This depends on the concept of moral agency, a concept still heavily debated (e.g. Floridi 2004, Himma 2007). We call this type of artefact an implicit ethical agent. STS researchers that hold with the 'neutrality' thesis will not be able to accommodate such a concept. Artefacts are neutral and thus cannot be said to act morally. The other three STS positions can deal well with IT-artefacts that act morally. The famous speed bump example, the 'artefacts as moral agents' position, assigns agency to a speed bump and asserts it acts to reduce speed. The other positions that allow moral significance directly in artefacts without assuming agency, or agency derived from human agency, will not object to the notion of moral action.

Subjecting an IT-artefact to moral evaluation is a next level. For most artefacts, it does make sense for us to be disappointed if it does not perform its function properly. To blame or praise it morally, however, seems to be something different entirely. Blame supposes a wilful misrepresentation of functionality offered, or a performance that falls short in a way that could have been avoided if 'it' had paid more attention, etc. Praise and blame often have educational, religious and social ends (see Floridi and Sanders 2004, for a detailed discussion of moral blame, responsibility and accountability in the context of artificial agents). This supposes intentionality on the side of the artefact. It supposes deliberation on various courses of action, and an ability to decide. With this ability would also come an ability to justify what it did. In a loose definition, justification is the ability to provide an account of the goals it pursued, their relative weight and its beliefs about the situation it found itself in, and the options open to it. Of the three STS positions left, all might have difficulty accommodating this notion. Position two, 'intrinsic value without agency', can obviously not accommodate this position since it excludes agency on the side of the artefacts. Assigning agency to a speed bump seems to indicate that moral evaluation of IT-artefacts is warranted. Researchers in position four, 'moral significance through human intentionality' might have difficulty accepting the full notion of agency. They will acknowledge that IT-artefacts make some sort of decision. But since that decision is wired into the artefact, complex though its behaviour might be, the artefact cannot be said to be truly making decisions. Of the four STS approaches, only ANT is able to make sense of this kind of artefact. Position four would deny that there is such thing as an explicit ethical agent. Of the three structures 'moral evaluation and justification' is the most challenging for theories in STS. Researchers in STS will have to extend their concepts to analyse the moral status of an artefact that can be morally evaluated and that is able to justify itself.

12.4   Are IT-artefacts (just) technical artefacts?

The distinction between IT-artefacts and technical artefacts is not clear-cut as we have seen. Some IT-artefacts are 'just' technical artefacts, whereas others are more complicated. Of Moor's four categories, two can be readily evaluated in this discussion. Ethical impact agents are artefacts that have an impact 'just' because of their very existence. Disk drives, calculator software, etc. have not been designed with any ethical considerations in mind. They might have an impact through their existence and the way they are constructed. As such, they are technical artefacts. There is no requirement for additional moral analysis equipment. Full ethical agents are artefacts that function at an equivalent human level of complexity. This includes notions of introspection, emotions, and what it means to live a full moral live. Whatever it is we mean exactly by full ethical agent, no IT-artefact can lay a claim to this status.

The remaining two categories interest us. Consider implicit ethical agents first. Implicit ethical agents are IT-artefacts that have moral decisions hard-wired into them. Operating systems are equipped with functionality for easy access for users that have a physical handicap. Thus, they ensure these users equal access to a computer and its capabilities, which is important for, say, equal chances on the labour market. Browsers are designed in such a way that they do (not) pass on particular information of the user while on the web, in order to prevent abuse. Key is that the functioning of the artefact is not subject to consideration by the artefact itself. Explicit ethical agents are artefacts that 'decide' about what they do. And they take ethical considerations into account when making their decision. Their intentionality might be of a second or even third order, e.g. have beliefs about beliefs. This is something that can not be said of the traditional technical artefacts as accounted for by the STS theories. As argued in the previous section, these theories might have difficulty accommodating this type of IT-artefact.

Let us consider a practical application of an explicit ethical agent, and see how STS theories might respond. Anderson and Anderson (2006) have developed a framework to derive moral decisions in situations where multiple prima facie duties apply and potentially conflict. The example deals with patient and physician decision-making procedures regarding a particular treatment. The decision-making process involves the weighing of various duties like

duties of Beneficence, Nonmaleficence and Justice . . . the principle of Respect for Autonomy, a principle that reflects the shift in recent years from a paternalistic model of the healthcare worker–patient relationship to one where the patient is given a more active role in his or her health care. For a decision by a patient concerning his/her care to be fully autonomous (Mappes and DeGrazia 2001), it must be based on sufficient understanding of his/her medical situation and the likely consequences of foregoing treatment, sufficiently free of external constraints (e.g. pressure by others or external circumstances, such as a lack of funds) and sufficiently free of internal constraints (e.g. pain/discomfort, the effects of medication, irrational fears or values that are likely to change over time). (Anderson and Anderson 2006)

If the patient refuses the proposed treatment what should the physician do? Try again to convince the patient, force the patient or leave the patient be, with, according to his judgement, detrimental consequences for the patient's health? Anderson and Anderson have proposed an automated decision-making framework to assess these situations. The framework learns from cases it is 'fed'. The researchers' intention is to construct an ethical advisor. They demonstrated how the framework can derive ethical principles from example cases, and apply them to new situations. Such an artificial advisor is limited in that the structure of the dilemmas is initially constructed by ethicists. Once it has 'learned' this, it is capable of absorbing and assessing new situations. It is a good example of an explicit ethical agent. It is capable of decision-making and weighing moral considerations (irrespective of whether we let it decide); it has some form of moral knowledge, and can abstract morally relevant information. It is certainly not a full moral agent because it relies on human agents to define the structure of class of problems.

Since it is capable of deriving principles from concrete instances, it is very well conceivable that, at some point in time, it might derive a principle we did not know ourselves, as indeed the authors claim it did. And what is more to the point, this principle might be one that we would not have approved of at design time, given our own limited understanding at the time, but that in fact reflects a better insight. Could the different approaches within STS accommodate this type of IT-artefact?

The approach of 'artefacts as neutral means to human ends' would not be able to deal with it. It would not be an artefact that is fully and exclusively operated by humans: it acts and has certain goals. Therefore it is not neutral. The 'intrinsic value without agency' approach allows for artefacts to be assigned value but denies its agency. An artefact carries meaning and, to some extent, helps define who and what we are, and what we do. This value is independent of human agency. One of the objections against this approach is that it is unclear how the non-physical value-laden properties can be explained if it is to be independent of human agency. Our IT-artefact might demonstrate how this can be understood. Moral properties are physical rather than non-physical as the objection supposes. This approach still denies the agency aspect of the ethical advisor. This STS approach is thus incapable of dealing with the ethical advisor.

ANT treats artefacts and humans at the same level as actants in a network. They all have agency, but the moral significance is only at the level of the network. Artefacts alter meaning in a network, they help create new or different values. For this approach, it would not be a problem to situate IT-artefacts as explicit ethical agents in the world. Since humans have no privileged position over technical artefacts, artefacts that are more complicated than technical artefacts do fit in.

In the last approach, 'moral significance through human intentionality', artefacts acquire moral significance. They have value of their own but only by virtue of human intentionality. The defining assertion is that only humans can have true intentionality. This intentionality defines the function of the artefact, which in turn is the source of its value. The ethical advisor would be a complicated expression of human design decisions. If we follow Dennett, and reject the distinction between original and derived intentionality, this approach will not be able to account for explicit ethical agents. The presentation of the developments in IT makes it clear that this approach will have increasing difficulty accommodating IT-artefacts as research progresses.

12.5 Artificial morality

In the preceding sections, traditional approaches in STS have been discussed. They deal with technical artefacts. These approaches have been considered insufficient by some researchers to deal with the new challenges that increasingly smart, autonomous and interconnected IT-artefacts pose. New analyses and theories have triggered intense debates. This section provides an overview based on four key questions.

(1) Do IT-artefacts require complex behaviour to merit moral consideration of some sort?
(2) Do IT-artefacts need some sort of mental states in order to be able to display behaviour that merits moral consideration?
(3) Can we ascribe mental states to IT-artefacts?
(4) If we can create IT-artefacts that display some sort of moral behaviour, should we?

These are the main issues that divide the field of (moral) philosophers of IT, researchers in STS and technical engineers.

12.5.1 Non-human moral actors

Traditional moral philosophy is anthropocentric and allows little room for artefacts. Philosophers in STS have paid ample attention to artefacts. Their analysis focuses on the artefact in relation to the users and designers. In this sense, they remain firmly in the anthropocentric mainstream. Few philosophers have developed theories to include animals, and more relevantly in our context, IT-artefacts (e.g. Floridi 1999b, see also Chapter 5). In order to do so a distinction is made between moral agents and moral patients. The latter are all entities that are on the receiving end of moral actions. Moral agents are the entities of which we say that they act morally. Humans are the example of, and in many theories the only, moral agents. In many of what Floridi calls the traditional macro-ethical theories, moral patients and agents coincide. It is, however, possible to argue that the class of patients is a superset of the class of moral agents. This means that all moral agents are also moral patients, but not vice versa. Floridi (1999b) argues that any information entity is a moral patient. Information is the 'true and universal patient of any action'. Floridi and Sanders developed their theory of information ethics in order to provide a framework of moral analysis for the many new situations that arise through the introduction of ICT. IT-artefacts are obviously information entities and as such at least moral patients.

12.5.2   Agency without mental states

Behaviour is an active form of moral expression. The question whether arte-facts need mental states in order to count as moral agents focuses on what is required for moral agency and, in particular, on whether IT-artefacts need mental states in order to be able to act morally. It is often argued that moral behaviour is something exclusively human (e.g. Bringsjord 2007) because it requires capacities that are exclusively human. Free will, consciousness, desires, intentions in general, are cited as the required capacities that IT-artefacts lack and bar them from moral agency.

Wallach and Allen (2008) argue that these capacities, the concepts that express them are mostly elusive and have escaped thorough scientific under-standing. The objection to artificial morality boils down to 'we humans have a free will and artificial agents do not, therefore they cannot be moral agents'. As this assertion escapes scientific assessment, they maintain that it does not bar us from creating artificial moral agents. And they add, in as far as there is something that humans do have and artificial agents do not have, we might create artificial behaviour that is functionally equivalent. For all practical purposes thus we may have an artificial agent: 'we predict that in the near term, (ro)bots will continue to converge toward human capacities while also showing considerable cognitive deficits. Nevertheless... the present state of AI, artificial life, and robotics is sufficient for the initiation of some interest-ing experiments in the design of AMAs [artificial moral agents]' According to Wallach and Allen so far no fundamental barriers to IT-artefacts becoming moral agents have been proven. In the meantime, they favour a pragmatic approach that is advocated by Floridi and Sanders. They argue for a mindless morality. Mental states or intentions are not required for moral agency.

Floridi and Sanders (2004) argue that given the appropriate level of abstrac-tion, i.e. how much knowledge about the artificial agent is abstracted, artificial agents can be moral agents if they meet the following conditions: they can interact with the environment; they display autonomous behaviour; they have adaptive capabilities. In addition, their actions must qualify as moral actions by being able to cause moral good or evil. Through their actions they can have moral impact. Note that Floridi and Sanders list fewer conditions than researchers in artificial intelligence usually require (e.g. Wooldridge 2000). Most notably, according to them mental states need not be assumed for agents to be moral agents *though it is required to be held morally responsible*. What the above researchers in fact argue is that the class of moral agents must be extended to include non-human agents.

The whole notion of artificial morality is a mistake according to other authors. Along lines similar to some of the STS researchers (position four, 'moral significance through human intentionality'), they argue that IT-artefacts are tethered to humans. Any meaning computer systems might have is meaning assigned to them through human convention. Even if the actions of a human and an artificial agent are functionally equivalent, they are achieved through different means. This is an important distinction, according to Johnson and Miller (2008). Their view is that even if, at certain levels of abstraction, IT-artefacts might be seen as autonomously operating entities, we cannot transfer moral concepts from one level – the human level at which they have been given meaning – to another level at which the IT-artefact operates autonomously. Computers have moral impact but they can never be conceived as moral agents. 'Users and their institutions are the beginning and ending point for all computer systems. Even computer subsystems that take their input from and deliver their output to other computer systems are ultimately connected to humans' (Johnson and Miller 2008).

12.5.3   Artificial moral agents with mental states

Most traditional philosophers maintain that moral behaviour requires mental states, consciousness, free will, that are (almost) exclusively human. Others, following Dennett, have argued that the behaviour of some IT-artefacts can be sufficiently rich to justify the assumption that they act as-if they have intentionalities. Many researchers (e.g. Boella and Torre 2004, Dastani, Wooldridge 2000, Wiegel *et al.* 2005, Wiegel 2006) taking this position are involved in research projects that involve the belief–desire–intention model by Bratman (1987) and are situated in the field of AI. In order to construct IT-artefacts with moral reasoning capabilities, intentions are 'constructed' or attributed to artificial agents. This attribution provides a workable mechanism in creating moral behaviour that is recognizable as such.

None of the researchers claim that the artificial intentions are human intentions. Nor is it claimed that these have (yet) reached levels of sophistication that are at all comparable to human intentions. Several researchers in this group have argued that the notions are as elusive in the human context as they are in the context of artificial agents. Wallach and Allen (2008) maintain that 'the question whether deterministic systems can be *real* moral agents is as unanswerable as the question of whether human beings *really* have free will'.

Moor (2006) argued against the idea that we can never have moral machines: 'no machine can have consciousness, intentionality, and free will. All of this is metaphysically contentious, but the simple rebuttal is that we have no idea whether machines of the future must lack these features.' There are two distinctive aspects to the above positions. It is pragmatic, in the sense that it provides a workable model, and it ignores the metaphysical questions claiming that the notions are too elusive at the current state of scientific knowledge. This position is also radical in its denial of human exclusivity in the domain of moral agency. The basis for this radical position has been laid by the ontocentric instead of anthropocentric philosophy of information that has been developed by Floridi (1999b).

12.5.4   Moral admissibility of artificial moral agents

Somewhat separate from the other questions is whether we should embark on the enterprise of creating artificial moral agents at all. The argument in favour highlights the already far-advanced presence of technologies that do have moral impact and act (quasi)autonomously. Sullins (2006b) argues that robotics technology becomes more ubiquitous and interactive and will become involved in morally laden situations. Together with a tendency to anthropomorphize robots, this creates situations that would be seen as moral. The question arises whether particular moral duties and rights will carry over if the caregiver is a robot rather than a human? For robust robots, he argues, that do complex moral reasoning the programmers are 'somewhat responsible but not entirely so'. In other words, 'the machine's programmers are not the only locus of moral agency in robots'.

Floridi and Sanders (2004) take a different line in arguing for moral accountability on the part of artificial agents. They argue against the traditional anthropocentric approach in which moral agency is confined to individual agents and is human-based. This would hinder 'the development of a satisfactory investigation of the distributed morality, a macroscopic and growing phenomenon of global moral actions and collective responsibilities resulting from the "invisible hand" of systemic interactions among several local agents at the local field'. Wallach and Allen (2008) argue along similar lines that 'The computer revolution is continuing to promote reliance on automation, and autonomous systems are increasingly in charge of a variety of decisions that have ethical ramifications.' Computer systems are involved in decision-making that involves value judgements. And as the systems become increasingly autonomous those decisions may not be guided by humans any longer. They conclude that 'Systems that are blind to the relevant values that should guide decisions in uncertain conditions are a recipe for disaster.'

It is therefore highly desirable that these artificial agents are provided with some moral awareness or even moral reasoning capacity. The argument goes even further in that it allows that sometimes artificial agents might be better moral judges than humans because of the exclusion of prejudices, emotional considerations and access to a wider knowledge base. The basic underlying argument in all above positions is that there is the widespread and continuing use and reliance on IT in situations that are morally charged.

The antagonists (e.g. Johnson and Miller 2008) to this position point to an 'assumed' technological determinism. The introduction of technologies that have moral impact is, they point out, not an accident but a human decision. The development of technology is driven by interest groups that have 'distinctively human interests in mind – more sophisticated and effective weapons, more global and efficient markets . . . Attributing moral agency to computer systems simply hides those groups and their interests.' Not only does the notion of artificial morality presuppose wrong notions about morality, it is a highly morally undesirable notion because it helps framing or hiding questions in such a way as to serve particular interest groups. An additional argument against creating artificial moral agents (AMA) is that creating them would provide humans an excuse for immoral behaviour on the part of the AMAs and absolve the designers of their responsibilities. Johnson and Miller (2008) argue that 'to conceptualize such systems as autonomous moral agents is to absolve those who design and deploy them from any responsibility for doing so. It is similar to absolving from responsibility people who put massive amounts of chemicals in the ocean on grounds that they didn't know precisely how the chemicals would react with salt water or algae.'

Grodzinksy et al. (2008) argue along similar lines, stressing the responsibilities of the designers. Creating artificial moral agents that reason about morality would let designers off the hook too easily. In their view, although a level of abstraction can be found in which an IT-artefact can be said to be a moral agent exhibiting learning and intentionality of some sort, the designer still remains fully responsible. 'The designer is in some sense responsible for all subsequent behaviours, whether or not they were planned or anticipated.' In order to fulfil this responsibility, the designers should limit the possibilities for autonomous action by the IT-artefacts. Their argument runs diametrically opposed to arguments in favour of artificial morality. The first group argues that, because IT-artefacts will operate more and more autonomously, we need to equip them with some sort of moral awareness and reasoning capabilities to prevent them from doing harm in situations that we cannot foresee at design time. The second group argues that, because we cannot foresee the behaviour, we should not create artificial agents that can act with such a degree of autonomy and impact. If we limit ourselves we have no need for artificial morality.

12.6   IT-artefacts as moral agents: no longer a privileged human position

The appearance of increasingly smart and autonomous IT-artefacts pose new questions that various researchers feel cannot be answered by the traditional approaches in STS that deal with technical artefacts. Some IT-artefacts are just technical artefacts. A growing subset of both implicit and explicit ethical agents, however, seems to escape the analysis of the traditional approaches.

The development of explicit ethical agents is still in its early engineering state. The successful deployment of explicit ethical agents is a possibility but not a foregone conclusion. We will see an increasing number of various IT-artefacts that have varying degrees of sophistication. Some of these will be relatively simple and can be treated as technical artefacts. Others will only be understandable if we treat them as if they were intentional entities or view them from a non-anthropocentric perspective. They will pose a considerable challenge to researchers in STS. ANT and information ethics (see Chapter 5) are two theories capable of accommodating the development of explicit ethical agents in its theoretical framework. The other approaches deny there can be such a thing as an IT-artefact that could lay claim to intentionality and moral decision-making.

We will need new theories, or extended theories, on how to deal with these entities, how to hold them to account. The moral status of the IT-artefacts will have to be addressed in much more detail than is currently done. And we might have to attribute them intentionality in order to make sense of them. But only if we can argue that it is morally admissible, or even obligatory, to create these kinds of IT-artefacts. And that is still an open question.

Special thanks to Peter Kroes for his ideas, comments and support. Thanks to Maarten Franssen, Bjorn Jespersen and Sabine Roessner for their comments. Of course all faulty reasoning remains solely my own.

13 Artificial life, artificial agents, virtual realities: technologies of autonomous agency

Colin Allen

13.1 Introduction

This chapter discusses ethical issues arising in connection with artificial life (non carbon-based), artificial agents (physically embodied robots and software agents or 'bots') and virtual reality. To different degrees, each of these technologies has a tinge of science fiction, but they are nevertheless all far enough advanced to raise current and pressing ethical issues. Each of them can be considered in the context of general ethical issues raised by philosophers of technology. These include worries about unintended harms, ranging from incremental erosion of human freedom and dignity as a result of overdependence on machines, to the danger of a huge catastrophe by technological failure. They also include general worries about the difficulty of assessing risks and rewards of technological development, and about the potential of technology to concentrate political and economic power in the hands of those who have privileged access or technical knowledge, creating a *de facto* technocracy or fostering economic injustice.

The specific ethical issues on which this chapter is focused arise from the potential for autonomous agency that is afforded by computational agents and environments. The chapter begins with a brief survey of the technologies involved, subdividing both artificial agents and virtual reality to produce a list of five different kinds of technology. Next comes a discussion of the notion of autonomy as it applies to people and to information-processing artefacts. The ethical issues arising in the context of each of the five technologies are then described, followed by some concluding remarks.

13.1.1 Introduction to the technologies

We begin by clarifying the kinds of technology to be discussed under the headings of artificial life, artificial agents and virtual reality.

Artificial Life may be 'wet' or 'dry'. *Wet ALife* is concerned with engineering new forms of life using for its substrate the same biochemical materials and reactions that constitute naturally evolved living organisms. In practical terms, this means engineering novel carbon-based life forms. *Dry ALife* is concerned with engineering new forms of life from materials and processes not currently known to constitute living organisms. This refers to the attempt to produce novel forms of life using the computational capacities and silicon-based circuitry of our most advanced electronics. Given that the context of this chapter is a volume on computer ethics, we restrict our attention to dry ALife. This is not to deny the essential role that computers play in the design of wet ALife, but a similar role is played in a great many ethically questionable technologies that are outside the scope of this chapter, for instance the design of nuclear weapons. A further division of ALife is possible, into physically embodied robots and virtual organisms operating entirely within computational environments. Although the concept of dry ALife stretches the boundaries of the concept of life, no attempt will be made to define life beyond the idea that it involves processes or entities that are adaptive, self-regulatory and capable of perpetuating their lineage through a process of self-replication (Schrödinger 1944, Farmer and Belin 1992).

Artificial Agents may be embodied or virtual. *Embodied artificial agents* are designed to operate autonomously in physical environments ranging from the nanoscale to the macroscopic domains of interstellar space. Autonomous robots are the most obvious examples of embodied artificial agents, but cyborgs and other forms of technologically enhanced human beings may also qualify as embodied artificial agents. *Virtual artificial agents*, sometimes known as software 'bots', are designed to operate inside computationally generated environments. These entities may be embedded in standalone applications, such as the artificially intelligent agents that have long been included in computer games. Or they may operate in networked environments, including the Internet as a whole and specific portions of the Internet that make up the so-called 'virtual worlds' for multiuser games (e.g., *World of Warcraft*) and multiuser social environments (e.g., *Second Life*). Like 'life', the proper definition of the term 'agency' is a matter of controversy, and the concept of artificial agent stretches ordinary usage. In this chapter, 'agent' will be used to refer to any system that can use information adaptively to achieve some goals. The ethics of both embodied and virtual artificial agents are discussed below.

Virtual Realities (VRs) are computer-generated environments designed to exploit the sensory systems of human beings so as to produce a sense of presence in those environments. *Machine-centred virtual realities* are computational environments that are designed to make things easy for computers. For instance, the Internet Protocol (IP) address space is a machine-centred virtual reality which is structured to make it easy for computers to pass messages across the Internet. Machine-centred virtual realities make little or no attempt to replicate the look or feel of physical environments for their human users. Nevertheless, early users of computer networks such as the ARPAnet (predecessor to the Internet) were often thrilled by the sense of remote presence provided by a virtual terminal connection to another computer that could be located hundreds or thousands of kilometres away. *Anthropomorphic virtual realities* are computational environments which attempt to make it easy (or engaging) for humans to interact with machines and other humans by replicating the kinds of experiences humans have of their physical (and social) environments. They vary in the degree to which the full range of human experience is replicated, and in the extent to which the faithful simulation of a physical environment is the end in itself, as for example in flight simulators, or an instrument for effective presentation of other kinds of information, as imagined by the original cyberpunk author William Gibson in his début novel *Neuromancer*.

13.1.2   Autonomous agency

Each of the five technologies just described contains the potential for autonomous agency either of the technological artefacts themselves or of humans operating within the virtual environments provided by the technology. There are divergent views among philosophers about how to understand the notion of autonomous agency.

The Kantian tradition within moral philosophy holds that genuinely autonomous agency is possible only for fully rational persons, and this is often taken to be restricted, at least on this planet, to mature, adult human beings. The Kantian conception is tied up with ideas about the importance of conscious reflection on reasons for beliefs and actions, and on the capacity to be guided by consciously adopted normative principles in the face of temptation or tendency to act differently. Such a conception is also entangled with the thorny notion of free will.

In contrast to the Kantian conception, there are deflationary accounts of autonomous agency which entail only that a reasonable selection is made among different behavioural options that take some account of the environmental challenges and contingencies but is not entirely determined by the environmental factors. Thus, for example, a rat faced with two food odours leading in opposite directions approaches one of them without that selection being strictly determined by the external cues. To say that the selection is *reasonable* is not to say that the agent is capable of self-consciously thinking about the reasons for choosing one way rather than another. Rather, it is to attribute the selection to the operation of a mechanism that has been deliberately designed or has evolved to make such decisions so as to satisfy some goals.

In this chapter, the phrase 'autonomous agent' is to be understood as something close to the latter 'deflationary' notion. If the Kantian insists, he or she can have the words. The important point is that our five emerging technologies represent something relatively new in the history of technology, namely artefacts which are not merely static, like bridges or buildings, and not mere vehicles for direct human agency, such as automobiles or can openers. These new technologies possess within them mechanisms that allow them to operate flexibly and without direct human supervision in a variety of conditions. On some views (e.g., Dennett 1987, Floridi and Sanders 2004) the agency of such artefacts is a matter of a stance taken by observers who are not mindful of the mechanistic principles by which they operate, and who may even be incapable of understanding them in such terms. On other views, the agency may be inherent to the structure of the mechanisms themselves (e.g., Wallach and Allen 2008). In other words, if an agent is a certain kind of complex mechanism, then it is not just a 'stance' but a proper description when agency is attributed to things having the right kind of complexity. For the purposes of this chapter it is not necessary to take a stand on this issue.

ALife and the technologies of embodied and virtual artificial agents obviously involve autonomous agency in the just-described sense. It may be less obvious how both forms of VR also involve this concept. Arguably, however, these technologies provide the environments where artificial autonomous agents have reached their most advanced forms. In machine-centred VR, millions of programs running on networked computers take ethically significant decisions without human oversight every millisecond of the day. Computers, for example, govern almost every credit card transaction on the planet, deciding whether to accept or decline charges without direct human supervision. Stock market trades are carried out by software using sophisticated analytical tools to determine the timing of sales and purchases. These programs are themselves artificial agents, but they are operating in a designed environment that allows them to make their decisions. A software trading system cannot operate unless the market provides pricing information directly to the software. Access to the data necessary for such agents to operate is part of what is afforded by the machine-centred VR. Thus, the ethics of constructing such environments cannot be separated from questions about the autonomy of the agents operating within it.

For anthropomorphic VR, the questions also include what kinds of entities should populate these environments. For instance, multi-user games in virtual environments gain some of their interest from the interactivity (and unpredictability) of the behaviour of other people operating within the same VR space. But people using VR also want artificial elements of these environments to behave in autonomous, interesting ways. Computer-generated characters inhabiting the space need to be as engaging as human-operated avatars. Furthermore, in anthropomorphic VR the autonomous agency afforded to people navigating the VR space can be technologically enhanced but it can also be artificially limited. The opening up of new possibilities for action and the closing down of other possibilities may have important consequences for the benefits and harms to people, whether directly internal to the virtual realms or indirectly through the effects on how people transfer what they have learned in the VR context to the real world. Thus, autonomous agency is also an important issue within anthropomorphic VR environments.

13.2   Ethics of virtual autonomy

We now turn to the particular ways in which issues of autonomy and agency play out in our five selected technologies.

13.2.1   ALife

During the 1960s, the exponential growth of speed and storage capacity in integrated circuits was recognized, giving us what is now known as Moore's Law (Moore 1965). The 1970s saw the introduction of 'genetic algorithms' (Holland 1975). Together, these developments suggested that the enormous power of evolution would soon be harnessed for computational purposes. In the 1980s, early proponents of ALife imagined that success was just around the corner. However, the task of engineering virtual computational environments in which ALife can flourish has proven much more difficult than its early advocates assumed. Partly this is due to the fact that ALife researchers started out with what we now know in hindsight to be overly simplistic ideas about the relationship between genotypes and phenotypes. For example, if an ALife researcher wanted to evolve artificial creatures whose artificial neural networks were capable of some task, they typically assumed it was appropriate to have one 'gene' for each connection in the network to determine the strength ('weight') of that connection. The fact that there aren't enough genes to code for every connection in the brain had been understood from at least the 1950s, even by computer scientists. But the one gene-one weight approach to ALife was nonetheless adopted as a reasonable simplifying assumption to allow modelling to begin.

This stance was partly based on the old dogma from biology that genes code for proteins in a one-to-one fashion. However, the genome mapping projects that were started in the 1990s and culminated with the publication of the first complete human genome in 2003 taught biologists that the development of organisms is far more complicated than this dogma suggests. The construction of cells and living organisms requires many resources not just from outside the DNA but from outside the cell and outside the organism itself. There is much machinery between transcription of a piece of DNA and the appearance of a specific protein in a cell. Furthermore, the so-called regulatory sequences of DNA need not code for proteins at all, and even those pieces of DNA that are used for the production of proteins do not directly specify the proteins expressed, but are subject to processes such as post-transcription editing by RNA. The result is that there is no one–one correspondence between genes and products, let alone between genes and phenotypic traits. The interactions are fearsomely complex, and it is part of the reason why humans and flatworms can be so different anatomically and behaviourally despite the fact that they have roughly the same number of genes, with many of those genes even being shared. So far this discussion has focused on the evolution of virtual organisms for computationally defined environments, but progress is also being made on evolvable hardware. Much of this work reinforces the lessons about the complexity of physical interactions and the surprising ways in which physical components can interact, even sometimes confounding the expectations of engineers (Thompson 1996, Lohn and Hornsby 2006).

Until the process of organismic development is more fully understood, ALife 'organisms' will remain but caricatures of actual living entities. Although there's plenty that's artificial about ALife, there's still not enough that's significantly life-like about it. Computer viruses and worms are sometimes claimed to be examples of successful artificial life forms; the extent to which such pieces of 'malware' successfully replicate themselves from one computer to another suggests a life-like process. However, these automatically propagating programs do not provide an example of an adaptive, self-regulatory process. They do not make use of (simulated) genetic mechanisms, and there is not a single case of a wild-type mutation in a virus or worm leading to an adaptive change in the means by which it propagates or infects vulnerable systems. Although 'polymorphic' and 'metamorphic' viruses are programmed to reorganize their code as a means to evade detection by virus scanners, these variations do not allow the viruses to adapt to changing ecological conditions, such as changes in the host operating systems, or transmission to entirely different operating systems, and they have no way to adapt to more sophisticated scanners.

Despite the utility of evolutionary algorithms for finding efficient solutions to difficult hardware and software design problems, these approaches yield systems that can be hard to analyse and understand. This lack of transparency, due to the complexity of the interactions involved, may be a source of worry about effective risk analysis for those who wish to deploy artificially evolved hardware or software. Nevertheless, current ALife technology is far from sustaining adaptive, self-regulatory and self-reproducing lineages of autonomous agents. The technological limitations noted here for both virtual and physically embodied ALife should, therefore, temper concerns about ALife somehow escaping the clutches of scientists, and running amok. Worries about the perils and ethical consequences of life *in silico* are destined to remain science fiction into the foreseeable future. Many commentators believe, however, that a more plausible path towards artificial life forms consists in hybridization of biological life forms with machines: cyborgs.

13.2.2   Embodied artificial agents

Embodied artificial agents are designed for operation in physical environments. Cyborgs are one main genus of embodied artificial agents, the other main genus being robots, which are completely inorganic in nature.

Cyborg technology covers a very wide spectrum of hybrid systems. It may be difficult to give a sharp definition that captures just what interests us about cyborgs in this context. A common dictionary definition, for example, identifies a cyborg as a 'person whose abilities are extended beyond normal human limitations by mechanical elements built into the body'. In this case, anyone with dental implants might count as a cyborg, if those artificial teeth are considerably stronger or more cavity resistant than their natural counterparts. Prosthetic devices of all kinds are capable of enhancing human abilities, and the 2008 case of whether double amputee Oscar Pistorius could compete in the Olympic Games with his 'Cheetah' blade legs highlighted the extent to which artificial limbs might provide an 'unfair' advantage because their material characteristics provide more efficient energy storage and return than natural legs. In the end, Pistorius failed to beat the qualifying time for entry to the 400 m event, although his time certainly put him well beyond average human running speed. Perhaps, however, the dictionary definition excludes Oscar Pistorius from the category of cyborgs on the grounds that his Cheetah blades were strapped on, not 'built into' the body. Still, it is not too much of stretch to imagine such prostheses soon being surgically implanted via an artificial knee or hip joint. Other borderline cases of cyborg technology include robotic exoskeletons that are being developed for military use (e.g., by the Utah-based robotics company Sarcos) and hybrid robots that use actual biological neurons grafted onto a multi-electrode array (MEA) to control simulated and embodied systems (Potter, Wagenaar and DeMarse 2006; as widely reported by news media, Potter trained 25,000 rat neurons on an MEA to control a flight simulator).

Setting definitional matters aside, the kinds of cyborgs that have the most interest for the purposes of this chapter are those which offer cognitive enhancements to humans through implanted computational devices. For many citizens of technologically advanced societies, cell phones, PDAs and pocket Wi-Fi devices have become indispensable external aids to our fallible memories and limited knowledge bases. Prototypes for cell phone implants have already been developed, but while these are physically embedded within the human body, they so far involve no direct links to the human nervous system. External readings of brain waves via EEG technology are being tested for the control of speech synthesizers, wheelchairs and avatars in virtual environments. The prospect of even tighter integration of information technology with human minds via direct implantation of devices to the human nervous system seems to offer enormous possibilities for cognitive enhancement. Neural-cognitive implants are being investigated mostly with medical applications in mind, but some for the sheer thrill of being at a technological frontier. Thus, brain–computer interfaces are being investigated for speech synthesis and brain-implanted electrodes have been used to control prosthetic limbs in monkeys and humans (Lebedev and Nicolelis 2006). At the more speculative and futuristic end of the spectrum, Kevin Warwick, professor of cybernetics at Reading University, has experimented with a variety of implants (Warwick 2004).

These technological developments raise some very general ethical issues that accompany the use of any technology. For example, the adoption of advanced technologies frequently widens the gap between haves and have-nots. Much has been made of the 'digital divide' between those who have access to computers and the Internet, and those who do not (see, e.g., Servon 2002). The 'cyborg divide' could be just as significant if these enhancements provide major advantages to those who adopt them. Specific enhancements also raise particular ethical issues. For instance, there are already hearing enhancers that can increase hearing sensitivity twentyfold, which means that you may no longer safely assume that a distant person cannot hear your private conversation. Human-cyborg technologies afford greatly enhanced agency in the real world through an increase in cognitive and physical capacities. If a cyborg human can do the physical work of ten men or the intellectual work of a team of experts, this has potentially profound consequences for increasing the freedom and autonomy of those who are enhanced, and decreasing the freedom and autonomy of those who are not.

While cyborgs are still mostly confined to the research laboratory, robots have long been a presence in the human environment. Industrial robots are very widely used, but these special-purpose machines are typically bolted to the factory floor where they do one job, and one job only. In non-industrial applications, however, autonomous or semi-autonomous robots that are free to roam and may have multiple capabilities are becoming mass-market consumer items as well as occupying more specialized niches. One morally significant area where the widespread use of robots is currently envisaged is in the burgeoning field of elder-care (Anderson and Anderson 2008). Technologically advanced countries are facing a large bulge in their elderly populations. Japanese society is particularly faced with the challenge of insufficient health care workers to take care of the aging population, and the introduction of robots in this context has been made an official government policy. So-called 'carebots' may be responsible for dispensing medicines, making sure they are taken, encouraging exercise and providing basic companionship (Floridi 2008a).

The field of robotics is also a major focus for military planners, for example the US Army's Future Combat Systems program. At the same time there is increasing penetration of semi-autonomous robots into homes, whether as programmable robotic toys (e.g., Sony's now-discontinued AIBO robotic dog, or current offerings such as Ugobe's Pleo robotic baby dinosaur) or as household appliances (e.g., iRobot's Roomba robotic vacuum cleaner). Roboticist and iRobot founder Rodney Brooks argues that there is presently an inverse relationship between price and autonomy (Brooks 2007). The expense of military robots means that there is an incentive to place them under human supervision to protect the investment. But home robots must be cheap to be commercially successful, and their owners do not want to have to supervise them continually. Neither does the average home contain the infrastructure that would be required for comprehensive monitoring and control. Thus the expensive robots that have been deployed for space exploration or military applications have thus far been almost entirely tele-operated, while the cheap robots intended for the mass market are relatively uncontrolled. Although Brooks may, for the time being, be right about the relationship about being cheap and out of control, the logic of military deployment nevertheless drives towards giving robots greater autonomy (Wallach and Allen 2008). For instance, the 'unmanned' drones that have been used extensively by the US military for missions in Afghanistan, Pakistan and Iraq, are in fact tele-operated from a base in Nevada by crews of four or more highly trained individuals. Increasing the autonomy of the drones would allow more of them to be flown with the same number of operators. The advantages for military superiority of having greater numbers of fighting units provides an incentive for increasing machine autonomy.

To work effectively with humans, robots need to engage human interest and maintain it. The field of human–robot interaction (HRI) investigates visual, linguistic and other cues that support engaging interactions. Among the characteristics that are systematically investigated by HRI scientists are the emotionally significant facial expressions and non-verbal properties of speech, such as rhythm or prosody, that play a significant role in human social interaction. These 'minimal cognition' cues are a focus of behaviour-based robotics (Breazeal 2002), and have proven surprisingly effective in giving people the sense that they are dealing with intelligent agents. However, some critics fear that the addition of such traits to robots is fundamentally deceptive, relying on the strong tendency of humans to anthropomorphize objects by projecting human-like characteristics onto things that don't have them. This may prove especially problematic in the context of elder-care, with people who are relatively starved of human companionship (Turkle 2005, Turkle *et al.* 2006).

All of these applications of robotics – whether home, military or healthcare – involve their own ethical issues. This is especially clear for military applications where there is considerable concern about ensuring that combat robots follow acceptable rules of war, as encoded by the Geneva conventions for instance (Arkin 2007), and for healthcare applications where the issue of patients' rights (for instance, to refuse medication) are of concern (Anderson and Anderson 2007). Arkin (2004) has also suggested that the likely military, service and sexual applications of robots may serve to revive callous attitudes towards life and liberty that characterized earlier stages of human history, thus undermining moral progress in domains such as the formal abolition of slavery. Arkin neatly captures these concerns with his title phrase, 'Bombs, Bonding, and Bondage'.

More generically, the presence of autonomous robots in real-world environments, where it may not always be possible to constrain their actions to well-defined contexts (robots do roam), raises questions about whether these machines will need to have on-board ethical decision-making capacities (Moor 2006, Turilli 2007, Wallach and Allen 2008). With the current state of robotics and artificial intelligence, the suggestion that artificial moral agents are possible, let alone necessary, may seem far-fetched. However, assessments of the autonomy and morality of artificial agents may hinge less on 'deep' metaphysical facts about moral agency, and more on the fact that people will adopt different stances towards artificial agency based on whether they understand (or care to understand) the underlying mechanisms (Floridi and Sanders 2004, Grodzinsky *et al.* 2008). The need is illustrated by the fact that artificial agents operating in virtual environments are already autonomously making decisions with potentially significant ethical consequences, even though they are blind to those consequences. The computer that denies your credit card purchase makes no prediction about whether this will ruin your day or your life, and gathers no information that might help it make such a determination.

Robotics thus forces us to think hard about whether and how autonomous agency might be located or replicated in the computer algorithms that control our most advanced technologies. The challenge of building machines that can be regarded as artificial moral agents raises not only questions about the ethics of doing so, but also raises questions about the nature of ethics itself, such as whether ethical rules and principles are the kinds of things that can effectively guide behaviour in real-time decision-making (Wallach and Allen 2008).

13.2.3   Virtual artificial agents

Virtual artificial agents (aka 'bots') already exist. They operate inside computationally generated environments ranging from the Internet as a whole, to electronic markets such as NASDAQ and eBay, to computer games, and they exist within networked virtual worlds such as *Second Life* that are designed primarily for entertainment, but are also increasingly being used for communication and education. Various kinds of autonomous systems have been built for these contexts. On the Internet as a whole there are information-gathering bots, for example the web crawlers used by search engines, which gather information with varying degrees of respect for the privacy of that information. In electronic markets, there are automated trading and bidding programs that carry out transactions based on formulas that in some cases are beyond the comprehension of those who rely upon them. Credit card approval decisions rely on the evaluation of multiple factors, whose combined effects may not have been fully appreciated or anticipated by their programmers, and that consider only general statistical patterns rather than the particular needs of the individual purchaser. Software games have long included agents with some degree of artificial intelligence, and the sophistication of these agents is continuously increasing.

The presence of bots in contexts where people are seeking social interaction has been a persistent concern to ethicists and technologists. These concerns predate the rich, virtual, multi-user environments exemplified by *Second Life*. They were raised in the context of the early text-based 'MUDs' (multi-user dungeons) and 'MOOs' (MUDS object oriented) that were constructed on early computer networks using only textual communication, and these concerns were raised even earlier than that in the context of artificial intelligence. A frequent concern is that people are easily tricked into forming social attachments to entities that are incapable of reciprocating them. This worry arose in the early days of artificial intelligence research in connection with ELIZA (Weizenbaum 1965), a program that simulated (or, perhaps, parodied) the question-asking technique of Rogerian psychotherapy, and that is credited as being the first 'chatterbot' or 'chatbot' – a piece of software which attempts to sustain a conversation with a human interlocutor. Carl Sagan enthusiastically suggested that in the future there would be computer psychotherapists available in street corner booths everywhere. Weizenbaum emphatically rejected this vision of the future and renounced his work on ELIZA, maintaining that computers would always lack the important human qualities of compassion and wisdom (Weizenbaum 1976).

The fact that people tend to overestimate the intelligence and complexity of computer programs is now known to AI researchers as the 'ELIZA effect'. It is a manifestation of the previously mentioned human tendency to anthropomorphize things. However, this tendency may be exacerbated by the much richer graphics-based virtual environments that have become common in the forty years since ELIZA's inception. Furthermore, in mixed virtual environments where some avatars are human-operated and others operated by autonomous software, it may be especially difficult to distinguish which are which. This is partly because the range of human actions in a virtual world is itself limited by the constraints on expression and action that are imposed by the rules of the virtual environment, a topic we shall return to in the following sections.

Although autonomous agents in virtual worlds are sometimes difficult for other users to distinguish from real human beings operating in those worlds, they are just as frequently all too easy to identify. And while there are many systems operating in virtual environments without direct human oversight, all of them are 'ethically blind' (Wallach and Allen 2008) in the sense that they lack specific information that would be relevant to ethical decision-making, they have no means of assessing the ethically relevant effects of their decisions, and they lack other capacities such as empathy that are important to human morality.

Work is also being done on virtual equivalents of cyborgs – on-screen avatars that combine tele-operation by humans with software enhancement. For instance, an on-screen avatar in a virtual reality context may derive its behaviour and appearance from the actions and facial expressions of a person connected to bodily motion sensors and cameras capable of providing enough information to render a three-dimensional model of the actor in the virtual setting. But such a tele-operated avatar can also be filtered through an intermediate layer of software and enhanced in specific ways, for instance by blending the appearance of the remote operator with the face of a famous person, or by enhancing and sustaining facial expressions that are known to influence the responses of other people to the avatar. The potential for 'persuasion' by non-verbal means is only just beginning to be investigated, but the potential for ethical abuse in such situations is already clear (Bailenson *et al.* 2008).

13.2.4   Machine-centred VR

We have already touched upon machine-centred VR in discussing the bots that operate there. While the autonomy of such agents is relatively limited at present, nevertheless the construction of machine-centred VR gives artificial agents an advantage compared to humans attempting to operate in the same environments. The simple example of online auctions illustrates this. Because the format in which information is presented favours machines, they are much more capable than humans of precisely timing a final bid to win an auction at the last second.

Of course, it is not all bad, and people reap benefits from having their software systems operate in environments that have been shaped so as to make it easy for the software rather than the people. Nevertheless, the design decisions involved in shaping such environments often have unintended effects, just as the shaping of our physical environments to accommodate motorized vehicles has had unintended effects on our ability to walk or use other modes of transportation, which in turn has both positive and negative consequences for general health and well-being. Similarly, the original use of the very limited set of characters belonging to the ASCII code made it easy for machines to process documents originally written in English, and for computers (and their English-speaking users) to communicate over networks. But the limitations of ASCII made it difficult for speakers of languages other than English to represent their documents in machine-processable formats and to communicate via email, instant messaging, and other information and communication technologies (ICTs). The adoption of Unicode, with its much richer character sets, has gone a long way towards rectifying these problems, of course, but not without the expense entailed in updating the software and revising archived materials so as to provide forward compatibility. Furthermore, ICTs embody other culture-specific assumptions about communication, such as the relative importance of words or text over non-verbal aspects of communication – for example, the facial and bodily gestures which in some cultures are important for showing proper respect to others. Thus it is important to recognize that technologies which appear to be value-neutral from one cultural perspective may in fact raise ethical issues in a different cultural context (Ess 2009).

The ethical issues raised by machine-centred VR environments are thus not just about the artificial agents operating within them, but concern the limitations placed by these environments upon people who attempt to operate within them. Current metaphors for information retrieval are frequently library-based metaphors, such as browsing and searching. Science fiction writers have long dreamed of technologies that would transform digitally encoded machine-centred VRs into information environments, epitomized by the brain–computer interface that the primary character of William Gibson's *Neuromancer* uses to 'enter', perceive and move around in cyberspace as if it were physical space. The field of information visualization is beginning to provide tools that support rich visual presentation of abstract information, and has been especially successful in providing visual representations of information networks. The much richer anthropomorphic VR access to the machine-centred underpinnings of the Internet envisaged by science fiction writers such as Gibson awaits the invention of appropriate physical, spatial and visual metaphors for the underlying information.

13.2.5   Anthropomorphic VR

Immersive, computer-generated environments attempt to present a 'realistic' world of experience to users. As with the previous section on machine-centred VR, our concern in this section is not with the agents populating these virtual realms, but with the ethical issues underlying the features of the environments themselves and the uses to which they are put (Brey 1999b). Anthropomorphic VR has been deployed for many purposes, including games, cybersex, teleconferencing, pilot training, soldier training, elementary school education, and it is under investigation for use in many more applications, for instance police lineups. These applications make different demands on the amount of realism involved. Flight simulators, for instance, aim to be realistic in almost all respects. Educational applications for anthropomorphic VR, do not always aim for full realism, since pedagogical objectives may lead their designers to limit both the range of actions that individuals can take within the virtual world, and to limit the range and complexity of responses to user actions. Consider, for example, all the ways that a school science project or field trip can go awry. A VR environment that is intended to substitute for a field trip may be deliberately designed so that it is less likely to fail (Barab *et al.* 2007). One might ask whether such a deliberate departure from realism teaches children the wrong lesson about how easy it is to do good scientific research, by oversimplifying the task of data collection and setting up in them the expectation that the world is more predictable than it actually is. But this seems like a relatively minor worry when the alternative might be no field trip at all because of the difficulty and expense involved.

VR-based games typically depart from realism in numerous ways. Games may, for instance, enable users to pretend that they have magical powers that can transcend the limitations of the physical world. It is hard to see how exercising the capacity to act out such fantasies would be harmful or unethical, except insofar as the activities are so intrinsically rewarding that they lead to addictive behaviour. A more worrisome aspect of anthropomorphic VR concerns what it affords to individuals by way of freedom to act out violent or coercive fantasies. When the person is operating as a single user within an isolated VR application, the ethical issues raised by actions within that environment are necessarily indirect. Their indirectness may not make them any less pressing, however, as concerns are widespread about how the ability to rehearse violent, misanthropic or misogynistic actions in video games may desensitize users to those issues in the real world, or even provide a training effect that makes game players more likely to engage in similar actions outside of the VR context. However, there is also a longstanding response that violent games actually divert antisocial propensities into a context where they are harmless. The scientific research on this topic remains controversial (but see Ess 2009 for a balanced treatment).

When the VR context involves networked computers and multiple users, the ethical issues take on a different character because there is the possibility of direct harm to other users. A case of 'cyberbullying' of a teenager by an adult in the United States using the *MySpace* social networking site allegedly led to the teenager's suicide, but resulted only in conviction in 2008 on misdemeanour charges of illegal computer access; a more serious charge of conspiracy was dismissed. Social networking in VR environments also allows users to simulate acts of violence or coercion that would be unethical or socially unacceptable outside the VR context. For instance, a case of virtual rape has been reported in *Second Life* and investigated by Belgian police. Also, real opportunities for fraud and for theft of valuable property are made possible with *Second Life*. The question of whether VR relationships can be adulterous has also been raised (Thomas 2004, Stuart 2008; see also Ess 2009), and regardless of the philosophical discussion of this point, there have been cases where online relationships have resulted in real-world divorce.

In affording the opportunity to transcend physical or social barriers, anthropomorphic VR provides technological enhancement of personal autonomy. Such opportunities are not ethically neutral, however. They may affect other individuals directly, or have indirect effects by training or reinforcing habits of action that may spill over into the real world.

13.3 Conclusion

In this fast-paced tour of the ethics of artificial life, artificial agents and virtual realities it has been suggested that the common theme uniting these technologies concerns the ethics of autonomous agency. For artificial life, robots and software bots, there are ethical questions concerning the agency inherent in these systems themselves, whether they can be made to respect ethical boundaries, and the ways in which, as these systems become more sophisticated, they may lead humanity down a path which reduces human freedom or autonomy. For virtual reality, the ethical questions concern the ways in which they may provide new opportunities for human agency, or they may restrict those opportunities, and whether they may habituate or desensitize people to violence and other acts of oppression, or perhaps train people to act in antisocial or unethical ways.

Neither the benefits nor risks of these technologies are easily predictable. The histories of both techno-utopianism and techno-pessimism are full of embarrassing overstatements. The best we can do is articulate long-term goals for these technologies while carefully monitoring the current developments to see how well those goals are being accomplished, to identify unanticipated problems before the technologies become so entrenched that they are difficult to change, and to make the designers of these technologies more cognizant of the extent to which their computer systems embody their values (Nissenbaum 2001), many of which are culturally specific (Ess 2009). It is with this approach in mind that the chapter has eschewed futuristic questions about whether our artefacts will ever themselves be appropriately condemned for their moral failings (Dennett 1996). Such speculations are entertaining and make for great discussions in undergraduate philosophy courses, but the more pressing ethical issues confronting us in the technologies of autonomous agency are those outlined above.

Acknowledgements

I thank Luciano Floridi and Wendell Wallach for their comments.

14 On new technologies

Stephen Clarke

14.1 Introduction

Ethical concerns about new technologies may be divided into two broad categories: concerns about newly introduced technologies, and concerns about technologies that might be introduced in the future. It is sometimes thought that we should focus exclusively on actual technologies and that concerns about possible future technologies are 'just science fiction' – mere speculations about what might be the case, which distract us from a proper consideration of what is the case. A contrary point of view is that we should attempt to anticipate ethical problems in advance of the implementation of new technologies. Instead of adapting norms and practices to accommodate new technologies after these have become available, we should try to produce new technologies that are in keeping with the values and practices we currently adhere to. In order to anticipate the ethical problems that new technologies will raise, we need to try to anticipate which of the possible future technologies that raise ethical concerns are likely to become actual, and try to respond to these.

In this chapter, we will consider prominent ethical concerns that have been raised about newly introduced technologies and about technologies that might be implemented in the future. In the case of newly introduced technologies, we will focus on concerns about privacy, individual autonomy and threats to safety. These are far from the only ethical concerns raised by newly introduced technologies, but they do appear to be the ones that have provoked the most discussion in the media and in academic circles. Concerns about privacy and threats to safety also feature prominently in discussions of future technologies, as do concerns about autonomy. A very prominent form of concern about threats to safety, in the discussion of possible future technologies, addresses catastrophic future scenarios. Concerns about autonomy have a tendency to become mixed up with concerns about the future of the human species, when our focus is on possible future technologies. This tendency will be reflected in our discussion.

Throughout this chapter the term 'information' is used broadly, to refer, roughly, to knowledge or facts, in the abstract or in the various ways in which knowledge or facts may be stored. There is a lack of agreement in the philosophical literature about the exact meaning of the term 'information'. For more on the different approaches to the philosophy of information, and the problem of defining information, see Floridi (2004).

14.2   Newly introduced technologies

14.2.1   Privacy

A host of recently available technologies enable governments, corporations and individuals to monitor individual activity in ways that would have been impossible only a few decades ago. Closed Circuit Television (CCTV) cameras transmit a signal to a restricted set of monitors and are used in the surveillance of specific locations. The Global Positioning System (GPS) utilizes satellite-based technology to accurately pinpoint the location of objects and individuals equipped with receivers, anywhere on the surface of the Earth. Radio Frequency Identity (RFID) tags can also be used to identify the location of objects and individuals. RFIDs are microscopic electronic tags that are mostly used by retailers to keep track of their products. They are either attached to the surfaces of products or implanted within them. They have also been implanted in animals and in a few cases in humans.

In 2004, the Food and Drug Administration approved the implantation of the *VeriChip* in humans (Foster and Jaeger, forthcoming). By 2006, these had been implanted in about 70 people in the US, mostly for medical reasons and to control access to high security areas (Waters 2006). It has been variously suggested that RFIDs should be implanted in employees of certain companies, immigrants and guest workers in the United States, sex offenders and US soldiers (Foster and Jaeger, forthcoming). Many commentators think that the use of RFIDs will become much more widespread soon. According to van den Hoven and Vermaas, 'Governments and the global business world are preparing for a large-scale implementation of RFID technology in the first decades of the 21st century' (2007, p. 291). Eastman Kodak has filed patent applications on a new technology that will enable RFID chips to be ingested (Tedjasaputra 2007). If this technology becomes readily available, it may become very easy to use RFID chips to monitor the whereabouts of individuals, without their consent, or even without them knowing that their movements are being monitored.

Unsurprisingly, the prospect of RFIDs being used to monitor the whereabouts of humans has met with fierce resistance from privacy advocates, such as CASPIAN (Consumers Against Supermarket Privacy Invasion and Numbering (www.nocards.org/)), and has prompted various publications warning of the threat to individual privacy. RFIDs are considered particularly suspect by some fundamentalist Christians, who see these as the 'Mark of the Beast' that we are warned about in the *Book of Revelations* (Albrecht and Macintyre 2006). In response to such concerns, three US states, California, Wisconsin and North Dakota, have passed laws prohibiting the forced implantation of RFIDs (Anderson 2007).

As well as technology that can monitor our movements, there are various technologies that can be used to interpret information collected about us. The interpretation of information provided by CCTV and other forms of video surveillance can be assisted by the use of face and gait recognition systems (Liu and Sarkar 2007). Information collected by aural surveillance devices can be interpreted using devices such as the 'Truth Phone', which analyses voice stress during telephone calls, in an attempt to detect lying (Davies 2003, p. 21). The 'love detector' operates similarly, identifying levels of excitement and arousal in speech, in an attempt to identify people's feelings for those that they are speaking to (see www.love-detector.com/index.php).

In addition to concerns about the aspects of our lives that are being monitored and concerns about how collected data can be analysed, there are concerns about who has access to personal data. Companies such as Acxiom specialize in buying data from businesses about their customers, integrating these into powerful data bases, and selling access to the data bases created to other businesses. Customers, who may be willing to accept that data about them may be made available to particular businesses that they have dealings with, may also be very unhappy about that data being passed on to other companies. Also of concern is the placement of data about individuals, such as court records, on the Internet. Enabling free and easy access to data that might otherwise be hard to access radically increases the number of their potential users and can alter the nature of their uses (Nissenbaum 2004).

It is widely accepted that individuals are entitled to certain forms of informational privacy and that certain information, such as personal financial data, which may find their way into some parts of the public realm, should be kept out of other parts of the public realm. Nissenbaum (2004) has argued that we should accept 'contextual integrity' as a benchmark for informational privacy in the public sphere. According to her, different contexts within the public sphere – the context of friendship, the context of the classroom and so on – are implicitly governed by particular norms of behaviour, including norms relating to respect for privacy. If her position is accepted, then information should not be made generally available, within a particular context, without due regard for the governing norms that implicitly shape our sense of what is appropriate within that context. Furthermore, information of a type that it is appropriate to make generally available in one context should not be transferred to a different context without due regard for norms that implicitly govern the flow of information between these particular contexts. Later, we will see that the scope of Nissenbaum's claims regarding the importance of contextual integrity stand in need of qualification, as Nissenbaum herself allows.

As well as debates about the right to informational privacy in general, there are debates about the right to informational privacy in the workplace. The surveillance of employee's emails, telephone calls and other forms of communication, by their workplace supervisors, is widespread. According to a recent survey, 73 per cent of American companies engaged in some form of electronic surveillance of their employees (Blackwell 2003). Although some commentators have argued that there is a presumptive right to privacy in the workplace, they generally acknowledge that this right needs to be balanced against the interests of employers, customers and other employees, all of whom have a legitimate interest in ensuring that employees are working effectively and are not using the workplace to conduct illegal activities (e.g. Miller and Weckert 2000). The topic will not be elaborated on here as the interested reader may find further information in Chapter 7.

14.2.2   Autonomy

One of the more important arguments for respecting the informational privacy of individuals is that, if people's activities are unknown to others then they cannot be deliberately interfered with by others. Therefore, they will be better able to act on their own life plans and devote their energies to satisfying their own preferences. In other words, they will be better able to realize the value of autonomy, a value which is deeply embedded in Western culture. Isaiah Berlin captured the core sentiments of the many of us who wish to live autonomously:

> I wish my life and decisions to depend on myself, not on external forces of whatever kind. I wish to be the instrument of my own, not of other men's acts of will. I wish to be a subject, not an object: to be moved by reasons, by conscious purposes, which are my own, not by causes which affect me, as it were from outside. (Berlin 1969, p. 131)

Of course, freedom from the external interference is not all there is to autonomy. Internal forces can also limit our ability to experience autonomy. Claustrophobics live with a fear of confined spaces. However, there may be some occasions when it is in the interest of a claustrophobic to enter particular confined spaces. If a claustrophobic is unable to overcome her fear when she decides that it is in her interest to do so, she has had her autonomy interfered with by an internal force.

In order, among other things, to ensure that people's autonomy is respected, interpersonal interactions in Western societies are typically structured around the ideal of mutual consent (Kleinig 1982). A business transaction can only occur when both buyer and vendor agree to complete that transaction. Similarly, a marriage can only occur when both bride and groom agree to the marriage. To provide 'effective consent' to an action, an agent must comprehend what they are consenting to, or at least have the opportunity to comprehend the major consequences of consenting to that action. Also, they must have sufficient, relevant information so that their consent can be the consequence of an informed autonomous decision. This is true of the many areas of human activity in which our governing norms of behaviour include consent requirements (Clarke 2001).

One way in which our autonomy can be compromised, when we are using new technologies, is that, sometimes, we may not understand what we are asked to consent to. An example of a complicated request for consent, that may be difficult to comprehend, is the request to consent to receive targeted behavioural advertising when a free *Gmail* email account is set up. New subscribers to free *Gmail* accounts are asked to consent to having the content of their emails mechanically scanned for keywords that are then used to select targeted advertisements, which appear alongside email messages. So, for example, if a *Gmail* user sends or receive emails containing an above average use of the word 'holiday', *Gmail* may direct advertisements for holidays to that user, rather than advertisements for some other product or service.

In medical contexts, it is a standard condition of the informed consent process that doctors discuss a recommended procedure or course of treatment with a prospective patient, so as to ensure that comprehension has been achieved (e.g. Wear 1998). It is not simply assumed that patients will comprehend complicated technical information disclosed for the purposes of enabling informed consent to be obtained. In the context of commercially provided software, it is perhaps unrealistic to suggest that companies should actively ensure that particular customers have comprehended technical information disclosed for the purposes of informed consent. However, it is reasonable to expect that companies do what they can to aid comprehension. Friedman *et al.* (2005, p. 515) describe the documents on *Gmail*'s registration and user interfaces as going 'a good distance toward helping ensuring comprehension'. And indeed the language used in the relevant documentation is admirably clear. Comprehension is more likely to be acquired as a result of reading the relevant documentation on *Gmail*'s registration and user interfaces than if this is not read. Nevertheless, there may be significant numbers of *Gmail* users who consent to use a *Gmail* account without properly comprehending what they are consenting to. They consent to use a *Gmail* account, but it is possible that they do not provide *effective* informed consent to the use of a *Gmail* account.

Targeted behavioural advertising seems set to become more confusing than it already is, due to new technology that will enable Internet service providers (ISPs) to track the websites visited by their customers in order to support targeted behavioural advertising. The current market leader in this area is a company called *Phorm* which has recently signed deals with the three biggest ISPs in the UK, *BT*, *Virgin Media* and *TalkTalk* to enable them to use their technology (see www.economist.com/science/tq/ displaystory.cfm?story_id=11482452). One's movements on the Internet can be tracked by HTTP cookies that have been downloaded onto computers, by search engines, by email providers and now by ISP providers. As well as raising obvious privacy issues, this situation raises significant concerns about autonomy. In order to provide effective informed consent to targeted behavioural advertising, computer users need to comprehend the means by which their behaviour is monitored. The fact that it may be monitored in a variety of different ways makes comprehension more difficult to achieve.

The introduction and uptake of new technologies creates a host of new social situations in which individuals have to decide how to behave. In such new situations, we may not have had time to collectively develop norms to guide behaviour. The rapid growth of information technologies has led to a slew of circumstances in which it is currently unclear what the appropriate norms of behaviour are and what the scope of consent should be. Should someone's consent be obtained before a photograph or a piece of video footage containing their image is posted on a site on the Internet (these days such visual images may be easily acquired without people's knowledge or consent using mobile camera phones)? Is it acceptable to post a document that has been created by another person, and forwarded to you, on a publicly accessible website, without their consent? Should I be allowed to create a website devoted to publicizing personal information about a third party, without obtaining their consent? The answers to these questions are not clear and answers that may be given will be contested.

Over time, as people interact with new technologies and with one another, norms can be expected to emerge that will guide behaviour. Alternatively, their development may be guided by the deliberate activities of policy makers, activists, lawyers and ethicists. Questions about the proper scope of consent have a clear ethical import. The answers to them that we generally accept will have a significant role in determining the scope of the sphere of individual autonomy. If we answer these questions without considering their ethical aspects then legal, institutional and practical considerations will do much to shape the norms that govern our behaviour at the expense of ethical considerations. The technology that we use will tend to shape the ethics that we accept, and the ethics that we accept will do little to shape the technology that we use. The reader interested in knowing more about recent discussions of the ways in which ethical standards are shaped by new technology and in which new technologies may be shaped by ethical considerations may wish to consult Budinger and Budinger (2006), Spier (2001), van den Hoven and Weckert (2008) and Winston and Edelbach (2008).

14.2.3 Threats to safety

There are many potential dangers associated with the use of new technologies. Some of these can be removed before particular new technologies are made publicly available. Still, there are usually going to be public concerns about the safety of some of the new technologies that are available. Public concerns about the safety of new information and communication technologies (ICT) have not received the same media attention as have public concerns about new biotechnologies. Nevertheless, concerns have been voiced about, for example, the safety of mobile phones and the radiation emitted by them and by the masts used to transmit phone signals, as well as about ICT human implants. The latter include cardiac pacemakers, cochlear implants, RFIDs that are implanted subcutaneously, and implantable neurostimulation devices, which are used, among other things, to manage chronic pain and to control seizures in epileptics. More broadly, there is growing concern about the increased use of nanotechnology. In particular, there is much concern about the consequences for humans of inhaling manufactured nanoparticles, or otherwise ending up with exotic nanoparticles in their bodies (Jones 2007, p. 75). Indeed, because of the importance of miniaturization in ICT, nanotechnology is playing an increasingly significant role in ICT. Nanotechnologies are already used in the production of computer chips, information storage technologies and optoelectronics. In the near future, nanotechnology is expected to play a role in other areas of ICT, including hard disk technologies and sensor technologies (Royal Society and the Royal Academy of Engineering, 2004, Chapter 3).

Those who voice concerns about the potential risks of using new technologies, including nanotechnology, often argue that we should apply the precautionary principle (PP) when evaluating their implementation. The PP is a conceptual tool, employed in risk management and in policy making in the face of uncertainty. The core intuition behind the PP is that, when in doubt, it is better to act precautiously, that is, it is 'better to be safe than sorry'. This is, of course, a commonsense saying, and the PP is often defended as simply being an extension of everyday reasoning (Sandin 2007), although this characterization is open to dispute (Clarke 2009). The Independent Expert Group on Mobile Phones (2000) recommends the application of the PP to mobile phone use and the European Group on Ethics in Science and New Technologies (2005) recommends the application of the PP to the use of ICT human implants (2005). Som *et al.* (2004) suggest that the PP should be applied more frequently to information technologies than it has been; while both the European Commission Scientific Committee on Emerging and Newly Identified Health Risks (2006, p. 54) and the ETC group (2005, p. 16) recommend a precautionary approach to the use of new nanomaterials.

The PP is often contrasted with cost–benefit analysis (CBA), an approach to risk management in which one attempts to determine the probability of benefits occurring as well as the probability of costs being incurred, when the implementation of a new policy is being considered. The expected balance of costs and benefits, for a given policy option, is then compared with the equivalent balances of costs and benefits that would be expected to result from the introduction of alternatives to that policy, and the policy with the overall best balance of expected benefits over expected costs is selected. While CBA involves weighing expected costs and benefits, application of the PP involves a more exclusive focus on the potential costs of introducing a new policy.

The common use of the phrase 'the precautionary principle' appears to suggest that there is one widely accepted formulation of the PP, but this is not the case. There are many versions of the PP and these can be quite distinct from one another. Although they are both considered to be statements of the PP, Principle 15 of the Rio Declaration on Environment and Development is quite different from the Final Declaration of the First European 'Seas at Risk' Conference (1994). Principle 15 of the 1992 Rio Declaration on Environment and Development states that:

In order to protect the environment, the precautionary approach shall be widely applied by States according to their capabilities. Where there are threats of serious or irreversible damage, lack of full scientific certainty shall not be used as a reason for postponing cost-effective measures to prevent environmental degradation. (United Nations Environment Programme 1992)

The Final Declaration of the First European 'Seas at Risk' Conference (1994) states that:

If the 'worst case scenario' for a certain activity is serious enough then even a small amount of doubt as to the safety of that activity is sufficient to stop it taking place. (1994, Annex 1)

There are many other variants of the precautionary principle that could also be listed here (e.g. Som *et al.* 2004, pp. 788–789).

'Principle 15' exemplifies what is sometimes referred to as the weak version of the PP. It does not replace CBA and can usefully be understood as offering us guidance in the interpretation of CBA. It advises us to ensure that CBA is not used in a selective manner and that risks which are only established with some degree of confidence are considered in any application of CBA, alongside risks established with 'full scientific certainty'. What weak versions of the PP have in common is that they instruct us to pay special attention to uncertainties, in one or other way, when formulating policy. The Final Declaration of the First European 'Seas at Risk' Conference, by contrast with 'Principle 15', is not compatible with CBA and is an example of what is sometimes referred to as a strong version of the PP. It advises us not to attempt to weigh the expected costs and benefits of a particular policy, but to formulate policy by considering the potential serious harms of a policy, under certain conditions, regardless of how potentially beneficial a particular policy may be, even if the estimated probability of the potential serious harms occurring is extremely low.

There is a well-known and seemingly devastating criticism of strong versions of the PP, which does not apply to typical weak versions of the PP (Sunstein 2005, Manson 2002). This is that strong versions of the PP, if applied consistently, lead to paradoxical outcomes. To see this, consider the application of a strong version of the PP to mobile phone use (note that the Independent Expert Group on Mobile Phones (2000) applies a weak version of the PP, so they would not go along with this line of reasoning). We do not know for sure what the risks to human health of exposure to radiation emitted by mobile phones and masts are, but they may be significant. So, an application of a strong version of the PP seems to lead to the conclusion that we should ban all mobile phones and masts until we have well-established data on what these effects are. However, if we do not have mobile phones and an operating system of transmitting mobile phone signals available, then individuals who find themselves in emergency situations may be unable to contact others to get help and human lives may be placed in jeopardy. Therefore, it seems that the application of a strong version of the PP leads to the conclusion that we should not ban mobile phones and masts. The consistent application of strong versions of the PP leads to the recommendation of contradictory policies and strong versions of the PP are, therefore, paradoxical.

There have been a number of attempts to defend strong versions of the PP from the charge of leading to paradox (e.g. Weckert and Moor 2006, Gardiner 2006). Although these appear to be unsuccessful (Clarke 2009), prominent defenders of the PP have not given up hope that a coherent version of the strong PP can and will be found (e.g. Sandin 2007, p. 102). Given that weak versions of the PP are not vulnerable to the charge of paradox, why do Sandin (2007) and others not simply adopt one of these and forego attempts to resuscitate strong versions of the PP? One answer to this question is that they may think that weak versions of the PP are too weak. If all the PP amounts to is a way of ensuring that the potential costs of a policy are fairly considered, then it must be allowed that these may sometimes be trumped by benefits when potential policies are being considered. If this is so, then applications of the PP may sometimes fail to recommend that we act precautiously. If the benefits of new mobile phone technologies, ICT implants and new nanomaterials are judged to outweigh costs, then, along with CBA, weak versions of the PP may end up recommending that we allow their use, subject to appropriate regulation. This may be good advice, but it is often not the advice those who advocate the PP hope to be able to recommend.

Much has been written on the management of risks associated with new technologies and this discussion has really just scratched the surface of that literature. For more on this subject see Bainbridge and Roco (2006), Fisher *et al.* (2006), Sunstein (2005) and Adler and Posner (2001).

14.3   Future technologies

14.3.1   Catastrophic future scenarios

Possible catastrophic scenarios receive widespread public discussion. This should not be surprising. We have a vested interest in considering the scenarios that are most important to us, and possible futures in which humanity is exterminated, or experiences a miserable existence, are of obvious concern. Perhaps, runaway technological development will lead us to become the authors of our own demise. Curiously, some of the most prominent science fiction dystopias are concerned not with the consequences of runaway technological development, but with technological development that has ceased to advance beyond the level that suits a future dictatorship. George Orwell's *1984* (1949) and Aldous Huxley's *Brave New World* (2006) [1932] fall into this category. We will return to consider these famous novels, which, in different ways, exemplify themes that are recurrent in much contemporary extemporizing about the dangers of future technology. But first, let us consider some catastrophic scenarios that may result from unfettered technological development.

Future developments in information technology offer us the prospect of creating genuinely powerful artificial intelligence (AI). A threshold in the development of AI will be reached if and when an artificial intelligence is able to act so as to improve its own intelligence. At that point, an artificial agent may be able to become extremely intelligent – and vastly more intelligent than humans – very rapidly. This prospect is of obvious concern, as it is unclear how a powerful artificial superintelligence would regard its much less intelligent, and much less powerful human creators. If the artificial superintelligence was ill-disposed towards humanity then the prospects for the latter could be grim. One way of heading off this possibility would be to seek to design 'friendly AI'. But it is unclear whether a friendly artificial agent that could rewrite its own programming would remain friendly for long. In any case, a powerful artificial agent that sought to act benevolently towards humans could not be guaranteed to act in ways that we would actually consider to be benevolent (Yudkowsky 2008).

An additional route to the possibility of inadvertently creating a malevolent superintelligence is via the possibility of uploading. An upload is a mind that has been transferred from a brain to a computer that is able to emulate the computational processes that occurred in the biological neural network located in the original brain. At present this is, of course, just a theoretical possibility, but it is one that has been taken seriously by some commentators for some time now (e.g. Hanson 1994). It could be much easier for an uploaded mind to increase its intelligence than it is for us biologically bounded beings. An uploaded mind which was connected to the Internet could access additional computational resources to dramatically improve itself (Bostrom 2002). In addition to worrying about the possibility of an artificial superintelligence that is ill-disposed towards us, we may need to be concerned about the possibility of a posthuman superintelligence that is ill-disposed towards us.

Another dramatic dystopian scenario, which is due to Eric Drexler (1986), is encapsulated in the 'grey goo problem'. Drexler (1986) speculates that advances in nanotechnology may lead to nano-scale assemblers that can be used to rearrange matter one atom at a time. With the aid of significant computing power, such assemblers could be used to turn physical items into completely different physical items; waste material into diamonds, and so on. A concern here is that we might program such assemblers to turn other things into themselves. If such assemblers were created, and they were able to turn all other things into themselves, then the entire Universe could end up being composed only of these assemblers (it would be 'grey goo'). Whether this is really possible is unclear, but the scenario is taken seriously by a number of commentators (Laurent and Petit 2005), and even a mild version of the grey goo problem, in which assemblers turned many other things into themselves, would be catastrophic.

It is difficult to know what to do about such speculative dystopian scenarios other than keep them in the back of our minds. Unless we have reason to think that these are at least somewhat likely to occur, then the chance that they might possibly occur does not seem sufficient to outweigh the benefits of conducting research in artificial intelligence, nanotechnology and general information technology. So, it seems that neither CBA nor weak versions of the PP could be used to recommend restrictions on research in any of these areas of technology, in light of the possibility of catastrophic future scenarios. As we have seen, advocates of strong versions of the PP argue that we should not consider the potential benefits of new technologies, in circumstances where significant harms are possible, when formulating policies to manage risk. So, it might be thought that strong versions of the PP could be used as the conceptual basis for restrictions on research in particular areas of technology, in light of the possibility of catastrophic future scenarios. However, the paradoxical consequences of applying strong versions of the PP appear when we attempt to apply strong versions of the PP to any scenario, so they will appear in catastrophic scenarios just as they do in non-catastrophic ones (Clarke 2005).

14.3.2   1984

The events described in George Orwell's *1984* take place in Oceania, one of three warring states, which rule all areas of the world in this dystopian novel. Oceania is an oppressive dictatorship, controlling its population with the aid of rigorous and systematic surveillance techniques. There is no possibility of privacy in the public domain in this society, as public areas are continuously monitored by cameras, hidden microphones and government spies. There is some possibility of privacy in the home – the traditional private sphere – but this is constantly under threat as children are indoctrinated to spy on their parents and others, and to report suspect activities to the 'Thought Police'. *1984* has become emblematic of the fears that people have that our future may become that of an all-encompassing surveillance society. Their fears are encapsulated in the slogan of Oceania: 'Big Brother is Watching You'.

Is the society depicted in *1984* particularly objectionable because the behaviour of its citizens is being continuously monitored or because the information obtained is collected by agents of a totalitarian government and used to oppress that society's citizens? This question is explored, in a general form, by David Brin in his *The Transparent Society* (1999). Brin argues that it is inevitable that our society is going to become an all-encompassing surveillance society. The important question for him is what sort of surveillance society we are going to become. He sees two broad alternatives. One sort of future society is the one familiar to Orwell's readers, in which surveillance technology is used to collect information about people's behaviour in public places and then transmitted to government agencies. In a second possible future society, the collected information is made available to everyone. In some ways, we seem to be evolving towards this second type of future society. Information about behaviour in public, including video footage, is now widely available on the Internet. Webcams, which can upload live feeds of video footage to the Internet, are increasingly common. And since 2007, *Google Maps* has offered a service called 'Google Street View' (see http://maps.google.com/help/maps/streetview/). This website currently contains regularly updated still photographs of streets in major American, Australian, French and Japanese cities, which are available for public access.

Brin (1999) argues that the second type of possible future society would be very different from, and much preferable to, the first; and it would also have many advantages over our current society. One advantage of such a society that he points to is that people, including employees of government agencies, would be deterred from attempting to commit crimes. In his view, the rise of CCTV cameras is already beginning to have this effect on our current society. Another example of our society taking a step in the direction of the second sort of surveillance society, which Brin (1999) points to, is the increasing popularity of 'Kindercam' (see www.kindercam.com), an online service that allows parents password-protected access to video cameras that monitor the day care centres hosting their children.

In effect, Brin (1999) is arguing that we will, and perhaps should, flout Nissenbaum's (2004) criterion of contextual integrity as a benchmark for privacy in the public sphere. One criticism that we might make of Nissenbaum (2004) is that a strict application of her criterion runs the danger of locking future societies into institutional structures that are geared around the norms of the present. Societies evolve and the norms that govern them can be expected to evolve accordingly. It is not hard to imagine that, in a future society, we will have little, or even no, expectation of privacy in the public sphere, and may care very little, or even not at all, for this type of privacy. Some argue that the very notion of a public sphere, with a set of attendant norms and expectations, is basically a product of modernity and so relatively recent in origin (Lyon 1994, p. 184). And if the notion of a public sphere is of relatively recent origin then so is the possibility of privacy in the public sphere. It may be that, as well as being a relatively recent phenomenon, privacy in the public sphere turns out to be a relatively short-lived phenomenon. Nissenbaum is aware that her position is susceptible to the charge of entrenching the status quo. She argues that, although it sets up a presumption in favour of the status quo, this does not mean that such a presumption cannot sometimes be overturned (2004, p. 127). Indeed, she argues that the status quo should sometimes be overturned, when we identify adequate reasons for doing so, grounded in fundamental social, moral and political values (2004, p. 129).

14.3.3   *Brave New World*

Orwell's *1984* is a dystopian novel portraying a repressive totalitarian state. Huxley's *Brave New World* is a dystopian novel portraying a benign dictatorship. In the future society, depicted in *Brave New World*, the vast majority of the populace is unremittingly happy and unthinkingly obedient to its government. Citizens in this society are bred, not born, in 'hatcheries'. A combination of selective breeding, and the use of drugs, administered as part of the process of foetal development, ensures the production of suitable proportions of members of a rigid hierarchy of castes, bred to perform distinct work roles. These citizens are uniformly promiscuous and do not form deep romantic relationships. They are encouraged to be good consumers and discouraged from seeking solitude. Negative feelings are soon drowned out by the use of the socially approved drug 'Soma'. In short, the lives of people who inhabit the society depicted in *Brave New World* are ones that we now think of as unrelentingly shallow.

In *1984* and in *Brave New World*, the potential for individual autonomy is much reduced from what it is today. In *1984*, individual autonomy is undermined mostly from without, by a repressive state. In *Brave New World*, the autonomy of ordinary individuals is undermined mostly from within. They lack the motivation and means to question the ways in which they are encouraged to live, as their upbringing renders them almost completely incapable of reflecting critically on their circumstances.

In recent times, a group of scholars, who have come to be known as 'bio-conservatives', has held up *Brave New World* as a warning of the potential dangers of 'enhancing' human beings. Bioconservative commentators, including Francis Fukuyama (2002), Leon Kass (2003) and Michael Sandel (2007), worry about the long-term, societal consequences of allowing enhancement technologies and worry that the use of these may result in us ceasing to be human and becoming 'posthumans'. However, 'transhumanists', such as Bostrom (2003), argue that the use of enhancement technologies is likely to be beneficial for us overall and that it would be a good thing for us, all things considered, if we were to be transformed into posthumans.

Roughly, enhancement is the use of technology to raise people's physical and mental capacities above the levels which these might otherwise reach. Enhancement is conventionally contrasted with therapy, which aims to restore lost functioning, although this distinction is somewhat problematic. Nowadays, humans can enhance themselves by using performance-enhancing drugs, various forms of cosmetic surgery, and some non-cosmetic surgeries, such as laser eye surgery, which can improve vision above and beyond natural levels (Saletan 2005). There is a plethora of ways in which it has been suggested that humans will become able to enhance themselves in the future, some of which involve possible future developments in ICT. These include the development of 'collective cortex' systems that aid in shared cognition, the development of software that will make human cognition more efficient and the development of software that mediates between the human mind and a wearable computer, a possibility that has been explored in some detail by Steve Mann (1997, 2001). If we understand the human mind very broadly, to include the 'exoself' of files, web pages, online identities and other personal information, then many other more conventional advances in ICT can be counted as contributions to human enhancement (Sandberg and Bostrom, 2007).

One recurrent theme in bioconservative scholarship is that there is a danger that, once we are sufficiently enhanced, we may cease to be autonomous individuals. Future beings may become so integrated in collective communication structures that they become incapable of operating as individual autonomous agents. Furthermore, future beings may cease to desire individual autonomy. They may become the unquestioning obedient subjects of *Brave New World*.

But while bioconservatives see the posthuman world as being something more like a bad combination of *Brave New World* and *1984*, Bostrom (2003) and other transhumanists imagine the posthuman world as a tolerant and liberal society, in which enhanced and unenhanced individuals live side by side and respect one another's choices and lifestyles. One thing that seems clear is that debates about the consequences of allowing enhancement technologies will not go away any time soon.

Thanks to Rafaela Hillerbrand, Steve Matthews and Luciano Floridi for helpful comments on an earlier version of this chapter.

Part V

Metaethics

15 The foundationalist debate in computer ethics

Herman T. Tavani

15.1 Introduction

> There are issues that are more abstract and basic than the substantive issues with which most information ethics theorizing is concerned. These issues are thought to be 'foundational' in the sense that we cannot fully succeed in giving an analysis of the concrete problems of information ethics (e.g. are legal intellectual property rights justifiably protected?) until these issues are adequately addressed. (K. E. Himma 2007a, p. 79)

Himma proposes one rationale for why foundational issues in information and computer ethics[1] warrant philosophical analysis. Independently of whether his provocative claim can be substantiated, however, we will see that there are many compelling reasons for examining foundational issues in computer ethics (CE). We will also see that various models for understanding CE's foundational issues have been proposed and continue to be debated.

This chapter begins with a brief analysis of a model defended by Floridi and Sanders (2002) for examining foundational issues in CE via five 'approaches'. Next, we propose an alternative model, which frames CE's foundationalist debate in terms of three principal questions. The remaining sections analyse these questions in detail. In proposing answers to each question, the chapter incorporates some insights from CE's leading theorists.

---

[1] Himma uses the expression 'information ethics' to describe the field of applied ethics that we refer to as 'computer ethics' in this chapter. The two expressions are often used interchangeably, but they can also refer to two distinct fields or sub-fields. Floridi (2008e) notes that 'information ethics' has 'come to mean different things to different researchers working in a variety of disciplines', from computer science to philosophy, to library and information science, and so forth. To avoid this ambiguity, we follow Floridi in using the expression 'computer ethics' in our analysis of the foundationalist debate. We will see that 'Information Ethics' (or 'IE') is used by Floridi (1999b) and others to refer to a particular macroethical theory/methodological framework for computer ethics, as opposed to a specific field of applied ethics.

15.2   The Floridi/Sanders model

According to Floridi and Sanders (2002, p. 2), the foundationalist debate can be viewed as 'a metatheoretical reflection on the nature and justification of CE and the discussion of CE's relationship to the broader context of metaethical theories'. The authors examine various conceptions of CE that have evolved from a 'random collection of heterogeneous computer-related ethical issues' to a discipline that is now more 'coherent and cohesive'. Floridi and Sanders articulate five distinct 'approaches' that have emerged in the evolution of CE as a field of applied ethics (see Table 15.1): the No-Resolution Approach (NA), Professional Approach (PA), Radical Approach (RA), Conservative Approach (CA) and Innovative Approach (IA).

In the NA approach, CE problems are seen as presenting us with 'unsolvable dilemmas' and thus are a 'pointless exercise [with] no foundation' (Floridi and Sanders, p. 2). However, the authors also point out that even though NA provides only a 'minimalist starting point', it is 'useful' because it prompts the other four approaches, and it sensitizes people both to the *fact that* computer technology has social and ethical consequences and to the *kinds of* ethical issues that arise from the use of computer technology.

PA stresses professional-responsibility issues affecting the development of computing technology. It has been defended by Gotterbarn (1995) and others (e.g., Buchanan 2004). Floridi and Sanders (p. 3) describe PA as a 'pedagogical methodology' that has been used in the instruction of computer science professionals, including software engineers. According to Gotterbarn, PA introduces computer science students to the 'responsibilities of their profession' and to the 'standards and methods used to resolve non-technical questions about their profession'. Floridi and Sanders note that PA takes seriously issues such as technical standards and requirements for professional guidelines, and thus stresses the vital importance of CE-education. A significant disadvantage of PA, however, is that its exclusive focus of professional-responsibility concerns provides us with a very narrow conception of CE as a field of applied ethics (Tavani 2007, 2010).

Both NA and PA can be construed as non-theoretical, or pre-theoretical, approaches in that they do not directly engage ethical theory in their analyses of CE issues. As such, they can be contrasted with the RA and CA approaches. Whereas RA stresses the novelty of CE's issues, suggesting that new ethical categories are needed, CA assumes that issues in CE can be handled by conventional ethical categories. Some proponents of RA, such as Maner (1996) and Barger (2008), claim that the use of computer technology has introduced new ethical issues or dilemmas, unique to computing. Advocates of CA, on the contrary, reject the view that CE has any new or unique features, even though some CE issues may initially seem to pose a challenge for 'ordinary ethics'. Johnson (2009) has defended a version of CA via an evolutionary metaphor

Table 15.1 **The Floridi/Sanders model for analysing foundational issues in CE.**

Name of approach	Focus of analysis for CE
NA (No Resolution Approach)	Suggests that CE's dilemmas are unsolvable because CE lacks a foundation.
PA (Professional Approach)	Views CE as a sub-field of professional ethics, whose focus is on pedagogy for training CS professionals.
RA (Radical Approach)	Focuses on aspects of CE that are allegedly new or unique.
CA (Conservative Approach)	Analyses CE in terms of traditional categories of ethics.
IA (Innovative Approach)	Proposes an alternative macroethical framework for CE.

(involving genus and species) in which ethical issues raised by computer technology are understood as 'new species' of (existing) generic moral problems. In this scheme, CE issues can be viewed as old (traditional) ethical problems, but with a new variation or new twist.

Floridi and Sanders defend a scheme called IA, as a mid-way position between CA and RA. IA is based on a macroethical framework that Floridi (1999b) calls Information Ethics (IE). Floridi and Sanders argue that IE is neither conservative nor radical, but rather 'innovative'. We will analyse IE in detail in Sections 15.5.2 and 15.6.2. The CA and RA positions are examined in Sections 15.5.1 and 15.6.1, while PA is briefly considered in Section 15.4. NA, however, will not be further examined because it is not essential to our analysis of the foundationalist debate.

Table 15.1 summarizes the five approaches in the Floridi/Sanders model, which inform our analysis of foundational issues in CE in the remaining sections of this chapter.

15.3 An alternative model for analysing the foundationalist debate

Whereas Floridi and Sanders frame CE's foundationalist debate in terms of the five 'approaches', identified above, the same debate may be analysed via three distinct, but related, questions:

(1) Is CE a legitimate field of applied ethics that warrants philosophical consideration?
(2) Are any aspects of CE new or unique in a philosophically interesting sense?
   (a) Have any new ethical issues or problems been generated?
   (b) Have any new ethical objects been introduced?

(3) Does CE require a new ethical framework?
  (a) Are any new normative ethical theories required?
  (b) Are any new meta ethical theories or methodological frameworks required?

Although each question is conceptually distinct, and thus deserves to be analysed independently, aspects of the three questions also intersect at some points or overlap at others. For example, an adequate answer to (1) may depend on answers to (2) or (3), or both. And (3) is significant if the answer to (2) is 'yes'. Questions 2 and 3 are each further subdivided into two sub-questions affecting the debate about foundational issues in CE. Questions 2(a) and 2(b) are analysed in Section 15.5, while Questions 3(a) and 3(b) are examined in Section 15.6. First, however, we consider Question 1.

15.4   Is CE a legitimate field of applied ethics that warrants philosophical analysis?

As already noted, some have questioned the legitimacy of CE as an independent field of applied ethics worthy of philosophical consideration. For example, Floridi (1999b) has suggested that CE's legitimacy as a philosophical field is threatened because it lacks an appropriate 'methodological foundation'. Others argue that CE should be conceived of simply as a branch, or sub-field, of professional ethics. According to PA, for example, CE can be understood as a sub-field of computer science concerned with identifying and analysing issues of ethical responsibility for computer professionals. PA's supporters draw some comparisons between the computer profession and other professional fields, such as medicine and law. They point out that in medical ethics and legal ethics, the principal focus of analysis has been on issues of moral responsibility that affect individuals as members of those professions. Continuing with this analogy, some proponents of PA support the view that the principal, and perhaps even the sole, focus of CE should be on issues of professional responsibility for computer-science and software-engineering professionals.

Defending the view that CE can best be understood as a branch of professional ethics (for the computing profession), Gotterbarn (1995) claims that many issues associated with CE are not really computer-ethics issues at all. He argues that computer-assisted crimes (that have captured the popular media's attention) should not be viewed as issues in CE, just as a crime involving a murder committed with a surgeon's scalpel should not be thought of as an issue in medical ethics. In the same way that medical ethics examines issues in the medical profession that are relevant for medical professionals, so too can CE be understood as a field that examines ethical issues that affect computer professionals.

Gotterbarn uses some instructive analogies to defend his version of PA. For example, he notes that, historically, the introduction of some technologies profoundly affected our daily lives. In particular, he mentions the printing press, the automobile and the airplane. He points out that each has had a significant, and arguably 'revolutionary', effect on our social institutions. But Gotterbarn also notes that we do not have categories such as 'printing press ethics', 'automobile ethics' or 'airplane ethics'. So, he asks why we need a field of computer ethics that is independent of a sub-field of computer science or professional ethics to examine issues in CE-proper, which are limited to ethical issues that affect the professionals responsible for the design, development and maintenance of computer systems. In other words, he questions the legitimacy of CE as something more than an area (of computer science) that examines ethical issues that affect computer professionals.

One might argue that, in the era of computing prior to the Web, the view of CE as mainly a field of professional ethics was plausible. During that period, a proportionately high number of computer users were also computer professionals; in fact, in the early days of computing, the majority of computer users may indeed have been computer professionals. But that phenomenon changed significantly with the advent of the personal computer in the early 1980s and especially with the widespread use of the Internet in the early 1990s. Because the number of ordinary computer users now far exceeds the number of users who are computer professionals, one might easily infer that, today, PA would seem to be a less plausible position than it might have been at one time (Tavani 2007, 2010).

If our critique of PA is correct, a different answer is needed for a positive response to the question posed at the beginning of this section: Is CE a legitimate field of applied ethics that warrants philosophical consideration? An insightful answer has been proposed by Moor (1985, p. 266) who describes CE as

the analysis of the nature and social impact of computer technology and the corresponding formulation and justification of policies for the ethical use of such technology.

First, we should note that Moor's definition goes beyond, but does not exclude, the principal claim of PA that CE must address ethical issues affecting computer professionals. His conception of CE as an academic discipline is much broader in scope than Gotterbarn's, and this difference is apparent in Moor's arguments for why CE is justified as an independent field of applied ethics. Moor argues that, because computer technology is 'logically malleable', it allows for new kinds of actions that were not previously possible. These actions sometimes stretch and strain our legal and ethical norms and introduce what Moor calls 'policy vacuums'. Before these vacuums or voids can be filled with either revised or new policies, we sometimes need to clarify one or more 'conceptual muddles' that can also arise (Moor, pp. 266–267). In Moor's view, one justification for continued research in CE as a separate field has to do with the number and kinds of policy vacuums that arise.

Others suggest that CE is justified as an academic field or discipline because it has some 'unique' aspects or dilemmas. For example, Maner (1996), whose arguments are examined in Section 15.5.1, claims that CE 'must exist as a field of study worthy of existence in its own right' because it has unique aspects. And Barger (2008, p. 14) argues that the 'nature of the computer and its operation gives certain dilemmas in computing a difference in degree that approximates a difference in kind and that certainly makes computer ethics a unique field of study'. Himma (2003) describes these views of CE as examples of the 'disciplinary thesis', and he questions the alleged logical relationship between the justification of CE as a discipline and the requirement that CE has some unique aspects. According to the disciplinary thesis,

ethical problems arising in connection with computer technologies represent a class that is indistinguishable in principle from other areas of applied ethics and should be studied by applied ethicists specializing in such problems. (Himma, p. 234)

In this view, CE is a legitimate field if and only if CE either (a) has some unique issues or dilemmas, or (b) requires a unique ethical theory. Himma rejects the view that such a logical relationship is required, arguing that CE could be justified as a distinct field of applied ethics independently of either (a) or (b). In doing this, he draws some comparisons between medical ethics and computer ethics, and he shows that just as the former field of applied ethics needs no unique ethical issues or new ethical theories to justify its philosophical worthiness as a distinct field of applied ethics, neither does the latter. Unlike Gotterbarn, however, Himma does not draw on professional-related ethical issues in his analogies involving medical ethics and computer ethics. Instead, Himma notes that just as some medical technologies, such as those affecting reproduction and cloning, have helped to define parameters of the field of medical ethics, so too have issues affecting computing technology itself contributed to the cluster of issues examined in CE. Thus, there is no compelling reason to believe that any unique ethical issues affecting computing technology are required to justify CE as a legitimate discipline. Like Himma, the present author (Tavani 2002, 2007, 2010) has also argued that the legitimacy of CE as an independent field of applied ethics is not contingent on the existence of any unique issues, properties, etc. (even if it turns out that such issues, properties, etc. are generated in CE).

We next consider the second of the three questions in our model for analysing foundational issues in CE.

15.5   Are any aspects of CE new or unique in a philosophically interesting sense?

As already noted, proponents of RA have argued that CE has some unique aspects, e.g., unique issues or dilemmas, unique attributes or properties, and so forth. Henceforth, we refer to the claim that *computer ethics is unique* (in some sense) as the CEIU thesis (Tavani 2002). In our examination of the arguments for and against this thesis, we will see that those who defend CA tend to reject CEIU, arguing that claims about the uniqueness of CE have been vastly overstated. RA's defenders, on the contrary, tend to embrace one or more elements of the CEIU thesis. For example, some suggest that CE is unique because it generates new ethical issues, while others claim that CE has some features that distinguish it from other fields of applied ethics.

Himma (2007a) argues that claims inherent in CEIU can be analysed in terms of four distinct 'theses', which he calls the Meta-ethical Thesis, the Normative-ethical Thesis, the Epistemological Thesis and the Properties Thesis. We will refer to these positions as MT, NT, ET and PT, respectively.

According to MT, 'there are acts in computer ethics that cannot adequately be characterized by the traditional metaethical concepts of obligatory, permissible, good, and supererogatory'. In the NT view, 'computer technologies present ethical problems that cannot, as an objective matter, be adequately resolved by recourse to existing normative-ethical first-principles'. According to ET, 'computer technologies present ethical problems that resist the analogies that enable us to see how ethical theories and first-principles apply in other fields of applied ethics'. PT has two variations: a 'strong' properties thesis, and a 'weak' one. In the latter variation, computers 'instantiate ethically significant properties' (including the possibility of 'moral personhood'), whereas the strong view asserts that computers instantiate ethically significant properties that are not instantiated by any other 'thing or being in the universe' (Himma, p. 80). We limit our discussion of PT to the view that Himma describes as the weak thesis. Himma's analysis of CEIU via the four theses informs our analysis of the foundationalist debate in the remaining sections of this chapter. Whereas aspects of ET and PT are examined in Sections 15.5.1 and 15.5.2, MT and NT are considered in 15.6.1 and 15.6.2. Table 15.2 summarizes Himma's model.

We next analyse the two components of Question 2: (a) Has computing technology generated any new moral issues/problems? (b) Has computing technology introduced any new moral entities/objects? These correspond to issues affecting ET and PT, respectively. We begin with an analysis of Question 2(a).

Table 15.2 **Himma's model for analysing CEIU via four theses.**

Thesis	Corresponding claim
ET (Epistemological Thesis)	CE presents problems that cannot adequately be analogized with other fields of applied ethics.
PT (Properties Thesis)	CE presents problems that cannot be easily resolved because computers instantiate ethically significant properties not found in other technologies.
NT (Normative Ethics Thesis)	CE presents problems that cannot adequately be resolved by recourse to existing first principles in morality.
MT (Metaethical Thesis)	CE presents problems that cannot adequately be characterized by the traditional concepts of obligatory, permissible, good and supererogatory.

15.5.1   Have any new ethical issues or problems been generated?

An issue/problem in applied ethics can be viewed as a controversial topic that warrants ethical analysis. Among the topical areas associated with controversies affecting computing technology are (general) categories such as security, anonymity, privacy, property, access and so forth. In this scheme, concerns affecting 'personal privacy' would be an example of a typical issue in CE that is also fairly general in scope – privacy concerns raise *ethical* issues because they typically involve one or more fundamental or core moral notions such as autonomy, fairness, justice and so forth. At a more specific level, privacy threats affecting spyware, cookies or RFID technologies are examples of some 'particular ethical issues' associated with privacy and computing technology.

Maner (1996) argues that computer technology has generated some moral issues that did not exist before the advent of computing technology and that could not have existed if computers had never been invented. It is unclear, however, which (specific) ethical issues he has in mind. If Maner meant that some new issues *qua topical areas* (in general) have been generated, it would have been helpful if he had explicitly identified them: but he has not done this. So perhaps he meant something less controversial – viz., that some new instances of existing moral issues (e.g. under traditional classificatory schemes such as personal privacy or intellectual property) have been introduced. In one sense ethical issues affecting RFID privacy or software piracy would have been impossible if computer technology had never been developed. Yet, this is true only in a trivial sense. The (general) underlying concerns of both issues – i.e., surveillance involving the unauthorized collection of personal information, and theft involving the unauthorized copying of proprietary information – existed long before the introduction of computing technology (Tavani 2007). If all that Maner meant was that new variations of (traditional) moral problems have been generated, one could reasonably ask whether his position differs in any significant respect from claims made by some who embrace CA, such as Johnson (2009), as opposed to those who defend the more radical claims in RA about CE's alleged uniqueness.

A second interpretation of what Maner meant is that computer technology possesses some unique features or 'properties' that are ethically relevant. For example, he points out that computers are 'uniquely malleable', 'uniquely complex', 'uniquely fast' and 'uniquely coded'. In focusing on the unique attributes or properties of computers, Maner can be interpreted as holding a variation of Himma's properties thesis (PT) regarding CEIU. However, one may wonder whether Maner's claim, so interpreted, entails the more controversial claim that computers have generated new ethical issues (qua topical areas or qua specific instances of topical areas). Although technological features, such as malleability, might indeed be unique to computer technology, it does not follow that any unique ethical issues have emerged *because of* this technology's malleability. Proponents of CEIU, who argue that CE issues must be unique because certain features or aspects of computing technology are unique, commit the 'computer-ethics-is-unique fallacy' (Tavani 2007, 2010): *computer technology has some unique technological features; the use of computer technology has generated ethical concerns; therefore, such ethical concerns must be unique.* This line of reasoning is fallacious because it mistakenly assumes that characteristics that apply to a certain technology must also be inherited by the ethical issues associated with it.

A third, and final, interpretation of what Maner intended in his defence of CEIU can be found in his remarks about the lack of an 'effective analogy' for understanding CE issues. There, he claims that our inability to find 'satisfactory non-computer analogies' for moral issues involving computers 'testifies to the uniqueness of computer ethics'. This claim would seem to correspond to the view expressed in Himma's epistemological thesis (ET) – i.e., the interpretation of CEIU stating that ethical problems generated by computers resist analogies with ethical problems handled by standard ethical categories and theories. But a claim about the lack of an effective analogy for understanding CE issues is a very different sort of claim from one asserting that CE has introduced new ethical issues that are also unique to computers. Also, we can ask why these analogies with ordinary ethics are unsatisfactory (even if computer technology has properties that are vastly different from those found in other kinds of earlier technologies). Unfortunately, Maner does not elaborate on why a lack of effective analogies with other technologies entails that CE issues are unique. So, it would seem that, when Maner's claims about the uniqueness of CE are examined from the perspective of ET, they fail to support CEIU.

If the CEIU thesis cannot be defended, does it follow that there is nothing special about CE or that CE does not merit the attention of philosophers and ethicists? Moor (1998) points out that CE raises some concerns that fall outside the scope of 'routine ethics'. It is important to note, however, that Moor does not claim that CE issues are unique ethical issues, even though he argues that computer technology has been used in ways that raise special ethical problems. Recall Moor's claims affecting the logical malleability of computer technology and the kinds of policy vacuums and conceptual muddles that result because of the malleable nature of that technology. Moor (1985) also argues that the use of computers has generated 'new possibilities for human action', which, in turn, raise ethical concerns. In determining whether these new possibilities for human action, made possible by computing technology, have also introduced any *new objects* that deserve moral consideration, we turn to Question 2(b).

15.5.2   Have any new ethical objects been introduced?

Jonas (1984) argued that 'modern technology' – though he does not specifically mention computer technology – has made possible certain kinds of actions which, in turn, have disclosed 'new objects of ethical consideration'. According to Jonas, our traditional scheme of ethics is no longer adequate in the era of modern technology because the nature of human action has changed in fundamental ways and this requires a change in ethics in which 'new objects' must be added. Prior to the twentieth century, most philosophers and moral theorists, at least in the West, assumed that the sphere of ethical consideration applied only to human beings. That view was eventually challenged by animal rights proponents, who argued that animals deserved moral consideration (because they are sentient beings), and by some environmentalists who believed that ethical consideration should also be extended to trees and plant life (because they are biological life forms). However, Jonas argued that the sphere of moral consideration needed to be expanded further to include additional 'objects', such as future generations of human beings as well as (the whole of) nature itself.

Floridi (1999b) argues that we need to extend the domain of moral consideration beyond the boundaries proposed by Jonas, because non-biological or inanimate objects can also have moral status and thus must be granted consideration. According to Floridi (2008e, pp. 10–11), all entities in the Universe can be viewed as 'clusters of data', which he calls 'informational objects'. Floridi defines these 'objects' as 'encapsulated packages' that are 'discrete' and 'self contained'. To understand why these objects warrant moral consideration, we need to analyse some key components of Floridi's Information Ethics (IE) framework, which he describes as a 'patient-oriented, ontocentric, ecological macroethics'. IE is a *macroethics* (as opposed to a microethics), Floridi argues, because it is like utilitarianism, Kantianism, and other standard theories of ethics in terms of their breadth of application. But he also shows why it is different from those conventional macroethical theories, which Floridi claims to be either anthropocentric or biocentric. Whereas utilitarian and deontological (macroethical) theories have tended to be anthropocentric (focusing on ways that human actions affect other humans), environmental and ecological macroethical theories are life-centred or biocentric (taking into consideration the interests of life forms in addition to humans). Like the ecological (macroethical) theory, IE avoids anthropocentrism; but IE goes one step further by replacing biocentrism with 'ontocentrism'.

According to IE, there is something more elemental than life – viz., *being* (i.e., what Floridi (p. 12) describes as the existence and flourishing of all entities and their global environment). And there is something more fundamental than suffering, viz., a condition that Floridi describes as 'entropy'. It is important to note, however, that Floridi's notion of entropy is not the same as the physicist's concept of thermodynamic entropy. For Floridi, entropy refers to 'any kind of disruption, corruption, pollution, and depletion of informational objects' which could result in any 'impoverishment of being'. IE is concerned with the well-being of the infosphere and the 'evil' (i.e., the harm) that can be suffered by objects in the infosphere. So, IE shifts the emphasis away from traditional concerns affecting *only* the well-being of humans, and in some cases *only* the well-being of biological life forms, to concerns about the well-being of the whole infosphere (and the informational objects that comprise it, including humans and biological life forms as well).

Although Floridi argues that all entities, qua informational objects, have intrinsic moral value, he also notes that the moral value of informational objects can be 'quite unusual' and that it is 'overridable'. But informational objects are nonetheless moral patients that are owed at least some 'minimal degree of moral respect'. Floridi (p. 12) also holds that duties owed to informational objects (as moral patients) by moral agents are evaluated either (i) 'positively', if an agent's actions contribute to the growth of the infosphere or (ii) 'negatively', if an agent's actions adversely impact the infosphere (i.e., through the depletion of informational objects, the degradation of information and informational resources, and so forth).

Floridi draws some important distinctions between moral patients and moral agents. In IE, both the infosphere and the informational objects that comprise it are moral patients that (a) need to be recognized as being at 'the centre of some basic ethical claims' and (b) are owed some respect by moral agents. As Floridi (p. 17) puts the matter, an agent's

decisions and actions should always be based on how the latter affects the well-being of the infosphere, that is, on how successful or unsuccessful they are

Table 15.3 **Four (sub)questions corresponding to Himma's four CEIU theses.**

(Sub)question	Corresponding thesis
2(a) Has CE generated any new moral issues/problems?	ET – CE issues are unique because they cannot be properly analogized.
2(b) Has CE introduced any new moral objects?	PT – CE is unique because computers instantiate unique properties.
3(a) Does CE require any new (normative) ethical theories?	NT – CE is unique because existing first principles cannot be applied.
3(b) Does CE require any new metaethical theories or methodological frameworks?	MT – CE is unique because it cannot be characterized by the traditional concepts of obligatory, permissible, etc.

in respecting the ethical claims attributable to information entities involved, and hence in improving or impoverishing the infosphere.

In this sense, IE suggests an 'ontological shift' in our thinking about the kinds of objects that can qualify for moral consideration and about the kinds of obligations that are owed to these objects qua moral patients by (human and non-human) moral agents.

Thus far, we have only briefly described some of the duties that moral agents have in preserving the well-being of the infosphere. In Section 15.6.2, we examine the concept of moral agency in more detail. We conclude Section 15.5 by summarizing some key points in our analysis of two interpretations of CEIU. First, we saw that there were no compelling reasons to believe that CE has generated any unique or new ethical issues. Next, we saw that, if IE is correct, a 'new' category of objects (viz., informational objects) deserve at least some moral consideration. But it is also important to note that IE does not claim that these objects either (i) have been introduced solely because of computer technology, or (ii) deserve moral consideration *because* they have some properties that are unique to computers.

Next, we turn our attention to the final question in our analysis of the foundationalist debate, Question 3, which also has two component parts. Whereas Question 3(a) asks whether a new (normative) ethical theory is needed for CE, Question 3(b) inquires into whether a new metaethical theory or a new methodological framework is needed. Both questions, as in the case of Questions 2(a) and 2(b), overlap with two of Himma's four 'theses' underlying CEIU (summarized above in Table 15.2). Table 15.3 describes the corresponding relationships that obtain between Questions 2(a) through 3(b) and Himma's four theses.

15.6   Does CE require a new ethical framework?

In answering this question, it is helpful to understand some of the claims that may be labelled as 'traditionalist' and 'expansionist' (Tavani 2005). Whereas the traditionalist position corresponds closely to Floridi and Sander's notion of CA, the expansionist position is similar to their category of RA. Traditionalists answer 'no' to Question 3 because they believe that our existing framework of ethics, including our standard concepts and theories, is adequate to analyse CE issues. Among those who defend the traditionalist view are Johnson (1994) and Gert (1999). Although Johnson views CE issues as a 'new species of existing moral problems', she also claims that 'ordinary ethics' is sufficient to handle these issues. Gert, who also believes that no new theory is needed, offers a different kind of rationale. Unlike Johnson and others, who embrace traditional ethical theories such as utilitarianism, Kantianism and so forth, Gert argues that his own system of 'common morality' is superior. He then shows how his system can be successfully applied to ethical issues in computing by examining the question whether it is permissible to copy proprietary software, and concludes that no new or special ethical theories are required to analyse issues in CE. Unfortunately, an examination of Gert's rich and interesting moral system, in the detail that it deserves, is beyond the scope of this chapter. The purpose in mentioning his theory, as well as the traditionalist's position in general, is to draw a contrast with the expansionist's claim that a new ethical framework is required.

We next examine some specific claims that expansionists have put forth with respect to Question 3(a).

15.6.1   Are any new normative ethical theories required?

Expansionists such as Adam (2005) and Górniak-Kocikowska (1996) claim that we need a new ethical theory to understand and resolve issues in CE. It is important to point out that neither Adam nor Górniak-Kocikowska argue that a new theory is needed *because* CE has any unique features or issues. It is also worth noting that they provide two very different accounts of the kind of ethical theory that is needed, as well as very different kinds of answers to the question of why a new theory is needed.

Adam argues that conventional ethical theories, such as utilitarianism and deontology, are insufficient for analysing CE issues because they have either ignored or greatly underestimated the importance of gender in CE. This, in turn, has resulted in gender issues being 'under-theorized' in CE research. Arguing that a gender-based ethical theory is needed to remedy this problem, she puts forth a theory that is based on a feminist ethics – in particular, on the 'ethic of care'. Adam then offers some reasons why an ethic of care can improve our understanding of gender issues affecting CE. For one thing, she claims that it helps us better understand ethical concerns and controversies affecting power and privacy. With regard to the former, a gender-informed framework enables us to see some of the relations of power that are involved in the development and use of computers. Regarding the latter topic, she holds that her theory can help us to see that the concept of privacy can be different for men and women. As a result, Adam argues that a gender-informed theory can help us to understand CE issues involving cyberstalking and Internet pornography in ways that the standard ethical theories cannot.

Even if we accept Adam's arguments for why the standard ethical theories used in CE are inadequate, it is still unclear why the gender-informed theory she articulates is peculiar to issues affecting computing per se, as opposed to broader areas of applied ethics that also are affected by controversies surrounding privacy and power. For example, ethical concerns affecting privacy and power for women could arise in other fields of applied ethics, such as legal ethics, bioethics and biotechnology ethics. So, her arguments for a new, gender-informed ethical theory for CE would also entail that such a theory would be required for other fields of applied ethics as well. In that case, Adam's thesis is as applicable to contemporary applied ethics in general, as it is for CE in particular. Thus, any need for a new ethical theory, based on the account that Adam provides, would not seem to arise solely from concerns affecting computer technology.

Górniak-Kocikowska presents a very different kind of case for why a new ethical theory is needed for CE. Her argument can be analysed into two stages. The first stage begins with a historical look at how certain technologies have brought about 'social revolutions'. For example, she notes that the 'revolution' brought on by the printing press affected both our social institutions and our (theorizing about) ethical values in profound and fundamental ways. She then draws some comparisons with the 'computer revolution', claiming that it too has affected our institutions and values in the same ways. The second stage focuses on the 'global' aspect of computing technology. Górniak-Kocikowska claims that, because the computer revolution is global in its impact, we need a 'new global ethical theory'. In particular, she argues that we need a new ethical theory that can respond to problems generated globally by computer technology, in much the same way that new ethical theories arose in response to social issues that resulted from technologies such as the printing press and the ensuing 'printing-press revolution'.

The first stage of Górniak-Kocikowska's argument suggests that new ethical theories might be required whenever a 'revolutionary technology' is introduced. But, what will count as a technology that is 'revolutionary' vs. one that is merely influential? For example, the automobile, when introduced, might have been viewed by many people as a revolutionary technology. Yet, we did not need a new ethical theory to address social issues affecting the impact of automobiles. Turning to the second stage of her argument, it would seem that new ethical theories are needed to handle technologies that have a 'global impact'. But is a new ethical theory needed for CE merely because of the global impact that computing has had to date? Consider that many other technologies, such as aviation, space travel or reproductive technologies (such as *in vitro* fertilization), have also had a global impact. However, no one has argued that we need a new (universal) ethical theory to account for their global impact. So, it is unclear how Górniak-Kocikowska's argument can convince us that a new ethical theory is needed for CE, at least on the basis of the evidence she provides. We next turn to Question 3(b).

15.6.2   Are any new methodological frameworks required?

While some novel, methodological frameworks have been proposed for CE, many proposals have also been based on the modification and extension of existing applied-ethics frameworks that can be tailored in ways to address specific concerns affecting CE. An example of the latter is articulated by van den Hoven (1997), who has argued for a method of 'reflective equilibrium', based on the model introduced by Rawls. Such a methodological scheme is applicable for CE (and for engineering ethics as well), van den Hoven claims, because it provides the appropriate levels of generality and particularity needed to 'shuttle' back and forth between specific cases affecting computing technology and general principle and theories that can be applied within and across the various cases.

Van den Hoven (2008, p. 59) has described some recent methodological trends in CE, as well as in engineering ethics, in terms of a 'design turn'. He notes, for example, that just as there was a shift in ethical analysis from metaethics to applied ethics in the second half of the twentieth century – i.e., an 'applied turn' in ethics – a more recent shift has occurred in that significant attention is being paid to the role that design decisions can play in the analysis of applied-ethics issues. For example, some ethicists now focus much of their early analysis of ethical problems involving technologies (and practices affecting those technologies) on the various kinds of values that can be either consciously or unconsciously built into those technologies. While some of the proposed methodological frameworks have been fairly modest, others include requirements that are more controversial. We next examine a model, 'disclosive computer ethics', introduced by Brey (2000) as a methodological framework for CE. It is relatively modest in terms of the required changes it proposes.

Brey argues that the standard methodology used by philosophers to conduct research in applied ethics needs to be modified for CE. The revised method that he proposes builds on some of the models advanced by analysts working in the area of 'value-sensitive design' (or VSD). For example, Friedman *et al.* (2008) have argued that implicit values, embedded in computing technologies, need to be identified at the design stage of their development. They claim that designers need to understand which kinds of values they are 'building in' to technologies they develop and implement. Brey argues that, in the case of computing technology, this requires some changes in the standard or 'mainstream' method of applied ethics. Because that model was developed to analyse (already) known moral controversies, Brey worries that it can easily fail to identify features and practices that may have 'moral import' but are yet unknown. He describes such features and practices as 'morally opaque', which he contrasts with those that are 'morally transparent'. While the latter kinds of features and practices are easily recognized as morally problematic, it can be difficult to identify some morally opaque features and practices affecting computer technology. For example, Brey notes that many people are aware that the practice of placing closed circuit video surveillance cameras in undisclosed locations may be controversial, from a moral point of view. Many people may also be aware that computer spyware can be morally controversial. However, Brey argues that other kinds of morally controversial practices and features involving computer technology might not be as easily discerned because of their opaqueness.

Brey notes that a practice or a feature affecting computer technology can be morally opaque for one of two reasons: (a) it is yet unknown, or (b) it is known but perceived to be 'morally neutral'. An example of (a) includes computerized practices involving cookies technology, which would be 'unknown' to those who are unfamiliar with Internet cookies. An example of (b) includes practices affecting online search facilities, a technology with which most computer users are familiar. However, users may not be aware that this technology is used in practices that record and store information about a user's online searches, which may be controversial from a moral point of view, as some learned for the first time in 2005, when the US Government subpoenaed the search records of users for Google, MSN and Yahoo.

According to Brey, an adequate methodology for CE must first 'disclose' any features and practices affecting computers that otherwise might not be noticed as having moral implications. Appropriately, he calls his methodology the 'disclosive method' of CE because its initial aim is to reveal any moral values embedded in the various features and practices associated with computer technology. It is in this sense that the standard applied-ethics methodology needs to be expanded to accommodate specific challenges for CE. It remains unclear, however, why the disclosive method should be limited to CE. For example, medical technology also includes features and practices that are morally opaque. Consider that *in vitro* fertilization and stem cell research are examples of medical technologies that, initially at least, had morally opaque aspects that needed to be 'disclosed'. So the methodological changes proposed by Brey for CE would seem to have far wider applications for applied ethics in general.

Because Brey's 'disclosive method' mainly expands upon the standard method used in applied ethics, it is not a radically new framework. However, others argue that we need an altogether different kind of methodological framework for CE. Perhaps the most provocative proposal is Floridi's Information Ethics (IE) methodological/macroethical framework.

We have already examined some important aspects of IE in Section 15.5.2, where our focus was on the status of informational objects that qualified as moral patients in the infosphere. In this section, our primary emphasis is on how IE also functions as a macroethical theory/methodological framework for CE. In Section 15.5.2, we saw how Floridi's IE macroethics was different, in several key respects, from standard ethical theories such as utilitarianism, Kantianism and virtue ethics. We next examine some of Floridi's arguments for why IE is a superior methodological framework for CE. They are based on distinctions he draws between: (i) macroethical vs. microethical issues; (ii) patient-centred vs. agent- and action-centred systems; and (iii) (non-moral) agency and moral agency. We begin with a brief look at Floridi's arguments involving (i).

Floridi (1999b) claims that one virtue of IE, as a methodological framework, is that it enables us to distinguish between macroethical and microethical aspects of CE. He argues that IE, as a macroethics, helps us to analyse specific microethical issues in CE, such as privacy, in a way that the standard macroethical frameworks cannot. Floridi notes that the concept of privacy is not well theorized by any of the standard macroethical theories used in CE, and he shows how IE can help us to understand some of the ontology-based considerations that need to be taken into account in analysing the concept of privacy and framing an adequate informational-privacy theory. Floridi (2005d) advances a theory, called the *ontological theory of informational privacy*, which he argues is superior to the classic theories of informational privacy. His ontological privacy theory is provocative for several reasons; for one thing, it shifts the locus of a violation of privacy away from conditions tied to an agent's personal rights involving control and ownership of information to conditions affecting the information environment, which the agent constitutes. In this sense, his theory provides us with a novel way of analysing the impact that digital technologies have had for informational privacy. However, one critique of Floridi's privacy theory is that it does not explicitly distinguish between descriptive and normative privacy regarding claims about privacy expectations for informational objects. As a result, one might infer that, in Floridi's theory, every informational object deserves normative privacy protection (Tavani 2008). Unfortunately, we cannot further examine Floridi's privacy theory here, since doing so would take us beyond the scope of this chapter.

We next examine some of Floridi's arguments for (ii). As we saw in Section 15.5.2, Floridi holds that one advantage that IE has, over the standard macroethics frameworks, is that the former is patient-centred, as opposed to being merely action-oriented or agent-oriented. Whereas virtue ethics is 'agent oriented' in that it focuses on the moral character development of individual agents, Floridi characterizes both utilitarianism and deontology as 'action oriented' because they are concerned with the consequences and motives of individuals engaged in moral decisions. And because action-oriented and agent-oriented theories focus primarily on agents and on the actions (and character development) of agents, Floridi claims that they do not adequately attend to the recipients of moral actions (i.e., moral patients). He argues that the IE methodological framework provides the conceptual apparatus needed to understand our role, as well as the roles of artificial moral agents, in preserving the well-being of the infosphere. This brings us to (iii), Floridi's accounts of agency and moral agency. We noted earlier that in IE, informational objects can qualify as moral agents (in addition to being moral patients).

How does IE differentiate a moral agent from a moral patient? Floridi (2008e, p. 14) describes a moral agent as an

interactive, autonomous, and adaptable transition system that can perform morally qualifiable actions. (italics Floridi)

By 'interactive', Floridi means that 'the system' and its environment 'can act upon each other'. A system is 'autonomous' when it is able to 'change state without direct response to interaction, i.e., it can perform internal transition to change its state'. To be 'adaptable', the system's 'interactions (can) change the transition roles by which it changes state'. Finally, an action is 'morally qualifiable' when it can cause some 'good or evil'. So any (interactive, autonomous and adaptable) individual or system that is capable of causing either good or harm in the infosphere qualifies as a moral agent in IE.

Floridi points out that the moral agents, inhabiting the infosphere, include 'artificial' agents, which are not only 'digital agents' but also 'social agents' (such as corporations). These artificial agents also qualify as (artificial) *moral* agents if they can be held 'morally *accountable* for their actions' (Floridi, 15). But we should note that in IE, accountability is not identical to moral responsibility. Floridi draws a distinction between moral *responsibility*, which requires 'intentions, consciousness, and other mental attitudes', and moral *accountability*, which he argues does not require these criteria. Whereas responsibility is associated with 'reward and punishment', Floridi argues that accountability can be linked to what he calls 'agenthood' and 'censure'. Thus, Floridi claims that there can be agency based only on accountability but in the 'absence of moral responsibility'.

In IE, humans are special moral agents, who have what Floridi and Sanders (2005) call 'ecopoietic responsibilities' – i.e., responsibilities towards the construction and well-being of the whole infosphere.[2] 'Ecopoiesis' refers to the 'morally informed construction of the environment', based on what Floridi describes as an 'ecologically neutral perspective'. Floridi (2008e) believes that humans, qua members of *Homo Poieticus*, have a moral obligation not only to be concerned with their own character development but also 'oversee' the 'well-being and flourishing of the whole infosphere'. More specifically, *Homo Poieticus*, as a human moral agent, has special responsibilities to the infosphere that are guided by four moral principles (Floridi, p. 17):

(1) entropy ought not to be caused in the infosphere;
(2) entropy ought to be prevented in the infosphere;
(3) entropy ought to be removed from the infosphere;
(4) the flourishing of informational entities as well as the whole of the infosphere ought to be promoted by preserving, cultivating and enriching their properties.

The four principles are listed in order of increasing value. In IE, a moral agent is accountable for any action that increases the level of entropy (defined in Section 15.5.2) in the infosphere. In particular, human moral agents can be held accountable for the evil produced – i.e., the harm caused to the infosphere (as well as harm caused to the ecosphere and to other humans). Because of this, Floridi argues that human moral agents have special moral responsibilities that exceed those of other moral agents (in the infosphere). And because of IE's attention to the roles that moral agents play vis-à-vis moral patients, Floridi argues that IE is able to address issues that the standard moral methodological frameworks are unprepared to handle.

IE provides a robust methodological framework for CE, but it has also been criticized on several grounds. Floridi (p. 18) notes that two general types of criticisms tend to recur in the CE literature: one that centres on conceptual challenges for IE's accounts of agency and moral agency;[3] and one based on the notion that IE is 'too abstract' to be useful in applied ethics. In responding to these criticisms, Floridi points out that IE is not intended to replace the standard macroethical theories. Instead, he proposes that IE can 'interact with those theories' and thus 'contribute an important new perspective' from which we can analyse CE issues (Floridi, p. 20). In this sense, IE can be construed as a methodological framework that is intended to supplement (rather than

---

[2] Floridi and Sanders distinguish between 'Homo Poieticus' and 'Homo Faber'. Whereas the latter is a tool maker who uses the infosphere as a resource, the former considers the well-being of the whole infosphere.

[3] For a critique of Floridi's notion of agency, see Himma (2007b). See Floridi (2008e) for a reply to some of his critics.

replace) the standard macroethical frameworks used in CE. So, Floridi claims that his IE framework is not as radical as some of his critics have suggested.

We conclude this section by summarizing some key points in our response to Question (3b). If IE is correct, then our standard or methodological framework for applied ethics, as well as Brey's method of disclosive computer ethics, will fall short. However, we have seen that IE has been criticized and thus has not been fully embraced, at least not yet, as the received methodological framework for CE. But we have also seen that one of IE's strengths is the way that it anticipates CE issues affecting agency and moral agency; even many of IE's critics are acutely aware of the controversial roles that artificial agents may soon be capable of performing. Also, Floridi argues that IE provides a 'common vocabulary' for identifying and analysing a wide range of microethical problems that will likely arise in the not-too-distant future, in connection with highly sophisticated 'bots' and other artificial agents. From the perspective of a new macroethics, IE arguably has heuristic value in that it causes us to question some key assumptions about many of our foundational metaphysical and ethical concepts, in addition to agency and moral agency. However, the question of whether a new methodological framework, such as IE, is *required* for CE research is one that still remains open.

15.7 Concluding remarks

In this chapter, we critically examined several claims underlying the foundationalist debate in CE. We framed that debate in terms of three principal questions. In our analysis of Question 1, we argued that CE qualifies as a legitimate field of applied ethics that warrants philosophical analysis. In our response to Question 2, we concluded that there were no convincing reasons to believe that computing technology has either (a) generated any unique or new ethical issues, or (b) introduced any new ethical objects. In answering Question 3(a), we argued that there are no compelling reasons to believe that a new normative ethical theory is required for CE. We also saw that Question 3(b) poses some challenges that are not as easily answered at this point. If IE's claims regarding agency and moral agency are correct, CE may require a more robust framework than what is currently provided in the alternative methodological approaches used in applied ethics.

Acknowledgements

In composing this chapter, I have drawn from material in some of my previously published works, including Tavani (2002, 2005). I am grateful to Lloyd Carr, Luciano Floridi, Frances Grodzinsky and Kenneth Himma for their helpful comments on an earlier draft of this chapter.

EPILOGUE
The ethics of the information society in a globalized world

Luciano Floridi

Introduction

The previous chapters have provided a detailed overview of the variety of ethical challenges posed by the development of ICTs. By way of conclusion, in this epilogue I would like to invite the reader to look into the possible future of Information and Computer Ethics. More specifically, I shall try to forecast how the convergence of two fundamental trends of our times, globalization and the development of the information society, may interact with the ethical problems analysed in this book. The exercise will not be based on some untenable technological determinism. Humanity is, and will remain, firmly in charge of its destiny and hence be responsible for it. Rather, it will mean adopting the farmer's view that, with enough intelligence, toil and a bit of luck, one might be able to tell today what one will probably reap tomorrow. Before trying to 'look into the seeds of time, and say which grain will grow and which will not' (Shakespeare, *Macbeth*, Act I, Scene III, 59–62), two clarifications might be in order.

First, the future of globalization is a phenomenon too complex even to sketch in this brief epilogue. For a synthetic, well-balanced and informed overview, the reader may wish to consult Held and McGrew (2001) and consider that this chapter is written from what Held *et al.* (1999)) have defined as a 'transformationalist perspective', according to which 'globalization does not simply denote a shift in the extensity or scale of social relations and activity. Much more significantly, argue the transformationalists, it also involves the spatial re-organization and re-articulation of economic, political, military and cultural power.'

Second, in the rest of this chapter I will highlight six key transformations characterizing the processes of globalization. I shall label them *contraction, expansion, porosity, hybridization, synchronization* and *correlation*. They provide the essential background for making sense of the suggestion that Information Ethics can provide a successful approach for coping with the challenges posed by our increasingly globalized reality.

Contraction

The world has gone through alternating stages of globalization, growing and shrinking, for as long as humanity can remember. Here is a reminder:

in some respects the world economy was more integrated in the late 19th century than it is today. . . . Capital markets, too, were well integrated. Only in the past few years, indeed, have international capital flows, relative to the size of the world economy, recovered to the levels of the few decades before the first world war. (*The Economist*, 18 December 1997)

The truth is that, after each 'globalization backlash' (think of the end of the Roman or British Empires), the world never really went back to its previous state. Rather, by moving two steps forward and one step back, some time towards the end of the last century the process of globalization reached a point of no return. Today, revolutions or the collapse of empires can never shrink the world again, short of the complete unravelling of human life as we know it. Globalization is here to stay.

Globalization has become irreversible mainly thanks to radical changes in worldwide transport and communications (Brandt and Henning 2002). Atoms and bytes have been moving increasingly rapidly, frequently, cheaply, reliably and widely for the past fifty years or so. This dramatic acceleration has shortened the time required for any interactions: economic exchanges, financial transactions, social relations, information flows, movements of people and so forth (Hodel *et al.* 1998). In turn, this acceleration has a more condensed life and a contracted physical space. Ours is a smaller world, in which one may multi-task fast enough to give, and have, the impression of leading parallel lives. We may regain a nineteenth-century sense of time and space only if, one day, we travel to Mars.

Expansion

Human space in the twenty-first century has not merely shrunk, though. ICTs have also created a new digital environment, which is constantly expanding and becoming progressively more diverse. Again, we saw in Chapter 1 that the origins of this global, transnational common space are old. They are to be found in the invention of recording and communication technologies that range from the alphabet to printing, from photography to television. But it is only in the last few decades that we have witnessed a vast and steady migration of human life to the other side of the screen. When you ask 'Where were you?' it is now normal and common to receive the answer 'Online'. Globalization also means the emergence of this sort of single virtual space, shareable in principle by anyone, any time, anywhere.

Porosity

An important relation between our contracting physical space and our expanding, virtual environment is that of *porosity*. Imagine living as a flat figure on the surface of an endless cylinder. You could travel on the surface of the cylinder as a two-dimensional space, like a shadow, but not through it. So in order to reach any other point on the cylinder, the best you could do would be to follow the shortest path (geodesic) on the cylindrical surface. The empty space inside the cylinder would be inconceivable, as a third dimension would. Imagine now that the surface became porous and hence that a third dimension were added. The geodesics would be revolutionized, for you could travel through the vacuum encircled by the cylinder and reach the other side, thus significantly shortening your journeys. To use the rather apt vocabulary of surfing, you would be *tubing*: space would be curling over you, forming a 'tube', with you inside the cylindrical space. From a two-dimensional perspective, you would literally come in and out of space. This sort of porosity now characterizes the relation between physical and virtual space. It is difficult to say where one is when one is 'tubing', but we know that we can travel through cyberspace to interact with other physical places in a way that would have been inconceivable only a few decades ago. Telepresence (Floridi 2005c) in our porous environment is an ordinary experience and this is also what globalization means.

Hybridization

We saw in Chapter 1 that the threshold between *analogue-carbon-offline-here* and *digital-silicon-online-there* is being constantly eroded. ICTs are as much re-ontologizing our world as they are creating new realities. The digital is spilling over into the analogue and merging with it. Adapting Horace's famous phrase, 'captive cyberspace is conquering its victor'. ICTs are as much modifying the essential nature of our world (re-ontologization) as they are creating new realities. Your next fridge (www.lginternetfamily.co.uk/homenetwork.asp) will inherit from the previous one your tastes and wishes, just as your new laptop can import your favourite settings from the old one; and it will interact with your new way of cooking and with the supermarket website, just as your laptop can talk to a printer or to another computer. We have all known this in theory for some time; the difference is that it is now actually happening in our kitchens. Globalization also means the emergence of this common, fully interactive and responsive environment of wireless, pervasive, distributed, *a2a* (anything to anything) information processes, that works *a4a* (anywhere for any time), in real time. Future generations will find it difficult to imagine what life was before becoming *onlife*.

Synchronization

In a world in which information and material flows are becoming so tightly integrated and enmeshed, it is not surprising to see global patterns emerging not only from well-orchestrated operations (consider the tedious experience of any launch of a major blockbuster, with interviews in magazines, discussions on TV programmes, advertisements of merchandise and by-products throughout the world, special food products in supermarkets and fast-foods, etc.), but also inadvertedly, as the result of the accidental synchronization of otherwise chaotic trends.

All of a sudden, the world reads the same novel, or wears the same kind of trousers, or listens to the same music, or eats the same sort of food, or is concerned about the same problems, or cherishes the same news, or is convinced that it has the same disease. Some of this need not be the effect of any plan by some Big Brother, a secret agency, a powerful multinational or any other mysterious source scheming behind the curtains. After all, worldwide attention span is very limited and flimsy, and it is very hard to compete for it. The truth is that at least some global trends may merely arise from the constructive interference of waves of information that accidentally come into phase, and hence reinforce each other to the point of becoming global, through the casual and entirely contingent interaction of chaotic forces. It may happen with the stock markets or the fashion industry or dietary trends. The recurrent emergence of temporarily synchronized patterns of human behaviour, both transculturally and transnationally, is a clear sign of globalization, but not necessarily of masterminded organization. There is no intelligent plan, evil intention, autonomy or purposeful organization in the billion snowflakes that become an avalanche. Social group behaviour is acquiring a global meaning. The distributed power that generates Wikipedia is the other side of the dark, mindless stupidity of millions of slaves of fashions and trends.

Correlation

Imagine a safety net, like the one used in a circus. If it is sufficiently tight and robust, the heavier the object that falls into it, the larger the area of the net that will be stretched, sending waves of vibration throughout the net. Globalization also refers to the emergence of a comparable net of correlations among agents all over the world, which is becoming so tight and sensitive that the time lag in the transmission of the effects of an event 'dropping' on it is fast shortening, to the point that sometimes there is almost no distinction between what counts as local or remote. Global often means not *everywhere* but actually *delocalized*, and in a delocalized environment social friction is inevitable, as there is no more room for agents that allows for absorption of the effects of their decisions and actions. If anyone moves, the global boat rocks.

Globalizing ethics

If we consider now the profound transformations just sketched, it would be rather surprising if they did not have serious implications for our moral lives (see Weckert 2001 and Ess 2002). In a reality that is more and more physically contracted, virtually expanded, porous, hybridized, synchronized and correlated, the very nature of moral interactions, and hence of their ethical analysis, is significantly altered. Innovative forms of agenthood are becoming possible; new values are developing and old ones are being reshaped or re-prioritized; cultural and moral assumptions are ever more likely to come into contact when not into conflict; the very concepts of what constitutes our 'natural' environment and our enhanced features as a biological species are changing; and unprecedented ethical challenges have arisen (a reference to the notorious problem of privacy is *de rigueur* here), just to mention some macroscopic transformations in which globalization factors, as sketched above, play an important role.

What sort of ethical reflection can help us to cope successfully with a world that is undergoing such dramatic changes? Local approaches are as satisfactory as burying one's head in home values and traditions. The ethical discourse appears to be in need of an upgrade to cope with a globalized world. Each ethical theory is called upon to justify its worldwide and cross-cultural suitability. This seems even more so if the theory in question seeks to address explicitly the new moral issues that arise from the evolution of the information society, as it is the case with Information Ethics (IE).

I shall say more about IE in the next two sections. The specific question that I wish to address is whether, in a world that is fast becoming more and more globalized, Information Ethics can provide a successful approach for dealing with its new challenges. I shall argue in favour of a positive answer. But to make my case, let me first clarify what *Global Information Ethics* may mean.

Global Communication Ethics vs. Global Information-Ethics

There are at least two ways of understanding Global Information Ethics: as an *ethics of global communication* (Smith 2002) or as a *global information-ethics* (Bynum and Rogerson 1996). Since I shall concentrate only on the latter, let me briefly comment on the former first.

Global Information Ethics, understood as an ethics of worldwide *communication*, may be seen as a commendable effort to foster all those informational conditions that facilitate participation, dialogue, negotiation and consensus-building practices among people, across cultures and through generations. It is an approach concerned with new and old problems, caused or exacerbated by global communications or affecting the flow of information. Global Information Ethics as Global Communication Ethics is therefore a continuation of policy by other means, and it does not have to be reduced to a mere gesture towards the importance of mutual respect and understanding (meeting people and talking to each other can hardly do any harm and often helps). It is, however, faced by the serious problem of providing its own justification. What sort of ethical principles of communication and information are to be privileged, and why? Is there any macroethics (e.g. some form of consequentialism or deontologism or contractualism) that can rationally buttress a Global Communication Ethics? Moreover, isn't any attempt at providing such a macroethics just another instance of 'globalization' of some values and principles to the disadvantage of others? Without decent theorization, the risk is that we will reduce goodness to goodiness and transform the ethical discourse into some generic, well-meant sermon. At the same time, a robust foundation for a Global Communication Ethics may easily incur the problem of failing to respect and appreciate a plurality of diverse positions. The dilemma often seems to be left untouched, even when it is not overlooked. The good news is that it may be possible to overcome it by grounding a Global-Communication Ethics on a Global Information-Ethics.

Global Information-Ethics and the problem of the lion

If we look at the roots of the problem, it seems that,

  (i) in an increasingly globalized world, successful interactions among micro and macro agents belonging to different cultures call for a high level of successful communication; but

 (ii) successful, cross-cultural communications among agents require, in their turn, not only the classic three 'e's – *embodiment, embeddedness* and hence *experience*, that is, a sense of 'us-here-now' – but also a shared *ontology* (more on this presently); and yet

(iii) imposing a uniform ontology on all agents only seems to aggravate the problem, globalization becoming synonymous with ontological imperialism.

By 'ontology' I do not mean to refer here to any metaphysical theory of being, of what there is or there isn't, of why there is what there is, or of the ultimate nature of reality in itself. All this would require a form of epistemological realism (some confidence in some privileged access to the essential nature of things) that is controversial and that, fortunately, is unnecessary here.

Rather, I am using 'ontology' to cover the outcome of a variety of processes that allow an agent to appropriate (be successfully embedded in), semanticize (give meaning to, and make sense of) and conceptualize (order, understand and explain) her environment. In simplified terms, one's ontology is one's world, that is, the world as it appears to, is experienced by and interacted with, the agent in question.[1]

Agents can talk to each other only if they can partake to some degree in a shared ontology anchored to a common reality to which they can all refer.[2] Imagine two solipsistic minds, α and β, disembodied, unembedded and devoid of any experience. Suppose them living in two entirely different universes. Even if α and β could telepathically exchange their data, they could still not *communicate* with each other, for there would be absolutely nothing that would allow the receiver to interpret the sender. In fact, it would not even be clear whether any message was being exchanged at all.

The impossibility of communication between α and β is what Wittgenstein (1953) had in mind, I take it, when he wrote that 'if a lion could talk, we could not understand him'. The statement is obviously false (because we share with lions a similar form of embeddedness and embodiment, and hence experiences like hunger or pain) if one fails to realize that the lion is only a place-holder to indicate an agent utterly and radically different from us, like our α and β. The lion is a Martian, someone you simply cannot talk to because it is 'from another ontology'.[3]

From this perspective, the famous Latin phrase *hic sunt leones* (here there are lions) acquires a new meaning. The phrase occurred on Roman maps to indicate unknown and unexplored regions beyond the southern, African borders of the empire.[4] In a Wittgensteinian sense, the Romans were mapping the threshold beyond which no further communication was possible at all. They were drawing the limits of their ontology. What was beyond the border, the *locus* inhabited by the lions, was nothing, a non-place. Globalization has often meant that what is not inglobate simply isn't, i.e. fails to exist.

We can now formulate the difficulty confronting a Global Information-Ethics as *the problem of the lion*: cross-cultural communication, which is the

---

[1] How an ontology is achieved and what sort of philosophical analysis is required to make sense of its formation is not a relevant matter in this context, but the interested reader may wish to see Floridi (forthcoming, c).

[2] More technically, this means that two agents can communicate only if they share at least some possible level of abstraction. On the method of abstraction see Floridi (2008b).

[3] If it took endless time and efforts to decipher the hieroglyphics, imagine what sense an extraterrestrial being could make of a message in a bottle like the plaque carried by the Pioneer spacecraft (http://spaceprojects.arc.nasa.gov/Space_Projects/pioneer/PN10&11.html).

[4] Unfortunately, we do not have African maps drawn from the 'lions' perspective'. The Da Ming Hun Yi Tu, or Amalgamated Map of the Great Ming Empire, the oldest map of Africa known so far, dates back 'only' to 1389.

necessary condition for any further moral interaction, is possible only if the interlocutors partake in a common ontology. When Crusoe and Friday meet, after twenty-five years of Crusoe's solitude on the island, they can begin to communicate with each other only because they share the most basic ontology of life and death, food and shelter, fear and safety. Agents may be strangers to each other. They do not have to speak the same language, empathize or sympathize. But they do need to share at least some basic appropriation, semanticization and conceptualization of their common environment, as a minimal condition for the possibility of any further, moral interaction.

Can Information Ethics provide a solution to the problem of the lion?

Global Information-Ethics and its advantages

We saw in Chapter 5 that Information Ethics endorses an environmental approach. As such, it offers the following four advantages.

(1) Embracing the new informational ontology.

Not only do we live in a world that is moving towards a common informational ontology, we also experience our environment and talk and make sense of our experiences in increasingly informational ways. *Information is the medium.* This calls for an ethics, like IE, that, by prioritizing an informational ontology, may provide a valuable approach to decoding current moral phenomena and orienting our choices.

(2) Sharing a minimal, horizontal, lite ontology.

There is a risk, by adopting an ontocentric perspective, as IE suggests, that one may be merely exchanging one form of 'centrism' (American, Athenian, bio, European, Greek, male, Western, you name it) with just another, perhaps inadvertently, thus failing to acknowledge the ultimate complexity, diversity and fragility of the multicultural, ethical landscape with which one is interacting. We saw how the problem of the lion may become a dilemma. This justified concern, however, does not apply here because IE advocates a *minimal* informational ontology, which is not only timely, as we have just seen, but also tolerant of, and interfaceable with, other local ontologies. Thick cultures with robust, vertical ontologies – that is, deeply seated, often irreconcilable, fundamental conceptions about human nature, the value and meaning of life, the nature of the Universe and our place in it, society and its fair organization, religious beliefs, and so forth – can more easily interact with each other if they can share a lite, horizontal ontology, as little committed to any particular vision of reality as possible. The identification of an absolute, ultimate, monistic ontology, capable of making all other ontologies merge, is just a myth, and a violent one at that. There is no such thing as a commitment-free position with respect to the way in which a variety of continuously changing agents appropriate, conceptualize and semanticize their environment. Yet the alternative cannot be some form of relativism. This is no longer sustainable in a globalized world in which choices, actions and events are delocalized. There simply is not enough room for 'minding one's own business' in a network in which the behaviour of each node may affect the behaviour of all nodes. The approach to be pursued seems rather to be along the lines of what IE proposes: respect for and tolerance towards diversity and pluralism and identification of a minimal common ontology, which does not try to be platform independent (i.e. absolute), but cross-platform (i.e. portable).

As in Queneau's *Exercises in Style*, we need to be able to appreciate both the ninety-nine variations of the same story and the fact that it is, after all, the same story that is being recounted again and again.[5] This plurality of narratives need not turn into a Babel of fragmented voices. It may well be a source of pluralism that enriches one's ontology. More eyes simply see better and appreciate more angles, and a thousand languages can express semantic nuances that no global Esperanto may ever hope to grasp.

(3) Informational Environmentalism.

The ontocentrism supported by IE means that at least some of the weight of the ethical interpretations may be carried by (outsourced to) the informational ontology shared by the agents, not only by the different cultural or intellectual traditions (vertical ontologies) to which they may belong. Two further advantages are that all agents, whether human, artificial, social or hybrid, may be able to share the same minimal ontology and conceptual vocabulary; and then that any agent may take into account ecological concerns that are not limited to the biosphere.

(4) Identifying the sources and targets of moral interactions.

One of the serious obstacles in sharing an ontology is often how the sources and targets of moral interactions (including communication) are identified. The concept of person or human individual, and the corresponding features that are considered essential to his or her definition, might be central in some ontologies, marginal in others, and different in most. IE may help foster communication and fruitful interactions among different, thick, vertical ontologies by approaching the problem with conceptual tools that are less pre-committed. For when IE speaks of agents and patients, these are neutral elements in the ethical analysis that different cultures or macroethics may

---

[5] On a crowded bus, a narrator observes a young man with a long neck in a strange hat yell at another man whom he claims is deliberately jostling him whenever anyone gets on or off the bus. The young man then sits down in a vacant seat. Two hours later the same narrator sees that same young man with another friend, who is suggesting that the young man have another button put on his overcoat.

be able to appropriate, enrich and make more complex, depending on their conceptual requirements and orientations. It is like having an ontology of agency that is open source, and that anyone can adapt to its own proprietary metaphysics.

The cost of a Global Information-Ethics: postulating the ontic trust

It would be silly to conclude at this point that a Global-Information Ethics may provide an answer to any challenge posed by the various phenomena of globalization. This would be impossible. Of course, there will be many issues and difficulties that will require substantial extensions and adaptations of IE, of its methodology and of its principles. The point is that such a great effort to apply IE as a global ethics would be fruitful and hence worth making.

It would be equally wrong to assume that the adoption of IE as a fruitful approach to global challenges may come at no conceptual cost. Every ethical approach requires some concession on the part of those who decide to share it and IE is no exception.

The cost imposed by IE is summarizable in terms of the postulation of what I shall define as the *ontic trust* binding agents and patients. A straightforward way of clarifying the concept of ontic trust is by drawing an analogy with the concept of 'social contract'.

Various forms of contractualism (in ethics) and contractarianism (in political philosophy) argue that moral obligation, the duty of political obedience, or the justice of social institutions, have their roots in, and gain their support from, a so-called 'social contract'. This may be a real, implicit or *merely hypothetical* agreement between the parties constituting a society, e.g. the people and the sovereign, the members of a community, or the individual and the state. The parties accept to agree to the terms of the contract, and thus obtain some rights, in exchange for some freedoms that, allegedly, they would enjoy in a hypothetical state of nature. The rights and responsibilities of the parties subscribing to the agreement are the terms of the social contract, whereas the society, state, group etc. is the entity created for the purpose of enforcing the agreement. Both rights and freedoms are not fixed and may vary, depending on the interpretation of the social contract.

Interpretations of the theory of the social contract tend to be highly (and often unknowingly) anthropocentric (the focus is only on human rational agents) and stress the coercive nature of the agreement. These two aspects are not characteristic of the concept of ontic trust, but the basic idea of a fundamental agreement between parties as a foundation of moral interactions is sensible. In the case of the ontic trust, it is transformed into a primeval, entirely hypothetical *pact*, logically predating the social contract, which all agents cannot but sign when they come into existence, and that is constantly renewed in successive generations.[6] The sort of pact in question can be understood more precisely in terms of an actual trust.

Generally speaking, a trust in the English legal system is an entity in which someone (the trustee) holds and manages the former assets of a person (the trustor, or donor) for the benefit of certain persons or entities (the beneficiaries). Strictly speaking, nobody owns the assets, since the trustor has donated them, the trustee has only legal ownership and the beneficiary has only equitable ownership. Now, the logical form of this sort of agreement can be used to model the ontic trust, in the following way:

- the assets or 'corpus' is represented by the world, including all existing agents and patients;
- the donors are all past and current *generations* of agents;
- the trustees are all current *individual* agents;
- the beneficiaries are all current and future *individual* agents and patients.

By coming into being, an agent is made possible thanks to the existence of other entities. It *is* therefore bound to all that already is, both *unwillingly* and *inescapably*. It *should be* so also *caringly*. *Unwillingly*, because no agent wills itself into existence, though every agent can, in theory, will itself out of it. *Inescapably*, because the ontic bond may be broken by an agent only at the cost of ceasing to exist as an agent. Moral life does not begin with an act of freedom, but it may end with one. *Caringly*, because participation in reality by any entity, including an agent – that is, the fact that any entity is an expression of what exists – provides a right to existence and an invitation (not a duty) to respect and take care of other entities. The pact then involves no coercion, but a mutual relation of appreciation, gratitude and care, which is fostered by the recognition of the dependence of all entities on each other. A simple example may help to clarify further the meaning of the ontic trust.

Existence begins with a gift, even if possibly an unwanted one. A foetus will be initially only a beneficiary of the world. Once she is born and has become a full moral agent, she will be, as an individual, both a beneficiary and a trustee of the world. She will be in charge of taking care of the world, and, insofar as she is a member of the generation of living agents, she will also be a donor of the world. Once dead, she will leave the world to other

---

[6] There are important and profound ways of understanding this *Ur-pact* religiously, especially but not only in the Judaeo-Christian tradition, where the parties involved are God and Israel or humanity, and their old or new *covenant* makes it easier to include environmental concerns and values otherwise overlooked from the strongly anthropocentric perspective *prima facie* endorsed by contemporary contractualism. However, it is not my intention to endorse or even draw on such sources. I am mentioning the point here in order to shed some light both on the origins of contractualism and on a possible way of understanding the approach advocated by IE.

agents after her, and thus become a member of the generation of donors. In short, the life of an agent becomes a journey from being only a beneficiary to being only a donor, passing through the stage of being a responsible trustee of the world. We begin our career as moral agents as strangers to the world; we should end it as friends of the world.

The obligations and responsibilities imposed by the ontic trust will vary depending on circumstances but, fundamentally, the expectation is that actions will be taken or avoided in view of the welfare of the whole world.

The ontic trust is what is postulated by the approach supported by IE. According to IE, the ethical discourse concerns any entity, understood informationally, that is, not only all persons, their cultivation, well-being and social interactions, not only animals, plants and their proper natural life, but also anything that exists, from buildings and other artefacts to rivers and sand. Indeed, according to IE, nothing is too humble to deserve no respect at all. In this way, IE brings to ultimate completion the process of enlargement of the concept of what may count as a centre of a (no matter how minimal) moral claim, which now includes every instance of *being* understood informationally, no matter whether physically implemented or not. IE holds that every entity, as an expression of *being*, has a dignity, constituted by its mode of existence and essence (the collection of all the elementary proprieties that constitute it for what it is), which deserve to be respected (at least in a minimal and overridable sense) and hence place moral claims on the interacting agent and ought to contribute to guiding and constraining his ethical decisions and behaviour whenever possible. The ontic trust (and the corresponding ontological equality principle among entities) means that any form of reality (any instance of information/*being*), simply by the fact of *being* what it is, enjoys a minimal, initial, overridable, equal right to exist and develop in a way which is appropriate to its nature. In the history of philosophy, a similar view can be found advocated by Stoic and Neoplatonic philosophers, and by Spinoza.

The acceptance of the ontic trust requires a disinterested judgement of the moral situation from an objective perspective, that is, a perspective which is as non-anthropocentric as possible. Moral behaviour is less likely without this epistemic virtue. The ontic trust is respected whenever actions are impartial, universal and 'caring' towards the world.

Conclusion

One of the objections that is sometimes made against IE is that of being too abstract or theoretical to be of much use when human agents are confronted by very concrete and applied challenges (Siponen 2004). Unfortunately, this is an obvious misunderstanding. Imagine someone who, being presented with the declaration of human rights, were to complain that it is too general and inapplicable to solve the ethical problems she is facing in a specific situation, say in dealing with a particular case of cyberstalking in the company that employs her. This would be rather out of place. The suspicion is that some impatience with conceptual explorations may betray a lack of understanding of how profound the revolution we are undergoing is, and hence how radical the rethinking of our ethical approaches and principles may need to be, in order to cope with it. IE is certainly not the declaration of human rights, but it seeks to obtain a level of generality purporting to provide a foundation for more applied and case-oriented analyses. So the question is not whether IE is too abstract – good foundations for the structure one may wish to see being built inevitably lie well below the surface – but whether it will succeed in providing the robust framework within which practical issues of moral concern may be more easily identified, clarified and solved. It is in its actual applications that IE, as a Global Ethics for our information society, will or will not qualify as a useful approach; although building on the foundation provided by IE is a challenge, it cannot be an objection.

References

Ackerman, B. and Fishkin, J. 2004. *Deliberation Day*. New Haven and London: Yale University Press.

Adam, A. 1998. *Artificial Knowing: Gender and the Thinking Machine*. New York and London: Routledge.

Adam, A. 2002. 'Cyberstalking and Internet Pornography', *Ethics and Information Technology* 4, 133–142.

Adam, A. 2005. *Gender, Ethics and Information Technology*. Basingstoke: Palgrave Macmillan.

Adam, A., Griffiths, M., Keogh, C., Moore, K., Richardson, H. and Tattersall, A. 2006. 'Being an it in IT – Gendered Identities in the IT Workplace', *European Journal of Information Systems* 15(4), 368–378.

Adam, A. and Kreps, D. 2006. 'Enabling or Disabling Technologies? A Critical Approach to Web Accessibility', *Information Technology and People* 19(3), 203–218.

Adams, J. 1998. *The Next World War: Computers Are the Weapons and the Front Line is Everywhere*. New York: Simon and Schuster.

Adler, M. and Posner, E. A. (eds.) 2001. *Cost-Benefit Analysis: Economic, Philosophical and Legal Perspectives*. Chicago: University of Chicago Press.

Agre, P. and Mailloux, C. 1997. 'Social Choice about Privacy: Intelligent Vehicle-Highway Systems in the United States', in Friedman, B. (ed.), *Human Values and the Design of Computer Technology*. Cambridge: Cambridge University Press.

Akrich, M. 1992. 'The Description of Technical Objects', in Bijker, W. and Law, J. E., (eds.), *Shaping Technology/Building Society*. Cambridge, MA: MIT Press.

Albrecht, K. and Macintyre, L. 2006. *The Spychips Threat: Why Christians Should Resist RFID and Electronic Surveillance*. Nashville: Nelson Current.

Albrechtslund, A. 2008. 'Online Social Networking as Participatory Surveillance', *First Monday* 13(3), 3 March. www.uic.edu/htbin/cgiwrap/bin/ojs/index.php/fm/article/view/2142/1949

Alexander, J. 1999. *Future War*. New York: St. Martin's Press.

Alterman, A., 2003. '"A Piece of Yourself": Ethical Issues in Biometric Identification', *Ethics and Information Technology* 5(3),139–150.

Anderson, M. and Anderson, S. L. 2006. 'Computing an Ethical Theory with Multiple Prima Facie Duties', in *Proceeding EthicALife/ALifeX*.

Anderson, M. and Anderson, S. L. 2007. 'Machine Ethics: Creating an Ethical Intelligent Agent', *Artificial Intelligence Magazine* 28(4), Winter, 15.

Anderson, M. and Anderson, S. L. 2008. 'Ethical Healthcare Agents. Advanced Computational Intelligence Paradigms', in Jain, L. C. (ed.), *Healthcare-3* pp. 233–257. Berlin: Springer.

Anderson, N. 2007. 'California Outlaws the Forced Subdermal RFID Tagging of Humans', http://arstechnica.com/news.ars/post/20070904-california-outlaws-forced-rfid-tagging-of-humans.html

Anscombe, G. E. M. 1958. 'Modern Moral Philosophy', *Philosophy* 33.

Arendt, H. 1958. *The Human Condition* (2nd edn). Chicago: University of Chicago Press.

Arendt, H. 1968. 'Crisis in Culture', in *Between Past and Future: Eight Exercises in Political Thought*, pp. 197–227. New York: Meridian.

Aristotle, *On the Motion of Animals, On the Soul, Nicomachean Ethics*.

Arkin, R. 2004. 'Bombs, Bonding, and Bondage: Human-Robot Interaction and Related Ethical Issues'. Paper presented at the First International Conference on Roboethics, San Remo, Italy, January 2004.

Arkin, R. 2007. *Governing Lethal Behavior: Embedding Ethics in a Hybrid Deliberative/Reactive Robot Architecture.* Technical Report GIT-GVU-07–11, College of Computing, Georgia Institute of Technology.

Arquilla, J. and Ronfeldt, D. 1997. *In Athena's Camp: Preparing for Conflict in the Information Age.* Santa Monica, CA: RAND.

Audi, R. 2007. *Moral Value and Human Diversity.* New York: Oxford University Press.

Avgerou, C. 2003. 'The Link Between ICT and Economic Growth in the Discourse of Development', in Korpeal, M., Montealegre, R. and Poulymenakou, A. 2003, *Organizational Information Systems in the Context of Globalization*, pp. 373–386. Dordrecht: Kluwer.

Bailenson, J. N., Yee, N., Blascovich, J. and Guadagno, R. E. 2008. 'Transformed Social Interaction in Mediated Interpersonal Communication', in Konijn, E., Tanis, M., Utz, S. and Linden, A. (eds.), *Mediated Interpersonal Communication*. Mahwah, NJ: Lawrence Erlbaum Associates.

Bainbridge, W. S. and Roco, M. C. (eds.) 2006. *Managing Nano-bio-info-cogno Innovations: Converging Technologies in Society.* Dordrecht: Springer.

Barab, S., Dodge, T., Thomas, M. K., Jackson, C. and Tuzun, H. 2007. 'Our Designs and the Social Agendas They Carry', *Journal of the Learning Sciences* 16, 263–305.

Barbaro, M. and Zeller Jr., T. 2006. 'A Face is Exposed for AOL Searcher No. 4417749', *The New York Times*, 9 August.

Barcan Marcus, R. 1987. 'Moral Dilemmas and Consistency', in Gowans (1987), pp. 188–204.

Barger, R. N. 2008. *Computer Ethics: A Case-Based Approach.* New York: Cambridge University Press.

Barlow, J. 1995. 'Coming into the Country', in Johnson, D. G. and Nissenbaum, H. (eds.), *Computers, Ethics and Social Value*, pp. 15–18. Upper Saddle River: Prentice Hall.

Barnaby, F. 1986. *The Automated Battlefield*. New York: The Free Press.

Barnes, S. B. 2006. 'A Privacy Paradox: Social Networking in the United States', *First Monday* 11(9). www.firstmonday.org/issues/issue11_9/barnes/index.html#author

Beauchamp, T. L. and Childress, J. F. 2001. *Principles of Biomedical Ethics*. Oxford: Oxford University Press.

Beckenstein, J. D. 2003. 'Information in the Holographic Universe', *Scientific American*, August, 58–65.

Beitz, C. 2001. 'Does Global Inequality Matter?', in Pogge, T. W., *Global Justice*, pp. 106–122. Oxford: Blackwell.

Bell, T. W. 1995. 'Anonymous Speech,' *Wired*, October, http://www.wired.com/wired/archive/3.10/cyber.rights.html.

Bellin, D. and Chapman, G. 1987. *Computers in Battle: Will They Work?* New York: Harcourt, Brace and Jovanovich.

Benhabib, S. 1992. *Situating the Self*. Cambridge: Polity Press.

Benkler, Y. 2001. 'The Battle over the Institutional Ecosystem in the Digital Environment', *Communications of the ACM* 44(2), 84–90.

Berlin, I. 1957. *The Hedgehog and the Fox: An Essay on Tolstoy's View of History*. New York: Weidenfeld and Nicolson.

Berlin, I. 1958. *Two Concepts of Liberty*: An Inaugural Lecture Delivered before the University of Oxford on 31 October 1958. Oxford: Clarendon Press.

Berlin, I. 1969. *Four Essays on Liberty*. Oxford: Clarendon Press.

Bijker, W. and Law, J. (eds.) 1992. *Shaping Technology/Building Society. Studies in Sociotechnical Change*. Cambridge, MA: MIT Press.

Black, H. C. 1990. *Black's Law Dictionary: Definitions of the Terms and Phrases of American and English Jurisprudence, Ancient and Modern* (6th edn). St Paul, MN: West Publishing.

Blackwell, A. H. 2003. 'Don't Expect Any Privacy in the Workplace', *WWWiz.Com*. wwwiz.com/issue45/

Bloor, D. 1976. *Knowledge and Social Imagery*. London: Routledge & Kegan Paul.

Boella, G. and Torre, van der L. 2004. 'Fulfilling or Violating Obligations in Normative Multiagent Systems', *IAT* 2004, 483–486.

Bohman, J. 1996. *Public Deliberation: Pluralism, Complexity and Democracy*. Cambridge, MA: MIT Press.

Boltuc, P. (ed.) 2008. *APA Newsletter on Computers and Philosophy*, Spring 7(2) and Fall 8(1).

Boran, M. 2007. 'Data Centres Make Big Carbon Footprint', *Siliconrepublic.com*, 10 October. www.siliconrepublic.com/news/news.nv?storyid=single9387

Boscarol, M. 2006. 'Working with Others: Accessibility and User Research', *Accessibility* 225, 9 October 09. http://alistapart.com/articles/workingwithothers

Bostrom, N. 2002. 'Existential Risks: Analyzing Human Extinction Scenarios and Related Hazards', *Journal of Evolution and Technology* 9, 1–30.

Bostrom, N. 2003. 'The Transhumanist FAQ, Version 2.1', www.transhumanism. org/resources/faq.html

Bourdieu, P. 1977. *Outline of a Theory of Practice*. Trans. R. Nice. Cambridge: Cambridge University Press.

Bowker, G. C. and Star, S. L. 1999. *Sorting Things Out: Classification and Its Consequences*. Boston: MIT Press.

Boyle, James. 2001. 'A Politics of Intellectual Property: Environmentalism for the Net?', in Spinello, R. A. and Tavani, H. T. (eds.), *Readings in Cyberethics*, pp. 231–251. Sudbury, MA: Jones and Bartlett.

Brandt, D. and Henning, K. 2002. 'Information and Communication Technologies: Perspectives and Their Impact on Society', *AI and Society* 16(3), 210–223.

Bratman, M. E. 1987. *Intention, Plans and Practical Reasoning*. Cambridge: Harvard University Press.

Breazeal, C. 2002. *Designing Sociable Robots*. Cambridge, MA: MIT Press.

Brey, P. 1998. 'The Politics of Computer Systems and the Ethics of Design', in van den Hoven, J. (ed.), *Computer Ethics: Philosophical Enquiry*. Rotterdam: Rotterdam University Press.

Brey, P. 1999a. 'Method in Computer Ethics: Towards a Multi-Level Interdisciplinary Approach', *Ethics and Information Technology* 2(3), 1–5.

Brey, P. 1999b. 'The Ethics of Representation and Action in Virtual Reality', *Ethics and Information Technology* 1(1), 5–14.

Brey, P. 1999c. 'Worker Autonomy and the Drama of Digital Networks in Organizations', *Journal of Business Ethics* 22(1), 15–25.

Brey, P. 2000. 'Disclosive Computer Ethics', *Computers and Society* 30(4), 10–16.

Brey, P. 2008. 'Virtual Reality and Computer Simulation', in Himma, K. E. and Tavani, H. T. (eds.), *The Handbook of Information and Computer Ethics*. Hoboken, NJ: John Wiley & Sons.

Briggle, A., Mitcham, C. and Ryder, M. 2005. 'Technology: Overview', in Mitcham, C. (ed.), *Encyclopedia of Science, Technology and Ethics*, pp. 908–1912. Detroit: Thomson, Gale.

Brin, D. 1999. *The Transparent Society: Will Technology Force Us to Choose between Privacy and Freedom?* New York: Perseus Books.

Bringsjord, S. 2007. 'Ethical Robots: The Future Can Heed Us', *AI and Society* (online).

Britz, J. 2007. 'The Internet: The Missing Link Between the Information Rich and the Information Poor?', in Capurro, R., Frühbauer J. and Hausmaningers, T. (eds.), *Localizing the Internet: Ethical aspects in intercultural perspective*, pp. 265–277. Munich: Wilhelm Fink.

Brooks, R. A. 2002. *Flesh and Machines: How Robots Will Change Us*. New York: Pantheon.

Brooks, R. 2007. 'Robotkind: On the Battlefield and in the Home', Lecture to the British Computer Society, June 2007. Video online at http:// 74.125.95.132/server.php?show=ConWebDoc.10440

Brown, C. 2003. *Lost Liberties: Ashcroft and the Assault on Personal Freedom.* New York: The New Press.

Buchanan, E. A. 2004. 'Ethical Considerations for the Information Professions', in Spinello, R. A. and Tavani, H. T., (eds.), *Readings in Cyberethics* (2nd edn), pp. 613–624. Sudbury, MA: Jones and Bartlett.

Buchanan, E. and Campbell, J. 2005. 'New Threats to Intellectual Freedom: The Loss of the Information Commons through Law and Technology in the US', in Spinello, R. A. and Tavani, H. T. (eds.), *Intellectual Property Rights in a Networked World: Theory and Practice*, pp. 205–242. Hershey, PA: INFOSCI.

Budinger, T. F. and Budinger, M. D. 2006. *Ethics of Emerging Technologies: Scientific Facts and Moral Challenges.* Hoboken, NJ: Wiley.

Burk, D. 2001. 'Copyrightable Functions and Patentable Speech', *Communications of the ACM* 44(2), 69–76.

Burk, D. 2007. 'Privacy and Property in the Global Datasphere', in Hongladarom, S. and Ess, C. (eds.), *Information Technology Ethics: Cultural Perspectives*, pp. 94–107. Hershey, PA: IGI Global.

Business Services Industry, 2007. 'TopTenREVIEWS Reports Worldwide Pornography Market at Least \$97 Billion; Every Second 28,258 Internet Users View Pornography', bNet Business Network (12 March). http://findarticles.com/p/articles/mi_m0EIN/is_/ai_n27186769

Butler, S, 1985 (1872), *Erewhon.* London: Penguin Books.

Bynum, T. W. 1985. Editor's Introduction to James Moor, 'What is Computer Ethics?', *Metaphilosophy* 16(4), 263–265.

Bynum, T. W. 1986. 'Aristotle's Theory of Human Action', a doctoral dissertation at the Graduate School of the City University of New York. www.southernct.edu/organizations/rccs/

Bynum, T. W. 2000a. 'The Foundation of Computer Ethics', *Computers and Society* 30(2), 6–13.

Bynum, T. W. 2000b. 'A Very Short History of Computer Ethics', Newsletter of the American Philosophical Association on Philosophy and Computing. www.southernct.edu/organizations/rccs/resources/research/introduction/bynum_shrt_hist.html

Bynum, T. W. 2001. 'Computer Ethics: Basic Concepts and Historical Overview', *Stanford Encyclopedia of Philosophy*, http://plato.stanford.edu/entries/ethics-computer/

Bynum, T. W. 2004. 'Ethical Challenges to Citizens of the "Automatic Age": Norbert Wiener on the Information Society', *Journal of Information, Communication and Ethics in Society* 2(2), 65–74.

Bynum, T. W. 2005. 'Norbert Wiener's Vision: The Impact of the "Automatic Age" on Our Moral Lives', in Cavalier, R. (ed.), *The Impact of the Internet on Our Moral Lives,* pp. 11–25. Albany, NY: State University of New York Press.

Bynum, T. W. 2006a. 'Flourishing Ethics', *Ethics and Information Technology* 8(4), 157–173.

Bynum, T. W. 2006b. 'A Copernican Revolution in Ethics?', in Dodig-Crnkovi, G. and Stuart, S. (eds.), *Computing, Philosophy, and Cognitive Science.* Newcastle upon Tyne: Cambridge Scholars Press.

Bynum, T. W. and Rogerson, S. 1996, 'Global Information Ethics: Introduction and Overview', *Science and Engineering Ethics* 2(2), 131–136.

Camp, J. 1999. 'Democratic Implications of Internet Protocols,' *The Information Society* 15, 249–256.

Camp, L. J. 2003. 'First Principles of Copyright for DRM Design', *IEEE Internet Computing* 7(3), 59–65.

Canellopoulou-Bottis, M. and Himma, K. E. 2008. 'The Digital Divide: A Perspective for the Future', in Himma, K. E. and Tavani, H. T. (eds.), *The Handbook of Information and Computer Ethics*, pp. 621–637. Hoboken, NJ: Wiley.

Castells, M. 2000. *The Information Age: Economy, Society, and Culture. Volume I: The Rise of the Network Society* (2nd edn). Oxford: Blackwell.

Chakraborty, R., Stivers, D. N., Su, B., Zhong, Y. and Budowle, B. 1999. 'The Utility of Short Tandem Repeat Loci Beyond Human Identification: Implications for Development of New DNA Typing', *Electrophoresis* 20(8), 1682–1696.

Chan, J. 2003. 'Confucian Attitudes towards Ethical Pluralism', in Madsen, R. and Strong, T. B. (eds.), *The Many and the One: Religions and Secular Perspectives on Ethical Pluralism in the Modern World*, pp. 129–153. Princeton: Princeton University Press.

Ciro, T. 2005. 'The Scarcity of Intellectual Property', *Journal of Information, Law and Technology*, www2.warwick.ac.uk/fac/soc/law/elj/jilt/

Clark, J. 2006. 'To Hell with WCAG2', *Accessibility* 217, 23 May 2006. http://alistapart.com/articles/tohellwithwcag2

Clarke, S. 2001. 'Informed Consent in Medicine in Comparison with Consent in Other Areas of Human Activity', *Southern Journal of Philosophy* 39, 169–187.

Clarke, S. 2005. 'Future Technologies, Dystopic Futures and the Precautionary Principle", *Ethics and Information Technology* 7, 121–126.

Clarke, S. 2009. 'New Technologies, Common Sense and the Paradoxical Precautionary Principle', in Duwell, M. and Sollie, P. (eds.), *Evaluating New Technologies: Methodological Problems for the Assessment of Technological Developments*, pp. 159–173. Dordrecht: Springer.

Clarke, S. G. and Simpson, E. 1989. *Anti-Theory in Ethics and Moral Conservatism.* Albany, NY: State University of New York Press.

Clouser, K. D. 1980. *Teaching Bioethics: Strategies, Problems, and Resources.* Hastings Center, Institute for Society, Ethics, and the Life Sciences.

Cockburn, C. and Ormrod, S. 1993. *Gender and Technology in the Making.* Thousand Oaks, CA: Sage.

Coeckelbergh, M. 2007. 'Violent Computer Games, Empathy, and Cosmopolitanism', *Ethics and Information Technology* 9(3), 219–231.

Coleman, S. and Gøtze, J. 2001/2004. 'Bowling Together: Online Public Engagement in Policy Deliberation, Hansard Society'. Online at bowlingtogether.net

Collins, H. M. 1990. *Artificial Experts: Social Knowledge and Intelligent Machines.* Cambridge, MA/London: MIT Press.

Collste, G. 2002. 'The Internet Doctor and Medical Ethics', *Medicine, Healthcare and Philosophy* 5(2), 121–125.

Combes, R. 2005. 'A Taxonomy of Technics', *International Philosophical Quarterly* 46, 5–24.

Couldry, N. 2003. 'Digital Divide or Discursive Design? On the Emerging Ethics of Information Space', *Ethics and Information Technology* 5(2), 89–97.

Cowan, R. S. 1989. *More Work for Mother: The Ironies of Household Technology from the Open Hearth to the Microwave.* London: Free Association Books.

Critcher, C. 2006. *Critical Readings: Moral Panics and the Media.* Maidenhead: Open University Press.

Cushman, M. and Klecun, E. 2006. 'How (Can) Nonusers Engage with Technology: Bringing in the Digitally Excluded', in Trauth, E. M., Howcroft, D., Butler, T., Fitzgerald, B. and DeGross, J. I., *Social Inclusion: Societal and Organizational Implications for Information Systems* (IFIP Volume 208), pp. 347–364. New York: Springer.

Dastani, M., Boer, F. de, Dignum, F., Hoek, W. van der, Kroese, M. and Meyer, J. J., 'Implementing Cognitive Agents in 3APL', www.cs.uu.nl/3apl/

Davies, S. 2003. 'New Techniques and Technologies of Surveillance in the Workplace', www.amicus-itpa.org//juneconf3.shtml

Davis, R. 2001. 'The Digital Dilemma', *Communications of the ACM* 44(2), 77–83.

De George, R. T. 1998. 'Computers, Ethics, and Business', *Philosophic Exchange* 1997–1998, 45–55.

De Landa, M. 1991. *War in the Age of Intelligent Machines.* Cambridge, MA: MIT Press.

Dennett, D. C. 1987. *The Intentional Stance.* Cambridge, MA: MIT Press.

Dennett, D. C. 1996. 'When Hal Kills, Who's to Blame?', in Stork, D. (ed.), *Hal's Legacy*, pp. 351–365. Cambridge, MA: MIT Press.

Dennis, L. 1997. 'Kant's Ethics and Duties to Oneself', *Pacific Philosophical Quarterly* 78(4), 321–348.

Devon, R. 2004. 'Towards a Social Ethics of Technology: A Research Prospect', *Techné: Research in Philosophy and Technology* 8(1), 99–115.

Dewan, S. and Riggins, F. J. 2005. 'The Digital Divide: Current and Future Research Directions', *Journal of the Association for Information Systems* 6(12), 298–337.

Dewey, J. 1927. *The Public and its Problems.* New York: Henry Holt & Co.

Dobransky, K. and Hargittai, E. 2006. 'The Disability Divide in Internet Access and Use', *Information, Communication and Society* 9(3), 313–334.

Donaldson, T. and Dunfee, T. W. 1999. *Ties that Bind: A Social Contracts Approach to Business Ethics.* Boston, MA: Harvard Business School Press.

Drexler, E. K. 1986. *Engines of Creation.* Garden City: Doubleday.

Dreyfus, H. L. 2001. *On the Internet.* London: Routledge.

Dryzek, J. 2001. *Deliberative Democracy and Beyond: Liberals, Critics, Contestations.* Oxford: Oxford University Press.

Dunnigan, J. 1996. *Digital Soldiers*. New York: St. Martin's Press.

Dusek, V. 2006. *Philosophy of Technology: An Introduction*. Malden: Blackwell.

Dyson, L., Hendriks, M. and Grant, S. (eds.). 2007. *Information Technology and Indigenous People*. Hershey, PA: Information Science Publishing.

Eickelman, D. F. 2003. 'Islam and Ethical Pluralism', in Madsen, R. and Strong, T. B. (eds.), *The Many and the One: Religious and Secular Perspectives on Ethical Pluralism in the Modern World*, pp. 161–180. Princeton: Princeton University Press.

Einstein, A. 1954. *Ideas and Opinions*. New York: Crown Publishers.

Elberfeld, R. 2002. 'Resonanz als Grundmotiv ostasiatischer Ethik' [Resonance as a Fundamental Motif of East Asian Ethics], in Elberfeld, R. and Wohlfart, G. (eds.), *Kamparative Ethik: Das gute Leben Zwischen den Kulturen* [Comparative Ethics: The Good Life between Cultures], pp. 131–141. Cologne: Edition Chora.

Electronic Frontier Foundation. www.EFF.org

Elgesem, D. 2005. 'Deliberative Technology?' in Thorseth, M. and Ess, C. (eds.), *Technology in a Multicultural and Global Society*, pp. 61–77. Trondheim: NTNU, Programme for Applied Ethics, publ. series no. 6.

Ellul, J. 1964. *The Technological Society* (trans. John Wilkinson). New York: Alfred A. Knopf.

Ess, C. 1996. 'The Political Computer: Democracy, CMC, and Habermas' in Ess, C. (ed.), *Philosophical Perspectives on Computer-Mediated Communication*, pp. 197–230. Albany, NY: State University of New York Press.

Ess, C. 2002. 'Computer-Mediated Colonization, the Renaissance, and Educational Imperatives for an Intercultural Global Village', *Ethics and Information Technology* 4(1), 11–22.

Ess, C. 2006a. 'Ethical Pluralism and Global Information Ethics', *Ethics and Information Technology* 8(4), 215–226.

Ess, C. 2006b. 'From Computer-Mediated Colonization to Culturally-Aware ICT Usage and Design', in Zaphiris, P. and Kurniawan, S. (eds.), *Advances in Universal Web Design and Evaluation: Research, Trends and Opportunities*, pp. 178–197. Hershey, PA: Idea Publishing.

Ess, C. 2007. 'Cybernetic Pluralism in an Emerging Global Information and Computing Ethics', *International Review of Information Ethics* 7 www.i-r-i-e.net/inhalt/007/11-ess.pdf

Ess, C. 2009. *Digital Media Ethics*. Malden, MA: Polity Press.

Ess, C. and Thorseth, M. 2006. 'Neither Relativism nor Imperialism: Theories and Practices for a Global Information Ethics', *Ethics and Information Technology* 8(3), 91–154.

ETC Group. 2005. 'A Tiny Primer on Nano-Scale Technologies and "the Little Bang Theory"', www.etcgroup.org/documents/TinyPrimer_English.pdf

European Commission Scientific Committee on Emerging and Newly Identified Health Risks. 2006. 'The Appropriateness of Existing Methodologies to Assess the Potential Risks Associated with Engineered and

Adventitious Products of Nanotechnologies', http://ec.europa.eu/health/ph_risk/committees/04_scenihr/docs/scenihr_o_003b.pdf

European Group on Ethics in Science and New Technologies. 2005. 'Ethical Aspects of ICT Implants in the Human Body', http://ec.europa.eu/european_group_ethics/docs/avis20_en.pdf

Fairweather, N. B. and Rogerson, S. 2001. 'A Moral Approach to Electronic Patient Records', *Medical Informatics and the Internet in Medicine* 26(3), 219–234.

Fallows, J. 2008. 'The Connection Has Been Reset,' *The Atlantic*, www.theatlantic.com/doc/200803/chinese-firewall

Farmer, J. D. and Belin, A. d'A. 1992. 'Artificial Life: The Coming Evolution", in Langton, C. G., Taylor, C. E, Farmer, J. D. and Rasmussen, S. (eds.) *Artificial Life II: Proceedings of the Workshop on Synthesis and Simulation of Living Systems*, Santa Fe, 1990. Redwood City, CA: Addison Wesley.

Farrell, G., Isaacs, S. and Trucano, M. 2007. 'The NEPAD e-Schools Demonstration Project: A Work in Progress. Washington, DC: infoDTheWorld Bank', www.infodev.org/en/Publication.355.html

Ferré, Frederick. 1995. *Philosophy of Technology*. Athens: University of Georgia Press.

Final Declaration of the First European 'Seas at Risk' Conference. 1994. www.seas-at-risk.org/n2_archive.php?page=9

Fish, S. 1994. *There's No Such Thing as Free Speech . . . and it's a Good Thing too*. New York: Oxford University Press.

Fisher, E., Jones, J. S. and von Schomberg, R. 2006. *Implementing the Precautionary Principle: Perspectives and Prospects*. Cheltenham: Edward Elgar.

Fishkin, J. 1997. *Voice of the People*. Yale University Press.

Flanagan, M., Howe, D. and Nissenbaum, H. 2005. 'Values at Play: Design Tradeoffs in Socially-Oriented Game Design', in *Proceedings of the CHI 2005 Conference on Human Factors in Computing Systems*. CHI 2005, 2–7 April, Portland, Oregon. New York: ACM Press.

Flanagan, M., Howe, D. and Nissenbaum, H. 2008. 'Embodying Values in Technology: Theory and Practice', in van den Hoven, J. and Weckert, J. (eds.), *Information Technology and Moral Philosophy*. Cambridge: Cambridge University Press.

Fleischmann, K. R. 2007. 'Digital Libraries with Embedded Values: Combining Insights from LIS and Science and Technology Studies', *Library Quarterly* 77(4), 409–427.

Floridi, L. 1995. 'Internet: Which Future for Organized Knowledge, Frankenstein or Pygmalion?', *International Journal of Human-Computer Studies* 43, 261–274.

Floridi, L. 1999a. *Philosophy and Computing: An Introduction*. London: Routledge.

Floridi, L. 1999b. 'Information Ethics: On the Philosophical Foundations of Computer Ethics', *Ethics and Information Technology* 1(1), 37–56.

Floridi, L. 2002a. 'Information Ethics: An Environmental Approach to the Digital Divide', *Philosophy in the Contemporary World* 9(1), 39–45.

Floridi, L. 2002b. 'What Is the Philosophy of Information?', in Moor, J. H. and Bynum, T. W. (eds.), *Cyberphilosophy: The Intersection of Computing and Philosophy*, pp. 117–138. Oxford: Blackwell.

Floridi, L. 2003. 'On the Intrinsic Value of Information Objects and the Infosphere', *Ethics and Information Technology* 4(4), 287–304.

Floridi, L. 2004. 'Open Problems in the Philosophy of Information', *Metaphilosophy* 35(4), 554–582.

Floridi, L. 2005a. 'An Interpretation of Informational Privacy and of Its Moral Value', *Proceedings of CEPE 2005 – 6th Computer Ethics: Philosophical Enquiries Conference, Ethics of New Information Technologies*, University of Twente, Enschede, the Netherlands.

Floridi, L. 2005b. 'Information Ethics: Its Nature and Scope', *Computers and Society* 36(3), 21–36.

Floridi, L. 2005c. 'Presence: From Epistemic Failure to Successful Observability', *Presence: Teleoperators and Virtual Environments* 14(6), 656–667.

Floridi, L. 2005d. 'The Ontological Interpretation of Informational Privacy,' *Ethics and Information Technology* 7(4), 185–200.

Floridi, L. 2006a. 'Four Challenges for a Theory of Informational Privacy', *Ethics and Information Technology* 8(3), 109–119.

Floridi, L. 2006b. 'Information Technologies and the Tragedy of the Good Will', *Ethics and Information Technology* 8(4), 253–262.

Floridi, L. 2006c. 'Informational Privacy and its Ontological Interpretation', *Computers and Society* 36(3), 37–40.

Floridi, L. 2007a. 'A Look into the Future Impact of ICT on Our Lives', *The Information Society* 23(1), 59–64.

Floridi, L., 2007b. 'Understanding Information Ethics', *APA Newsletter on Philosophy and Computers* 7(1), http://76.12.57.18/publications/newsletters/v07n1_Computers_04.aspx

Floridi, L. 2008a. 'Artificial Intelligence's New Frontier: Artificial Companions and the Fourth Revolution', *Metaphilosophy* 39 (4/5), 651–655.

Floridi, L. 2008b. 'The Method of Levels of Abstraction', *Minds and Machines*, 18(3), 303–329.

Floridi, L. 2008c. 'Replies to "Commentaries on Floridi"', *APA Newsletter on Philosophy and Computers*, 72.

Floridi L. 2008d. 'Information Ethics, its Nature and Scope', in van den Hoven, J. and Weckert, J. (eds.), *Information Technology and Moral Philosophy*, pp. 40–65. Cambridge: Cambridge University Press.

Floridi, L. 2008e. 'Foundations of Information Ethics' in Himma, K. E. and Tavani, H. T. (eds.), *The Handbook of Information and Computer Ethics*, pp. 3–23. Hoboken, NJ: Wiley.

Floridi, L. 2008f. 'A Defence of Informational Structural Realism', *Synthese* 161(2), 219–253.

Floridi, L. (forthcoming, a). 'The Information Society and Its Philosophy', *The Information Society*.

Floridi, L. (forthcoming, b). Response to S. Hongladarom in special issue of *Floridi and his Critics*

Floridi, L. (forthcoming, c). *The Philosophy of Information*. Oxford: Oxford University Press.

Floridi, L., and Sanders, J. W. 1999. 'Entropy as Evil in Information Ethics', *Etica & Politica, special issue on Computer Ethics* 1(2).

Floridi, L. and Sanders, J. W. 2001. 'Artificial Evil and the Foundation of Computer Ethics', *Ethics and Information Technology* 3, 55–66.

Floridi, L. and Sanders, J. W. 2002. 'Mapping the Foundationalist Debate in Computer Ethics,' *Ethics and Information Technology* 4(1), 1–9. A revised version is printed in Spinello, R. A. and Tavani, H. T. (eds.), *Readings in Cyberethics* (2nd edn), pp. 84–95. Sudbury, MA: Jones and Bartlett.

Floridi, L. and Sanders, J. W. 2004. 'On the Morality of Artificial Agents'. *Minds and Machines* 14(3), 349–379.

Floridi, L. and Sanders, J. W. 2005. 'Internet Ethics: The Constructionist Values of Homo Poieticus', in Cavalier, R. (ed.), *The Impact of the Internet on Our Moral Lives*, pp. 195–214. Albany, NY: SUNY Press.

Foot, P. 1967. 'The Problem of Abortion and the Doctrine of the Double Effect', *Oxford Review* 5, 5–15.

Foster, K. R. and Jaeger, J. (forthcoming). 'Ethical Implications of Implantable Radiofrequency Identification Tags in Humans', *American Journal of Bioethics*.

Frankena, W. 1973. *Ethics* (2nd edn). Englewood Cliffs, NJ: Prentice-Hall Inc.

Freud, S. 1917. 'A Difficulty in the Path of Psycho-Analysis', *The Standard Edition of the Complete Psychological Works of Sigmund Freud*, XVII(1917–1919), pp. 135–144.

Friedman, B. (ed.) 1997. *Human Values and the Design of Computer Technology*. Cambridge: Cambridge University Press.

Friedman, B. and Freier, N. 2005. 'Value Sensitive Design', in Fisher, E., Erdelez, S. and McKechnie, E. (eds.), *Theories of Information Behavior: A Researcher's Guide*. Medford, NJ: Information Today.

Friedman, B., Howe, D. and Felten, E. 2002. 'Informed Consent in the Mozilla Browser: Implementing Value-Sensitive Design', in *Proceedings of the Thirty-Fifth Annual Hawai'i International Conference on System Sciences*. Abstract, p. 247; CD-ROM of full-paper, OSPE101. Los Alamitos, CA: IEEE Computer Society.

Friedman, B. and Kahn, P. 2003. 'Human Values, Ethics, and Design', in Jacko, J. and Sears, A. (eds.), *The Human-Computer Interaction Handbook*. Mahwah, NJ: Lawrence Erlbaum Associates.

Friedman, B., Kahn, P. H. Jr. and Borning, A. 2006. 'Value Sensitive Design and Information Systems' in Zhang, P. and Galletta, D. (eds.), *Human-Computer Interaction in Management Information Systems*. Foundations, New York: M. E. Sharpe.

Friedman, B., Kahn, P. H. Jr. and Borning, A. 2008. 'Value Sensitive Design and Information System', in Himma, K. E. and Tavani, H. T. (eds.), *The Handbook of Information and Computer Ethics*, pp. 69–102. Hoboken, NJ: John Wiley & Sons.

Friedman, B., Lin, P. and Miller, J. K. 2005. 'Informed Consent by Design', in Cranor, L. F. and Garfinkel, S. (eds.), *Designing Secure Systems that People Can Use*. O'Reilly.

Friedman, B. and Nissenbaum, H. 1996. 'Bias in Computer Systems', *ACM Transactions on Computer Systems* 14(3), 330–347.

Friedman, T. 2005. 'It's a Flat World, After All', *New York Times*, 3 April. www.nytimes.com/2005/04/03/magazine/03DOMINANCE.html

Froomkin, A. Michael. 2001. 'The Collision of Trademarks, Domain Names, and Due Process in Cyberspace', *Communications of the ACM* 44(2), 91–97.

Fukuyama, F. 2002. *Our Posthuman Future*. New York: Farrar, Straus and Giroux.

Fulcher, G. 1989. *Disabling Policies?* London: Falmer Press.

Gall, C. and. de Waal, T. 1998. *Chechnya: Calamity in the Caucasus*. New York: New York University Press.

Gallie, W. B. 1956. 'Essentially Contested Concepts', *Proceedings of the Aristotelian Society* 56, 167–198.

Galston, W. A. 2002. *Liberal Pluralism*. New York: Cambridge University Press.

Gardiner, S. M. 2006. 'A Core Precautionary Principle', *Journal of Political Philosophy* 14(1), 33–60.

Gemmey, J., Bell, G., Lueder, R., Drucker, S. and Wong, C. 2002 'MyLifeBits: Fulfilling the Memex Vision', *ACM Multimedia '02*, 1–6 December 2002, Juan-les-Pins, France, pp. 235–238. Retrieved January 2008 from http://research.microsoft.com/apps/pubs/default.aspx?id=64165

George, Carlisle E. 2006. 'Copyright Management Systems: Accessing the Power Balance', in Zielinski, C., Duquenoy, P. and Kimppa, K. (eds.), *The Information Society: Emerging Landscapes (IFIP WG 9.2 Proceedings)*, pp. 211–222. New York: Springer.

Gert, B. 1998. *Morality: Its Nature and Justification*. Oxford: Oxford University Press.

Gert, Bernard. 1999. 'Common Morality and Computing', *Ethics and Information Technology* 1(1), 57–64.

Ghemawat, P. 2007. 'Why the World Isn't Flat', *Foreign Policy* 159 (March/April), 54–60.

Global Forum for Health Research. 'The 10/90 Gap', www.globalforumhealth.org/

Goggin, G. and Newell, C. 2000. 'An End to Disabling Policies? Toward Enlightened Universal Service', *The Information Society* 16, 127–133.

Goggin, G. and Newell, C. 2006. 'Disability, Identity, and Interdependence: ICTs and New Social Forms', *Information, Communication and Society* 9(3), 309–311.

Goode, R. 2004. *Commercial Law* (3rd edn). London: Penguin Books.

Goodstein, A. 2007. *Totally Wired: What Teens and Tweens are Really Doing Online*. St Martin's: Griffin.

Goodwin, I. 2004. 'Book Reviews: The Virtual Community', *Westminster Papers in Communication and Culture* 1(1), 103–109.

Górniak-Kocikowska, K. 1996. 'The Computer Revolution and the Problem of Global Ethics', *Global Information Ethics* (a special issue of *Science and Engineering Ethics*) 2(2), 177–190.

Gotterbarn, D. 1995. 'Computer Ethics: Responsibility Regained', in Johnson, D. G. and Nissenbaum, H. (eds.), *Computers, Ethics and Social Values*, pp. 18–24. Englewood Cliffs, NJ: Prentice Hall.

Gowans, C. W. 1987. *Moral Dilemmas*. New York: Oxford University Press.

Greco, G. M. and Floridi, L. 2004. 'The Tragedy of the Digital Commons', *Ethics and Information Technology* 6(2), 73–82.

Greenhill, A. and Wilson, M. 2006. 'Haven or Hell? Telework, Flexibility and Family in the E-Society: A Marxist Analysis', *European Journal of Information Systems* 15(3), 379–388.

Grier, D. A. 2005. *When Computers Were Human*. Princeton, NJ: Princeton University Press.

Griffin, J. 1993. "How We Do Ethics Now', in Phillips Griffiths, A. (ed.), *Ethics*. Cambridge: Cambridge University Press.

Griffin, J. 1996. *Value Judgement: Improving Our Ethical Beliefs*. Oxford: Oxford University Press.

Griffiths, M. and Light, B. 2008. 'Social Networking and Digital Gaming Media Convergence: Consequences for Appropriation in Habbo Hotel', *Under the Mask: Perspectives on the Gamer Conference*, the Research Institute for Media, Art and Design, University of Bedfordshire.

Grodzinsky, F. S., Miller, K. W. and Wolf, M. J. 2008. 'The Ethics of Designing Artificial Agents', *Ethics and Information Technology* 10, 115–121.

Grundy, F. 1996. *Women and Computing*. Exeter: Intellect.

Gutman, A. and. Thompson, D. 1996. *Democracy and Disagreement*. Cambridge, MA: Belknap Press.

Habermas, J. 1983. *Moralbewußtsein und Kommunikatives Handelns*. Frankfurt am Main: Suhrkamp.

Habermas, J. 1990. *Moral Consciousness and Communicative Ethics*. Cambridge, MA: MIT Press.

Habermas, J. 1993. 'Remarks on Discourse Ethics', in *Justification and Application*, pp. 19–113. Cambridge, MA: MIT Press.

Hacker, K. and Mason, S. M. 2003. 'Ethical Gaps in Studies of the Digital Divide', *Ethics and Information Technology* 5(2), 99–115.

Haga, S. B. and Willard, H. F. 2006. 'Defining the Spectrum of Genome Policy', *Nature Reviews Genetics* 7(12), 966–972.

Haldane, J. H. 2003. 'Natural Law and Ethical Pluralism', in Madsen, R. and Strong, T. B. (eds.), *The Many and the One: Religious and Secular Perspectives on Ethical Pluralism in the Modern World*, pp. 89–114. Princeton: Princeton University Press.

Hallion, R. 1992. *Storm Over Iraq.* Washington, DC: Smithsonian Institution Press.

Hamilton, E. and Cairns, H. (eds.). 1989. *Plato, The Collected Dialogues.* Princeton: Princeton University Press.

Hanson, R. 1994. 'If Uploads Come First', *Extropy* 6(2). http://hanson.gmu.edu/uploads.html

Hare, R. M. 1984. 'Supervenience'. Paper read at Aristotelian Society Supplementary Volume 56.

Harvey, L. 1990. *Critical Social Research.* London: Unwin Hyman.

Held, D. and McGrew, A. 2001. 'Globalization' in Krieger, J. (ed.), *Oxford Companion to Politics of the World.* Oxford and New York: Oxford University Press. Also available online at www.polity.co.uk/global/globocp.htm.

Held, D., McGrew, A., Goldblatt, D. and Perraton, J. 1999. *Global Transformations: Politics, Economics and Culture.* Cambridge: Polity Press.

Henwood, F. 1993. 'Establishing Gender Perspectives on Information Technology: Problems Issues and Opportunities', in Green, E., Owen, J. and Pain, D. (eds.), *Gendered by Design? Information Technology and Office Systems*, pp. 31–49. London: Taylor and Francis.

Hepburn, R. W. 1984. *'Wonder' and Other Essays: Eight Studies in Aesthetics and Neighbouring Fields.* Edinburgh: Edinburgh University Press.

Herold, K. 2005. 'A Buddhist Model for the Informational Person', *Proceedings of the Second Asia Pacific Computing and Philosophy Conference*, 7–9 January, Bangkok, Thailand.

Herring, S. 1996. 'Posting in a Different Voice: Gender and Ethics in CMC', in Ess, C. (ed.), *Philosophical Perspectives on Computer-Mediated Communication*, pp. 115–145. Albany NY: State University of New York Press.

Heymann, P. 2003. *Terrorism, Security, and Freedom.* Cambridge, MA: MIT Press.

Himanen, P. 2001. *The Hacker Ethic and the Spirit of the Information Age.* London: Secker & Warburg.

Himma, K. E. 2003. 'The Relationship between the Uniqueness of Computer Ethics and Its Independence as a Discipline in Applied Ethics', *Ethics and Information Technology* 5(4), 225–237.

Himma, K. E. 2004. 'There's Something About Mary: The Moral Value of Things Qua Information Objects', *Ethics and Information Technology* 6(3), 145–159.

Himma, K. E. 2007a. 'Foundational Issues in Information Ethics', *Library Hi Tech* 25(1), 79–94.

Himma, K. E. 2007b. 'Artificial Agency, Consciousness, and the Criteria for Moral Agency: What Properties Must an Artificial Agent Have to be a Moral Agent?', SSRN: http://ssrn.com/abstract=983503

Himma, K. E. and Tavani, H. T. (eds.) 2008. *The Handbook of Information and Computer Ethics.* Hoboken, NJ: John Wiley & Sons.

Hinman, L. 2002. 'The Impact of the Internet on Our Moral Lives in Academia', *Ethics and Information Technology* 4(1), 31–35.

Hinman, L. 2004. 'Virtual Virtues: Reflections on Academic Integrity in the Age of the Internet', in Cavalier, R. (ed.), *The Internet and Our Moral Lives*, pp. 49–68. Albany, NY: SUNY Press.

Hinman, L. 2008. *Ethics: A Pluralistic Approach to Moral Theory* (4th edn). Belmont, CA: Thomson-Wadsworth.

Hobsbawm, E. 1969. *Bandits.* London: Weidenfeld and Nicolson.

Hodel, T. B., Holderegger, A. and Lüthi, A. 1998. 'Ethical Guidelines for a Networked World under Construction', *Journal of Business Ethics* 17(9–10), 1057–1071.

Holland, J. H. 1975. *Adaptation in Natural and Artificial Systems.* Ann Arbor: University of Michigan Press.

Hollis, D. 2007. 'Rules of Cyberwar?', *The Los Angeles Times*, 8 October.

Hongladarom, S. 2004. 'Making Information Transparent as a Means to Close the Global Digital Divide', *Minds and Machines* 14(1), 85–99.

Hongladarom, S. 2007. 'Analysis and Justification of Privacy from a Buddhist Perspective', in Hongladarom, S. and Ess, C. (eds.), *Information Technology Ethics: Cultural Perspectives*, pp. 108–122. Hershey, PA: Idea Group Publishing.

Hongladarom, S. 2008. 'Floridi and Spinoza on Global Information Ethics', *Ethics and Information Technology* 10(2–3), 175–187.

Hoque, K. and Noon, M. 2004. 'Equal Opportunities Policy and Practice in Britain: Evaluating the "empty shell" hypothesis', *Work, Employment and Society* 18(3), 418–505.

Howard, M., Andreopoulos, G. and Shulman, M. 1994. *The Laws of War.* New Haven: Yale University Press.

Huizinga, J. 1998. *Homo Ludens: A Study of the Play-Element in Culture.* Abingdon: Routledge. First published in 1938 with the title *Homo Ludens : Proeve Eener Bepaling Van Het Spel-Element Der Cultuur.* Haarlem: H. D. Tjeenk Willink.

Huxley, A. 2006. *Brave New World.* New York: Harper Perennial Modern Classics.

Ihde, D. 1990, *Technology and the Lifeworld.* Bloomington/Minneapolis: Indiana University Press.

Ihde, D. 1998. *Expanding Hermeneutics.* Evanston, IL: Northwestern University Press.

Independent Expert Group on Mobile Phones. 2000. 'Mobile phones and health', www.iegmp.org.uk/

Inness, J. C. 1992. *Privacy, Intimacy, and Isolation.* New York: Oxford University Press.

International Herald Tribune, Europe. 2008. 'Heathrow Begins Requiring Iris scans, Fingerprints from Some Passengers', the Associated Press. 1 February. www.iht.com/articles/ap/2008/02/01/europe/EU-GEN-Britain-Heathrow-Biometric-Data.php

Internet World Stats: Usage and Population Statistics. 2008. World Internet Users: March 2008. www.internetworldstats.com/stats.htm

Introna, L. 2005. 'Disclosive Ethics and Information Technology: Disclosing Facial Recognition Systems', *Ethics and Information Technology* 7(2), 75–86.

Introna, L. 2007. 'Maintaining the Reversibility of Foldings: Making the Ethics (Politics) of Information Technology Visible', *Ethics and Information Technology* 9(1), 11–25.

Introna, L. 2008. 'Phenomenological Approaches to Ethics and Information Technology', in Zalta, E. N. (ed.), *The Stanford Encyclopedia of Philosophy* (Fall 2008 edition).

Introna, L. and Nissenbaum, H. 2000. 'Shaping the Web: Why the Politics of Search Engines Matters', *The Information Society* 16(3), 1–17.

Jackson, P., Gharavi, H. and Klobas, J. 2006. 'Technologies of the Self: Virtual Work and the Inner Panopticon', *Information Technology and People* 19(3), 219–243.

Jerrard, A. A. and Chang, T. Y. 2003. 'A Case Study of How Technology and Trust Enable the Projectized Team-Based Organization', in Joia, Luiz Antonio (ed.), *IT-Based Management: Challenges and Solutions*, pp. 111–129. Hershey, PA: Idea Group Publishing.

Johnson, D. G. 1985. *Computer Ethics.* Englewood Cliffs, NJ: Prentice Hall. (2nd edn, 1994; 3rd edn, 2001.)

Johnson, D. G. 1997. 'Is the Global Information Infrastructure a Democratic Technology?', *Computers and Society* 27, 20–26.

Johnson, D. G. 2000. 'Should Computer Programs be Owned?', in Baird, R. M., Ramsower, R. and Rosenbaum, S. E. (eds.), *Cyberethics – Social and Moral Issues in the Computer Age*, pp. 222–235. New York: Prometheus Books.

Johnson, D. G. 2006. 'Computer Systems: Moral Entities but Not Moral Agents', *Ethics and Information Technology* 8(4), 195–204.

Johnson, D. G. and Miller, K. W. 2008. 'Un-making Artificial Moral Agents', *Ethics and Information Technology* 10, 123–133.

Johnstone, J. 2007. 'Technology as Empowerment: A Capability Approach to Computer Ethics', *Ethics and Information Technology* 9(1), 73–87.

Jonas, H. 1984. *The Imperative of Responsibility: In Search of an Ethics for the Technological Age.* Chicago, IL: University of Chicago Press.

Jones, R. A. L. 2007. 'Debating Nanotechnologies', in Allhof, F., Lin, P., Moor, J. and Weckert, J. (eds.) *Nanoethics: The Ethical and Social Implications of Nanotechnology*, pp. 71–79. Hoboken, NJ: Wiley Interscience.

Jordan, T. and Taylor, P. A. 2004. *Hacktivism and Cyberwars: Rebels With a Cause?* London and New York: Routledge.

Kant, Immanuel 1952. *The Critique of Judgment.* Trans. J. M. Meredith. Oxford: Clarendon.

Kass, L. 2003. 'Ageless Bodies, Happy Souls: Biotechnology and the Pursuit of Perfection', *The New Atlantis*, Spring, 9–28.

Kim, T. K. 2005. 'Electronic Storm: Stormfront Grows a Thriving Neo-Nazi Community', Intelligence Report, Southern Poverty Law Center, Summer 2005. www.splcenter.org/intel/intelreport/article.jsp?aid=551

Klein, N. 2000. *No Logo: No Space, No Choice, No Jobs.* London: Flamingo.

Klein, Naomi. 2008. 'China's All-Seeing Eye', *Rolling Stone Magazine* (29 May). www.rollingstone.com/politics/story/20797485/chinas_allseeing_eye

Kleinig, J. 1982. 'The Ethics of Consent', in Neilsen, K. and Patten, S. C. (eds.), *New Essays in Ethics and Public Policy*. Guelph, Ontario: Canadian Association for Publishing in Philosophy.

Korsgaard, C. M. 2003. 'The Dependence of Value on Humanity', in Raz, J., *The Practice of Value*, pp. 63–86. (ed.) R. J. Wallace. Oxford: Clarendon Press.

Kreps, D. and Adam, A. 2006. 'Failing the Disabled Community?: The Continuing Problem of Web Accessibility', in Zaphiris, P. and Kurniawan, S. (eds.), *Human Computer Interaction Research in Web Design and Evaluation*. Hershey, PA: Idea Group Publishing.

Kroes, P. (forthcoming). *The Moral Significance of Technical Artefacts*.

Kroes, P. and Meijers, A. 2006. 'The Dual Nature of Technical Artefacts', *Studies in History and Philosophy* 37, 1–4.

Ladd, J. 2000. 'Ethics and the Computer World – A New Challenge for Philosophers', in Baird, R. M., Ramsower, R. and Rosenbaum, S. E. (eds.), *Cyberethics – Social and Moral Issues in the Computer Age*, pp. 44–55. New York: Prometheus Books.

Latour, B. 1992, 'Where are the Missing Masses? – The Sociology of a Few Mundane Artefacts', in Bijker, W. E. and Law, J. (eds.), *Shaping Technology/Building Society*, pp. 225–258. Cambridge, MA: MIT Press.

Latour, B. 2002. 'Morality and Technology: The End of the Means', *Theory, Culture and Society* 19(5–6), 247–260.

Laurent, L. and Petit, J. C. 2005. 'Nanoscience and Its Convergence with Other Technologies', *Hyle* 11(1), 45–76.

Law, J. and Hassard, J. 1999. *Actor Network Theory and After*. Oxford and Malden, MA: Blackwell.

Lebedev, M. A. and Nicolelis, M. A. L. 2006. 'Brain Machine Interfaces: Past, Present, and Future', *Trends in Neurosciences* 29(9), 536–546.

Leone, R. and Anrig, G. 2004. *The War on Our Freedoms: Civil Liberties in an Age of Terrorism*. New York: Public Affairs Press.

Leopold, A. 1949. *The Sand County Almanac*. New York: Oxford University Press.

Lessig, L. 1999. *Code and Other Laws of Cyberspace*. New York: Basic Books.

Lessig, L. 2006. *Code: Version 2.0*. New York: Basic Books.

Lewis, S. 2004. 'How Much is Stronger DRM Worth?', in Camp, L. J. and Lewis, S. (eds.), *Economics of Information Security*, pp. 53–57. Dordrecht: Kluwer.

Libicki, M. 2007. *Conquest in Cyberspace: National Security and Information Warfare*. Cambridge: Cambridge University Press.

Lieven, A. 1998. *Chechnya: Tombstone of Russian Power*. New Haven: Yale University Press.

Liu, Z. and Sarkar, S. 2007. 'Outdoor Recognition at a Distance by Fusing Gait and Face', *Image and Vision Computing* 25(6), 817–832.

Lloyd, S. 2006. *Programming the Universe*. New York: Knopf.

Lohn, J. D. and Hornsby, G. S. 2006. 'Evolvable Hardware: Using Evolutionary Computation to Design and Optimize Hardware Systems', *IEEE Computational Intelligence Magazine* 1, 19–27.

Lü, Y. 2005. 'Privacy and Data Privacy Issues in Contemporary China', *Ethics and Information Technology* 7(1), 7–15.

Ludlow, P. 1996. *High Noon on the Electronic Frontier: Conceptual Issues in Cyberspace.* Boston: MIT Press.

Ludlow, P. and Wallace, M. 2007. *The Second Life Herald: The Virtual Tabloid that Witnessed the Dawn of the Metaverse.* Boston: MIT Press.

Lyman, P. and Varian, H. R. 2003. 'How Much Information?', www.sims. berkeley.edu/research/projects/how-much-info-2003/execsum. htm#summary

Lyon, D. 1994. *The Electronic Eye: The Rise of Surveillance Society.* Cambridge: Polity Press

MacKinnon, R. 2008. 'Asia's Fight for Web Rights', *Far Eastern Economic Review*, April. www.feer.com/essays/2008/april/asias-fight-for-web-rights

Maner, W. 1980. *Starter Kit in Computer Ethics.* Hyde Park, NY: Helvetia Press and the National Information and Resource Center for Teaching Philosophy. (Originally self-published in 1978.)

Maner, W. 1996, 'Unique Ethical Problems in Information Technology', *Global Information Ethics* (a special issue of *Science and Engineering Ethics*) 2(2), 137–154.

Maner, W. 2004. 'Unique Ethical Problems in Information Technology', in Bynum, T. W. and Rogerson, S. (eds.), *Computer Ethics and Professional Responsibilty*, pp. 39–59. Oxford: Blackwell Publishing.

Mann, S. 1997. 'Wearable Computing: A First Step Toward Personal Imaging', *Computer* 30(2), 25–31.

Mann, S. 2001. 'Wearable Computing: Toward Humanistic Intelligence', *IEEE Intelligent Systems* 16(3), 10–15.

Manson, N. A. 2002. 'Formulating the Precautionary Principle', *Environmental Ethics* 24, 263–274.

Manson, N. C. and O'Neill, O. 2007. 'Rethinking Informed Consent', in *Bioethics.* Cambridge: Cambridge University Press.

Marber, P. 2005. 'Globalization and Its Contents', *World Policy Journal*, Winter 2004/2005, 29–37.

Markoff, J. 2005. *What the Dormouse Said: How the 60s Counterculture Shaped the Personal Computer.* New York: Viking Adult.

Marquie, J. C., Jourdan-Boddaert, L. and Huet, N. 2002. 'Do Older Adults Under-estimate Their Actual Computer Knowledge?', *Behaviour and Information Technology* 24(4), 273–280.

Mason, R. O. 2000. 'Intellectual Property and Open Systems', in *Proceedings of the 33rd Hawaii International Conference on System Sciences.*

Mather, K. 2005. 'Object Oriented Goodness: A Response to Mathiesen's "What Is Information Ethics?"', *Computers and Society* 34(4).

Mathiesen, K. 2004. 'What Is Information Ethics?', *Computers and Society*, 32(8), www.computersandsociety.org/sigcas_ofthefuture2/sigcas/subpage/sub_page. cfm?article=909&page_number_nb=901

McCalman, J. 2003. 'What Can We Do for Corporate Nomads? IT and Facilities Management', in Joia, Luiz Antonio (ed.), *IT-Based Management: Challenges and Solutions*, pp. 130–142. Hershey, PA: Idea Group Publishing.

McCormick, M. 2001. 'Is It Wrong to Play Violent Video Games?' *Ethics and Information Technology* 3(4), 277–287.

McFarland, M. C. 2001. 'Intellectual Property, Information, and the Common Good', in Spinello, R. A. and Tavani, H. T. (eds.) *Readings in Cyberethics*, pp. 252–262. Sudbury, MA: Jones and Bartlett.

McKenzie, D. and Wajcman, J. (eds.) 1999. *The Social Shaping of Technology*. Milton Keynes: Open University Press.

McLaughlin, B. and Bennet, K. 2005. 'Supervenience', *Stanford Encyclopedia of Philosophy*, http://plato.stanford.edu/entries/supervenience/

McSorley, K. 2003. 'The Secular Salvation Story of the Digital Divide', *Ethics and Information Technology* 5(2), 75–87.

Mellor, C. 2004. 'Google's Storage Strategy', *TechWorld* (6 April).

Michelfelder, D. 2001. 'The Moral Value of Informational Privacy in Cyberspace', *Ethics and Information Technology* 3(2), 129–135.

Microsoft-Research 2005. 'The Towards 2020 Science'.

Midgley, Mary. 1996. 'Trying Out One's New Sword', in Arthur, J. (ed.), *Morality and Moral Controversies* (4th edn), pp. 116–119. Upper Saddle River, NJ: Simon and Schuster.

Midgley, M. 1985. 'Persons and Non-Persons', in Singer P. (ed.), *Defence of Animals*, pp. 52–62. Oxford: Basil Blackwell.

Mill, J. S. 2007. *On Liberty and The Subjection of Women*. New York: Penguin Classics.

Miller, S. and Weckert, J. 2000. 'Privacy, the Workplace and the Internet', *Journal of Business Ethics* 28, 255–265.

Moor, J. H. 1985. 'What is Computer Ethics?', *Metaphilosophy* 16(4), 266–275.

Moor, J. H. 1998. 'Reason, Relativity and Responsibility in Computer Ethics', *Computers and Society* 28(1), 14–21.

Moor, J. H. 1999. 'Just Consequentialism and Computing', *Ethics and Information Technology* 1(1), 65–69.

Moor, J. H. 2001. 'Just Consequentialism and Computing', in Spinello, R. A. and Tavani, H. T (eds.), *Readings in Cyberethics*, pp. 98–105. Sudbury, MA: Jones and Bartlett.

Moor, J. H. 2006. 'The Nature, Importance, and Difficulty of Machine Ethics', *IEEE Intelligent Systems* 21, 18–21.

Moore, G. 1965. 'Cramming More Components onto Integrated Circuits', *Electronics* 38, 114–117.

Moores, T. T. and Chang, J. 2006. 'Ethical Decision Making in Software Privacy: Initial Development and Test of a Four-Component Model', *MIS Quarterly* 30(1), 167–180.

Morgan, R. 2008. 'Juicy Campus: College Gossip Leaves the Bathroom Wall and Goes Online', *International Herald Tribune*, 18 March. www.iht.com/articles/2008/03/18/arts/gossip.php

Moser, I. 2006. 'Disability and the Promises of Technology: Technology, Subjectivity and Embodiment within an Order of the Normal', *Information, Communication and Society* 9(3), 373–395.

Moss, J. 2002. 'Power and the Digital Divide', *Ethics and Information Technology* 4(2), 159–165.

Naess, A. 1973. 'The Shallow and the Deep, Long-Range Ecology Movement', *Inquiry* 16, 95–100.

Nagel, T. 1986. *The View from Nowhere.* Oxford: Oxford University Press.

Nagel, T. 1987. 'The Fragmentation of Value', in Gowans, C. W. *Moral Dilemmas*, pp. 174–187. New York: Oxford University Press.

Nakada, M. and Tamura, T. 2005. 'Japanese Conceptions of Privacy: An Intercultural Perspective', *Ethics and Information Technology* 7(1), 27–36.

Nash, R. F. 1989. *The Rights of Nature.* Madison, WI: The University of Wisconsin Press.

National Institute of Health. 'Nuremburg Code' http://ohsr.od.nih.gov/ guidelines/index.html.]

Nature. 2006, '2020 – Future of Computing', 440.

Nietzsche, F. W. 2003. *Beyond Good and Evil: Prelude to a Philosophy of the Future.* R.-P. Horstmann (ed.); Judith Norman (trans). Cambridge: Cambridge University Press.

Nissenbaum, H. 1998. 'Values in the Design of Computer Systems', *Computers and Society*, March 1998, 38–39.

Nissenbaum, H. 2001. 'How Computer Systems Embody Values', *IEEE Computer* 34, March, 118–120.

Nissenbaum, H. 2004. 'Privacy as Contextual Integrity', *Washington Law Review* 79, 119–158.

Nozick, R. 1993. *The Nature of Rationality.* Princeton: Princeton University Press.

Nuffield Council on Bioethics. 2003. *Pharmacogenetics: Ethical Issues.* London: Nuffield Council On Bioethics.

Ofcom 2008. 'The Communications Market 2008', www.ofcom.org.uk/ research/cm/cmr08/

O'Neill, O. 2004. 'Modern Moral Philosophy and the Problem of Relevant Descriptions', in *Modern Moral Philosophy*, pp. 301–316. Cambridge: Cambridge University Press.

O'Reilly, T. 2005. 'What Is Web 2.0 – Design Patterns and Business Models for the Next Generation of Software', www.oreillynet.com/pub/a/ oreilly/tim/news/2005/09/30/what-is-web-20.html

Ortega Y Gasset, J. 1961. 'Man the Technician', in Weyl, H. (trans.), *History as a System: And Other Essays Toward a Philosophy of History*, pp. 87–161. New York: W. W. Norton & Company.

Orwell, G. 1949. *Nineteen Eighty-Four.* London: Secker and Warburg.

Ossorio, Pilar N. 2006. 'About Face: Forensic Genetic Testing for Race and Visible Traits', *Journal of Law, Medicine and Ethics* 34(2), 277–292.

Pape, R. 1996. *Bombing to Win*. Ithaca: Cornell University Press.

Parker, D. 1968. 'Rules of Ethics in Information Processing', *Communications of the ACM* 11, 198–201.

Parker, D. 1979. *Ethical Conflicts in Computer Science and Technology*. Arlington, VA: AFIPS Press.

Parker, D. *et al.* 1990. *Ethical Conflicts in Information and Computer Science, Technology and Business*. Wellesley, MA: QED Information Sciences.

Paterson, B. 2007. 'We Cannot Eat Data: The Need for Computer Ethics to Address the Cultural and Ecological Impacts of Computing', in Hongladarom, S. and Ess, C. (eds.), *Information Technology Ethics: Cultural Perspectives*, pp. 153–168. Hershey, PA: Idea Group Publishing.

Patton, M. F. J. 1988. 'Tissues in the Profession: Can Bad Men Make Good Brains Do Bad Things?', *Proceedings and Addresses of the American Philosophical Association*, 61(3).

PBS Online. 1998. 'Nerds 2.0.1: Wiring the World', www.pbs.org/opb/nerds2.0.1/wiring_world/

Pearson, C. and Watson, N. 2007. 'Tackling Disability Discrimination in the United Kingdom: The British Disability Discrimination Act', *Journal of Law and Policy* 23: 95–120. http://law.wustl.edu/Journal.index.asp?ID=5697

Pennell, C. 2001. *Bandits at Sea: A Pirates Reader*. New York: New York University Press.

Pennings, J. 1998. 'Innovations as Precursors of Organizational Performance', in Galliers, R. D. and Baets, W. R. J. (eds.), *Information Technology and Organizational Transformation: Innovation for the 21st Century*, pp. 153–178. Chichester: John Wiley & Sons.

Phillips, A. 1995. *The Politics of Presence*. Oxford: Oxford University Press.

Phillips, J. and Firth, A. 2001. *Introduction to Intellectual Property Law* (4th edn). London: Butterworths LexisNexis.

Plant, S. 1997. *Zeros and Ones*. London: Fourth Estate.

Plato. 1993. *Symposium*, Robin Waterfield (ed. and trans.). Oxford/New York: Oxford University Press.

Pohl, F. 1981. *The Cool War*. New York: Ballantine Books.

Posner, R. A. 1997, 'Problematics of Moral and Legal Theory', *The Harvard Law Review* 111, 1637–1637.

Potter, S. M., Wagenaar, D. A. and DeMarse, T. B. 2006. 'Closing the Loop: Stimulation Feedback Systems for Embodied MEA Cultures', in Taketani, M. and Baudry, M. (eds.), *Advances in Network Electrophysiology Using Multi-Electrode Arrays*, pp. 215–242. New York: Springer.

Putnam, H. 2004. *Ethics Without Ontology*. Cambridge, MA: Harvard University Press.

Putnam, R. 2001. *Bowling Alone: The Collapse and Revival of American Community*. New York: Simon & Schuster.

Rattray, G. 2001. *Strategic Warfare in Cyberspace*. Cambridge, MA: MIT Press.

Rawls, J. 1993. *Political Liberalism*. New York: Columbia University Press.

Rawls, J. 1999. *A Theory of Justice* (rev. edn). Oxford: Oxford University Press.

Rees, T. L. 1998. *Mainstreaming Equality in the European Union*. London and New York: Routledge.

Reidenberg, J. R. 2000. 'Resolving Conflicting International Data Privacy Rules in Cyberspace', *Stanford Law Review* 52, 1315–1376.

Rheingold, H. 2000. *The Virtual Community: Homesteading on the Electronic Frontier* (2nd edn). Cambridge, MA and London: MIT Press.

Rosen, J. 2004. *The Naked Crowd: Reclaiming Security and Freedom in an Anxious Age*. New York: Random House.

Ross, D. *et al.* (eds.) 2000. *Dennett's Philosophy*. Cambridge, MA: MIT Press.

Royal Society and the Royal Academy of Engineering. 2004. 'Nanoscience and Nanotechnologies: Opportunities and Uncertainties', www.nanotec.org. uk/finalReport.htm

Rucker, R. 2006. *The Lifebox, the Seashell, and the Soul: What Gnarly Computation Taught Me About Ultimate Reality, the Meaning of Life, and How to Be Happy*. New York: Basic Books.

Saletan, W. 2005. 'The Beam in Your Eye: If Steroids are Cheating Why isn't LASIK?', *Slate*, 18 April. www.slate.com/id/2116858/

Samuelson, P. and Scotchmer, S. 2002. 'The Law and Economics of Reverse Engineering', *The Yale Law Journal* 111(7), 1575–1673.

Sandberg, A. and Bostrom, N. 2007. 'Cognitive Enhancement: A Review of Technology', www.enhanceproject.org/documents/Cognitive% 20Enhancement%20Tech%20Review.pdf

Sandel, M. 2007. *The Case Against Perfection: Ethics in the Age of Genetic Engineering*. Cambridge, MA: Harvard University Press.

Sandin, P. 2007. 'Common Sense Precaution and Varieties of the Precautionary Principle', in Lewen, T. (ed.), *Risk: Philosophical Perspectives*, pp. 99–112. London: Routledge.

Saponas, T. S., Jonathan, L., Carl, H., Sameer, A. and Tadayoshi, K. (eds.) 2007. Special issue on 'Devices That Tell on You: Privacy Trends in Consumer Ubiquitous Computing', *USENIX Association*.

Schelling, T. 1966. *Arms and Influence*. New Haven: Yale University Press.

Schiffman, B. 2008. 'Turns Out Porn Isn't Recession-Proof', *Wired Blog Network*, http://blog.wired.com/business/2008/07/turns-out-por-1.html

Schneiderman, F. B. (ed.) 1999. *Trust in Cyberspace*. Washington, DC: National Academic Press.

Schrödinger, E. 1944. *What is Life? The Physical Aspect of the Living Cell*. Cambridge: Cambridge University Press.

Seife, C. 2006. *Decoding the Universe: How the New Science of Information is Explaining Everything in the Cosmos, from Our Brains to Black Holes*. New York: Viking, the Penguin Group.

Servon, L. 2002. *Bridging the Digital Divide: Technology, Community, and Public Policy*. Malden, MA: Blackwell.

Severson, R. J. 1997. *The Principles of Information Ethics*. New York: Armonk and London: M. E. Sharpe.

Shakespeare, T. 2006. *Disability Rights and Wrongs*. London and New York: Routledge.

Shapira, N., Barak, A. and Gal, I. 2007. 'Promoting Older Adults' Well-being through Internet Training and Use'. *Aging and Mental Health*, 11(5), 477–484.

Shrader-Frechette, K. and Westra, L. (eds.) 1997. *Technology and Values*. New York: Rowman & Littlefield.

Sicart, M. 2005. 'On the Foundations of Evil in Computer Game Cheating', *Proceedings of the Digital Games Research Association's 2nd International Conference – Changing Views: Worlds in Play, June 16–20*, Vancouver, British Columbia, Canada.

Sicart, M. and Studies, G. 2009. *The Ethics of Computer Games*. Cambridge MA: MIT Press.

Siponen, M. 2004. 'A Pragmatic Evaluation of the Theory of Information Ethics', *Ethics and Information Technology* 6(4), 279–290.

Siponen, M. and Vartiainen, T. 2002. 'Teaching End-User Ethics: Issues and a Solution Based on Universalizability', *Communications of the Association for Information Systems* 8, 422–443.

Small, Luc. 2007. 'Theft in a Wireless World', *Ethics and Information Technology* 9, 179–186.

Smart, A., Martin, P. and Parker, M. 2004. 'Tailored Medicine: Whom Will it Fit? The Ethics of Patient and Disease Stratification', *Bioethics* 18(4), 322–343.

Smart, J. J. C. and Williams, B. A. O. 1987. *Utilitarianism: For and Against*. Cambridge: Cambridge University Press. (First published 1973, reprinted with corrections and supplementary bibliography.)

Smith, M. M. 1996. 'Information Ethics: An Hermeneutical Analysis of an Emerging Area in Applied Ethics', PhD thesis, The University of North Carolina at Chapel Hill, Chapel Hill, D.C.

Smith, M. M. 2002, 'Global Information Ethics: A Mandate for Professional Education', *Proceedings of the 68th IFLA Council and General Conference*, Glasgow. Also available online at www.ifla.org/IV/ifla68/papers/056-093e.pdf.

Som, C., Hilty, L. M. and Ruddy, T. F. 2004. 'The Precautionary Principle in the Information Society', *Human and Ecological Risk Assessment* 10, 787–799.

Spencer, R. 2008. 'Footprints Faked, Admit Organizers', *The Age*, www.theage.com.au/news/latest-news/footprints-faked-admit-organisers/2008/08/11/1218306780009.html

Spier, R. M. 2001. *Science and Technology Ethics*. London: Routledge.

Spinello, R. A. 2000. *Cyberethics: Morality and Law in Cyberspace*. London: Jones and Bartlett.

Spinello, R. A. 2003. 'The Future of Intellectual Property', *Ethics and Information Technology* 5(1), 1–16.

Spinello, R. A. and Tavani, H. T. 2005. 'Intellectual Property Rights: From Theory to Practical Implementation', in Spinello, R. A. and Tavani, H. T. (eds.), *Intellectual Property Rights in a Networked World: Theory and Practice,* pp. 1–65. Hershey, PA: INFOSCI.

Stahl, B. C. 2005. 'The Impact of Open Source Development on the Social Construction of Intellectual Property', in Koch, S. (ed.) *Free/Open Source Software Development,* pp. 259–272. Hershey, PA: Idea Group Publishing.

Stahl, B. C. 2007. 'Social Justice and Market Metaphysics: A Critical Discussion of Philosophical Approaches to Digital Divides', in Rookby, E. and Weckert, J. (eds.) *Information Technology and Social Justice,* pp. 148–170. Hershey, PA: Idea Group Publishing.

Stahl, B. C. 2008a. 'Empowerment through ICT: A Critical Discourse Analysis of the Egyptian ICT Policy', in *Proceedings of the Human Choice and Computers 8 Conference,* 25–27 September 2008, Pretoria, South Africa.

Stahl, B. C. 2008b. *Information Systems: Critical Perspectives.* London: Routledge.

Stahl, B. C. 2008c. 'The Ethical Nature of Critical Research in Information Systems', *Information Systems Journal* 18(2), special issue on 'Exploring the Critical Agenda in IS Research', Brooke, C., Cecez-Kecmanovic, D. and Klein, H. K. (eds.), 137–163.

Stallman, R. 1995. 'Why Software Should Be Free', in Johnson, D. G. and Nissenbaum, H. (eds.), *Computers, Ethics and Social Values,* pp. 190–200. Upper Saddle River: Prentice Hall.

Stanton, J. M. and Julian, A. L. 2002, 'The Impact of Electronic Monitoring on Quality and Quantity of Performance', *Computers in Human Behavior* 18(1), 85–101.

Stienstra, D. 2006. 'The Critical Space between: Access, Inclusion and Standards in Information Technologies', *Information, Communication and Society* 9(6), 335–354.

Stuart, S. 2008. 'From Agency to Apperception: Through Kinaesthesia to Cognition and Creation'. (Special issue on Kant and Information Ethics), *Ethics and Information Technology.*

Sullins, J. P. 2006a. 'Ethics and Artificial Life: From Modeling to Moral Agents'. *Ethics and Information Technology* 7(3), 139–148.

Sullins, J. P. 2006b. 'When Is a Robot a Moral Agent?', *International Review of Information Ethics* 6, 23–30.

Sullins, J. P. 2007. 'Friends by Design: A Design Philosophy for Personal Robotics Technology', in Vermaas, P. E., Kroes, P., Light, A. and Moore, S. A. (eds.), *Philosophy and Design: From Engineering to Architecture.* Dordrecht: Springer.

Sullins, J. P. 2008. 'The Role of Artificial Moral Agency in Technoethics', in *Handbook of Research on Technoethics,* New York: Idea Group Inc.

Sunderland City Council 2008. 'Digital Challenge', www.sunderland.gov. uk/wherepeoplematter/

Sunstein, C. 2001. *republic.com.* New Jersey: Princeton University Press.

Sunstein, C. 2005. *Laws of Fear: Beyond the Precautionary Principle.* Cambridge: Cambridge University Press.

Tavani, H. T. 1999. 'Informational Privacy, Data Mining, and the Internet', *Ethics and Information Technology* 1(2), 137–145.

Tavani, H. T. 2002. 'The Uniqueness Debate in Computer Ethics: What Exactly Is at Issue, and Why Does it Matter?', *Ethics and Information Technology* 4(1), 37–54.

Tavani, H. T. 2005. 'The Impact of the Internet on Our Moral Condition: Do We Need a New Framework of Ethics', in Cavalier, R. (ed.), *The Impact of the Internet on Our Moral Lives*, pp. 215–238. Albany, NY: SUNY Press.

Tavani, H. T. 2007. *Ethics and Technology: Ethical Issues in an Age of Information and Communication Technology* (2nd edn). Hoboken, NJ: John Wiley & Sons.

Tavani, H. T. 2008. 'Floridi's Ontological Theory of Informational Privacy: Some Implications and Challenges', *Ethics and Information Technology* 10(2–3), 155–156.

Tavani, H. T. 2010. *Ethics and Technology: Controversies: Questions and Strategies for Ethical Computing.* (3rd edn) Hoboken, NJ: John Wiley & Sons.

Taylor, C. 2002. 'Democracy, Inclusive and Exclusive', in Madsen, R., Sullivan, W. M., Swiderl, A. and Tipton, S. M. (eds.), *Meaning and Modernity: Religion, Polity, and Self*, pp. 181–194. Berkeley: University of California Press.

Tedjasaputra, A. 2007. 'Digestible RFID Tag: An Alternative for Your Internal Body Monitoring', RFID Community in Asia: www.rfid-asia.info/2007/02/digestible-rfid-tag-alternative-for.htm

Thaler, R. H. and Sunstein C. R., 2008. *Nudge: Improving Decisions about Health, Wealth, and Happiness.* New Haven: Yale University Press.

The Economist, 18 December 1997, '1897 and 1997 – the Century the Earth Stood Still'.

The High Court of Australia: Dow Jones and Company Inc v Gutnick [2002] HCA 56; 210 CLR 575; 194 ALR 433; 77 ALJR 255 (10 December 2002), www.austlii.edu.au/au/cases/cth/HCA/2002/56.html

Thomas, J. 2004. 'Cyberpoaching behind the keyboard: Uncoupling the ethics of "virtual infidelity"', in Waskul, D. D. (ed.), *net.seXXX: Readings on Sex, Pornography, and the Internet*, pp. 149–77. New York: Peter Lang.

Thomas, T. 1997. 'The Threat of Information Operations: A Russian Perspective', in Pfaltzgraff, R. and Shultz, R. (eds.), *War in the Information Age*. London: Brassey's.

Thomasson, A. L. 2003. 'Realism and Human Kinds', in *Philosophy and Phenomenological Research*, LXVII (3), 580–609.

Thompson, A. 1996. *Hardware Evolution: Automatic Design of Electronic Circuits in Reconfigurable Hardware by Artificial Evolution.* London: Springer-Verlag.

Thorseth, M. 2006. 'Worldwide Deliberation and Public Use of Reason Online', *Ethics and Information Technology* 8(4), 243–252.

Thorseth, M. 2007. 'Ethical Pluralism', in Collste, G. (ed.), *Perspectives on Applied Ethics (Studies in Applied Ethics 10)*, pp. 41–55. Linköping: Centre for Applied Ethics, Linköping University.

Thorseth, M. 2008. 'Reflective Judgment and Enlarged Thinking Online', *Ethics and Information Technology* 10(4), 221–231.

Torremans, P. 2005. *Holyoak and Torremans Intellectual Property Law* (4th edn). Oxford: Oxford University Press.

Turilli, M. 2007. 'Ethical Protocols Design', *Ethics and Information Technology* 9, 49–62.

Turilli, M. 2008. 'Ethics and the Practice of Software Design', in Waelbers, K. Brey, P. A. and Briggle, A. (eds.), *Current Issues in Computing and Philosophy*, pp. 171–183. IOS Press.

Turing, A. M. 1950. 'Computing Machinery and Intelligence', *Mind* 59, 433–460.

Turkle, S. 2005. 'Relational Artifacts/Children/Elders: The Complexities of Cyber-companions'. In 'Toward Social Mechanisms of Android Science. A CogSci-2005 Workshop', *Cognitive Science Society* 62–73. www.androidscience.com/proceedings2005/TurkleCogSci2005AS.pdf

Turkle, S., Taggart, W., Kidd, C. D. and Dasté, O. 2006. 'Relational Artifacts with Children and Elders: The Complexities of Cybercompanionship', *Connection Science* 18, 347–361.

Turner, E. 1998. 'The Case for Responsibility of the Computing Industry to Promote Equal Presentation of Women and Men in Advertising Campaigns', *ETHICOMP98*, Rotterdam.

Turner, E. 1999. 'Gender and Ethnicity of Computing, Perceptions of the Future Generation', *ETHICOMP99*, Rome.

UNDP (United Nations Development Programme) 1998. *Human Development Report 1998*. New York, Oxford: Oxford University Press.

United Nations. 1948. 'Universal Declaration of Human Rights', www.un.org/Overview/rights.html

United Nations Environment Programme. 1992. 'Rio Declaration on Environment and Development 1992', www.unep.org/Documents.Multilingual/Default.asp?ArticleID=1163&DocumentID=78&l=en

US Patent and Trademark Office. 2007. 'United States Patent Application 20070300174' Kind Code, A1, Macbeth; Steven, W. *et al.*, (http://patft.uspto.gov) re US Patent Application 20070300174.

van Amerongen, M. 2008, 'The Interpretation of Artefacts', Simon Stevin series in the *Philosophy of Technology*, Delft.

Van Caenegem, W. 2003. 'Intellectual Property Law and the Idea of Progress', *Intellectual Property Quarterly* 3, 237–256.

van Delden, J., Bolt, I., Kalis, A., Derjiks, J. and Leufkins, H. 2004. 'Tailor-made Pharmacotherapy: Future Developments and Ethical Challenges in the Field of Pharmacogenomics', *Bioethics* 18(4), 303–321.

van den Hoven, J. 1995. 'Equal Access and Social Justice: Information as a Primary Good', *ETHICOMP9*, Leicester: De Montfort University.

van den Hoven, J. 1997. 'Computer Ethics and Moral Methodology', *Metaphilosophy* 28(3), 234–248.

van den Hoven, J. 2005. 'E-democracy, E-contestation and the Monitorial Citizen', *Ethics and Information Technology* 7(2), 51–59.

van den Hoven, J. 2008. 'Moral Methodology and Information Technology' in Himma, K. E. and Tavani, H. T. (eds.), 2008. *The Handbook of Information and Computer Ethics*, pp. 49–69.

van den Hoven, J., Miller, S. and Pogge, T. (2010, forthcoming). *The Design Turn in Applied Ethics*. Cambridge: Cambridge University Press.

van den Hoven, J. and Rooksby, E. 2008. 'Distributive Justice and the Value of Information: A (Broadly) Rawlsian Approach', in van den Hoven, J. and Weckert, J. (eds.) *Information Technology and Moral Philosophy*, pp. 376–397. Cambridge: Cambridge University Press.

van den Hoven, J. and Vermaas, P. 2007. 'Nano-technology and Privacy: On Continuous Surveillance outside the Panopticon', *Journal of Medicine and Philosophy* 32(3), 283–297.

van den Hoven, J. and Weckert, J. (eds.) 2008. *Information Technology and Moral Philosophy*. Cambridge: Cambridge University Press.

Verbeek, P. P. 2005. *What Things Do: Philosophical Reflections on Technology, Agency, and Design*. PA: Penn State Press.

Verton, D. 2003. *Black Ice: The Invisible Threat of Cyber-Terrorism*. New York: McGraw-Hill.

W3C. 2004. 'HTML and XHTML Frequently Answered Questions'. Available at www.w3.org/MarkUp/2004/xhtml-faq

Waddington, D. 2007. 'Locating the Wrongness in Ultra-violent Video Games', *Ethics and Information Technology* 9(2), 121–128.

Wajcman, J. 2004. *TechnoFeminism*. Cambridge, UK and Malden, MA: Polity.

Wallach, W. and Allen, C. 2008. *Moral Machines: Teaching Robots Right from Wrong*. New York: Oxford University Press.

Walsham, G. 1995. 'Interpretive Case Studies in IS Research: Nature and Method', *European Journal of Information Systems* 4(2), 74–81.

Walsham, G. 2001. *Making a World of Difference – IT in a Global Context*. Chichester: Wiley.

Waltz, K. 1959. *Man, the State, and War*. New York: Columbia University Press.

Walzer, M. 1977. *Just and Unjust Wars*. New York: Basic Books.

Warschauer, Mark. 2003. 'Dissecting the "Digital Divide": A Case Study in Egypt', *The Information Society* 19, 297–304.

Warwick, K. 2004. *I, Cyborg*. Champaign, IL: University of Illinois Press.

Warwick, S. 2001. 'Is Copyright Ethical? An Examination of the Theories, Laws, and Practices Regarding the Private Ownership of Intellectual Work in the United States', in Spinello, R. A. and Tavani, H T. (eds.), *Readings in Cyberethics*, pp. 263–279. Sudbury, MA: Jones and Bartlett.

Waters, R. 2006. 'US Group Implants Electronic Tags in Workers', *Financial Times*, 12 February, www.commondreams.org/headlines06/0213-07.htm

Wear, S. 1998. *Informed Consent: Patient Autonomy and Physician Beneficence within Healthcare* (2nd edn). Dordrecht: Kluwer.

Weckert, J. 2001. 'Computer Ethics: Future Directions', *Ethics and Information Technology* 3(2), 93–96.

Weckert, J. 2002. Trust, Corruption, and Surveillance in the Electronic Workplace', in Brunnstein, K. and Berleur, J. (eds.), *Human Choice and Computers: Issues of Choice and Quality of Life in the Information Society, 17th IFIP World Computer Congress, Montreal*, pp. 109–120. Boston: Kluwer.

Weckert, J. 2005. 'On-line Trust', in Cavalier, R. (ed.), *The Impact of the Internet on Our Moral Lives*, pp. 95–117. Albany, NJ: SUNY Press.

Weckert, J. (ed.) 2005. *Electronic Monitoring in the Workplace: Controversies and Solutions*. Hershey, PA: Idea Group Publishing.

Weckert, J. 2007. 'Computer Ethics' *The International Library of Essays in Public and Professional Ethics*. Aldershot: Ashgate.

Weckert, J. and Moor, J. 2006. 'The Precautionary Principle in Nanotechnology', *International Journal of Applied Philosophy* 20(2), 191–204.

Weimann, G. 2006. *Terror on the Internet*. Washington, DC: The United States Institute of Peace Press.

Weinert, F. 2009. *Copernicus, Darwin, and Freud: Revolutions in the History and Philosophy of Science*. Oxford: Blackwell.

Weizenbaum, J. 1965. 'Eliza – a Computer Program for the Study of Natural Language Communication between Man and Machine', *Communications of the Association for Computing Machinery* 9, 36–45.

Weizenbaum, J. 1976. *Computer Power and Human Reason*. San Francisco: W. H. Freeman.

Westin, A. F. 1968. *Privacy and Freedom*. New York: Atheneum.

Wheeler, D. 2006. 'Gender Sensitivity and the Drive for IT: Lessons from the NetCorps Jordan Project', *Ethics and Information Technology* 8(3), 131–142.

Wheeler, J. 1990. *Information, Physics, Quantum: The Search for Links*. Boulder, CO: Westview Press.

White, H., McConnell, E., Clipp, E., Branch, L. G., Sloane, R., Pieper, C. and Box, T. L. 2002. 'A Randomized Controlled Trial of the Psychosocial Impact of Providing Internet Training and Access to Older Adults', *Aging and Mental Health* 6(3), 213–221.

White, L. J. 1967. 'The Historical Roots of Our Ecological Crisis', *Science* 155, 1203–1207.

Wiegel, V. *et al.* 2005. 'Privacy, Deontic Epistemic Action Logic and Software Agents', *Ethics and Information Technology* 7(4), 251–264.

Wiegel, V. 2006, 'Building Blocks for Artificial Moral Agents', in *Proceeding EthicALife/ALifeX*.

Wiegel, V. 2007, *Sopholab, Volker Stevin Series in Philosophy of Technology*. Delft: Delft University of Technology.

Wiener, N. 1948. *Cybernetics: or Control and Communication in the Animal and the Machine*. Cambridge, MA: MIT Press.

Wiener, N. 1950. *The Human Use of Human Beings: Cybernetics and Society*. Houghton Mifflin.

Wiener, N. 1954. *The Human Use of Human Beings* (2nd rev. edn). New York: Doubleday Anchor.

Wiener, N. 1964. *God & Golem, Inc.: A Comment on Certain Points Where Cybernetics Impinges on Religion.* Cambridge, MA: MIT Press.

Winner, L. 1986. *The Whale and the Reactor: A Search for Limits in an Age of High Technology.* Chicago: University of Chicago Press.

Winner, L. 1997. 'Cyberlibertarian Myths and the Prospect for Community', *ACM Computers and Society* 27(3), 14–19.

Winner, L. 1999. 'Do Artefacts Have Politics?', in McKenzie, D. and Wajcman, J. (eds.) *The Social Shaping of Technology*, pp. 2–40. Buckingham: Open University Press.

Winston, M. and Edelbach, R. 2008. *Society, Ethics and Technology.* (4th edn) Florence, KY: Wadsworth.

Wittgenstein, L. 1953. *Philosophical Investigations*, G. E. M. Anscombe and R. Rhees (eds.), G. E. M. Anscombe (trans.). Oxford: Blackwell.

Wonderly, M. 2008. 'A Humean Approach to Assessing the Moral Significance of Ultra-violent Video Games', *Ethics and Information Technology* 10(1), 1–10.

Wooldridge, M., 2000. *Reasoning about Rational Agents*, Cambridge, MA: MIT Press.

York, P. F. 2005. 'Respect for the World: Universal Ethics and the Morality of Terraforming', PhD Thesis, the University of Queensland.

Young, I. M. 2000. *Inclusion and Democracy.* Oxford: Oxford University Press.

Yudkowsky, E. 2008. 'Artificial Intelligence as a Positive and Negative Factor in Global Risk', in Bostrom, N. and Circovic, M. (eds.) *Global Catastrophic Risks*, pp. 308–345. Oxford: Oxford University Press.

ZDNet. 2007. 'Facebook Users Open to Cyberattacks, ID Theft?', ZDNet, http://news.zdnet.com/2100-1009_22-157855.html

Index

Locators for headings which also have subheadings refer to general aspects of that topic only
Locators in **bold** refer to major content
Locators in *italics* refer to figures and tables